The New Radical Theatre Note book

AN APPLAUSE ORIGINAL
THE NEW RADICAL THEATRE NOTEBOOK by Arthur Sainer
Copyright © 1975, 1997 by Arthur Sainer.
Published by arrangement with the author.

Library of Congress Cataloging-In-Publication Data
Sainer, Arthur
The new radical theatre notebook / by Arthur Sainer
    p.   cm.
ISBN 1-55783-168-8 (pbk.)
1. Experimental theater--United States--20th century
I. Title.
PN2193.E86S25 1997
792'.022--dc21   97-12185
                                                 CIP

Applause Books

211 West 71st Street
New York, NY 10023
Phone: (212) 595-4735
Fax: (212) 721-2856

A&C Black

Howard Road, Eaton Socon
Huntingdon, Cambs PC19 3CZ
Phone: 01480-212666
Fax: 01480-405014

First Applause Printing, 1997

The New Radical Theatre Notebook

New, Expanded, Revised Edition.

ARTHUR SAINER

APPLAUSE
NEW YORK • LONDON

ACKNOWLEDGMENTS

Terminal © 1971 by Susan Yankowitz/The Open Theater. All rights reserved. No performances or readings of this work may be given without the express authorization of the authors' agent, Mary Harden, Harden-Curtis Associates, 850 Seventh Ave., Suite 405, New York, NY 10019.

Spring Offensive © 1975 by Arthur Sainer. For permission to perform this work, contact the author's agent, Ann Edelstein, 404 Riverside Drive, New York, NY 10025.

Commune is used by permission of the Performance Group; © 1975 by Wooster Group, Inc. Anyone interested in producing the play should contact the Performance Group, 33 Wooster Street, New York, NY 10013.

Still Falling by The Firehouse Theater is used by permission of the author. © 1975 by Nancy Walter. For permission to perform or reprint the work, contact Norah Holmgren, 1394 San Anselmo Dr., San Anselmo, CA 94960.

Los Siete (Bart) is used by the permission of The San Francisco Mime Troupe. © 1970. Script by Steve Friedman. For permission to perform or reprint the work contact The San Francisco Mime Troupe, 855 Treat Street, San Francisco, CA 94110.

Fire by George Dennison. First published in *The Drama Review*, Vol. 14, No. 3 (T47), 1970. © 1970 by *The Drama Review*. Reprinted by permission. All rights reserved.

"Spectacles and Scenarios" by Lee Baxendall. First published in *The Drama Review*, Vol. 13, No. 4 (T44), Summer 1969. © 1969 by *The Drama Review*. Reprinted by permission. All rights reserved.

"About Little Trips" by Norman Taffel. First published in *The Drama Review*, Vol. 15, No. 3a (T51), Summer 1971. © 1971 by *The Drama Review*. Reprinted by permission. All rights reserved.

Terminal by Paul Ryan. First published in *The Drama Review*, Vol. 15, No. 3a (T51), Summer 1971. © 1971 by *The Drama Review*. Reprinted by permission. All rights reserved.

"El Teatro Campesino: Interviews with Luis Valdez," by Beth Bagby. First published in *The Drama Review*, Vol. 13, No. 4 (T44), Summer 1967. © 1967 by *The Drama Review*. Reprinted by permission. All rights reserved.

Arthur Sainer is a playwright, novelist, and former drama critic for the Village Voice. He has taught playwriting at Bennington, Wesleyan, Hunter, and Middlebury Colleges, and is currently a member of Sarah Lawrence's Theatre Faculty. His plays include *The Spring Offensive, Images of the Coming Dead, The Celebration: Jooz/Guns/Movies/The Abyss, The Thing Itself, Charley Chestnut Rides the I.R.T.,Cruising Angel, After the Baal-Shem Tov, Carol in Winter Sunlight, The Burning Out of 82,* and *Jews and Christians in the End Zone.* As a playwright, he has been associated with the Bridge Collective and the Theater for the New City, whose production of his *The Children's Army Is Late* was performed at the International Theatre Festival of Parma in 1974. He has been a recipient of playwrighting grants from the Office for Advanced Drama Research and the John Golden Prize at the University of Minnesota, the National Foundation for Jewish Culture, and the Ford Foundation. He is also the author of *Zero Dances*, a study of Zero Mostel. He is also a member of PEN American Center.

Acknowledgments

I am indebted to Jacques Chwat, Carol Saltus, Margo Sherman, Reva Snilkstein Joseph Chaikin, Geraldine Lust, Peter Schumann, Michael Brown, Joan Holden, Richard Schechner, Sydney Walter, Susan Yankowitz, Peter Mayer and Mafia Carvainis for their aid in making this book happen. And to Glenn Young, Rachel Reiss, and Emily Franzosa of Applause Books for guiding this work into its new life. And to my wife, Maryjane Treloar, and to director–designer Donald Brooks, both of whom tracked down the manuscript for this expanded edition which was sitting on the floor of my office while I was in the rehab unit at NYU Medical Center, recovering from open–heart surgery.

This work is dedicated to the memory of Saul Gottlieb, a brave soul who fought in the vanguard of the new theatre movement he so strongly believed in. And to Julian Beck and Judith Malina. And to Joe Chaikin.

Shalom, peace, choose life.

CONTENTS

PART III: TO THE RADICAL THEATRE COMMUNITY

PART IV: TOWARD THE MILLENNIUM

INTRODUCTION

I write these notes for a book which is essentially a new work, both expanding on and absorbing a work which first saw the light of day in 1975. The earlier *Radical Theatre Notebook*, as I look at it now, spoke to a time of hope in which the premises of both theatre and Western society were held up to a radical scrutiny and both found wanting, and to a world in which anything seemed possible for those who believed in a reordering of priorities.

We spoke then of what we still speak of, truth and justice, though we were hardly of a single mind when we held up those comforting abstractions. We? The "we" is also misleading, suggesting a cohesive radical or alternative theatre community, but that extended community never really existed. What did exist in the sixties and into the seventies were parallel efforts by artists and companies that at times supported and at other times worked at cross-purposes from one another. We certainly had the rhetoric but too often we were like "the real world." Unfortunately, "radicalness" hardly negates "self-centeredness," even when the latter comes with a dollop of guilt.

Today, long after Vietnam, Watergate, Nicaragua, El Salvador, Iran-Contra, Grenada, Panama—easy to make these sounds, the litany seems endless, metaphors for moments in which truth and justice were consigned to the dustbin. Long after we "settled" Asia, Central America and the US constitution, lo and behold we flexed our muscles once again to orchestrate a New World Order. But even Reagan-Bush, after Kennedy-Johnson-Nixon-Ford, have hardly been isolated from the phenomena of terror. One can't discount the players in the sad and troubled Middle East, the embattled forces in Afghanistan and Rwanda, the adversaries in Northern Ireland, India, Somalia and . . . and . . . and . . .

Even as I compose these words there has been the genocidal theatre of horror played out in Sarajevo and other "safe areas" in Bosnia, the breakup of the USSR and its attendant civil wars, the many unifications and deunifications in the East and West, the promise of more tribal warfare into the next century, and the degeneration and destruction of this planet's resources—plants, air, soil, people, underwater species we never suspected even lived for an instant—and on and on. After all this contamination, this defoliation, these endless massacres, it nevertheless appears that anything is still possible. That even art is possible, because there are incorrigible beings who want, like that persistent nuisance the Ancient Mariner, to tell us something. Or perhaps they want only to tell something to that inner being they carry each waking and sleeping moment and are reinventing the wheel yet again, little realizing that Sophocles and Shakespeare and Chekhov and Ibsen and Brecht and The Living Theatre have already invented it twice over. And good thing, too, that they don't realize this over-invention of the wheel, because their arrogance and energy and naiveté are essential to the formation of something further to tell somebody.

Troubled times, and we thought that art was going to collaborate in the development of... of what? Of more beautiful, noble, sensitive, just beings? Didn't Chekhov intimate something to that effect? Didn't many of us in the radical theatre movement propose a symbiotic relationship between a new artistic consciousness and a planet in which one could sit in relative peace under one's fig tree?

Will some Donald Trump or Rupert Murdoch of the future buy up all the fig trees on planet earth and rent them out at prices nobody can afford? Or rent out the fig-tree hallucination (e.g., virtual reality) to those bent on the latest narcotic?

I suspect there is an edge of self-congratulation to that early work known as *The Radical Theatre Notebook*, although I had struggled for some objectivity as I tunneled into those journals and notes and diaries that I had been sporadically keeping about the work. To what degree we took as gospel our ability to change the world is a question not readily answered. There were serious changes at work, past the overblown rhetoric of change. Those sixties peaceniks and flower children might have grown to accommodate the powers-that-be, or in some cases might have metamorphosized into the powers-that-be. But whether subsumed into the latter-day aging radical or sober accomodator, for each of us something of the events of the sixties filtered into a consciousness that could never fully slough off what had been felt and spoken and, on occasion, even acted upon.

One has to only see the more recent theatre of the Becks or Joe Chaikin or Peter Schumann to know that if they had evolved from their work of the sixties, they had not so much evolved away from earlier visions but rather worked through them to the next stage. This does not mean that they took the bulk of the working theatre with them, or even necessarily that the next stage maintained the quality of the earlier work, that it was even "any good," but what they understood as truth and justice was not to be dismissed even if it was to be recast, even if truth and justice presented them with a complexity that seemed at times all but impossible to recast.

The artist, sooner or later, comes to understand that what is impossible must be lived with. One must find a way to come to terms with a condition that seems to offer no terms, and that in the face of what is impossible one must continue the struggle for those obstinate, maddening saints: truth and justice.

As for the mainstream, with its cowardice, its denial, its greed, and its refusal to grow into responsibility, it has pursued its fortunes as if on a perpetual date with the mid-forties. The mainstream may have changed its vocabulary, and to some extent it has become issue-oriented—certainly AIDS has pushed it into a new sobriety, and there are probably environmental concerns surfacing—but its vision of theatre as a way of illuminating the world, hasn't moved much from the point where William Saroyan and Tennessee Williams gracefully decimated the aesthetics of Ibsen. For the mainstream, Antonin Artaud is solemnly acknowledged behind repressed laughter as an hallucinating pest, an icon to whom one pays lip service, or he remains a rumor of madness or infantilism with which to titillate the good Philistines at stag parties. Jerzy Grotowski is recalled as some mythical figure, some Ariel who flew too close to the sun, someone who made outrageous remarks on each of his junkets to the West, encouraging young to relinquish the theatrical Caesar for the theatrical Christ—abandon your material careers, theatre needs your spiritual energies, not your agents and head shots! In short, Artaud and Grotowski, as well as the cigar-smoking ideologue Bertolt Brecht, in his own sinister fashion, were always disturbing the neighborhood and creating disciples who never quite seemed to wash or finish school but were always running off to start some revolution of sorts. Well the mainstream could deal with this commotion, this often inflated rhetoric, as long as no one took these self-proclaimed revolutionaries seriously. Judging by the merchandise currently packaged for the theatrical marketplace, a good nap on the Great White Way and a major snooze among its minor league affiliates has been pretty well secured.

The New Radical Theatre Notebook, which you are presently holding in your hand, presumes to take a new look at where experimental, alternative, "developmental"—a neutral term, so how could one take offense?—or political theatres have been, where they are now, and where they might possibly be heading. The latter concern is blatant presumption—where they might possibly be heading? Note the equivocation. How can we possibly have a fix on that possibility? For people and events are always surprising us, and if we are not as insightful as Isaiah—prophecy is a fool's game—then probably we should leave it in the hands of Artaud.

The earlier volume focused on experimental ensembles in the United States, but two decades have gone by since then. Movements and people have come and gone, while others have stayed. The Happenings grew silent, the performance artists grew raucous. A new formalism came into being with artists like Robert Wilson, who dreamed the unconscious into post-Rhinehartlike spectacles, Richard Foreman, who dreamed Wittgenstein and wiggling beauties, and Bix Beiderbeck, who dreamed into a kind of twitching, irrational logos and in parallel channels Meredith Monk and Ping Chong synthesized, each in their own way, narrative and film and dance and sound. Lee Nagrin added the artist painting in time as an integral part of the event, and Joseph Dunn did away with lights. Mabou Mines created a cerebral choreography with puppets and ritual combat. And out of the womb of The Open Theatre came Medicine Show and the Talking Band and The Winter Project. Out of the womb of The Living Theatre came the reconstituted Living Theatre, moving from Brecht toward a holistic communal life where theatre threatened its own existence. And out of the womb of the Bread and Puppet Theatre came The Ninth Street Theater, until recently a store-front operation. Peter Schumann and the ongoing Bread and Puppets came to town from Glover, Vermont, and brought Peter's disciples together for Nativities and Resurrections. They summoned the Ninth Street contingent and others from the Bay Area to Cologne, up to the Glover farm for the annual summer Bread and Puppet Circus. Finally, there was the Wooster Group emerging from the Performance Group, and there were groups and individuals who disappeared, died (Bob Carroll, Maurice Blanc, Wil Leach, John Braswell, Jenny Hecht, Joe Papp, Geraldine Lust, Murray Levy, Victor Lipton, Julian Beck, Charles Ludlum, George Ashley, Jane Yoeckel, Charles Stanley, Johnny Dodd, Donald Kvares) or discovered new careers, like Ric Zank, who founded the Iowa Theatre Lab and went into real estate; Sydney Walter, who left directing at the Firehouse Theater to study with a Zen master and discovered the presumed blessings of psychotherapy; Linda Mussman, who seems to have dissolved her Time and Space Theatre for what new endeavors I can't even begin to imagine. There are others who will appear in this book: Margo Lee Sherman, Helen Duberstein, Stuart Sherman, Marjorie Melnick, Anne Bogart, Joe Dunn, Spiderwoman, Herbert Blau and his Kraken ensemble, Mabou Mines, the perversely beautiful Squat Theater that started in Budapest and eventually broke up on West Twenty-third Street in Manhattan. And there are groups and individuals you and I, or at least I, have never heard of. Some of them—I hear rumors about the Broome St. Theatre in Madison—may find their way into our consciousness, if not immediately into this book. So—as they are wont to say—let the play begin, let the once-upon-a-time have its day.

Anything is still possible.

—*Arthur Sainer, 1997*

Photo: The Living Theatre Collection

Julian Beck and The Living Theatre in *Six Public Acts*

INTRODUCTORY DIALOGUE

The following are excerpts from an hour-long conversation between Joseph Chaikin and Arthur Sainer, recorded on January 22, 1974. It came shortly after the breakup of the Open Theatre, which Chaikin had headed for over ten years.

SAINER: I was wondering what the last ten years have done for all of us. I kept thinking that somehow we've gotten into the kind of theatre we have because of a dissatisfaction both with theatre and, for some of us, with society. I wonder how much the new work has helped us, and has it been primarily for us, and how much of it has gone beyond us to make some impact on the culture at large?

CHAIKIN: There are two things I think about when you say that. What I had been learning up to then [the advent of the Open Theatre] was that an actor acts like a person with a given function in a situation. A person who is in an office acts in one particular function, a person in a love relationship acts in another, and one recognizes the actor by his function in the life circumstances. Whereas I felt, without knowing clearly what I had in mind, that there was a way in which the body and the voice in fact could give testimony to other kinds of experiences and conditions. I wanted to see if it was possible to make that testimony, and the experiments were very clumsy, very complicated, without any navigating. I mean, the initial part was just sort of moving around. But I think that particular exploration, which other people were doing as well, was pretty far–reaching. I think that theatre is no longer looking simply to reflect people as they appear in an office or at a meal. Sometimes one wants to do that. But one of the things that was very necessary then and is not necessary now, in fact is in the way now, is to go into oneself... into oneself in one's group, one's collaborators, and say, "What can we do that has vitality for us?" without any interest in what has vitality for any community of people we're playing for. There was no audience, there was no community, there was no nothing, there was just, Let's get together and play around and try these things. And I think that probably was necessary, [because] if one started with the idea of "What should we do for them?," you know, there would have been a break in something organic. But now it seems to me that the reverse is true—that is, it seems to me absolutely essential that people not only ask themselves, "How can I work from myself in a true way?" but also, "And in what way does this connect to my community or to my whatever—you know, whatever group that I would also perform for?" You can't do it alone anymore...

SAINER: I had this thought the other day, and it's the first time I've been able to articulate it, that a lot of the experimental work had the sense of playing overtones, and that what you're talking about now [Chaikin had just spoken about his interest in the Greeks, in Chekhov, Shakespeare, and Brecht] is getting back to the tones.

CHAIKIN: I don't have so clear a critical perspective on what actually happened, but it does seem to me that one of the things that practically everybody in the sixties was working with was to create resonance in the work, and that people would tune in on different parts of themselves to one or another overtone that was created, that the overtone was where the address was. And if you're going to take that chance of doing overtones, you must also know that a lot of people won't tune in, because a lot of people are going to tune in strictly to the pitch itself. . .

SAINER: Does the continuation of a collaborative effort [within an ensemble] that starts with a blank page, does that feel like a structure you want to go on with?

CHAIKIN: No . . . no. For example, that's more or less what we've been doing at the Open Theatre — the blank page. In other words, saying "The material doesn't exist," and we all put our heads together and our bodies together and see what we can bring into existence. Then we say, "What's, so to speak, a theme, or what's the central idea or image of the thing?" And the idea is that the theme has to be something which we can connect to, all of us can connect to equally, with equal vitality, and something which at any given, living moment concerns us — not something which concerns us in the summertime, or just before we're getting into the army, or just returning home from summer camp, but at any given moment. At least, that's been my criterion. In *Terminal*, it was the theme of dying, in *The Mutation Show*, about changing, in *Nightwalk*, about sleeping or levels. And then in some cases, there were ideas I had that just aborted, they didn't bring anybody else's interest out, and I found them eventually academic and not ideas that activated anything. But anyway, that's more or less the way we proceeded. And then we had the skill of a writer coming in and working in relation to us — we didn't have that skill, not any one of us had the skill and in combination we didn't have the skill — and, to me, the weakness of the work was generally the degree that the writer was not participating. In any case, working on Lear or Chekhov is a very, very different thing — working on existing material — because each element in it has a kind of inevitability. And what one is doing there is not saying, "What do I bring into existence?" but "How do I discover the inevitability of this particular moment, of this particular thing?" It's like a musical score, which already exists, of Mahler. And you don't say, "Here's this pitch on high C — I think I'll change it to E." You don't begin at all with variations, not at all. And, for example, although I've worked a lot improvisationally to bring about certain kinds of things, in working on a text I don't believe in it at all. I believe one should do no improvisations, none — except in an emergency. I think that one can only make a distance between the text and the performance. I don't believe at all that you start and say, "How can I create on top of *Waiting for Godot* or *King Lear* — what can I do with it?" To me the question is, "In *The Seagull*, are all the clues in the text — entirely there?" And what one does is try to uncover the clues to give visibility and to embody them — to bring one's body into it — which is different from what you do if you're getting together and saying, "What kind of piece can we work up in terms of such and such a theme?"

SAINER: Do you feel that working on an existing text can be a satisfying process for the actors who've been working in an ensemble group?

CHAIKIN: I think it can be very satisfying, because it's like detective work — it's a very exciting process, especially for people who've been doing that other kind of open, open, open stuff — you know, where nothing exists and . . . I mean, it's a kind of ballast, in a way, to do both things.

SAINER: I've found that some of the people I've worked with in the past couple of years have resented a script existing, it has seemed presumptuous to them. Other people I've worked with have resented the fact that I've asked them to think about anything. So there still seem to be both those tendencies.

CHAIKIN: Well, you know, when you work improvisationally a lot, the actors do certain improvisations and they have sensations as they do them. Mind you, this is nothing I knew five years ago, or certainly ten years ago, but they have extremely strong sensations, they make great discoveries, and they see each other opening out and opening out and discovering parts of themselves that had no expression before. And then a writer comes in and restricts that expression and says, "Look, say this or do this — don't do anything under the sun," which was more or less what they were trying to do, which was anything. And they say, "You're straitjacketing me, who needs you, it was just going very beautifully before you stepped into it." And my experience is that, initially, the actor resents the writer, and eventually the actor realizes there's no other way to do it. I mean, those improvisations don't become a piece and those sensations are not to be preserved — they're not to be denied, either, but one can't preserve them . . .

SAINER: Joe, do you have any sense about yourself continuing to work in this culture, this America 1974, with all that it implies about the government and the tensions on the street?. I'm thinking partly of the Becks' charge that one is helping the culture go on, that one is making the powers that be and all their adjunct forces feel good, and that the theatre has generally existed as a way to make all these forces feel good.

CHAIKIN: Yes . . . as a kind of handmaiden. Well, first of all, it hasn't been my impression that the theatre has made anybody feel good at this time. I think it's either making people feel bad or feel nothing at all. To start with, I think it's a good thing to feel. I don't know, the Becks and I have a running argument about that, because I really value art deeply. To me, art's like a window, it's like living somewhere and there's a window in that place, or there isn't a window. And from what I understand, I think that Chinese art is no window. I don't think that China is a model, I don't think that Russia is a model, I don't think that for me the Becks' work is a model, because, to me, the problem with their work — now, right now, I don't mean before, because the Becks have been the real groundbreakers and really just extraordinary as an inspiration to so many people in spite of a lot of bugle–playing that they do, too, which is, to me, empty some of the time — the problem right now is that they're trying to play for them. They have made a certain separation between themselves and their potential audience and they're playing for them, for the other, the outside other. In that sense, there's not their own relationship to their work, they don't inhabit their work mixing the other and them in one community. I don't feel in a sense that it's for their community, but for the enemy, for the adversary. Or for the worker — in that case, the unenlightened other. And this, to me, is what their way of combating what you talk about is — they say, "I'm not going to make people feel good, I'm not going to serve this culture which I see to be a deadly one." I mean, I think that their indictment of the culture and their relationship to the art of the culture are things that I don't agree with at all. We had once a really terrific argument about Mozart, because they said Mozart was this racist, classicist pig . . .

SAINER: Anti–Semitic, and playing for the courts . . .

CHAIKIN: And playing for the courts. And I don't see that, it just seems to me that one lives continually with absolute contradictions. I think you could easily get elitist about art, and yet I think that to say that art should be simply propaganda, or art should be simply that which serves the subversive forces is, to me, not true. Among the people I most admire politically today is an activist, Grace Paley, whose stories, interesting to note, have very little, if anything at all, to do with her political understanding. I don't feel that it's the requirement of anybody to take sides on issues, it's the requirement of people to work organically and from a kind of human center, and then all the problems come up — what's your relationship to money, what's your relationship to the commercial salability of what you've got, what's your relationship to grants if you receive them or if you don't receive them, et cetera? And then come the absolutely contradictory things that throw you continually off balance.

SAINER: In a way, Chekhov's work encompasses all those human problems, even as they're talking about how they're going to get by day by day, how they're going to find a way of living with husband, wife, child — all those other questions come up without his needing to force them.

CHAIKIN: Yes — you see, what I meant, though, was the company's relation to money, to each other, to the manager, et cetera. But, you know, one thing about the theatre that's really interesting is that since theatre is about people and about situations to some degree, the political question continually comes up, heated. But one doesn't say about a flute player that he should play only marches or only certain hymns, became music is thought to be another language. And, in a way, theatre also must have the leeway, the margin, to be like flute–playing, it also must be able to be a kind of song.

∽

PART ONE

AN EXPLORATION OF
THE DECADE

Photo: Karl Bessinger

Julian Beck and Judith Malina in San Paolo
Visions, Rituals, and Transformations

1. THE RADICAL LOOSENING

In a critique of Jack Gelber's *The Connection*, which opened at the Living Theatre on July 15, 1959, the British drama critic Kenneth Tynan reported that "the people with whom it is concerned are beyond the reach of drama, as we commonly define the word."

Beyond the reach of drama Tynan had struck a chord, the implications of which he perhaps did not fully appreciate. It was a prophetic if ambiguous statement. Tynan's explanation for this "beyondness" was that the characters were "heroin addicts, from which it follows that they are almost totally passive as human beings." That is, only "the fix" and everything pertaining to the fix could move them to action.

But what Tynan apparently failed to perceive was that the "passivity" in *The Connection* began with and then went beyond the situation of junkies waiting for the fix, that it went beyond character. That in the most radical sense it was not passivity at all but an absence of drama, that it had to do not with character being made but with performers ceasing to make performances.

The spectator in 1959 who could not comprehend this radical absence of drama was not unusual. The change was barely perceptible. In fact the performers may not have been conscious of it themselves, nor Judith and Julian Beck, founders and directors of the Living Theatre. But whether its participants were fully aware of it or not, the Living Theatre production fluctuated, in the subtlest manner, between performers performing and performers not performing, between performers making character and performers being selves. As characters, they waited for the next fix, they waited to be taken out of themselves. But as selves, the performers were in themselves, comfortably in the context of self until those moments when Gelber's script called for them to take themselves out of self and back into the play, into the area almost beyond the reach of drama.

Thus, what none of us seemed to realize at the time was that some essential loosening, some radical loosening of the fabric of drama was taking place before our eyes. A double loosening was taking place, first involving the immobility of character in situation, which Tynan correctly perceived, and then, more radically still, involving the attitude of performer offering self rather than character.

There was no precedent in American theatre for this loosening. The Method technique, evolved from the aesthetics of Stanislavski, dictated that the performer derive character from analogous areas of self, from analogous experiences in self; but the concern was always to build the character and to build within a situation that would result in the modification either of character or situation. The theatre in America, since the advent of Eugene O'Neill, first with the Provincetown Players in 1919, then with the Theatre Guild in 1925, had in its most serious efforts been a theatre of character, character embedded in situation. O'Neill had been deeply influenced by Freud (*Desire Under the Elms, Strange Interlude*) and by the Greeks (*Mourning Becomes Electra*) and believed in character determined by fate, at times in the grip of the unconscious, at times in the grip of Higher Powers. In Clifford Odets' plays of the 30s, character was still in the forefront, but the major influence had shifted from fate, genetic inheritance, and the unconscious to a generally destructive socioeconomic force, symbolically represented in the Great Depression. In the early 40s, William Saroyan's gently rhapsodic characters (*My Heart's in the Highlands, The Time of Your Life*) moved through a wan, middle–class sunlight, rarely affected by environment, generating character through some intuitive sense of the godliness in men. Saroyan's people seemed transfixed into dumb saintliness by some benign, indeterminate force in the universe.

With Tennessee Williams and *The Glass Menagerie* in 1945, the world began to grow dark and untenable, but there was still character, stricken character, timidly hopeful, remembering the never–to–be–fulfilled promises of the past. The world of Southern gentility, hard drinkers, and social climbers hovered and waited while Williams' people — Tom, the narrator in *The Glass Menagerie*, and Blanche DuBois in *A Streetcar Named Desire* — flagellated self over some now impossible dream, over the personal failure of self which tainted whatever opportunity the world might have offered for salvation. In Arthur Miller (*All My Sons, Death of a Salesman*), there was a return to the failures of society. Men failed because they accepted the ethic of a competitive culture which envisioned humanity as a series of interchangeable consumers, none possessing intrinsic worth. Miller's Willy Loman feels worthless because he judges his own being according to the standards of the marketplace. Unlike an Odet's character, Willy is never smart enough to question the moral climate.

From O'Neill's fated heroes to Miller's victims of the marketplace, there is always character struggling to survive or to modify the circumstances of his existence. But with *The Connection*, partly through the absence of character but more through the presence of performer, something new begins to infect our theatre. Both the play and the performers militate against the Western notion of progress–solution, of beginnings and end-ings. In terms of the play, the plight of the junkie is unresolved, he neither succumbs to his habit nor kicks it. The structure of *The Connection* resem-bles those of Gorky's *The Lower Depths* and Beckett's *Waiting for Godot*, the latter being one of the first dramas in the West to puncture the notion of men leading meaningful lives. (In *The Lower Depths*, members of humanity fail. In *Godot*, humanity fails.) In *Godot*, games are played while Didi and Gogo wait for the possibly existent Godot to make a change in their presently futile lives. Didi and Gogo make some kind of life while waiting, they make a life of waiting. But Gelber's people, waiting for *The Connection*, waiting to be connected to a source of energy, play nothing while waiting, are not so much passive as absent. Gelber's junkies aren't even retreating, retreat is too active, but are more not there than there. Like Didi and Gogo, who will go on waiting tomorrow, will speculate futilely about the efficacy of hanging themselves, the junkies will go on waiting for the next fix. For the fix is the critical action of the play and also the recurring one. Character isn't changed and condition is only momentarily modified, therefore not modified. Unlike O'Neill's heroes, who are either destroyed by higher forces or by their own inner turmoil, or Odets' Depression–rid-den heroes who leave the bourgeois hearth to go forth to battle the System, Gelber's junkies simply go from the fix into a state of euphoria, into a har-mony with some universal inertia until their *private systems* tell them that they are in need of the next fix.

But of even greater import for the future is the attitude of the Living Theatre performer in absenting himself from his character. The performer is watching the performance; he becomes a third party, a bridge between audience and character, an intelligence which breaks in on the illusion of the continuous action of the drama. No longer is there a perfect universe of character embedded in stage setting, like the universe of every important dramatist from O'Neill to Miller. Now there comes into play a spillover of life tainting illusion, the attitude of the performer. The attitude of a par-ticular kind of socially conscious theatre begins to modify the illusion of the drama. If the given problem has a solution, the attitude of the performer as self will keep us from believing that any resolution within the experience of the performance will be adequate.

This becomes a critical point. Like good Brechtian disciples, the Becks have been uneasy about self–enclosed drama, a drama that is too perfectly illusionistic, that does all the work for the audience. In the Gelber play is the seed that is later to flower in *Mysteries* and *Paradise Now*. The attitude of the performer as self causes the responsibility for the world to be thrown back onto the audience, to be shared with the performer. Thus the radical loosening was underway in 1959; and within ten years it would challenge our dramaturgical standards, as exemplified by playwrights like O'Neill, Williams and Miller and by institutions like Broadway and its satellite, Off Broadway. Changes came rapidly, sometimes with a peremptory abruptness. Everything came into question: the place of the performer in the theatre; the place of the audience; the function of the playwright and the usefulness of a written script; the structure of the playhouse, and later, the need for any kind of playhouse; and finally, the continued existence of theatre as a relevant force in a changing culture. The questions are still being asked, but the inability to answer them hasn't at all slowed the tide of change. The changes occurred because the theatre as we had known it, the theatre of character, of problems and solutions, the theatre of beings uttering intelligently formed, balanced utterances, the theatre of significant scenes, of fortuitous events, was no longer working for many of us.

We began to understand in the sixties that the words in plays, that the physical beings in plays, that the events in plays were too often evasions, too often artifices that had to do not with truths but with semblances. At best they were about something rather than *some* thing; they were ideas describing experiences rather than the experiences. At the beginning of the 60s, there was the Living Theatre, beautifully floundering behind its proscenium toward some open life it was dimly beginning to sense. And a few people like Julie Bovasso, schoolgirl–actress, who at the age of twenty brought Jean Genet's work to the United States in the form of *The Maids*. A number of us were sensing the need for change; but, by and large, the vehicles and the mechanism for change weren't available. Grotowski had just begun to happen in 1959, but he was in Poland and unknown to us. Artaud had happened in the 20s and 30s, but in the early 60s he was barely more than a name. Meyerhold had happened in Czarist and then in Soviet Russia some fifty years earlier, but he was encrusted in legend. Beckett had happened on Broadway with *Godot* and Off Broadway with *Endgame* and *Krapp's Last Tape*, and Ionesco was happening everywhere. But a new American theatre was just sending down its roots; it was beginning to nourish a new uncertainty, beginning to ask questions that had to do with the presumptions with which humankind lived conscious and subconscious lives. We were trying to find a new way to express what we had begun to understand about character and society; we had to find a new way to express who we were becoming or who it was that we wanted to become as spectators, more responsible beings, not mesmerized by fictional creatures set in little jewel boxes carrying out their own lives; as writers, directors, and performers, beings who were more aware of the workings of our inner lives and more responsive to the social and political forces at work around us. We are still only at the beginning of that search.

2. ENSEMBLE BEGINNINGS

The sixties saw the slow development, then proliferation, of the ensemble. The disenchantment with commercial theatre paralleled a broader disenchantment with the culture at large, with America as a world power, with material well–being, with the ethic of the isolated figure laboring to merit the approval of society.

The case is overstated — it's likely that some went into ensembles for the comforts of belonging; some perhaps smelled the advantages of a coming thing — but a significant number who were also disaffected with the myth of success and with the United States as infantile if global thug discovered that the ensemble not only allowed for a serious critique of the culture, but also for sustained, therefore serious, work; and further, that the ensemble tended to make irrelevant the problem of individual glory.

The complaints against Broadway and later Off Broadway were many and familiar. Actors felt their talents were exploited in the cause of a commercial product, that aesthetic and social considerations ran a bad second to the needs of the box office, that the practice of bringing together a new package of artists for each production militated against the possibility of serious work because much rehearsal time was used up learning to adjust to one another's work habits. They also felt that the rehearsal period was far too short — on Broadway it was normally three to four weeks to allow the production to deepen sufficiently. Playwrights and directors felt that the commercial theatre barely contained the vestiges of a serious art form, that the significant concerns of their lives simply could not be dealt with in any depth in the commercial theatre. All of them — directors, writers, performers — felt the need for a new approach.

But the ensemble was not always a conscious creation, at least not in the case of the Open Theatre. Below are my notes on the beginnings of the Open Theatre, one of the early and most significant of the ensemble theatres in this country.

❖❖❖

OPEN THEATRE, EARLY DAYS. Beginning of '63, winter. Michael Smith, fellow *Village Voice* critic, invites me to join the playwrights. The Open Theatre is then in a loft in the East 20s, subletting from A.P.A.

Playwrights include Earl Scott, Megan Terry, Michael, and myself. Jean Reavey and Jean Claude von Itallie will come in later.

Nice group of people but no apparent focus. On Sunday afternoons, for example, we sit through endless scenes of Chekhov, Williams, Beckett, and then discuss performances and concepts. How is this different from any other acting group? There's also a great deal of fuss about a constitution.

The group came into being as a result of the departure from New York of acting teacher Nola Chiltern. Many of her students wanted to stay together.

"The Open Theatre," says Robert Pasolli in his book on the group, "limped into existence during the first half of 1963. The first session of record occurred on February 1st in the borrowed auditorium of the Living Theatre. Seventeen actors and four writers declared themselves to be a new theatre group, did some warm–up exercises and two improvisations... then went across the street for coffee."[1]

Well into the spring, not much more was happening.

Members at that time include Catherine Mandas, Joe Chaikin, Mike Bradford, Peter Feldman, Murray Paskin, Gerry Ragni, Lee Worley, Isabelle Blau, Sydney Walter, Paul Boesing, Ira Zuckerman, Jim Barbosa, Barbara Vann, Ron Faber, Mimi Cozzens, Sharon Gans, Jordan Hott, Lynn Kevin, and Valerie Belden.

We talk, perform small projects, but no focus. But at some point Joe Chaikin begins a workshop to deal with the problems of actors learning how to work with non–naturalistic material. It's a time when the Absurd is coming into its own in America.

Always something innocent about Joe. In the workshop sessions he's inarticulate, not essentially inarticulate but peripherally so. Painful but exciting to watch him trying to verbalize impulses to form axioms to concretize what's buzzing inside him. And the actors listen with extraordinary patience, and with devotion.

But still no focus. A number of us are restless. But we are beginning to scratch at something. A catalyst appears on the scene that spring — Geraldine Lust, one of the producers of Genet's *The Blacks*. She was later to write about conversations she and I had during that period:

> Among the themes we explored were two which struck firm chords in both of us: one, the conviction that theatre should be functioning at a point beyond that which the community has reached, although this is

[1] Robert Pasolli, *A Book On the Open Theatre* (Indianapolis: Bobbs-Merrill, 1970), p. 2

a reversal of the traditional relationship in which theatre reflects the events around it; it seemed to us that our times were moving so swiftly that we could not afford to let the most effective voice be the tardy one. This led to an examination of what is community in the 1960s .and what is leadership for it, and we wondered how it might be possible to create, through theatre, ideas for a community.

The second exciting discourse concerned the theatre as a function of man which enriches him by bringing into consciousness the unspoken levels of our human experience the theatre being midwife to dreams, an Artaudian concept. [2]

Thus man in the community, man in the *polis*, man in his collective unconscious. Brecht, and Artaud out of Jung.

A series of conferences over the late spring leads to the decision to run several workshops. There will be Joe's, and also workshops by Peter Feldman, a performer who had come from the Living Theatre, and by Geraldine Lust. Also, Jordan Hott, a director, will organize a series of plays around the theme of the Absurd.

The Absurd has taken some hold on the group, but in fact it is not that strong. Joe's head is seething with ideas relating to socio–psychological problems. All of us consider it of paramount importance to develop what Grotowski was later to call the psycho–physical life of the performer.

Joe is obsessed by the theme of alienation in modern society. Many of the techniques developed are ways of counteracting within the performer this sense of alienation from self, just as many of the themes explored are about the alienation of the individual and the mass.

Ultimately the Absurd is incorporated predominantly as an idea for a counteraction. Unlike Ionesco and his non sequiturs, exploration in the Open Theatre is not principally verbal but is *sometimes* through the word and more often through the body.

Geraldine Lust's workshop runs for about two months. I recall her leaning somewhat more toward the Arcadian Man as opposed to the political Mass Man of the early Chaikin, but in fact both are very concerned with the subconscious. Joe was later to write, "We are joined to each other by forces ... of two kinds. The first are political–social forces which move irrevocably through all of us who are alive at the same time in history. We are further joined by other forces: unanswerable questions to do with being alive at all."[3] And this aliveness has partly to do with man the

[2] Geraldine Lust, Introduction, in Arthur Sainer, *The Sleepwalker and the Assassin* (New York: Bridgehead Books, 1964).

[3] Joseph Chaikin, *The Presence of the Actor* (New York: Atheneum, 1972) pp. 11, 12

half–formed, man the grotesque, and man the dreamed. Man is what he is dreaming, he is both the dreamer and the dreamed. And here the radical theatre is trying to dredge up the life of the race. New body movements, new sounds, a new awareness must be formed in order to make comprehensible this underground life of the race.

The Open Theatre at the time of its sometimes floundering beginnings was a place to work, and to experiment in order to perfect the work. To experiment in order to deepen self, work, and ultimately, the community. To. this end we not only ran workshops but also held general discussions. We met, for instance, one Sunday afternoon after John Kennedy's assassination because we wanted in some way to share our feelings about the murder that had just taken place.

The concern in those early months: to move closer to reality. Public performances were far from the thinking of the ensemble, certainly far from Joe's mind. But under the persuasion of Gordon Rogoff, who, along with Richard Gilman, had become one of two advisers, the group gave its first public performance or demonstration on a Monday night in December 1963 at the Sheridan Square Playhouse. The evening consisted of a collection of exercises, improvisations, and short pieces written for the ensemble. It became the first of a number of Monday nights, at the Sheridan Square Playhouse and the Martinique Theatre.

The ensemble in those early performances leaned heavily on social satire. An obsessive cuteness not evident in the workshops plagued the performances. Partly it stemmed from the notion that "performing" was synonymous with "pleasing the audience," as if the spectator had to be wooed. It was one of the dangers of performing publicly, and it took the Open Theatre several years to get past that problem, remnants of which still existed in *The Serpent*, in 1968, the work in which the ensemble truly seemed to mature, to find a physical life for its early concepts.

❖❖❖

If the developing notion of ensemble seemed congenial to artists in the theatre who wanted to do serious work, its appeal also began to be felt by those who were planning for or already working in areas far from theatre. Students with divergent interests (e.g., in physics, in political science) and older people already launched in other careers found themselves drawn to the ideas of ensemble as a new and unique way of expressing ideas about self and society, as a new way of being with the community. One of the earliest of such non–theatrical groups was the Bread & Puppet Theater. Throughout its life it has been staffed predominantly by young students, but its personnel has also included a general practitioner, Dr. Irving Oil, a housewife, Pearl Oil, a professor of sociology, Jules Rabin, as well as a handful of "professionals": Murray Levy, who had worked in commercial theatre before going on to the Free Southern Theatre; Carol Grosberg, performer and coordinator of the Angry Arts Week in New York; Robert Nichols, playwright, poet and landscape architect; and Margo Sherman, director and actress.

The Bread & Puppet Theater was founded at the beginning of the 60s by Peter Schumann, German–born (in Breslau, later Poland's Wroclaw, where Grotowski's Polish Laboratory Theatre was to work). Schumann had been both a puppeteer and a choreographer and had taught at the progressive Putney School in Vermont by the time he came to New York. His first New York production was *Totentanz* (*Dance of Death*); it was given several performances in the city, one of which this writer witnessed on a freezing afternoon in the winter of 1962 at the Sheridan Square Playhouse. That performance was part of a week–long series of demonstrations, lectures, and performances sponsored by the General Strike for Peace. (*Totentanz* is discussed in Chapter 3, "Ritual and Ceremony.") Within two years Schumann had built a permanent troupe and was performing regularly in a loft on Delancey Street. Word began to spread about the troupe; its performance of *Fire*, a work inspired by the self–immolation of several Americans in protest against the US involvement in Vietnam, began to be discussed among the theatrical underground. Audiences were intrigued by the troupe's combined use of massive puppets, at least twice the size of human, with sometimes grotesque, sometimes noble countenances, tiny rod puppets, and human figures, often masked. And by the combination of rude humor, lyric gentleness and almost archetypal violence in the stories. Soon the troupe began to be seen on the streets as well as in its Delancey Street headquarters, creating masked processions and plays during peace demonstrations.

With the Bread & Puppets as a spearhead, the idea of the non–theatrical or nonprofessional ensemble began to take hold. By 1965 the Pageant Players had come into being, and by the end of the decade there was the Theatre for the Burning City, the Stomachache Theatre, the It's All Right to Be a Woman Theatre, the East Bay Sharks, the Moving Men, the Ontrabanda Company, and numerous others — all enthusiastic, some short–lived.

The Pageant Players were formed by a group of young people who wanted to use theatre as a forum for their political beliefs. The political orientation was primarily Marxist, the predominant view was that the US was imperialistic abroad and repressive and smothering at home. The Pageant

Players also wanted no part of a traditional theatre building; their plays were performed both indoors and out, at political demonstrations, at sit–ins (e.g., the student takeover at Columbia University in 1968), at schools, in parks, on the street, and once, back in 1966, in a laundromat.

From what this writer is able to gather (I never saw their early work), there was a certain rough edge to the first offerings of the Pageant Players. They had a kind of inspired amateurishness, relying heavily on energetic beliefs and a simple, anti–illusionistic rhetoric. Their initial production was *The Paper Tiger Pageant*, first presented in November of 1965, a "dance/movement and music" piece, as Michael Brown, one of the founders of the Players, describes it, a kind of "anti–imperialist analysis," performed at peace rallies. *King Con* was performed both outdoors and in during the summer of 1966, and dealt with giant corporate power behaving irresponsibly in terms of the economic and ecological life of the community. In the fall of 1966, the *Laundromat* play was developed, treating US aggression in Vietnam in allegorical terms. Several performers, pretending to be customers in a laundromat, begin to quarrel among themselves in front of legitimate laundromat customers who become, unknown to themselves, audience members.

During the next few years, the Pageant Players moved from a reliance on enthusiasm and political beliefs to a serious concern with spiritual and bodily disciplines as a way of clarifying their theatrical statements and as a way of deepening their commitment to the social problems of the day. But by the end of the decade the troupe as such had come to an end, some of its members going west to Oregon to found a new company, some to the Bay Area to found the Moving Men, others remaining in New York to found the Painted Women Ritual Theatre.

Some groups, like the Bread & Puppets, combined professional performers and amateurs. The OM–Theatre Workshop began, in 1967, as an acting class for young people in the Boston area who were not necessarily interested in theatre as a profession. But after some months it was felt that a production was necessary to further the learning process and professional considerations soon modified the original intentions. The work that evolved, under the direction of Julie Portman, who had been conducting the class, was called *Riot*. It opened late in 1967 in the basement of the Arlington St. Church in downtown Boston, was acclaimed by local critics, proved to be a box–office hit, and after its initial run, reopened, played a long engagement in Boston, toured the outlying areas and eventually, in late 1968, came to New York.

Riot begins with a panel on the question of racial harmony. The participants, black radical, white liberal, black liberal and white conservative, begin with reasonable if sometimes hostile give–and–take; but the dialogue degenerates into a fist–fight, at which point the entire theatre is shaken by a simulated riot perpetrated by other members of the company.

By the time of *Riot*, the company had become more oriented toward production. And because several professionals were brought in specifically for the production, the nature of the organism became somewhat diffuse. Were the actors amateurs making social statements or professionals making "good" theatre? Probably both. Also, it was Julie Portman's idea that the company would create the production, that the script would be an ensemble creation. Ultimately, however, the script was written by first one, then another, professional writer, and the action conceived primarily by the director and a young choreographer, Elizabeth Martin.

The hope of the OM was to deal with social issues and to use experimental techniques in company–conceived productions. Some of these goals were partially fulfilled. For example, the church service it performed in May 1968 (described in detail in Part Two) provided the company with a chance to explore new techniques. However, even here, under the pressure of a deadline, the scripted section of the service was finally composed by this writer and the movements predominantly by Portman and Martin.

Julie Portman's theatrical focus was on the physical but always in connection with the spiritual. Yoga exercises were employed as warm–ups for each session, and the sounding of om was central to the warm–ups. Also employed were trust exercises (now traditional with ensembles), one of which has a performer moving with eyes closed, trusting that his colleagues will keep him from danger. As for technical skills, they were principally confined to music and movement. Like most ensemble groups at this period, little if any emphasis was given to traditional acting — for example, to the problem of building character. Primary attention was devoted to the spirit — of the individual performer, of the group.

During the summer of 1968, this writer arranged for the OM troupe to run a six–week workshop at Bennington College, where I was then part of the drama faculty. We worked intensively on *Hunger*, an idea concerned with mass starvation, and finally gave a twenty–minute demonstration piece before an invited audience.

At Tulane University in the mid–60s, Richard Schechner, along with Franklin Adams and Paul Epstein, formed the New Orleans Group. Its best known work was Ionesco's *Victims of Duty*, produced in June of 1967. As Schechner, who was a member of the Tulane drama department and editing the *Tulane Drama Review* at the time puts it, "The theatre department blew up in 1967." TDR, with Schechner, moved to New York, to become

The Drama Review at New York University, and Schechner set out to find his way in the New York theatrical scene. In October of 1967 he was involved in the staging of a guerrilla–warfare piece, simultaneously taking place at twenty–seven locations both in theatres and on the street. In November he began a workshop with some forty performers but in January of 1968, when he began work on *The Bacchae* of Euripides, the number of performers was down to fifteen. The company decided to call itself the Performance Group, and in March it moved to a garage on Wooster Street in lower Manhattan. Also in March, the company presented the birth–ritual section of *Dionysus in 69*, as their adaptation of *The Bacchae* had come to be called, at Washington Square Methodist Church in Greenwich Village.

The complete *Dionysus* opened at the Performing Garage on June 6. The spectator had the sense that he could help make the production, he was encouraged to get into the play, to participate in the rituals, to chant, march, touch, strip and be fondled. The spatial design of the theatre, with its various levels of scaffolding, served to integrate the audience with performer action on the stage, so that the spectator might further feel he was always, potentially, involved in the action.

In *Dionysus* the performers made biographical references to themselves, thus going in and out of their mythical and legendary characters. They often referred to one another by their own names. They would move from formalized ritual action to ordinary, "non–theatrical" action, as if they had left the play. They would also move from a formal rhetoric (lines from Euripides) to an assumed spontaneity manifested through the colloquialisms of the contemporary hipster. In fact, in developing the play, Schechner had laid down the following rehearsal rules — the Dionysus performer, a god, was allowed to improvise and to use hip language, but the Pentheus character, man, had to stick to the script, to the formal language of his time. The script, then, evolved partly through what Euripides had to say, partly through what the performers and Schechner had to say about themselves and current social problems (e.g., sexual liberation).

The aesthetic ideology of the Performance Group, as well as that of the OM and of the Open Theatre, embraced a communal creation, the impetus for which seemed in part a reaction to the paternalistic behavior of the US establishment.

On the West Coast, in 1959, a time when the radical movement in the East was represented only by the Living Theatre (and it was not yet an ensemble), the San Francisco Mime Troupe came into existence. It began as a unit of the San Francisco Actor's Workshop, and was called the R.G. Davis Mime Troupe, after its founder and director, Ronnie Davis. According to Joan Holden, currently one of the moving forces in the Mime

Troupe, "the name was changed [to the S.F. Mime Troupe] when the Troupe left the Workshop in 1962, but it remained R.G. Davis's Mime Troupe until 1970."

According to an old program note, the Troupe "inaugurated the first outdoor *commedia dell'arte* shows on the West Coast. In 1960–61 we went outdoors with a small stage and presented free *commedia dell'arte* (Italian popular and bawdy comedy) to the people in the parks."

In 1963 the Mime Troupe opened an indoor theatre with Jarry's *Ubu Roi*, some original plays, and happenings. The Troupe had always had an impulse toward radical politics, and by 1965 it was offering a political evening, Brecht's *The Exception and the Rule* together with a talk on Vietnam by journalist Robert Scheer. Also in 1965, it toured its famous *Minstrel Show* or *Civil Rights in a Cracker Barrel*. "We have worked on this show," say the notes for *Cracker Barrel*, "improvising, writing and reworking the material for nine months. We began with a desire to deal with racial issues in the theater, but the plays we read and the material available did not talk about what we knew, and feared. The Minstrel form lends itself to some of the subjects that confront us. It is an epic form, an open–stage form where social subjects can be bounced around and not reduced to 'adjustment psychology.'"

"The old Mime Troupe's best show," says Joan Holden, "was . . . *Civil Rights in a Cracker Barrel* but its mainstay and training ground was *commedia dell'arte*. We did classical comedies in *commedia* style, rewriting them to connect them with the present and give them our tone and line which — looking back on it — was anarchist; now it's Marxist. In the course of this change the company became a collective and Ronnie left.

"We performed our *commedias*, as we still do all our shows, in the parks, passing the hat. The avant–garde theatres stayed in their cellars, which is probably why the Mime Troupe is now the oldest theatre in San Francisco. We thought of ourselves as outside agitators; outside the establishment, obviously, but also — in our roles as artists — outside the movement, despite our sympathy for it. Now, if there were a Red Army, we would be an 'art and propaganda team.' In the absence of an army, we work with different groups as occasions arise." Such as Los Siete de La Raza, the seven Latinos charged with shooting a San Francisco policeman in 1969. (See *Los Siete (BART)* in Part Two.)

In the Midwest, in 1969, the Firehouse Theater of Minneapolis decided to move to San Francisco. It published a booklet at that time in which Marlow Hotchkiss, managing director of the Firehouse Theater, talked about the company's "spiritual history" and its "years of experimentation and exploration."

August 21, 1963, 8:30 p.m. *The Connection* by Jack Gelber, direction by Charles Morrison, set design and program notes by Marlow Hotchkiss, opened the newly formed Firehouse Theater, Inc. July 12, 1969, *A Mass Actors and Audience on the Passion and Birth of Doctor John Faust According to the Spirit of Our Times*, text by Marlow Hotchkiss, the Firehouse Theater Company, and others, direction by Sydney Walter, was given as the last performance in the old Firehouse Theater...A community theater with a professional director, but relying on open auditions among a pool of local amateur actors, students, and housewives, confronts severe limitations. Its rationale is primarily social and at best it will reflect the values and mores of its community. In setting up, the Firehouse Theater initially on such a community model, we assured the complete frustration of any artistic or political vision on the part of its founders. Our goal, which was hardly more specific than a desire to be relevant, and which practically meant that we staged last year's better Off–Broadway offerings (e.g., *The Connection, The Caretaker, The Brig*), became lost in a morass of budget blunders, inept talent, PR fiascoes, petty emotionalism and alienated audiences. Who wanted contemporary, relevant plays when they only succeeded in embarrassing you?

In two years the Firehouse Theater moved from a vague promise of relevance to spiritual bankruptcy. Ironically, the solution to this problem was found in yet another New York model, Off–Off–Broadway. When Sydney Walter took over artistic leadership of the Firehouse, he brought with him a legacy of experimentation from the Open Theatre, as well as a belief in an ongoing improvisational workshop, as the watershed of an ensemble growth.

In improvisational workshops and in productions, the actors continued to ask basic questions about character, role, personality and identity. A premium was placed on freedom and flexibility, on being able to take imaginative leaps, to establish a character *in relation* to another actor's creation, and then to transform to a completely new relationship, changing in an instant all givens of role, situation, character, motivation, etc. The result: techniques of insanity which nonetheless looked more naturalistic to us than the conceits of Zola and Chekhov. In three years our exploration became a hydra–headed affair, going everywhere and arriving nowhere. We tried multimedia productions with Ionesco and New York playwright Arthur Sainer; we staged Beckett with strobe lights and performed two plays simultaneously on the same stage; we tampered with the classics, doing *Peer Gynt* as a freewheeling athletic production, and *Iphigenia* as a transformation play, complete with audience participation, choral improvisations, and a popsicle–beer party at the end. We mounted Megan Terry's *Jack-Jack* with original music, a nude scene, and film projections. We explored a broad commedia style, taking Brecht's *A Man's a Man* into Minneapolis parks. Through all these experiments ran the thread of transformation and our preoccupation with an ongoing definition for ego and role. For the company and audiences alike this was a period of wild growth and unpredictable changes. Audiences were alternately amused and distressed to find the foundations of our work shifting from production to production. For the acting company this was an intense period of self–discovery. Because of the multi–directional aspect of the work, many of the self–discoveries meant that an actor found himself interested in a specific type of theater that no longer interested the rest of the company and therefore had to leave. This coming and going was part of the excitement of the theater at this time, and the changes in personnel only served to reinforce the multi–directional nature of the work.

"If someone in the world is being hit, why not me? I always hoped to get something back."

(Rags, Nancy Walter)

With the production of *Rags*, written by a member of our company, the exploration took on a more specific direction. The themes and the techniques of transformations became redefined. The actor was now seen as a willing victim of the various specific situations in the script and in the staging. The actor as victim meant that he was not so much the agent of action as the one who is acted upon. By surrendering willingly to the situations of the moment, the actor can deal with what is really happening on stage and in the auditorium as well as what is fictionally happening. Role and role player become one, but one who is constantly in the process of changing to a different one.

The history of the Firehouse is a history of an impulse which is larger than the sum of the individuals who are collected together at any one time. From no vision to a hopeful and viable vision of the theater as a force for change, that anonymous impulse begins to take on new life. Where the theater was once a "community" theater, we are now a communal theater. We live together. Our work, after *Faust*, becomes more risky; we ask our .audience to take these risks with us. I don't believe that theater can ever change a person's politics or ethical values; at best it can merely reflect the coming changes in values. But it is capable, if we are willing to commit ourselves to each other and to. the moment, of changing people's perceptions, of radically altering the ways in which we see ourselves and each other. I and Thou.[4]

As the Mime Troupe grew out of the Actors Workshop, so El Teatro Campesino grew out of the Mime Troupe. At least its use of agitprop and its guerrilla–theatre esprit provided inspiration for Luis Valdez, a young theatre student from San Jose State College who worked with the Mime Troupe for a time before he organized Teatro. But Teatro also grew out of a specific economic action — the 1965 grape strike in Central California. And unlike every other ensemble discussed in this volume, Teatro was not a middle–class or student company but, with the exception of Valdez him-self, a theatre of farm workers. Farm workers playing for other farm work-ers, dramatizing the condition of Chicanos in the fields.

In an interview with Beth Bagby in the Summer 1967 issue of the *Tulane Drama Review*, Valdez describes his initial attempt to start a theatre of farm workers. The first meetings were at the Delano, California, head-quarters of the United Farm Workers Organizing Committee:

> I talked for about ten minutes, and then realized that talking wasn't going to accomplish anything. The thing to do was do it, so I called three of them over [student volunteers, not farm workers — Valdez was disappointed], and on two hung *huelgista* [striker] signs. Then I gave one an *esquirol* sign, and told him to stand up there and act like an esquirol — a scab. He didn't want to at first, because it was a dirty word at that time, but he did it in good spirits. Then the two *huelgis-tas* started shouting at him, and everybody started cracking up. All of a sudden, people started coming into the pink house from I don't know where; they filled up the whole kitchen. We started changing signs around and people started volunteering. "Let me play so and so," "Look this is what I did," imitating all kinds of things. We ran for about two hours just doing that. By the time we had finished, there were people packing the place. They were in the doorways, the living room, and they were outside at the windows peeking in . . .

> That was the beginning. The effects we achieved that night were fan-tastic, because people were acting out real things. Then I got together an original group of about five, and we started working on skits — this was all done after picketing hours, by the way. Sometimes we would-n't get started until eight or nine . . .

> There's a dramatic theory — we used to talk about it in the Mime Troupe. I think we've put a different use to it in the Teatro just out of necessity, but it is that your dramatic situation, the thing you're trying

---

[4] Marlow Hotchkiss, "A Spiritual History," in *Firehouse Theater*, privately printed booklet by the Firehouse Theater, 1969.

to portray on the stage, must be very close to the reality that is on the stage. You take the figure of DiGiorgio standing on the backs of two farm workers. The response of the audience is to the very real situation of one human being standing on two others. That type of fakery is not imitation. It's a theatrical reality that will hold up on the flatbed of a truck.[5]

Comedy has been a principal element in the work of the Teatro. Satire, slapstick, clowning. But recently El Teatro Campesino has added an element of mysticism. In its first full–length, collective work, *La Carpa de Los Rasquachis* ("Tent of the Underdogs"), Teatro introduces two *mitos* (myths) through the figures of Jesus and of the Aztec god Quetzalcoatl, whom the Mexicans and the Chicanos await in his resurrection. The spiritual values inherent in these figures reinforce the sense that political action cannot do it alone, that the forms of action needed to make a free society entail more than labor, the picket line and political awareness.

The seventies saw the development of new companies. André Gregory's Manhattan Project, with its initial performance of *Alice in Wonderland*, based at the NYU School of the Arts. Medicine Show, also operating out of New York, the creation of former Open Theatre members, including James Barbosa and Barbara Vann. The Iowa Theatre Lab, from the University of Iowa, the offspring of Ric Zank. In the Bay Area, the Moving Men, mentioned earlier in this chapter, the child of several of the male Pageant Players and Burning City performers.

The Bridge Collective began as this writer's brainchild. It came into existence because of my own need to create theatre with an ensemble. Most ensembles are essentially directors' companies, with playwrights, when used at all, functioning as adjunct forces. (The Firehouse, since its move to San Francisco and the emergence of Nancy Waiter as writer–director, is an exception.) I needed an ensemble where I could operate as one of the guiding forces, testing out my own ideas rather than simply providing a text for the ideas of others. Before the birth of the Bridge Collective, I had felt trapped between writing for existing ensemble troupes who were wary of written scripts and the more–or–less traditional theatrical scheme where a play is chosen and a group of people who have not previously worked together as a unit are assembled for the limited goal of making one play happen.

The Bridge Collective began work in the spring of 1972. Its personnel included former Open Theatre performers, Kay Camey Ralph Lee, and Ron Faber, as well as the Bread & Puppets' Maurice Blanc. We worked out

[5] Beth Bagby, "El Teatro Campesino: Interviews with Luis Valdez," in the *Tulane Drama Review* (T 36), Vol. 11, No. 4, Summer 1967

of St. Clement's Church for several months, with Kay conducting warm–ups and the workshop itself divided between myself, Maurice and Kay. I had stressed that I wanted the group to have a political orientation. That is, I wanted its existence to indicate that it was somehow in touch with the life of the streets, with what was happening in Washington, DC, and the world at large. I had grown very tired, I stated, and was to state again when the Group reformed at the end of the year, of making theatre that was going to be judged solely as theatre, as a work which the audience felt impelled to *judge* — that is, if *anything* impelled it to do *anything* — to judge rather than be with. I wasn't interested in demonstrating aesthetic niceties, in showing how well we could make theatre, but was interested in *making something happen* that related to the world outside.

In this connection I began using workshop sessions to try out ideas for a collective work, *Attica Lives!*, which would deal with the political and psychological sense of America today. I made the assumption that the group wanted to create a collective work before I myself begin creating a script for them. After two months I was disabused of this notion. In a talk session, I was exhorted to sit down and simply write a play that the company could then work on.

So I spent the summer writing. Not one play but two. *The Spring Offensive* and *Attica Lives!* But by the fall it became more and more obvious that the group was not holding together. Kay Carney was no longer available, Maurice Blanc and Ron Faber went on to do other shows, and Ralph Lee rejoined the Open Theatre. In the January of 1973 the group started taking shape again. Nancy Gabor, a former Open Theatre actress who had been an integral part of the development of *The Serpent*, joined the Collective as director of the workshop and, along with me, as artistic co–director. With Nancy came Calvin Holt who became managing director and a key figure in the workshop, conducting movement–and–sound based on yoga principles. In February we began work on *The Spring Offensive*, and in June we opened the play for a three–week run at Super Nova, a gallery in New York's Soho district.

The Open Theatre disbanded after its fall 1973 tour. By the beginning of 1975, the Bridge Collective had suspended its operations. The Firehouse Theater no longer functions as an ensemble but as a loose alliance of theatre people, coming together for individual projects. Peter Schumann's Bread & Puppets has also been transformed into a loose alliance. Joe Chaikin works with similar alliances.

Finally, the Living Theatre. A strange phenomenon, because it pre-dates all the other groups but was a comparative latecomer to ensemble work. *The Brig*, the last work before the company's shutdown by the

Internal Revenue Service in 1963 and its subsequent exile from the US, did suggest the beginnings of an ensemble at work through the obsessively if unconsciously coordinated movements of the prisoners in the brig; but it was not until its nomadic life in Europe began, in 1964, that the company began to explore with any depth the psycho–physical life of the performer, that it began to experiment in workshop, that it began to think of the whole company in the collaborative process of making the play. As Joe Chaikin in his days as performer with the Living Theatre had been influenced ideologically by Judith and Julian Beck, so later the Becks were influenced by Joe's ensemble experiments with the Open Theatre. The sound and–movement exercise, which the Open Theatre developed extensively in its early days, was taught to the Living Theatre by Lee Worley, an Open Theatre member who was in Paris while the Living Theatre was performing there in 1964. The sound–and–movement exercise became scene seven of *Mysteries and Smaller Pieces.*

According to Saul Gottlieb, "*Mysteries* was born almost accidentally, when the company was asked to give an evening's entertainment in exchange for free rehearsal space at the American Center for Students and Artists in Paris."[6] *Mysteries* has no script, many of the scenes are exercises and improvisations, and almost all of the evening foregoes dialogue, instead concentrating heavily on sounds and on movements of the body. In *Mysteries and Frankenstein*, and later in *Antigone*, the Living Theatre began to develop the use of the physical mass — performers collectively forming a larger–than–life being or a collective being or sometimes an object. By 1968, in *Paradise Now*, the first piece truly developed by the whole company, the ensemble in its collective physical life had become a dominant feature.

Until *Paradise Now*, the Living Theatre never asked for participation by the spectator — it was not an aesthetic principle of the company's, though by 1968 it had become a political one. Gottlieb reports that during the plague scene in *Mysteries*, in which almost everyone in the ensemble "dies," in which "violent assaults occur, bodies roll off the stage into the audience, the actors gasping, blubbering, sputtering and wailing," and in which the bodies, in death, are later piled up on stage, first side by side, then on top of one another, "forming a pyramidal body–pile," the spectators found themselves getting into the performance. "Most people get out of their seats, mill about, laugh, cry, shout, touch the bodies of the actors, pull and push them, even sometimes beat them. Some people die with the

---

[6] Saul Gottlieb, "The Living Theatre in Exile: *Mysteries, Frankenstein.*" In *Tulane Drama Review*, (T 32), Vol. 10, No. 4, Summer, 1966.

actors and permit themselves to be put in the body–pile — in Brussels, fifty people took part in the scene."[7]

Unlike the other ensembles, the Living Theatre has echoed the history of avant–garde theatre and then gone past it, has gone through multiple changes, a veritable lifetime of changes. The theatre began in the Becks' living room with performances of poetic dramas and moved into theatres; then, many years later, out of theatres into the street; and finally, past the street into primitive villages (in Brazil) where the drama as we have known it gave way to an attempt to form new rituals, where the attempt to enlighten has been joined by the attempt to make the revolution.

❖❖❖

A word needs to be said about contemporary European influences on the early ensembles. During the formative years of the Open Theatre, the Firehouse, and other ensembles functioning through the first half of the 60s, the influences were from the recent past, from Artaud and Brecht. No European ensemble had any influence on the American theatre in those years.

And there was barely a movement. Grotowski began his Polish Laboratory Theatre in 1959, but he was hardly known in his own country, much less in ours. Grotowski had never seen our theatres and we had never heard of his. The first word of him that came through to the US was by way of Jim Hatch, a New York writer who, while in Egypt in 1964, sent to the *Tulane Drama Review* Grotowski's program notes for the Polish Laboratory Theatre's production of *Doctor Faustus* (T24). The following year TDR printed Ludwik Flaszen's article on the Polish Laboratory Theatre's *Akropolis* (T27), and the revealing photographs of an obviously disciplined ensemble sent reverberations through the US. experimental theatre. Needless to say, within the next few years Grotowski's influence became enormous.

About the time that Grotowski became known in the US, at least known through texts and photographs, the Peter Brook production of *Marat/Sade* made its assault on New York. The Royal Shakespeare version of the Peter Weiss play gave New York a sense of what Brook and Charles Marowitz had been doing in London since 1963 in their Theatre of Cruelty Workshop. At its best, *Marat/Sade* was moved by the principles of Artaud. At its worst, the production affected a sense of ensemble performance that never seemed authentic. But the departure from traditional theatre shook New York audiences and theatre people who had never seen or

---

[7] Ibid.

heard of the Open Theatre. Along with the rumored work of the Polish Laboratory Theatre, Brook's Theatre of Cruelty production helped to expand the sense of a new theatre.

Generally, experimentation in European theatre seemed to be in the hands of lone artists, the happening artists and men like Hermann Nitsch, who carved up previously slaughtered animals in his performances. As late as January 1968, the one experimental company I saw in Europe was Connie Hans Meyer's Komodianten Theatre in Vienna. But Meyer's theatre worked exclusively in a Brechtian mode and was, therefore, something of an exciting throwback. If there were other experimental ensembles working in Europe in the first half of the decade, many of us in the U.S. were unaware of them.

On the other hand, the Living Theatre, an American export, self-exiled to London and the Continent, had an enormous impact on the European theatre and, like the Polish Laboratory Theatre, was responsible for the proliferation of European ensembles in the second half of the decade.

3. RITUAL AND CEREMONY

Artaud called for ritual in theatre, but how was one to respond? Theories and ideologies may be calls to action, but to initiate action is another thing. One responds to necessity, not to causes.

In the fifties many of us felt that the our theatre was drying up, that its concentration on the ordinary, albeit the ordinary in crisis, was weighing it down, that we needed what in fact Artaud had cried for: magic, spectacle, incantation, ceremony, ritual. The confines of the psychological drama, the sense that theatre was shriveling beneath the surface drabness of character and the ordinariness of place and event, fed the need for some other approach; but how could a need, beyond the need for ideology, be sufficient to make something else happen? How, for example, could ritual happen, past ideology, past need? The theatre, despite Artaud's plea, did not find ritual. Instead ritual found the theatre.

I've chosen to use the terms ritual, rite and ceremony. I conceive of ritual as a dynamic process that employs ceremony to heighten occasion and the sense of occasion, rather than as a series of prescribed acts handed down from an earlier time.

The emptiness in *Waiting for Godot* did not create ritual; but the absence of linear events, of traditional psychological promptings as we had known them, emptied the theatre sufficiently so that something else could take place. The scattered devices employed to combat emptiness *became* ritual — in the emptiness ritual became organic content. Didi and Gogo do not decide to create ritual, but the repetition of their game–playing, the use of game–playing to begin with, transforms the action into ritual. In the Living Theatre production of Kenneth Brown's *The Brig*, the formalized prison composed procedures begin as barbarous reality, but through repetition and intensity they become ritualized. The nature of the continuing act (e.g., prisoners' constant request for permission to cross the white line in language that must be repeated without change and sounded at an inhumanly high volume) transforms the act, even as it retains its original nature, so that the act is unmoored from its impetus and takes its place in the world as a ceremony no longer dependent on cause and effect.

(Playwrights and ensemble groups have also manufactured ritual, as one markets fashion, but the best work — the plague section of the Living Theatre's *Mysteries*, the Open Theatre's *Terminal*, the Bread & Puppets'

Fire—has been fostered by the need, not to make ritual, but to understand the nature of events and sometimes to change circumstances. The ritual is inherent in certain subjects and in certain ways of theatricalizing a vision.)

The characteristics of ritual and ceremony, sometimes contradictory, include a formalized action and often a repetitive one. The formality is one of attitude: the performer has a sense or awareness of occasion, is being called on to allow the manifestation of an act, a gesture which is set off from those acts which are taken for granted. The ritualized or ceremonious action is always seen as extraordinary, whether or not it is separate from the daylight world. Often the action also appears to set itself off, to conflagrate itself. We lose the sense of response to a prior event. The act–or, maker of the act, appears as the carrier of the act; the act appears to be maintained for its own sake, not for the sake of its maker. The action is thus liberated from causality, from prior action, and from its own actor.

The making of the action becomes its own primary purpose, that is to say, it becomes "purposeless." It is there for no good, it begins to be there because it must be there, it carries no moral connotation, it is its own cause, its own defense. The action is still, however, in the world, making the action is a way of being in the world. But simultaneously the action is outside the world, the world of the familiar, and its maker–carrier is outside the world.

The use of repetition tends to make the action sacramental. In certain events, the memory of a previous action fortifies the present with a curious sense of what has been accomplished and, conversely, never accomplished. We have the memory of the action, therefore the memory of having accomplished it. But we are also repeating the action as if we had not accomplished it. Something is impelling us to this repetition and we begin to understand that though we accomplish the action a hundred times, that is, though we complete it, we will never *really* accomplish it, never *really* complete it. For the action takes us nowhere but back to its own necessity. We come in time to be partners or accomplices in the action, and our partner is the action itself. We act for the sake of the action, and it acts for no sake, it is both mysterious (sacred) and necessary.

As anyone who has ever repeated words over and over knows, constant verbal repetition tends to wipe out symbolic meaning. This sounding remains outside the area of ritual and ceremony. Certain repetitive social acts —I am thinking here of the early plays of Jean–Claude von Itallie (*America Hurrah!*) and Megan Terry (*Calm Down, Mother*), in which characters repeat pat phrases—point up the absurdities in social intercourse but lack mysterious character. The action in these plays may be "ritualized" but it is also and purposely trivialized. We see less of the unknown rather than more of it.

It is important to return to Beckett and Genet as earlier writers employing ritual and ceremony. In Beckett the action operates as a denial of its own efficacy even as it supports its necessity. In *Endgame*, in *Happy Days*, in *Act Without Words II*, the day is apportioned into a series of ceremonial acts. Hamm, the blind and impotent kinglike figure in the wheelchair, has his painkiller, plays with his toy dog, is moved about the room. Winnie has her song and her shopping bag. A and B have brushing of teeth, prayers, and physical exercises. The acts are referral points, landmarks in a desert. They are stabilizers, reassurances, operating much as the crutch of closely and regularly positioned lampposts might operate for a cripple whose only mobility comes through staggering from one post to the next. Between the posts, emptiness. Also, the potential abyss. But the acts are also subverting. They can't change the condition of things, they promise what they can't deliver. One is always expectant — one is always disappointed. The acts must be repeated; disappointment and weariness undermine even as the acts fortify. But the acts reinforce themselves, there is nowhere else to go but to the act, no other way to be, no other action as efficacious. Thus the acts are both saviors and subtle destroyers, pseudo–healers and slow killers.

In Genet, prior to *The Screens*, the ritual is not so much an action as a gesture. While Beckett's acts may have symbolic overtones, they are nevertheless literal acts. Winnie doesn't pretend to sing, she sings. Didi and Gogo don't pretend to play games or wait for Godot, they do play and do wait. But Genet's rituals are pretenses. The blacks make the gesture of murder, in *The Maids* Claire and Solange take turns at pretending to be Madame. In fact, Genet calls for male actors to pretend to be female actors who. pretend to be other females (Claire, Solange) who in turn pretend to be Madame. For Genet the gesture is a mechanism for driving the outside world from the life of the play. Beckett's people are perennially involved in a Cartesian attempt to analyze their condition, to understand. But Genet's people act as if they implicitly understood; they are not reaching for what the world has to offer, they are trying to supplant it. For Genet the value of an action is judged in terms of the action's intensity and the grace of its brutality. In *Our Lady of the Flowers*, Genet writes that the importance of an action lies in "the resonance it sets up within us . . . in the degree to which it makes us move toward asceticism."

Thus the innovators. But the radical theatre in the U.S. has moved away from the kind of private ritual used by Beckett and Genet and toward a more impassioned, more assertive, more public ritual. Perhaps the collective nature of the ensemble has had a hand in this change; perhaps, also, the sense that the performer and the spectator are intimately caught up in today's convulsive events has demanded a correlative theatrical intimacy. (I find that I am veering away from references to the playwright's ritual to that of the ensemble. But considering the history of the 60s, this is a natural tendency.)

The Bread & Puppet Theater, under the direction of Peter Schumann, was one of the earliest ensembles to employ ritual. Here is a brief study I made of *The Totentanz*, which the troupe performed in 1962 at the Sheridan Square Playhouse, the first time they were seen in New York.

❖❖❖

The Totentanz, a ritual dance of death, performed by young men and women and one or two children, all in black garments. To the accompaniment of a steady percussive beat, they circle about and leap, circle about and leap until one by one they drop, until one by one they are symbolically dead. And then, after death, they rise, to die again. A constant death and resurrection.

But what is so effective, so moving about this troupe is the commitment to the dance, the concentration, the belief in the efficacy of the theatrical statement. All performed wordlessly, anonymously. The action goes past energy to belief, it isn't the will that's engaged but the soul that wills. Something is taking place that goes beyond theatre that becomes theatre because it goes beyond it: it goes through theatre and, leaving it, striking at an atavistic nerve, it becomes theatre. Becomes what it's almost become indifferent to, gets there by going past it.

And so gets to us, affects us because we become incapable of seeing it as theatre, we move into the essential area of simply seeing and feeling, we lose the power and the need to judge, we can't ask of it because we're caught up in answering it. And what it asks of us is not to see it but to see ourselves. And we do see ourselves by seeing it. We see the death of man and simultaneously see one man, each his own man, from death to resurrection, the resurrection of all to that of each. In some way the death embodies us so that we begin to partake of it, and also of the resurrection. It's not that we include ourselves through a logical extension, that we rationally see ourselves in the scheme of death, but rather that, like seeing an auto accident that wrenches us, we are shaken into a comprehension of the terms of the universe, not its intent but its effect. We come to see ourselves dying ourselves. We are died and dying. We comprehend and are comprehended. We are watching and the witnesses are being witnessed.

❖❖❖

Several years after *Totentanz*, the Bread & Puppets were to utilize a similar structure for what is now called *Grey Lady Cantata 1*, but in 1967 was called *Bach Cantata 140 — Wake Up*. It was performed in conjunction with the Judson Chamber Ensemble and took place at the Village Theatre (later called the Fillmore East.) "Across the width of the huge stage of the Village Theatre," I wrote in the February 16, 1967 issue of the *Village Voice*,

masses of men and women (puppets) silently stand, silently observe — a pounding begins, the guns of the enemy (kettle drum) break the stillness, the enemy has come to make victories — the masses of men and women begin to fall, hit by the persistent pounding of the unseen enemy — as they have silently stood, so they silently fall, and so at last they silently die. A hand is seen, here and there, raised, trembling. In the end the kettle drum wins victims.

But as they fall, these monumental stricken puppets (many are seven feet high) reveal the chamber ensemble standing behind them, waiting to perform. Their dying bodies have uncovered the mourners who, sooner or later, always follow victims. But these are not only mourners, they are believers (beyond belief!) in the goodness of God. They are celebrants conveying hope beyond hope over the silent victims.

It is not possible to say where the God of Bach has gone to. But before our eyes some force resurrects the victims of the slaughter. They are rising, even as we watch, to their feet, the victims come silently to life. But the kettle drum returns, the enemy returns. Death is crying over the silent voice of God.

But the victory of the kettle drum can only be a temporary victory, for it can do nothing but repeat itself, its resourcefulness has strict limits — it can destroy but as long as anything remains, itself remains, or rather the force energizing itself remains. It cannot permanently put an end to existence. Whereas the puppet–victims in conjunction with the chorale–celebrants not only are enveloped by similar energizing forces which strike almost haphazardly like bacteria, and are admittedly destructive more often than not, but are also charged with the need to seek out life, sustain life, synthesize agitated particles into some cohesive, sometime individual, sometime collective form.

Schumann's puppets, in their gray, almost shapeless garments, with their large, stolid faces and enormous laborer's hands, convey not only a remarkable sense of patience but suggest that what is dignifying them, what is allowing them to come back from the dead is that they take unto themselves not only the suffering of the victim but the guilt of the destroyer. It is not that they understand what the destroyer is doing, nor even so much that they forgive, though they do seem to forgive — it is that they cannot really make a separation between victim and destroyer, that some faith beyond hope has imprisoned them in the very action of being. In their bodies they feel death. In their bodies they feel the destroyer, the destruction, feel ultimately all human endeavor, God's love and deceit, all in their bodies as they rise inevitably but not finally, masses rising and voices rising, in grayness, in want, in a beautiful and imprisoning delusion, but if a delusion, one that liberates us all to one another, where the only enemy is absence.

In *Grey Lady* the ritual has not dictated the action; rather the vision, whether the troupe has ever articulated it or not, sets in motion the action which then becomes the ritual.

The OM–Theatre Workshop, in its experimental church service, *OM, a sharing service*, also developed certain ritualistic acts. The event was performed one Sunday morning in place of the traditional service at Arlington St. Church in Boston. The entire impulse of the experimental service was toward a psychophysical contact between performer and spectator. The extension of the performer's fingers, the act of reaching out to touch, became one the dominant motifs. In an early section of the piece, the performers slither along the carpeted aisles and, as they do, their fingers reach up toward and over the high, boxlike pews. While reaching, they sometimes come in contact with the fingers, sometimes with the face of a spectator. At the conclusion of the service, each performer, eyes closed, is permitted to enter a pew. Those who do are also permitted to reach out physically toward the spectators. Sometimes the fingers of the "sightless" performer and those of the sighted spectator touch for a moment.

In both cases — performers reaching up over the doors of the pews and performers reaching toward spectators while in the pews — there is a sense of a dynamic occasion made possible by the confrontation between a premeditated act and an unpremeditated response. The dynamics of the performer unleashes those of the spectator. Through an act of will, the spectator coheres the action or breaks (rejects) it. In coherence, the occasion is not only heightened, it is actually memorialized — that is, it takes its place in the souls of both performer and spectator as perpetual ceremony. Its first occasion is so charged with feeling that the act becomes a memorialization of itself; it appears to have taken place a thousand times before, though in fact this is its initial unfolding. The act is thus ritualized through sheer density of feeling and almost nothing else. It miraculously creates, through this density, its own legendary past.

In the Firehouse Theatre's 1969 production of Nancy Walter's *Rags*, the performance opens and closes with each member of the ensemble choosing a segment of the scattered audience and reciting to it, in a semi-whisper, a short monologue about some personal aspect of his own life. Paul Boesing addresses himself to his growing preoccupation with the undermining of discipline in theatre. Marlow Hotchkiss recites a letter in which a close friend painfully evaluates their friendship. The performers offer up an intimacy to the spectators. On the surface the event reads also like a rote action, but despite its preset formality it is a soul–baring event.

The personal revelation that opens the evening is then repeated word for word at the conclusion of the performance. It becomes a sacrificial symbol, the performer's symbolic baring of self is thrust upon the audience, twice, unasked. The act is arbitrary and fixed, without cause and without respite. The spectator, like Coleridge's wedding guest, is doomed to bear witness to the personal revelation. The performer, like the mariner, is doomed to repeat the revelation over and over. The act has transcended both performer and spectator.

One of the critical moments of the Performance Group's *Dionysus in 69* is the enactment of the birth ritual. The ensemble forms what it refers to as the birth canal. Four naked members of the company sprawl on the ground. Four other naked members stand over them. The first four hump their backs to form an arch, the second four face at right angles to them and squat. The one to be born crawls and is pulled along over the humped backs and under the squatters until pulled, thrust, dragged past all the bodies to the front of the canal and is born.

The ensemble combines the contemporary and the eternal, the informal and the formal. The actor performing the god Dionysus introduces himself as himself, states a few biographical facts, and then enters the birth canal in order to be born. Bill Finley, on the evenings he performed *Dionysus*, addressed the audience as follows:

> Good evening, I see you found your seats. My name is William Finley, son of William Finley. I was born twenty–seven years ago and two months after my birth the hospital in which I was born burned to the ground. I've come here tonight for three important reasons. The first and most important of these is to announce my divinity. The second is to establish my rites and my rituals. And the third is to be born, if you'll excuse me.[1]

Joan Macintosh, another ensemble member who sometimes performed Dionysus writes:

> The first speech as Dionysus is the hardest part of the play for me. To emerge vulnerable and naked and address the audience and say I am a god ... Told [Richard Schechner] I felt like a fraud, doing that. He said expose that, deal with that anguish and fraud — don't cover it up and be phony.... The absurdity of telling 250 people that I am a god makes me laugh and the audience laughs with me and gradually the strength comes and the self–mockery fades away.... In this scene I am totally Joan MacIntosh. I have not begun to become a god. The play is a series of revealments in which I find out that I am a god ...
> I enter the birth canal Joan Macintosh and emerge invested with

[1] Richard Schechner, ed., *Dionysus in 69* (New York: Farrar, Straus and Giroux, 1970), pages unnumbered.

god–power.... Throughout the play I am both Joan in the garage
[Performing Garage] and Dionysus in Thebes. But the birth ritual is
a giving over of myself, totally, to the bodies of the men and women
of the Group. It is remaining passive and yet open and receptive, like
the womb, to their back and their hands, their sweat and their sounds.
These fill me and when I emerge I am more than when I went in....
One night I remembered my own birth. I was me and I was being born
from my own mother's womb. It was hard and painful. I screamed.[2]

The ritual claims its own. We are no longer, as in Genet, in the domain
of the performer offering the gesture primarily for the spectator. The performer now becomes vulnerable to the ritual of one's own making. The
theatre is striking back. The primordial aspect is tainting and undermining
the surface certainties of the contemporary self. The contemporary performer is calling upon the power of ritual, and occasionally the power of
ritual is answering back past one's expectations. One begins as self, not as
character, but goes into the ritual as self tentatively examining character —
and the ritual seizes the character and assaults the heart of the self.

In the Open Theatre's *Terminal*, the performers — as generalized rep-
resentations of humanity — exhort the dead to take possession of them, to
come forward, to speak, to make an action:

Let the dead come through
Let them take my body
Let them use my tongue

The performance is permeated by this ritual call, this sense of exhortation, and by the performer's response to the effects of exhortation. The
performer incants, cries to be taken into the life of the dead, and then his
demeanor suggests that somehow it has happened, that the sobering energy
of the departed has begun to flow into him. This is more than an idea in
the head of the performer, it is also an idea of which he has become no
longer the instigator but the recipient. He is also the embodiment of that
being who sees the dead and the dying. Thus the dead once again live their
dying and their death through the surrogate witnesses.

The Living Theatre, in *Paradise Now*, created a series of what it saw as
eight rituals or rites, each of which comprises the opening section of a series of eight "rungs" that divide the play. Each rung has a rite, followed by
a "vision," followed by an "action." The rites are: the Rite of Guerilla
Theatre, the Rite of Prayer, the Rite of Study, the Rite of Universal
Intercourse, the Rite of the Mysterious Voyage, the Rite of Opposite
Forces, the Rite of New Possibilities, the Rite of I and Thou.

In the Rite of Guerilla Theatre, the performers go from spectator to

[2] Ibid.

spectator, repeating a phrase with ever–increasing volume. "I am not allowed to travel without a passport." The performer, according to Judith and Julian Beck, uses whatever response he gets from the spectator to "increase his expression of the frustration at the taboos and inhibitions imposed on him by the structure of the world around him."[3] His voice rises in the repetition of the phrase until all the actors go beyond words into a collective scream. Then the pattern begins again with a second phrase. There are five phrases, including "I don't know how to stop the wars," "You can't live if you don't have money," "I'm not allowed to smoke marijuana" and "I'm not allowed to take my clothes off." For each phrase the voices rise and the collective scream terminates the phrase. Near the end of the fifth phrase, "I am not allowed to take my clothes off," the performers tear their clothes off, "the forbidden areas of their bodies covered, the rest exposed. It is an active demonstration of the Prohibition."[4]

In the Rite of Prayer each performer moves quietly through the theatre, addressing a spectator here and there.

He may speak of a part of his body or face, a piece of his clothing, or occasionally of one of the objects in the room. Moving through the auditorium quietly, from person to person, the actors praise whatever they come in contact with, and the sound of their voices, their words of praise and prayer float through the space of the theatre. Holy hand. Holy shin. Holy store. Holy teeth. Holy hair. Holy asshole. Holy chair. Holy feet.

It is a prayer of praise. A prayer of the sacredness of all things. It rises gently toward a very quiet ecstasy, ending when the feeling of the prayer, the feeling of universal identification, or oneness, has filled each of us. When the holy relationship has been established. [5]

One of the pervasive beliefs, then, among the theatre ensembles in America, is not only that the rite, the ritual, the ceremony changes the spectator, awakening him to certain perceptions and insights, but also that the performer has the potential for transcending his present state and attaining greater purity. The performer wants to make a change and be changed. The ritual is his tool for allowing the community of performer–spectator, ensemble–audience to succumb to something larger and nobler than itself.

---

[3] Judith Malina, Julian Beck, and the Living Theatre, *Paradise Now* (New York: Random House, 1971), p. 15

[4] Ibid., p. 19.

[5] Ibid., p. 36.

4. ENVIRONMENT

Where should a play happen? The theatrical event always happens within a space, but only sometimes is space itself an event. Too often space is a tired housewife, shapeless, wandering, taken for granted. Like the classic repertoire that each age needs to rediscover in its own way, traditional space needs to be re–energized conceptually by each age. As for radical space, the new girl in town, it needs to be charged with necessity if it isn't simply to function as window dressing disguising worn–out concepts.

No space is impossible and no space is sacrosanct or a herald proclaiming the millennium. The ancient Greek amphitheater is as viable as the most radical environmental space Off–Off–Broadway. We have had church sanctuaries, processional wagons, courtyards, great halls, village squares, art galleries, caves, mountains, islands, rooftops, parking lots and railroad stations. We have had prosceniums, thrusts and open spaces. All are viable. Perhaps less efficacious in our own time is the old proscenium jewel box with its sense of performer as donor and spectator as recipient, representing as it distressingly does the manipulatory performer–spectator relationship.

Recent departures from conventional theatrical interiors are of two natures: the traditional auditorium reconstituted, utilizing radical spatial concepts; and nontheatrical interiors, found interiors (the church, the laundromat), which do not become surrogate theatres but maintain their own identities. All manner of found exteriors, from sidewalks and parks (traditional) to parking lots and exteriors of government buildings (radical), become thinkable. But one must always question the efficacy of the space. Its location and structure may tell us something about the expectations the performers may have of their spectators.

One of the sixties early and striking examples of the experimental use of theatrical space occurred in Elaine Sommers' *Fantastic Gardens*, a dance–film–music–sculpture spectacle performed for two nights in the Sanctuary at Judson Memorial Church in New York in February 1964. For this event Sommers employed the entire sanctuary as playing space. She seated spectators in irregular patterns throughout the room and then, halfway through the performance, repositioned them. Large works of sculpture were set among them, sometimes partially blocking their view of the action. In and among spectators and sculpture were woven the performers and the various sequences of film. The event invited a rethinking of relationships between performers, spectators and works of art. For sculpture became a member of the audience and film took on the character of a caress as it settled on heads and shoulders of those watching. Spectators took on the aspect of works of sculpture and of living, breathing screens for film.

Later in the decade, some of the ensembles began seriously to break down heretofore fixed spatial relationships. After five years of maintaining its modified proscenium thrust, though rudely violating it with occasional bustling incursions in the aisles, the Firehouse in 1968 took its entire lovely old Minneapolis auditorium and ravaged it. The result was an approximation of free–form open space. All rows of seats were removed but the stage was kept intact.A ramp spanned the center of the auditorium from the rear to the front. Supported by steel scaffolding, the ramp was high enough at its front end to allow performers to stand beneath it. Spectators could sit on what had been the stage, or in the auditorium, on the ramp or under it. Thus the entire theatre became potential working and viewing space.

The Living Theatre had been experimenting since the early sixties with its own invasions of the proscenium. (Much earlier in the century, Max Reinhardt's Grosses Schauspielhaus was so constructed that its arena seating for five thousand "made it easy to send crowds of actors surging into the aisles to mingle with the audience.")[1] Though the proscenium was maintained, Living Theatre performers were violating its threshold. The early invasions were timid. During *The Connection*, the actors playing the producer and the author made their entrances down the aisle, through the audience. In Gelber's later play, *The Apple*, performers mingled with the spectators in the lobby during intermission. Later violations were more daring. During Brecht's *Antigone* ('67–'68), performed primarily in vast, conventional theatres in Western Europe, Henry Howard, playing a soldier, spent the bulk of the play on his stomach crawling along the aisles. At intervals he would rise to his feet and "fire." Towards the conclusion of the long evening he became involved in a hand–to–hand battle with an enemy soldier. They wrestled in the aisles, at the feet of nearby spectators. In *Mysteries and Smaller Pieces*, "dead" performers were carried through the aisles and piled up on stage. Arrests were made in the aisles during *Frankenstein*.

By 1968, in *Paradise Now*, the boundaries between stage and audience, performer and spectator were finally dissolved. The performances took place in areas as varied as the traditional proscenium theatre at the

[1] Lee Simonson, *The Stage is Set* (New York: Theatre Arts Books, 1963) p. 40.

Brooklyn Academy of Music and the open space of the Carriage Barn at Bennington College. For the most part, the demarcation lines readily broke down, performers and spectators at times literally exchanging space or joining (sometimes with great physical intimacy) in space.

The Performance Group extended the open–space concept with their 1968 production of *Dionysus in 69* by constructing an "environment" that allowed performers and spectators many levels throughout the space. (They purposely refer to the space not as a theatre, nor as an auditorium, but as an environment.) Through a series of wooden scaffoldings, multiple vertical levels afforded spectators varied views of the action they could be watching from positions on the floor or perched six feet over the performers. The performers could move through the center of the space or, employing ladders and ramps, could navigate and perform among, beneath the feet, or over the heads of the spectators. With *Makbeth*, the Performance Group created another environment based upon open–space principles; and a new element was added: at certain performances spectators were encouraged to move about the room, trailing the action of the moment.

In Juan Carlos Uviedo's New York production of Mario Fratti's *Che Guevara*, offered in the summer of 1971, a large loft was broken into a number of playing areas where simultaneous action occurred. No specific area was designated for spectators; as in *Makbeth*, they were encouraged to follow the action about the room.

The Pageant Players' *Laundromat* show exemplifies theatre–making that maintains the integrity of the non–theatrical space. The performers actually brought laundry into an actual laundromat, where there were actual customers, hardly suspecting that a play was about to ignite in front of and for them. When two customer–performers, on cue, began to quarrel, the *Laundromat* play was underway.

As for exteriors I've chosen to discuss the street as a separate genre in a later chapter — mountains have become favorite sites these past few years, for the Bread & Puppets *The Cry of the People for Meat*, for Robert Wilson's *Ka Mountain and Gardenia Terrace*. Other sites, some traditional, include islands, meadows, courtyards, gardens, exteriors of public buildings. Concerning *Ka Mountain*, performed at the Iranian Festival of Shiraz–Persepolis in 1972[2]. George Ashley, former president of Wilson's Byrd Hoffman Foundation, reports in a newsletter that the work

ran continuously for 7 days and 7 nights, in the open air, at the base,

[2] The Peter Brook, Ted Hughes *Orghast* production also took place on a mountain during the Shiraz-Persepolis Festival the year prior to Robert Wilson's *Ka Mountain and Guardenia Terrace*.

on the sides and, finally, at the very top of the Haft–tan mountain. 168 hours of plays, dances and stories done in platform stages as well as on the sandy, rocky incline of the mountain with the performers and the audience ascending further each day to observe the activities and the imagery, cut–outs and three–dimensional forms, walking along pathways indicated by colored banners and painted rocks.[3]

But to return now to the efficacy of the space. What is the space good for? Who is it that this space is good for? If, for example, the proscenium tends to promote the idea of spectator–as–recipient, what are the possibilities inherent in the freer structures mentioned above? The most obvious will be explored in Chapter 6, "The Spectator Participates." Here are some other thoughts.

The proscenium, like the picture frame and the movie frame, tends toward a visual two–dimensionality which the open space obviously diminishes if not wipes out. The open space makes significant inroads on the virtues as well as the limitations of the proscenium. (The Open Theatre and the Bread & Puppets normally retain the proscenium effect. The Open Theatre's approach is particularly frontal.) With three–dimensionality, the underside of the performance becomes visible. We begin to sense more of the kinesthetic life of the performance, new stresses are in evidence, we begin to locate the performers less as mobile voices, themselves vessels for the dialogue and moral stances of the playwright, and more as beings in the world. These beings also tend to take on more of the aspect of temporal conditions as performers, as characters and less of fixed, perennial beings unearthed for the evening. A three–dimensional Lear becomes more vulnerable, if perhaps less noble. The condition of the earth becomes more vulnerable. The theatre becomes more "real" and simultaneously more "artificial" as the artifice of the performer comes into closer physical proximity with the spectator.

Related to this is the question of focus. Life — one another, the context of our lives begins — to make inroads on the performance. The life of the play begins to vie with the life of life; they overlap, they taint and enrich each other. Life is no longer the distraction that diminishes the purity of the play; instead it sometimes becomes the context in which the play is perceived, just as the play sometimes becomes the context in which we perceive one another. Distraction has less meaning because everything sensed in the room weighs importantly — we can't be taken away because *there is no away.* Instead of a constant focus on the perhaps marvelous living mu-

---

[3] Ashley's letter, dated December 30, 1972, was addressed to various people who had in some way aided Wilson during his detention in Greece the summer of 1972 on possession of drugs.

seum that is proscenium at its worst, we are caught up in a radically shifting focus that keeps us in the world even as it also transcends the world. It
isn't, incidentally, that the life of the spectator witnessing the proscenium
play is of less consequence — how can it be? it's the same life — but that the
proscenium demands all our attention; and the life, except in its function as
recipient, is felt to be a distraction and an encumbrance. But in the open
space, more of the world is present, *everything means*, we are bombarded by
the riches of two worlds, wherever we look we are in the presence of an aspect of two worlds.

The open space extends new aesthetic possibilities. Close–ups become
viable, visual angles become more varied, subtleties in aural modulation
multiply, and there is the sometimes abused but exciting possibility of
touch. The new aesthetic potential is as revolutionary as D.W. Griffith's
suddenly mobile camera and the advent of sound in film. However, aesthetic impact in the theatre varies with the position of each spectator as it
does not with film. Though this variability is also true to some extent of the
proscenium theatre — obviously the closer you are to the stage, the larger
the image becomes, the more audible the sound becomes, barring dead
spots — the new spaces radically intensify these differences. So that one
spectator may perceive a figure as a remote object while another may be in
almost microscopic range of the outer membrane of the object's nose.

What are the virtues of the non–theatrical interior (the church, the
laundromat)? A certain enriching tension is set up when the space is employed as itself but is simultaneously something else: the church that isn't
transformed into a theatre for a night but in which theatre nevertheless
happens, and the laundromat in which theatre suddenly erupts both demand that the spectator understand that life is less capable than usual of
protecting him from art, that the demands of the imagination, with its audacious risks and its disturbing confrontations, have pursued him as it were
into his own home. As the spectator finds that he cannot insulate himself
from their demands, he is forced to consider more seriously than ever an
adequate response to the often unarticulated questions and nonverbal demands made on him. The life of the play is more than ever backing his own
life into a corner, and he can break free only by shutting himself off or by
taking risks — that is, by freeing his imagination, by resorting to courage.
(The following chapter looks at some of the the deteriorating factors of the
too–lifelike–performance.)

What about the outdoor performance? It is faced with the vulnerability connected with the outdoors, with landscape, weather and all the acci-
dental occasions of life. Here the spectators and the performers are equally
under the sway of the sometimes benign, sometimes threatening aspects of

the outdoors. We are all smaller and more than ever equal under the stars. No one is host, all are visitors on the planet. The performance, if it is true to the outdoors, is in the grip of the outdoors.

My own outdoor experience is connected with the prologue to my play, *Boat Sun Cavern*, performed on the lawn at Bennington College, where the ensemble moved through a series of prescribed physical actions and a sequence of chanted phrases. The participants were faced each night with the varying tints of the gathering dusk, with the sound of the wind, and the growing chill in the air, with the dew, with the dogs that seemed to know it was time for the performance and descended in barking packs. The performance, the performers, the spectators, and even the dogs had come together under the larger, recurring movements of the coming night. What truth the play was making had to be revealed under that other unutterable but nevertheless persistent truth. It thus becomes more difficult to fabricate an action or to avoid the naggingly profound questions of life under the evidence of the outside world.

But we are still left with the question of who the spectator is, who it is that is having the experiences that so many have put so much energy into making happen. The question will be dealt with more fully in Chapter 6, "The Spectator Participates," and in Part 3 of this book. But for now it is important to state that if so much energy is expended principally for the edification of bourgeois, middle–class spectators and theatre connoisseurs, those who have constituted the bulk of theatre audiences in the West in recent centuries, and this because the performance site chosen is not physically, psychologically or economically accessible to the poor, the old, the half–literate and the generally alienated, then we are like children playing at danger in the safe confines of our parents' houses, then the world will truly pass us by as it goes about its serious and truly perilous business. If space is an event, then art is a larger social action effecting that event and the dynamics of the community.

ᐤ᠎᠎ᢓᢓ

5. THEATRE IN THE STREET

$\overline{A}$rtaud wanted a theatre which would generate the kind of electricity that is generated when a mob rushes into the street. But there is no substitute for the passion of the street. The street is urgent, it is capable of fear and cowardice; but even in its moments of hypocrisy, the street is incapable of essential falsehood.

On November 7, 1917 (October 25, Old Style), the Bolsheviks stormed the Winter Palace in Petrograd and overthrew Kerensky's Provisional Government. On the second anniversary of that action, Nikolai Evreinov replayed the event, called *The Taking of the Winter Palace*, at its actual site, employing eight thousand Red Army soldiers, sailors, professional actors, and workers.[1] The intent of the first action was the revolutionary displacement of an existing if tenuous order (itself revolutionary), that of the second the fortifying of the new order.

The second action was celebratory; like the first it thrived on a theatrical ambiance natural to mass demonstrations, but unlike the first it was essentially symbolic. In principle celebratory theatre would not seem to be an adequate response to Artaud's plea for a dynamic analogous in spirit to that of the mob. But the street has a way of transforming goals, it sets up a confusion between life in its theatricality and theatre in its lifelikeness. In another Soviet spectacle similar to Evreinov's celebration and taking place in the same year, N.G. Vinogradov, head of the Red Army Workshop for the Theatre and Playwrights, mounted a work called *Krasnyi god* ("The Red Year") which was performed at the civil war front, in various buildings, and inside the lobby of the Winter Palace. In *The Theater in Soviet Russia*, N.A. Gorchakov reports that "the Red Army men" in the audience . . . weapons in hand, joined the 'performers' involuntarily."[2] Thus two years after the October Revolution the spectators apparently could be counted on to celebrate and fortify the new political order. But spontaneity by definition means a radical shift in control, and the enthusiasm that caused an armed audience to join in the action could at other times, under different circumstances, work against the existing order. Theatre or no theatre, weapons

---

[1] Nikolai A. Gorchakov, *The Theater in Soviet Russia* (New York: Columbia University Press, 1957), pp. 149, 150.

[2] *Ibid.*, p. 133

have a way of dredging up deeper needs, of making needs more needful and the street, as we have said, has its own dynamic.

✧✧✧

Christmas in the middle sixties, New York City. The country is torn over the Vietnamese War. The Bread & Puppet troupe holds an antiwar vigil in front of St. Patrick's Cathedral. Among the props arranged on the sidewalk is a figure of Jesus, the size of a small doll. During the proceedings a male passerby snatches up the Jesus and runs off into the crowd. Some troupe members pursue him for blocks and see him disappear at last into a precinct house. The theatrical Jesus is thus literally kidnapped by the local police. A trivial incident? Maybe. But one of symbolic import. It sees the life of the street clashing with the theatre.

On the day of Richard Nixon's inauguration as the thirty–seventh President of the United States, January 20, 1969, the New Left held what it termed a Counter Inaugural in the streets of Washington. The Counter Inaugural was an anti–celebration, reflecting the peace movement's revulsion toward the new White House occupant. The more theatrical elements (according to Marc Estrin of the American Playground, who was one of the strategists) never came to pass, so that the Counter Inaugural as it finally manifested itself was composed of placards held aloft, hurled epithets sounding in the air, and militant figures stationed along the route of the Nixon inaugural procession. The drama of the Counter Inaugural was a life drama, the dissident witnesses testifying in the streets, but the theatricality of the event was in its ceremoniousness. Yet alongside the relentless reality of the transferring of administrative power that constituted the true inaugural, the Counter Inaugural at best expressed a displeasure wrapped in theatrical flamboyance. Though its impulses were admirable, its art was feeble and its political import proved negligible.[3] And yet the sixties have grimly reinforced for us the sense of the government's vulnerability when it is in the streets. Fortification via ceremony has given way to displacement via the assassin's bullet.

In the sixties the theatre more and more found its way into the street and into politics. While some groups mounted raw protests, others mounted guerrilla theatre (the term was first used by Peter Berg of the San Francisco Mime Troupe), often a hit–and–run affair composed of unexpected action, and accompanied by chants, signs, political slogans, and a quick dispersal before the police could break up the unauthorized perfor-

---

3 The March Against Death, on January 20, 1973, staged during Nixon's second inauguration, was a more effective protest action.

mance; or else an extended performance in the streets or in a park, in the fashion of the Mime Troupe or the Bread & Puppets.

The performances were often one–shot or random occasions, e.g., Schechner's group performing Robert Head's *Kill Viet Cong* at the Port Authority Bus Terminal in New York, asking passersby to "kill the enemy" (a performer). Sometimes the performances were part of a continuing repertoire: the Pageant Players' *King Play*, which was performed on Manhattan street comers. Often the police would arrive before the group could disperse and thus become part of the performance or event. Sometimes, when the group was not dispersed, political discussions would ensue. Sometimes there were angry confrontations. The methods were provocative, designed to call attention to a condition.

> During the 1970 election day stuff," Michael Brown of the Pageant Players reports, "we were performing on a Manhattan street corner. Big crowd. Almost at the end of the play and a cop comes to break us up. Well, we start doing a number on him. One of us had an arm around him and is facing the crowd explaining his position to them, telling them they should really leave 'cause it's the law and he's a nice guy doing his job. Other Players are running around on milk boxes and with cardboard guns from the play, acting like nasty cops and saying split or get busted! Still others are screaming like banshees, but laying a reverse trip on them: You're a bunch of freaks, how come you want to see a play on the street, go home and watch TV alone, get a haircut, no fun allowed on the street, go home. Well, these folks were beautiful! They didn't budge, not one of them, not a muscle moved. The cop's telling them to leave and they don't move. They were having a good time and they're pissed and confused. The cop must have put in a call before coming over, because suddenly there's flashing red lights from all over, so we gather the props, bid the crowd a formal good–bye, thank them for their militancy, remind them to keep up the fight for this kind of thing, and with props dangling, *King Play* robes flying in the breeze, run like hell down 6th Avenue, and just get away around a couple of convenient comers. Movement is relative.[4]

And here is Ronnie Davis reflecting on some of the uses of street theatre. In a discussion of agitprop he remarks:

> Still further removed from agitprop are those so–called guerrilla the-
> ater groups who surprise people in the midst of their daily routines by
> creating a theatrical situation where performers and audience are
> mixed. Often the skit happens so rapidly that the audience doesn't
> know it has been hit until the piece is over. The people, mildly duped,

4 Michael Brown, article on the Pageant Players. Also published in Henry Lesnick, ed., *Guerilla Street Theater* (New York, Avon Books, 1973).

are supposed to become conscious of their responsibility and guilt. Acting more like bandits than guerrillas, and, like newspaper headlines, shouting images rather than telling news, these groups try to "sell" their product through moral suasion and personal confrontation — both ideals of bourgeois culture...

When the Mime Troupe first went to the streets to do short skits, crankies (paper movies a la Peter Schumann), and puppet plays, we didn't try to insult or assault people; we decided to teach something useful. We began by teaching general city–folk how to stuff parking meters with tab–tops, using a simple puppet–and–actor skit to inform them of the free use of parking meters. Another skit in this vein, telephone credit cards, was also designed to teach people something useful...

But . . . agitational propaganda is not revolutionary art. It supports rather than examines, explains rather than analyzes.[5]

The 1967 March on the Pentagon was neither a hit–and–run affair nor a form of theatre superimposed on an essentially political event but, instead, represented a massive political demonstration which proved in some of its more radical moments to be theatrically audacious. "One of every 2,000 Americans," writes Lee Baxandall in *The Drama Review*,

...marched across the Potomac and up to the malls of the Pentagon, where cyclone fences, topped with barbed wire, had been erected. Swiftly the fences went down as "demonstrators" moved to confront, close beneath the building's Mussolinian facade, an involuntary cast placed there by Robert Strange McNamara: several thousand paratroopers, military police and federal marshals. The scenario was to disrupt Pentagon operations as fully as possible without resort to arms...Scaling ropes, flanking maneuvers, inundation by sheer numbers were but part of the repertoire of this humoristic, motley and audacious legion. The yellow submarine of the hippies, 12 feet long, was passed over heads toward the doors. Smaller contingents of troops were surrounded, talked to, pressed in so tightly they could not use their weapons, allowed to retreat only in disorderly flight, perhaps with helmets swiped or a flower in a rifle barrel. Posters and slogans remembering Che appeared on abutments. Tens of thousands alternated "America the Beautiful" with an ironic "Sieg Heil!" salute chanted to commanding officers on the battlements. Yippies, banners proclaiming solidarity and a victory more pyrrhic (We Have One), moved upon the portals chanting: "Out, Demon, Out!" to a strange music. Everywhere there pervaded a spirit of Epic Theatre (so many

[5] R.G. Davis, "1971: Rethinking Guerilla Theater," in *Performance* (1) Vol. 1, No. 1, December 1971.

actions and performers, so much detached awareness of one's deeds even as one acted), even to a Brechtian "narrator" who stood with a bullhorn where he had a commanding view and laconically interpreted events for the majority who could not summon a whole view. The troops tried to seize the narrator; with a little help from his friends he evaded them, not once losing his cool; his ironic commentary set the context for the besiegers.[6]

Spectacle, narration, exhortation, analysis. The theatricalization of politics and, sometimes, theatre overturned by politics. But it is important to watch one's footing in the murky waters where the boundaries between theatre and life grow indistinct. Definitions at their worst may circumscribe actions, but at their best they help us to understand them. Drama may be an enlightened and generous mistress, but she is nevertheless jealous about her priorities.

The dynamism of the street may take us past theatre, the logic of events may inevitably lead to a necessary displacement, to a radical purging, but the theatre cannot chart its own overturn, it can only give way to it. So while the action of theatre can set off the action of life (the Red Army spectators could be driven to a life action, the passerby at St. Patrick's Cathedral could be driven to a real theft), one pays a price for too closely identifying theatre and life and for relegating theatre to the position of a theatricalizing function of life. The theatre must always see about its own life, and we must try to understand something of that life and try to serve its nature so that it may simultaneously serve our nature.

If we place a premium on theatre as cause in a simplistic cause–and–effect action, we begin to dismiss that sense of distance (artifice) that allows us to play out what life in many of its often brutalizing aspects (exceptions: art, religion, the dream life) does not allow. This playing out involves the symbolic enactment of our collective myths and the tapping of the subconscious levels of existence. Art has its own way of enriching life, and the notion that it acts essentially as a shell to be broken into in order to get at life is a false and withering idea. The figure of Jesus on the sidewalks, the puppet figures of slain Vietnamese peasants moving down Fifth Avenue constitute symbols that instantly connect us to the ideas of atrocity, violence, nonviolence, and redemption. But as surrogate images of transcendent victims, they also help connect us to all humanity, to the idea of self as a precious gift offered not only to self but to collective self. This is political in an essential sense, and if it leads to action it does so through an awakened conscience. Action and illumination: one displaces, one fortifies.

[6] Lee Baxandall, "Dramaturgy of Radical Activity," in *The Drama Review* (T 44), Vol 13, No. 4, Summer 1969.

In the case of the exorcising of the Pentagon, the primary force is the symbolic action, not the literal one, the ritual that purports to cast out the demon from the military. Here the participant is also the primary spectator, and the action is theatrical with religious borrowings. Because the Pentagon cannot literally be purged of its demons or at least was not on that occasion the action is a mock service, which serves as a way of liberating the feelings of its performer–spectators. But because the street has a way of recasting action, it is also possible for the ritual to function as a consciousness–raising mechanism on members of the military, who were there to defend the institution of the Pentagon. The "exorcising" might thus prove to be prophetic.

The street ultimately enriches and endangers theatre as the symbol collides with the concrete world. In the confines of a theatre, this collision is to some extent mitigated by an inhibiting decorum. All things may be permitted within its walls — nudity, blasphemy, violence — but its walls nevertheless seem to protect. But the street offers no such protection, the street only leads to the street, extending itself indefinitely. The collision of symbol with literal event means that the participant–spectator in the symbolic action can no longer be assured of safety, of immunity. Unlike R.D. Laing's patient inside the mental home, the participant–spectator is no longer free to "break down" with impunity. The efficacy of the symbol may thus be impaired; or if the spectator or participant–spectator dares to embrace it fully, he must dare it in the face of a literal reality that may claim him more intensely by virtue of his very commitment to the symbol.

Many of the ensembles in the radical theatre have radically recast the role of the spectator. This recasting is offering new, life–giving blood to the theatre, and its prospects are enormously exciting. But simultaneously its dangers are also enormous as we noted, for in the co–minglings of life and theatre, we have to be alert to the possibility that we are draining theatre of its own life. Theatre exists to serve life; if we bastardize and drain theatre sufficiently in the supposed cause of life, we lose an enriching and essential aspect of life in the process.

∽

6. THE SPECTATOR PARTICIPATES

The spectator makes a difference. He always participates, the play is always in part dependent on his perception of it. In *The Sleepwalker and the Assassin*, I wrote that "each [*King*] *Lear* is a real *Lear*. There may be lesser *Lears* and greater *Lears*, but the reality of *Lear* as experience, in other words as total Idea, is different for each spectator. There are, in fact, as many *Lears* as there are spectators watching it, and for the same spectator a new *Lear* each time he sees the play. Part of *Lear* is where you are seated, what you have eaten — not only this evening but all your life — what the morning papers have warned you about, who your companion is."[1]

Thus the life of the spectator in the traditional theatre. But the radical theatre has thrust the spectator into a more physically active role. In *Fantastic Gardens* the activity was conservative but nevertheless indicated the first twinges of a convulsion which was already radicalizing the spectator/performer relationship in the Living Theatre's *Mysteries* in Europe. Hand mirrors were given to the spectators. The shifting of the mirrors caused a constant change in the light patterns throughout the room; the spectators were relighting each other, relighting the performers, the sculptures, the film, the general environment. The involvement was in decor. Later productions would make room for the psyche.

The Pageant Players took that bold leap in the mid–sixties, thrusting into the public arena not only the physical spectator but his psyche — as subject matter. They developed a piece called *The Dream Play*. After several members of the troupe relate dreams, which the others then physicalize through improvisations, members of the audience are called upon to offer their own dreams. At the GI Coffee House in Fort Dix, Michael Brown relates:

> We were so overwhelmed with the intensity and meaning of these soldiers' dreams, especially the Vietnam vets, our movement improvisations were almost paralyzed at times. Every dream about killing innocent oriental faces; or facing death; or fear and rebellion against officer–type authority figures. It was incredible. One of the men could

---

[1] *The Sleepwalker and the Assassin*, p. 20.

[2] Michael Brown, *op. cit.*

barely get his words out and had to be encouraged by us to keep going. It was like an exorcism for him and he wouldn't quit.[2]

Brown believes *The Dream Play* is the most important theatrical contribution made by the Pageant Players. In the spring of 1971, Norman
Taffel's 70 Grand St. Theatre reintroduced the spectators' dreams as theatrical subject matter. The structure of Taffel's *Dream Arena* was similar to
that of the Pageant Players' *The Dream Play*, though the two groups were
apparently unaware of each other's work. In reviewing Taffel's play, I voiced
serious reservations about its use of dreams:

> ... a new group of ensemble players have been performing *The Dream
> Arena* ... I'm not sure perform is the right term to use in relation to
> what they are after. The night I saw the piece, the group began with
> one of its members narrating a dream ... [and then] followed the nar-
> ration with some theatrical development. The evening was then
> opened up to the spectators, several of whom came forward with their
> own dreams which the ensemble proceeded to build upon. I find that
> I am fluctuating among several terms: perform, develop, build upon.
> And my uncertainty stems from the uncertainty of the ensemble,
> members of which had varied ideas as to what they were doing ...
> [This] came out clearly in the discussion that followed ... It was not
> clear, to the group or to the spectators, whether the dreams were to
> provide jumping off points for the ensemble, that is, simply provide
> material which the ensemble could then free–form according to lines
> that satisfied its own aesthetics, or whether the dreams were to be so
> developed that the theatricalization of them would provide the origi-
> nal dreamer with insight into the original dream and thus into him-
> self. It seemed to me that the latter wasn't happening and I also
> wonder now whether it's at all possible for such insightful develop-
> ment actually to happen, and if possible whether it's at all appropriate
> for it to happen in the environment of theatre. It boils down to the
> difficulty of interpreting dreams and also the decorum of dream–in-
> terpretation. It seems to me that the dreamer ought to be left with his
> dreams, either left totally alone with them or left alone with them in
> the company of his therapist, that he should be left alone with his
> dream as he ought to be left alone with his conscious experience, that
> if the dream is anything it's valuable as material which the dreamer
> consciously re–forms in his head and thus reveals to himself. He then
> has the original dream, the reformation of the dream and the experi-
> ence of making the reformation. The possible good that may come
> from the dream–reforming by the theatre ensemble seems to me infi-
> nitely inferior in its worth to the dreamer, though it may provide rich
> material for the ensemble.

[3] *Village Voice*, August 5, 1971.

As for using the dream essentially as a jumping–off point, as material for the ensemble without necessarily having to relate the material back to the dreamer and his own needs, that seems to me somewhat like taking the material of the earth and not sufficiently respecting its characteristics.[3]

The spectator as creator? Yes. But the spectator ransacked for his dreams? Dream images are rich sources, but the dream taken wholesale can impoverish the dreamer.

I spoke in the chapter on ritual of the spectator's role in *OM, a sharing service*, of how he coheres the action or breaks it through his acceptance or rejection of the performer's presence in the pew. The performers in this case acted with great discretion. They were instructed not to enter a pew unless there were positive signs — vibrations, since they could not use their eyes — that they were wanted in the pew. Insofar as they could be known, the wishes of the spectator were respected. So the spectator, given his own makeup, was comparatively free to take a truthful stand in relation to the performer. The spectator could reach out to the performer in a way that protocol discouraged him from reaching out to strangers "in life?" The theatrical situation both encouraged and protected him. He could be comfortable and truthful.

Near the conclusion of *A Mass for Actors and Audience on the Passion and Birth of Doctor John Faust according to the Spirit of Our Times*, the Firehouse performers offered the audience a choice. "Would you like to see Faust or be Faust?" Those who chose to "see" Faust kept their roles as spectators. Those who chose to "be" Faust were enclosed in a vast communal bed-sheet, given a powdered soap with which to perform a ritual handwashing of one another, and then brought into close physical contact for up to thirty minutes as they swayed back and forth to an om–like chant.

It isn't entirely clear how much of the final action of Faust was dictated to the spectators, how much they initiated on their own. They seemed to come physically together, to hold each other and sway together because circumstances were conducive to those actions. By thus coming together, they became a self–enclosed unit. The play was no longer necessary to them, instructions by the cast were no longer necessary. They had found a kind of communal womb which sometimes they consciously, even self–consciously, protected from alien forces, but by and large simply allowed to be. That is, within a public arena and without much prodding and without much immediate preparation (other than that communal–encounter syndromes were "in the air"), a number of spectators took over the play by leaving the play, took over the space by forgetting themselves in the space. They became the play; they no longer saw the play but felt it in a new way, felt it because they now were the play.

By the time of *Dionysus in 69*, the spectator had plans of his own. Here is Joan Macintosh on one event:

> One Sunday night when I was playing Dionysus, a woman came out to Bill Shephard and satisfied him. I went to break it up and get on with the play. Bill said, "I'm sorry, Joan, you lose." I answered, "Well, what are you going to do now?" And Bill got up and left the theatre with the woman. I announced that the play was over. "Ladies and gentlemen, tonight for the first time since the play has been running, Pentheus, a man, has won over Dionysus, the god. The play is over."[4]

And here is Schechner on another event:

> On one other occasion people have planned and successfully changed the ending of the play. In June 1969, a small group of young people, led by some who had seen the play before, dragged Pentheus from the theatre. McDermott was playing Dionysus; and Shephard, Pentheus. It was not as clear cut as the time when Katherine took Bill away. This time Bill was comatose and a fistfight almost broke out between Jason, acting on Dionysus' behalf, and several of the kids taking Pentheus out. After Shephard was dragged from the theatre, he came back but did not want to continue performing. Jason was very upset and went upstairs. Other performers were confused, blaming both McDermott and Shephard for an unresolved situation. I was not there at the start of the performance and walked into the theatre as Shephard was being dragged out. I sensed a bad scene developing and, perhaps unwisely, spoke to both performers and audience. I explained what had happened, how rare it was, and asked for a volunteer Pentheus from the audience. A young man who had seen the play five times volunteered. We asked him a few questions, explained what was expected of him, put in an improvised scene in which the performers, instead of reciting the death speeches, voiced their reactions to the night's occurrences and went on with the play.[5]

And here is Pat McDermott on audience participation:

> Some of the best moments of *Dionysus*, and some of the worst, have been created by individual spectators who sought to participate tangibly. Tangible participation, spontaneous or invited, does not necessarily mean deeper audience involvement. Involvement depends on the symbolic consciousness, or creativity, of the spectator. Involvement may or may not become tangible. If it does, the spectator pulls him-

---

[4] *Dionysus in 69.*

[5] *Ibid.*

self, along with actors and other spectators, out of the show; or he may plunge himself, and them too, deeper into it. Participation is a challenge to the ability of both actors and audience to create symbols. Rituals can be created and the scope of symbolism expanded. Ritual involvement reveals the audience. The reciprocal privacy of stage and auditorium is not maintained. Ritual assembles; it dispels the illusions of routinization and privacy. It does not pretend to the public performance of private acts.[6]

❖❖❖

In the Living Theatre's *Paradise Now*, the spectator became an active, physical entity in the play. The most publicized actions were those in which spectators joined the company by taking their clothes off. But spectators also joined in ritual activities, the most graphic being the flying event, in which the "flier" descends through the air into the waiting arms of six to eight performers below. Spectators also engaged in dialogue with the company, e.g., the scene at Yale Theatre on September 27, 1968, in which the discussion inside was about the crowd outside waiting to gain admittance to the performance:

Open the doors.

Free the people.

Don't go out into the street and put your head in front of a police club . . .

Last night the Living Theatre went on. And tonight the revolution is dead, right?

The Living Theatre is a bunch of cowards.

Wait a minute. Let's think a minute. There are two people here who, if the doors are open and there's a violation, will go to jail for five years. Let's think about human life.

If you want someone to go to jail, if you want someone to get clubbed, let that someone be you. But don't force that penalty on others. Get those fucking liberals out of the house. I only want revolutionaries here . . .

A member of the cast: Let me ask you an honest, serious question. Let me ask you a question. Who here is not going to pay his taxes this year?

A man in audience: I'm not.

---

[6] *Ibid.*

A member of the cast: Who here is not going to vote?

Cries from audience: Me. Here. Here. Yeah.

Member of cast: The rest of you please go outside and let the other two hundred people in. (*Cheers*)[7]

Norman Taffel's *Little Trips*, produced at 70 Grand St. in 1970, required the spectator to perform a series of specified actions which on the most productive nights would lead him to a series of original actions. The play is structured as a series of physical "progressions," which are repeated an indeterminate numbers of times. There are two performers: Cassandra, the Trojan prophetess, and a guide, who is there to direct Cassandra through the progressions. "In developing *Little Trips*, " says Taffel,[8] "I searched for a new structure that would function for both actor and audience. I did not want to get the audience to dance for five minutes, only to have the actors then abandon, push, or intimidate them off the stage..." As *Trips* finally developed, the guide instructs Cassandra in a series of simple rituals based on Cassandra's life, e.g., an attempt to throttle the infant Paris, the rape of Agamemnon. The cycles are repeated a number of times, and each time the spectators are encouraged to take over more and more of the guide's actions, to play the physical roles in the rituals opposite Cassandra. As the actress playing Cassandra reacts more and more to what the spectators are doing as she "opens" her inner actions, making them larger and larger, [as] her gestures become more emotional, less mimetic,"[9] as she begins in short to break away from her role, the spectators, at times disturbed by Cassandra's breaking away, begin their own breaking away, that is, they attempt to keep the ritual going — and as Cassandra plays her part less and less, the spectators through enthusiasm or disgust further take over the action of the place. Or at least that is what is supposed to happen. And some nights it did.

Trips, as I wrote in a retrospective *Voice* column,

> is one of the few shows I know of that actually cannot happen without an audience. The show depends on an audience for its development, it simply cannot go anywhere without one. The repeated rituals of certain events from the Cassandra story, or rather the repeated attempts of the actress trying to fulfill those rituals, really is deadened without the audience. On its best evenings, the show was developed by the audience into the show it wanted, or at least the audience made

[7] "The Living Theatre," *yale/theatre*, Vol 2, No. 1, Spring 1969.

[8] Norman Taffel, "About Little Trips," in *The Drama Review* (T 51), Vol. 15, No. 3a, Summer 1971.

[9] *Ibid.*, p. 108.

changes, wanted or not, simply because the show was creatively vulnerable enough to be changed, to be fulfilled in accordance with the audience's momentary needs.

[The Performance Group's] *Commune* seems to me the kind of show in which the audience has the opportunity for participation, but which nevertheless can fulfill itself without any overt action from the audience. It contains itself and can be colored in varying ways, its orchestration modified by the audience, but inherent in its structure is the fulfillment of the show which has originally been planned. The audience can be seen as offering improvisations on a given theme, as opposed to *Trips* in which audience improvisations can make a new play rather than embellishing the given play. There is no value judgment implicit in this analysis, the audience taking the play away from the performers does not per se make for better theatre, though some of my colleagues (directors, playwrights) would argue this . . . [10]

As I myself might have at one time.

In the early summer of 1971, director Juan Carlos Uviedo staged Mario Frati's play *Che Guevara* as a multi–focus work that forced the spectator into making constant choices. My *Voice* review of June 24 reported that

Uviedo has constructed two worlds, the decadent world, as he sees it, of the Bolivian ruling class and its satellites, and the world of the dedicated guerrilleros, and they are both in action simultaneously. While Che and his followers are planning or fulfilling actions in the Andes, musing, raiding, tending to the wounded, the generals and socialites and entertainers and whores are involved in torture and nightly debauchery. And, in fact, Uviedo has broken it down even further, so that at one time there may be three separate guerrillero scenes as well as several debauchery and/or torture scenes. And no designated places for the audience, we move around as at a street fair, we choose what it is we want to see at a given moment Schechner, in *Makbeth*, wanted the audience on its feet, following the action about the environment, though most nights the production wasn't played with a mobile audience, and the *Orlando Furioso* troupe (from Milan) offered the spectator the choice of two simultaneous actions. Uviedo utilizes multiple actions with at times great effect, the play is considerably energized by this device, it is always in motion, but the spectator is also energized, the spectator has the choice of motion or rest, of creating his own distances from the several actions; he can come in for close–ups, go out for long shots, or simply remain stationary and be exposed, in full or in part, to whatever actions happen to come his way. Furthermore, if

[10] Village Voice, July 15, 1971.

he wants to, he can completely go out of the play, shut if off, find a place to be "in Bolivia" but outside all action.[11]

In 1971 the Living Theatre began developing *The Legacy of Cain*, a 150–play play, created and performed with students and villagers in various towns and villages in Brazil. Here they took another radical step in making a closer alliance with the spectator. No longer were they simply bringing the play to the spectator, encouraging or allowing him to join or interrupt as in *Paradise Now*, now they had begun to bring the spectator into the conceptual process of their work from the beginning. (See the dialogue with Steve Israel, in Part Two, on the development of *The Mother's Day Play*, one of the works in *The Legacy of Cain*.) In *The Favela Project 1, Christmas Cake for the Hot Hole and the Cold Hole*, an actor playing Death binds the wrists and gags the mouths of all in the playing area. "Everyone is bound. Everyone waits. No one can move except the people [villagers witnessing the play]. Everyone waits until the people begin the Rite of Liberation. The rite is performed by the inhabitants of the community where the play is being performed. As the inhabitants of the community untie the actors, the actors begin a choral sound of joy and liberation."[12]

Judith Malina reports[13] that in one village, no one moved, the favellados (villagers) watched. They understood, without being told, what was expected of them. But they also were well aware that the performance was illegal — all outdoor performances in Brazil, unless sanctioned by the government, are illegal and that by participating in the symbolic liberation of the performers, the spectators were risking imprisonment as criminals. And not only imprisonment, but torture, a commonplace occurrence in Brazilian prisons today. But the favellados moved at last, and began to untie the performers. And one favellado, shyly untying Judith, whispered to her, "Tomorrow the favellados will free the people of the whole world." "At that moment," Judith reports, "this man became capable of hope, of another (perhaps greater) action."

The spectator today has the potential for radically modifying the play or even replacing it. As I noted earlier, his overt movement doesn't necessarily make for a better experience, but it certainly makes for a different one. Basically what has changed are the assumptions of the spectator. He can no longer assume almost anything on entering the theatre. The possibilities, from the moment of his entrance, are numerous. The world of the

[11] Village Voice, June 24, 1971.

[12] Living Theatre, *The Favela Project 1, Christmas Cake for the Hot Hole and the Cold Hole, Scripts*, Vol. 1, No. 1, November 1971.

[13] During forum at Hunter College, New York City, on "Theatre and Revolution," March 15, 1972.

play no longer automatically promises to let him be, to rescue him for an hour or two from life. But in fact no significant theatre ever promises that rescuing; the only difference is that we thought it did. *Lear* always brings us back to our life. But the new theatre does provide a new tension as the old assumptions die; it refuses to assure us that we have a fixed place in the event.

Is the spectator thus more responsible in the new theatre? He is differently responsible. He is less the voyeur, less the spectator reaching into his own heart. He has been given the chance to physically test out the illusory figures performing for him and to discover that these figures may be no more illusory than he himself is, may be realer than he, may be part of a trick being played on him, may in fact be fraudulent, may be neither illusory nor symbolic at all but nervous, vibrating, questioning creatures who, like himself—the spectator—are trying to find their way in the play. The spectator in the radical theatre may be finding something that the play has been unable to find before his appearance on the scene. As the play breaks down many of the barriers between life and art, the spectator may find out something about his life through his physical entrance into art. If in *Lear* he learns some exalted and terrible truths about the human condition, in the new theatre he may learn something of value about his personal self in a given moment in history. His growth as a person ultimately involves both these revelations.

ᔕ

PART TWO

SCRIPTS, NOTES, LOGS, DIALOGUES

7. THE OM–THEATRE WORKSHOP, BOSTON

During the time that this writer functioned as playwright with the OM–Theatre Workshop, the group worked on two pieces: *OM, a sharing service* was completed, *Hunger* remained a work in progress. In the following section, I attempt to describe the working process for both pieces, to focus on the aesthetic as well as personal concerns of the troupe. "The Litany of Touch in a Theatre of Pews," about the OM production, was published in the *Village Voice* and obviously written for public consumption. The *Hunger* log is a diary kept during a period of much frustration over our inability to bring that work into focus and also during a period of growing personal stress. Since the log was written originally as a private diary, it is to me (more than to the reader, perhaps) a particularly valuable document on that period.

OM, a sharing service was developed for a specific occasion, thus it began with a concrete goal, to do the Sunday morning service. Most theatres begin with more general goals to make good theatre, to entertain, to excite.

The occasion of the church piece also set up an implicit relationship between performer and spectator, that of sharing, of being together in worship. Unlike many theatre pieces in which the ensemble wants spectator participation out of principle but has to find a specific reason to bring it into the piece, OM had that participation as a built–in element — it had only to uncover it and understand it.

❖❖❖

OM, A SHARING SERVICE. A collective work created by the OM–Theatre Workshop, Boston. & Directed by Julie Portman • Text by Arthur Sainer • Sound by Philip Corner • Choreography by Elizabeth Martin

OM, a sharing service, *was developed collectively by the ensemble and performed as the Sunday morning service at Arlington St. Church in downtown Boston on April 21, 1968. Those involved in its creation included Philip Corner, Edward Dennis, Marda Dennis, Stan Latham, Barbara Linden, Elizabeth Martin, Jaimie Midwinter, Bob Miller, Bonnie Miller, Julie Portman, Arthur Sainer, James Tenney. Additional performers included Mark Aronson, Tom Badgett, Tommie Ann Braun, Veda Daly,*

Stephanie Engel, Tom Gardner, Malcolm Goldstein, Amy Gordon, Mark Gordon, Marsha Green, Jayne Lappin, Dorothy Noland, Cathy Payne, Liz Preyer, Helene Schwartz, Howard Schwartz, Debby Seltzer, Leon Setti, Adriane Sheff, Joe Topin, Ken Werner, and Patty Woodruff. The stage manager was Tom Gardner.

TEXT FOR INVOCATION: Bell, tree, bridge, sun, leaf, bright, day. Morning. Morning. Sharing. Sharing this morning, sharing this light, sharing this space. We've thought of sharing, of who we are, and in what way, if any way, we are or might become one another.

We thought of words like "play," like "form," like "space." You come together, each week, each Sunday, come together, in this space, on those seats, in those pews, five, six or seven in each pew. What is it like to be separate and together? How is the space really shared? What do the seats feel like? What does the air feel like? What do the sounds feel like?

I make a sound, I hear a sound, I share a sound. I hear the idea and I hear the sound that has been formed to communicate, or to try to communicate the idea. Does my mind, hearing the idea, when I sit beside you hear the idea that you hear? Does my mind, hearing the sound, when I sit beside you hear the sound that you hear? Hearing that idea, hearing that sound that is made to make the idea, do we then become part of one another — or do we then take what is common and embrace a part, reject a part? In what vessel do we store the idea and the sound of the idea?

I make a form, I see a form, I share a form. I see pillars bodies, pews, windows, ceiling, light, shadow, altars, smiles, furrows, nearer, further, closer and higher. I see the form and I see the gesture. Does my mind, seeing the form, when I sit beside you, see the form that you see? Does my mind, seeing the gesture when I sit beside you, see the gesture that you see? Seeing that form, seeing that gesture, do we then become part of one another or do we then take what is common and embrace a pan, reject a part? Into what vessel do we store the form and the gesture?

I reach out to touch, I touch, I share touching. I touch pillows, books, doors, the fingers of other people. I touch and am touched. Does my mind, sensing what I touch, if I sit beside you, sense what is being sensed by what I touch? Does my mind, sensing that I am being touched, when I sit beside you, sense what you are sensing when you touch me? Touching that form, being touched by that form, do we them become part of one another. or do we then take what is common and embrace a part, reject a part? Into what vessel do we store the sense of touching and being touched?

The play, to play, to make a play. It is another way to hear a sound, see a form, sense an idea, and perhaps touch one another. It is another way to hear what we have always heard, but do not hear at any moment, another way to see what we have always seen but do not see at any moment, another way to touch what we have always heard and always seen, but never, never touched. It is another way to remind us that, whatever we are, we are together in the light and in the darkness, another way to discover one another, another way to discover ourselves. And as we gather together, sharing ignorance and wisdom, gather together sharing minds and bodies, gather together sharing ourselves with ourselves, sharing courage and despair, we will always be separate — but perhaps we can find a way of coming closer in our various, beautiful, desperate, tranquil and trembling separateness.

❖❖❖

Village Voice, May 16, 1968

THE LITANY OF TOUCH IN A THEATRE OF PEWS . . . Another way to hear a sound, see a form, sense an idea, and perhaps touch one another . . .

I met Julie Portman back in February. I'd gone to see the OM–Theatre Workshop's creation called *Riot* at Arlington Street Church in Boston, and Julie, the group's director (a dynamo, a love, now my dear friend), invited me to help create an experimental church service. We performed the event several Sunday mornings ago. I can't review that service but I can describe what it was, how it happened, and how it felt to us.

What did we begin with? A time, 11 a.m., Sunday, April 21; a space, the vast auditorium of Arlington Street Church; a congregation, characteristics specifically unknown to us, except that we assumed they were mostly Unitarians, thought to be generally liberal, and had housed (supported?) the draft resistance movement in the persons of Spock, Coffin et al., and had allowed (condoned?) the burning of draft cards in the sanctuary. We were warned, however, not to ask too much of the congregation.

We had no name for our piece, no theme, no events in mind, no specific images. We had plenty of good will, were delighted at being asked to do the service and to be offered the space.

The delight deteriorated rapidly. We discovered that the space made stringent, at times seemingly impossible demands. Every idea we tried seemed appropriate for some other space. Every action was stymied by the space. We developed concepts but couldn't work out actions stemming from them. We developed actions but couldn't find concepts unifying them.

The auditorium of Arlington Church is deep; formidable rows of pews in box–like formations fill it solidly. The wooden boxes, each literally surrounding some half dozen members of the congregation, come shoulder–high on a fairly tall person. One unlatches the door and steps into the pew as into a steam bath; one's head is free to peer ahead at the pulpit.

What areas were available to us? The pulpit, the aisles, the balcony. We tried working in the aisles and discovered that most of what we attempted simply couldn't be seen. We tried working at the front of the balconies, which run parallel to the pews along the length of the church, but most movement couldn't be seen and that which could be seen proved to be dangerous — for instance, we became seriously concerned that performers, standing at the edges and breathing deeply, might become kinetically assured that they could levitate and attempt to float over the auditorium. Since the aisles and the balcony limited our actions, we were left with the pulpit, for at least everyone could see the pulpit and it wasn't dangerous. But it also wasn't that rewarding, for it set up the kind of aesthetic and psychological funneling that ultimately was not what we were about. We were not there to preach or to draw power from the congregation, we sensed that much, but rather to "be" and hopefully to share. We were not there to "do" anything to them. To be there in a particular way became more and more important to us. "Sharing" became a word we used over and over. Sharing, being, and perceiving the space.

We tried a lot of things. At the moment I can't remember half of them. One had to do with acting out or responding to newspaper stories or advertisements or phrases. We tried one phrase, "I am not about to" (about what LBJ, in '64, wasn't about to do in Vietnam), and the performers worked out some interesting sounds based on it. But it proved not to be satisfying enough, that is, the use of the LBJ phrase and others like it came to seem like game–playing, a kind of low–keyed, self–satisfied, cynical game which expressed our attitude about events from which the audience was essentially excluded. It became little more than a demonstration of our position. We worked with a men's clothing advertisement, something to do with dapper dressing, to which the performers were to react on impulse. Within three minutes, every member of the ensemble was sprawled in the aisle before the pulpit, savagely undressing his neighbor. Again, satisfying but for whom?

Phil Corner, who made the trek from New York every weekend, spent a great deal of time on sound. Human voices sounding the "OM" (the Hindu utterance) and chords proved to be a stabilizing force. During the first weeks, when movements and verbalizing only frustrated us, the OM sounds, involving the full concentration of body and mind, did much to anchor the piece, to give us the sense (to shift the metaphor) of having reached a high and generously broad plateau.

Meanwhile we kept improvising with words and gestures. We threw words at one another, transformed them, moved sounds from one performer to another. Very nice, all very nice, but why were we doing it? Again it seemed self–serving.

The first break came when Elizabeth Martin, our choreographer, devised an exercise in which the troupe went scampering along the center aisle, under terms demanding that one part of their bodies always be in contact with the pews. For many nights we worked on variations of this, the troupe rubbing against the doors, moving hurriedly or slowly, softly or savagely against the doors of the pews. The doors presented physical problems, they swung open unexpectedly, they resisted contact by offering hard and broken surfaces, performers kept bruising themselves against the hinges, etc. But something about the doors compelled us not to abandon them.

For many nights Julie, Elizabeth, and I watched the door exercises from inside the pews. We were fascinated by being able to hear but not see bodies, by being able to see what appeared to be disembodied hands running along the tops of the doors. I suspect now that our rubbings and brushings and hurtlings had not only to do with exploring the space but with those brutish circlings and barkings a dog makes when it is after something and those equally brutish pointings and gruntings humans make when they want to effect something but cannot speak the native tongue. In this light, the as yet non–existent pew dwellers could be seen to be "wearing" their pews as shell fish wear their shells. Our bodies thus could be seen as operating on the animal level of indicating a "wanting" and our hands, those disembodied hands, symptomatic of a finer intelligence, involved in exploring and sensing.

And the hands running along the tops of the pews led us at last to hands "reaching," to hands reaching over the tops and down into the pews, attempting to feel what could not be seen. One night I sat just inside a pew and watched a performer's hand coming over. I knew I wanted something, that something was wanting of me, and knew what it was, but hesitated, confused suddenly as to whether I was a legitimate spectator, uncertain what my response would do to the performer. But then I did what I wanted and simply touched the hand. We touched fingers, feeling each other's fingers. On a later occasion, again seated just inside the pew, I watched a hand reaching over and then felt it exploring the surfaces of my face. I neither

knew whose hand touched my face (I might easily have found out by leaning over, but didn't) nor did the performer know whose face he was gently
touching. All I can say is that it was extraordinarily beautiful, and that both
of us wanted to go on touching and being touched.

Reaching. Touching. Later on the not seeing led to further reaching
and touching sequences, with eyes closed. For the piece at last came into
focus, to have to do with making contact, with being in the same space and
being in the same space in a particular way. It seemed to us that what we
wanted and what the as yet unknown congregation would want of us was
the sharing of being. Finally we began working on what we knew would be
the most chancy element of the service the moving into the pews. For it
seemed right that at some point near the conclusion of the service we
should unlatch the doors and move into where the congregation was. But
how were we to do it? And what were we to do once we were inside?

It seemed right to some of us that we should be "blind," that is, move
with closed eyes. It made the movement into the pews less presumptuous,
made it a "feeling" movement, the concentration on "sensing" the pews
and occupants, not "invading" them.

What were we to do once inside? Not behave like victims, not go in
helplessly nor stand helplessly — but simply stand, simply be.

We discussed the movement into the pews for a long time. Julie's idea
was that we should not enter a pew if we sensed we were not wanted. When
we sensed that we might move in, we were to do so.

What would the congregation do once we were in the pews, before
them? We couldn't know. We had to be enough with them so that we could
be open to what they then wanted to do. They might want to seat us, to
touch us, to ignore us. We couldn't know but had to enter with courage.

How long were we to stay in the pews? Again we couldn't know. Until
we felt it was time to leave, that's all we knew, until we felt that the relationship (performer/selves congregation–selves) had been satisfied. How
were we to go? We were simply to go, as simply as we had entered. To go
with closed eyes, down the aisle, into the street.

What would the congregation do? They would leave. How would they
know the service was over? They would know. If they didn't know, then the
service obviously would not be over.

Following is a brief account of the proceedings as they actually occurred the morning of the service (noting, of course, that each performer
would have a varied account).

Prelude: congregation is greeted at entrance to church. Jim Tenney had come up from New York with several other musicians. They joined some dozen and a half of us in front of the church, all with rhythm sticks. We comprised a rhythm band, playing in identical beats, sensing when the beat was changing, greeting the gathering congregation on the steps of the church and in the vestibule with our rhythm sticks.

A lady in the vestibule, pointing to the hand drum I was keeping the beat with, querulously asked, "Why are you doing that?"

I thought. "To give you pleasure," I said.

She thought. "I have one of those things at home I could have brought." She wasn't pleased.

Most people were.

The OM congregation stands in center aisle of church. And some spilled over onto the sides and top of the pulpit — 450 people, packed into the aisles and up the pulpit. And watched eight performers, in lotus positions on the balconies, sounding the OM. Philip picked up the sound on the organ, it grew in volume while the performers, still seated, moved through a series of slow, formal gestures with heads, arms, and torsos. They were beautiful and noble beings at that moment.

Congregation is seated. To the sound of a series of vibrating bells, each sounding alone.

The Chord. I went to the pulpit and delivered — what? Invocation? Sermon? Prose poem, more likely, about why we thought we were there. The eight performers, still in the balcony but no longer visible, began to pick up the sounds of my words. All their sounds, while my words continued, were transformed into the word "become," and they left the balcony and walked down the center aisle, sounding their word, until at last all 20 of them joined me on the pulpit, all of us by now sounding the word "become." Which was then cut off suddenly, and we made a circle and each picked a note and formed a chord from the sounding of our different notes and dispersed with our notes down through the aisles, slowly moving to the balcony and then drifting out of sight and our chord at last drifting away.

Fifteen seconds of silence.

Reaching. Those in the pews heard footsteps running down the balcony steps, heard bodies scurrying against the sides of the pews and saw hands running along the tops. Then heard the shuffling of hands and feet on the carpet throughout the interior of the church. Then hands began slowly reaching into the pews, the shuffling noises still heard, and some hands were touched and some ignored and some watched and one or two kissed.

Silence.

Performers at the front, with eyes closed, began moving up the pulpit steps. Others followed, eyes closed, and stopped when they made contact with another body. And another, eyes closed, would follow and move until he made contact. Thus a web was at last formed. At the rear of the auditorium, another blind group moved up the center aisle and created a similar web. At last several groups of blind performers stood still in several webs. Silence.

And the webs dissolved and each blind performer sought the pews and the congregation. All in silence, all of us with eyes closed, slowly groping past one another, feeling for a pew, stopping, sensing the pews. No sounds. Unlatching the pews. No sounds. Entering the pews.

No sounds.

I listened, I could hear nothing. Did the people in the pew before which I had stopped want me to enter or not? I couldn't tell. I felt no resistance. But not only that, I also felt no people. Were there actually no people? And opened the latch and entered the pew. And could feel something. But could not be sure. Some presence? Writing this now, I'm still not sure. Not sure. Something. And stood there. A minute? Several? A simple gong sounded, from one of the musicians, reverberated through the church — and as it almost died, another, from another area of the church, sounded. I could sense (sense?) performers slowly leaving pews. (Very likely I heard bodies, heard doors.) Another gong picked up the sound. I tentatively reached out my hand, swung it slowly, tentatively, several times. Someone then touched it, took it, held it. I held that other hand. For perhaps 10 seconds that hand and my hand held one another. I don't know whose hand it was. A moment later I moved slowly out of the pew, slowly down the center aisle. I could feel the air of the street.

Congregation leaves the church. After us. We were ecstatic. On Boylston Street, in front of the church, Ann Guerlac and I (she like a young Giulietta Masina), eyes fully open, pounded each other on the back, laughed like children. In the basement of the church, we were joined by others — touching, kissing, grinning. Everyone had a story to tell, everyone had had something happen that was special. Members of the congregation came down to tell how it had been in the pews. Stories. Everyone had stories. What can I say? The most exciting theatre event I've ever seen? No. But one of them. (After all, I didn't see half of this one.) But I've never sensed a theatre event in which so many were glowing at the end. Glowing. Really feeling so damned good. Really damned damned good.

We touched one another.

Julie wants to do it again, at night

... to hear a sound, see a form, sense an idea, and perhaps touch one another...

❖❖❖

HUNGER, A WORK IN PROGRESS In the summer of 1968, following the successful church service, the OM Theatre Workshop spent six weeks at Bennington College in Vermont, in workshop sessions and in the creation of a new work, to be called *Hunger*. We had, as the title implies, a very general theme, but thought most particularly of physical hunger, mass starvation throughout much of the world, a dire and supposedly imminent prospect. We worked throughout the day on ideas for the piece — it was to be written by the entire ensemble — on physical and vocal exercises, on yoga, on mime, first in the Carriage Barn, later in Commons Theatre. Many of our evenings were devoted to discussion of the political and economic ramifications of mass starvation.

The six–week workshop was the OM's first attempt at communal living. Most of the company was housed in the servants' quarters at .the Governor McCullough Mansion in North Bennington. We worked on campus during the day and had dinner in the dining area of the North Bennington Catholic Church at 8:30 each night.

Participants included Philip Corner, Ed and Marda Dennis, Tom Gardner, Lois and Shephard Ginandes, Harvey Grossman, Ann Guerlac, Margo Jefferson, Ricky Juda, Barbara Linden, Jamie Midwinter, Bonnie Miller, Gerry Nathanson, Murray Paskin, Julie Portman, Arthur Sainer, Howard Schwartz and Ann Willard. Diana Robbins, my senior playwriting student, acted as an observer and contributed ideas for *Hunger*.

During that summer, this writer kept a day–by–day log of ideas and events concerned with the making of *Hunger*. It is reproduced here almost in its entirety.

❖❖❖

HUNGER LOG, LOOSE PAPERS, ETC. At the start of the workshop Julie asked me to create a piece of nonsense prose for the workshop. I find that creation my first entry.

July 7, 1968

Mushko moon ate squaggles in the fence. Mushko moon told never days, says lance me no parroteels. Oh never, fungo boy, never strike till the sputter's all gone and the wist wends abar, cuchawking the lay dong.

Cuchawking, cuchawking till the spencer's arift in the shmout, till the globbel's kinking itself in the earster, till the rouser's gunhole and the fark's melking in the crod. Oh then, oh then, oh mushko moon, only then will we gax why the jawg's a–jowling through the earplatoons and the liolet's bealing through swealth. Did you never know prinkles in brool? Did you never know assrouts in brod? And whang of the melly owkers that never got slaced in the crake? Whang of them? Mushko moon, thy squeegles and parroteels have unfurmenced my crowling easht. Hulloose, hulloose, and never the shpeets shall gartz. Hulloose, hulloose, and never the gazamunds shall blenk. Nevermore gartz, nevermore blenk. And whale, oh whale will you be cuchawking then, oh mushko moon. Landsaving?

July 9

OM Workshop summer workshop at Bennington began Sunday. Philip working with scales (minors, Eastern) and rounds. Julie yoga in a.m., improvs in afternoon.

For Sunday afternoon I wrote a gibberish prose piece which was then to be used to make "scenes." Not too satisfactory results, scenes clever enough but too traditional. People hung up with script. Julie's suggestion that they improvise. May try it today.

Touching — Sunday, with eyes closed, feeling a partner all over. Except inhibitions prevented "all over" from happening, and we weren't explicitly told "all over."

But yesterday we (they) were. Much beauty. Each partner took turns being still and being touched.

Murray conducted sound and gesture yesterday.

Image of dead bodies, from Sunday exercises, still with me.

Undated

Tape or film Fulbright on foreign aid.

Howard: A job is the difference bet. life and death.

(Bogota)

Starve the tenant farmers out of the rural areas so they'll go to the cities.

Giving — the changes, from constant giving to apathy. Howard's comments on his Peace Corps experience in Bogota: most outsiders begin with great feeling for those suffering malnutrition, but the latter are so many that the outsiders grow apathetic, partly to preserve their sanity.

July 12

Open with the end—all the dead bodies, discovered by audience. Hold for some time after audience seated. Then blackout. (Return to it at end.) When lights come up, it's the beginning—all alive, active.

What activity? Life's. Each doing his thing, particular—labor, love.

At some point for each, food ceases to be available. How is this to be shown? Perhaps each has his own "feeding box"? Or is symbolically bereft of food by a symbolic figure who simply taps him or closes his mouth or . . . ?

Starvation slowly sets in for each at different stations, leading to:

theft

violent quarrels

cannibalism

despair

At intervals throughout the play, films, slides and tapes document moments of famine throughout history: Calcutta, Ireland, Biafra, etc., ending with America and the world in 1999.

July 13

The vultures perch, waiting.

July 16

One starving person at beginning. How do others relate?

July 18

Fruit. "Multitudes" of fruit. Bananas?

Everybody has a tin bowl and a spoon. All same size bowls but varied embroidery, etc. Each one's food supply in bowl.

Central, huge bowl from which everyone dips. At last it runs dry.

Events—little by little they become of less and less import as the central bowl and then subsidiary bowls run dry:

sex

entertainment

politics

work

MURRAY: Styles of eating. People around the dinner table. Attitudes.

July 19

HOWARD: I could see going to war against one's people. Mexico — ten percent of the rich (including government) fighting the rest. Starving people in the cities won't die quietly, will try to raid the food supply. Keep them off with machine guns.

JULIE: Concentration camps: ledger of the hungry.

Cults of starvation.

July 22

Eating rites: Breaking of the bread: sharing. (Also symbolic digestive action?)

Exercise: utterance on outbreath (groan). Stagger movement on sound.

Cold exercise: shiver, rub, blow, etc.

Limp body crawling, use only of arms.

Swaying, body contacts only at 1 point.

July 26

Don't hide idea of actors. They talk, etc., to audience at beginning, then do their thing.

July 27

The haves and have–nots.

Attitudes about poor, from poor.

Audience arbitrarily divided into haves and have–nots.

Slogans, headlines, etc.:

Bet you can't eat just one.

Savarin is too good to be sipped.

Double your flavor, double your fun.

Good to the last drop.

You don't have to be Jewish to like Levy's.

Victor of Pie–eating Contest Dies During 58th Pie

Cranberries Found Cancerous

Physicians Found Weight over 350 Dangerous

WBAI Stages Fat–in in Central Park

Russian statement. Times (July 22):

The little black coffins in Brazil.

Arranging the dead.

July 28

Orchestrated voices, litany.

July 29

Borrow garments from members of audience.

Dying amidst artifacts: color TV sets, etc.

The living mouth: at walls, audience.

"The population bomb keeps ticking."

August 4

The amoeba calling out to audience. Actual names.

How make audience understand everyone's detachment?

How break down, modify detachment?

Amoeba. Battling over (food?). Comforting. Changing face. Hoarding. Impotent love.

JULIE: What do you mean, too real?

BONNIE: There's a sharpness in the listlessness of hungry people.

Fuel

Nutrition   Mother's Breast

Comfort

Audience to sit on blankets, pillows, etc., stuff to be taken for props.

Walls: flags, campaign posters, ads for good living?

Undated

Living program:

Wilt thou be fat?

The battle to feed humanity is over... Sometime between 1970 and 1985 the world will undergo vast famines — hundreds of millions of people are going to starve to death. That is, they will starve to death unless plague, thermonuclear war, or some other agent kills them first.

Who are these bastards trying to kid? They're as well fed as you and I.

"If all men were fat, there would be no wars."

Empty boxtops.

"What if they gave a war and nobody came?"

Undated

THE WAR ON HUNGER IS OVER.

The gestures from the breaking of the bread. Begin with actual loaf. (Later use loaf for Jamie and Bob.)

The group mouth, to:

A cry (in darkness?) (light?), cries? A genuine cry in which mouths ask, really ask, of one another, of themselves, of audience:

WHAT DO YOU WANT?

WHY ARE YOU DOING THIS?

LEAVE ME ALONE!

I WANT

I WANT

August 10

I believe Bob Miller found the key yesterday, that the piece must be a continual attempt to understand and be understood: understand the nature, not of hunger, but first (what we've all been saying) our attitudes toward hunger, toward hungry people, toward the coming mass starvation.

No more dates were recorded.

LITANY

Audience steps over performers.

The breaking of the bread, given to the haves and have–nots. (Arbitrarily given to audience and performers.) This could lead, after a suitable interval, to Jamie rushing Bob for his bread. By this act, perhaps everybody's bread is threatened. 1. Audience. 2. Performers with bread. Now what actions do performers with and without bread make?

ICES

The following lettered blocs, G.E. etc., indicate ideas for slogans and actions.

G. 1. 1st symptom: dry mouth, increased urination.

2. Second: rapid loss of fat, desire to chew constantly.

1. Depression, apathy, fetal position.

2. The young become old.

1. Life stops. Death comes silently.

2. Fuck death.

Someone's going to die.

I can't save everybody.

E   1. Half a million Biafrans may die before the end of August.

2. We can't save everybody.

3. We can't save anybody.

4. If All Men Were Fat, There Would Be No Wars.

Solutions are socially and politically unacceptable.

An unexamined belly isn't worth filling.

We'll always have famines.

Maybe the next famine's desirable.

What about the protein pill?

Feeds one, feeds all.

When famine comes, we decide who gets.

Food is power.

Poor people make a point of starving too publicly.

It hurts to watch.

We're only human.

J   1. We'll always have famines.

2. The war on hunger is over.

K   1. Hunger is caused by the deterioration of human beings.

Group Mouth . . . to Eyes Closed

JULIE: You must work on people's eyes.

   I do not understand little children who let God die by the sweat of his brow.

   I do not understand the exhausted fields.

   I do not understand.

   I want to make a litany but I don't know how.

I want to say that I want to understand but I don't know how to begin to want it.

I want you to help me but I don't know how to want it badly enough. I don't know how to begin.

And he saw, he saw, he really saw that it was good. And then what did we do? What did we do then?

ME: What is to give Ann a sense of form when she doesn't have a sense of what is forming?

PHIL: That's Ann's problem.

ME: Isn't it Julie's?

PHIL: It is if Ann can't solve it.

What kind of dress? What do leotards and blue jeans tell me? But then, what does anything tell me, more than partially, about ... ?

if two–thirds of world's starving people black, what's relationship of 1 black starving performer saying it? Margo Jefferson only black performer in workshop. Maybe a relationship but do we have a sense of what and how we're using it? Enough that Margo feels it? Has to be true?

Group mouth now so fucking static, seems self–indulgent. Can't see if others have analogous movement.

✧✧✧

INVITATION TO THE PERFORMANCE READ AS FOLLOWS:
You are invited to attend a run–through of *Hunger*, a work in progress being developed by the OM Theatre Workshop of Boston Friday, August 16, at 9:00 p.m. in Commons Theatre. Please use the Northeast entrance to Commons (there will be signs). You may bring guests. Pillows are advisable.

8. THE OPEN THEATRE

T*erminal* represents the Open Theatre in full maturity. Along with *The Serpent, The Mutation Show*, and *Nightwalk*, the Open Theatre's last play, the work exemplifies a flowering of the collective process of creation. All four works were written in collaboration with playwrights, but all forcefully utilized the creative powers of the performers in developing concepts.

Terminal's contemporaneity is flavored with a choral–mythic quality that is at times lovely, at times chilling, always haunting. My belief is that the play never really comes to grips with the complex feelings of our culture toward death, that it settles for obvious answers about surface attitudes; but the work is nevertheless extraordinarily impassioned and demanding, both of its performers and its audience.

The script for *Terminal* is followed by two interviews. The one with Roberta Sklar, co–director of the piece, looks at the collective process that went into determining the eventual subject matter. The one with Susan Yankowitz, last of several playwrights to work on *Terminal*, underscores the special problems the playwright has in working with an ensemble, when all stages of the work are meant to be a collective creation.

❖❖❖

TERMINAL. *A collective work created by the Open Theatre Ensemble.* • *Co–directed by Joseph Chaikin and Roberta Sklar* • *Text by Susan Yankowitz (1971)*
    The ensemble: Raymond Barry, Shami Chaikin, Tom Lillard, Jo–Ann Schmidman, Tina Shepard, Paul Zimet.
    Musician: Ellen Maddow; Production manager: John Dillon. Costumes: Gwen Fabricant; Lighting designer: Arden Fingerhut. Electrician: Howard Meyer. Administrative director: John Stoltenberg.

Note from the Open Theatre In a collective work there are stages equal in significance to the performance stage. When the ensemble begins to prepare directly for the performing stage, it relies entirely on the initial investigations. We would like to acknowledge the following people for their participation in the development of *Terminal*: Dick Peaslee and Stanley Walden, composers; Marc Kaminski, Nancy Martin and Sam Shepard, writers; Joyce Aaron, James Barbosa, Brenda Dixon, Ron Faber, Sharon Gans, Jayne Haynes, Ralph Lee, Peter Maloney, Mufial Miguel, Mark Samuels, Ellen Schindler, Barbara Vann, Lee Worley, actors; and

Dale Whitt, Joseph Campbell, Mossa Bildner, Kesang–tomma, Ronald Laing and Muir Weisinger.

Terminal is the product of a collaboration among actors, directors, and writers. It evolved out of a collective investigation into human mortality and a consideration of both personal and societal responses to the fact of death. The piece was conceived from its inception as a theatrical work; the text cannot be fully understood apart from its production. Visual and verbal patterns are interwoven; word, sound, and image reinforce and elucidate each other.

This scenario documents the results of more than a year's intensive work. The process through which we arrived at these results can only be suggested in these pages. Any group that wishes to perform *Terminal* will have to rediscover the material for itself; it will need to use, adapt, reject, and recreate. This text is, then, a skeleton which a new group of performers will have to flesh. It is intended as a framework and guide and, to that end, attempts to reconstruct as clearly as possible the details of the Open Theatre production.

Style and Structure The style of the piece is presentational. It is constructed of general sections within which are a series of fragments. Each fragment is a self–contained entity which relates to the others and to the whole through juxtapositions and associations. Every section and fragment is introduced by a title. A single actor, or several, may perform this function during the course of the play. Blackouts are used to define the beginning and end of major sections. These blackouts not only delineate distinct thematic areas, but provide a stylistic counterpart to the cycle of life and death, presence and absence. The movement from fragment to fragment shifts the piece back and forth through various levels of experience.

The Actors and the Space The actors are always present. When an actor is not directly engaged in the events on stage, he moves into a defined area around the periphery. This space may be considered an onstage offstage area in which the actor rests, prepares, changes costume, waits. From this periphery, an actor may spontaneously enter the acting area and join in an action. The line between the onstage and offstage area may be crossed. There is only one space in which the actors are always visible.

Properties and Lights Like the actors, all theatrical props and materials are visible. Lights are hung in plain view of the audience. Nothing is hidden or disguised, but everything can be transformed. A pallet is a bed when placed horizontally on the floor. It is a wall when upright. A rack is a structure for hanging clothes. It is also an instrument of torture. Lights may be

used as spotlights or instruments of interrogation; they may be fixed overhead or held by the actors. All objects are real objects. And what is constructed for the piece is obviously makeshift. Everything is part of the
theatrical world and derives its functions from the needs of that world.

The Roles All roles are multiple and interchangeable. The living are also
the dying; the dying are potentially the dead. And the dead will become living matter. The Guide straddles the space between the living and the dead.
His presence inspires the dying to make contact with the dead. The Dying
are close to death and sensitive to spiritual forces. Their heightened awareness makes possible their possession by the dead. The Team supervise the
institutions of life; they are the hospital attendants, the wardens, the embalmers. They may be portrayed by one person or by many, but they, too,
are the dying.

The Music Music is used in its broadest definition: it is pure sound and
rhythm. Meaning does not accompany music, but is contained within it.
Some music is simply an extension of the human voice. The actors become
instruments; they find and produce sounds which communicate emotions
and experiences outside the usual range of human expressions. Some music is an extension of the human body. Hands and feet become instruments
for eliciting music from surfaces — floors, walls, beds. Language becomes
incantation and incantation becomes music. Words dissolve into fragments
and sounds. Repetition of lines, sounds, and gestures recur as a means of
suggesting associations between seemingly unrelated passages and evoking
resonances which enrich meaning. When conventional instruments are
used, they are always simple — harmonicas, tambourines, drums, sticks.
The clavis maintains a regular rhythm, measuring time.

The Costumes The piece is concerned with death and, therefore, with the
body. As a part of nature, the body must be revealed by the costume. As a
part of society, it must also be concealed. In our production, simple white
garments are worn by the actors. Each differs from the others in cut and
style, but creates an overall impression of uniformity. The costumes evoke
many associations: they suggest hospital wear, uniforms, mummy clothes,
bones. Strips of black tape appear on the faces of the actors during the first
section. Here, an eye is covered; there, a mouth or two eyes. Each taped
feature represents the loss of its function. Nothing more is worn — no jewelry, shoes, or makeup.

The Setting A proscenium arch or some other well–defined frame reinforces the presentational style of the piece. Two spotlights, which will later
be held by the actors, lie downstage and illuminate the acting area. Five

beds — bare slabs of wood on metal legs — are lined up at the rear. They are raked at different angles and stand at varying heights. The beds will be used as pallets for the dying and embalming tables for the dead; as alternate stage levels for the actors to walk upon; as walls; and as graves. A clothing rack and ladder are visible. Stools, equal in number to the actors, stand to the right and left of the stage area in the periphery. Beneath the stools lie sticks and musical instruments which will later be used by the actors. The general effect is deliberately ambiguous. The setting is a theatrical arena, a hospital ward, a graveyard, a nameless home to which people come to die and, perhaps, to be transformed.

I. THE DANCE ON THE GRAVES OF THE DEAD

Silence. Overhead lights and two small spots illuminate the beds, the stools, the empty space. A trumpet blast. Music. A light, rhythmic melody. The procession begins. The actors move down the aisle under a makeshift red canopy. They repeat the melody on simple instruments. The actors reach the stage and face the audience. The GUIDE *steps forward and starts the incantation. His words break through the music and charge the space with a different energy. The music stops. The canopy is placed against the rear wall where it will remain, The actors move to the stools and sit. The* GUIDE *continues his incantation.*

THE GUIDE: We come among the dying to call upon the dead.
There are graves beneath this house — we call upon the dead.
Let them take my body, let them use my tongue.
There are bones beneath this floor — we call upon the dead.
Let the dead come through
and let it begin with me.

Individual actors begin to join in the calling. Each carries two sticks, like divining rods. All the actors eventually participate. They call up the dead in every corner of the globe facing each compass point. Their voices and movements merge and overlap, filling the space with sounds and words.

THE ACTORS: We come among the dying
There are graves beneath this house
We come among the dying
We call upon the dead
There are graves beneath this house
There are bones beneath this floor
We call upon the dead
We come
We come among the dying to call upon the dead

We come
            Let them take my body   We come
Let them take my body, let them use my tongue
            Let the dead come through
Let them take my body, let them use my tongue
                        We come among the dying
                        There are graves beneath this house
                        There are bones beneath this floor
Let the dead come through and let it begin with me
                        and let it begin with me
                        and let it begin with me
            Let the dead come through
                        Let them take my body
                        Let them use my tongue
We come among the dying to call upon the dead
Let the dead come through
            Let the dead come through
                        and let it begin with me

*The words become increasingly fragmented. A single syllable evokes the en-
tire incantation. The sound of the calling becomes its meaning. Cacophony.
One actor grows silent. Then another. Then all. They collapse from the
waist; the sticks dangle from their hands. Silence. The* GUIDE *moves among
the actors. His physical presence brings them into contact with the spirits
they have invoked. The actors straighten and stiffen. They raise their arms
in a stylized position, as if in a trance, still holding the sticks. Drumbeat.
The dance begins. Hands, feet, and sticks drum on every surface. The actors
knock on the floor, walls, and beds — on the graves of the dead. They dance
individually and, linking upraised arms, in pairs. From time to time, they
lie on the floor to let the dead come through. Dance and knocking merge
with fragments from the incantation. The drumbeat increases in volume.
The dance builds in pace and pitch, reaches a peak, and ceases. Silence.
Tableau.*

II. THE PREGNANT DYING

When the title is announced, the actors return to the periphery. THE PREG-
NANT DYING *is alone onstage, stretched out on a bed. Her swollen body is
seen in profile. She breathes evenly. Her large belly rises and falls with sudden, sharp motions. She lies there, silently breathing, as the other fragments
are enacted.*

Note: *The* PREGNANT DYING *provides a focal image for this section of the* *piece. She is a tunnel in which the living and the dying come into contact for a moment and then pass each other. Each fragment in this section isolates a single bodily activity which is necessary to sustain life. The succession of images are all united in their relationship to our basic biological functions.*

The Private Case *The Masses of dying people huddle together. They are crowded on beds and floor. There is a great distance between them and the* PRIVATE CASE. *The* PRIVATE CASE *is propped up on his own bed. He is attended by two* MEMBERS OF THE TEAM *who hold his hand and buff his nails. The hoarse, collective breathing of the* MASSES *is heard.*

Motion *The* PRIVATE CASE *and the* MASSES *remain on their beds. Four actors come forward. Three run in place. One paces in a narrow circle. All participate in some form of pure movement.*

Taking In and Eliminating *Two actors stand side by side and squat. They grimace and contract their pelvic regions. They simulate defecation. At the same time, the* PRIVATE CASE *is being fed by the* TEAM MEMBERS. *One spoons the food into his mouth. The other smoothes it down his throat. The* PRIVATE CASE *swallows regularly, with a gulping sound. The movements of the ones who are eliminating are in a rhythmic relation to the gulping sound of the one who is eating.*

Breathing *Two actors step forward. They walk ahead almost imperceptibly, breathing. A third breathes loudly and with much difficulty. The only audible sound is the rhythmic intake and exhalation of breath.*

The Last Biological Rites *One actor faces the audience. A* TEAM MEMBER, *impassive and matter-of-fact, stands at his side.*

TEAM MEMBER: This is your last chance to use your eyes.

The actor uses his eyes. He looks, he sees. His vision fails.
He can see no more.
The TEAM MEMBER *hands him a piece of black tape. The blind man seals off his eyes.*

TEAM MEMBER: This is your last chance to use your voice.

The actor makes a sound which presses out into the space and recedes. His voice fades. He can speak no more.
The TEAM MEMBER *hands him a piece of black tape. The dumb man seals off his mouth.*

TEAM MEMBER: This is your last chance to use your legs.

The actor stumbles forward an weak legs. His legs give way. He can walk no more.

The TEAM MEMBER *lifts his legs into a small cart and seats him on his knees.*

His chest rises and falls. The only function remaining to him is breathing.

The actors on the beds breathe audibly. All motion has ceased.

The TEAM MEMBER *and the dying man face the audience. Tableau.*

Reprise: The Second Calling *The tableau is interrupted by the voice of* ONE ACTOR *who begins the second calling. Others join. They raise their sticks and move in a trance–like rhythm. Fragments of the calling are repeated. Gestures and movements from the dance appear and reappear throughout* THE STATE OF THE DYING; *they are emblematic of the incantation.*

THE ACTORS: Let the dead come through
    Let the dead come through
    Let the dead come through
        and let it begin with me
            with me
      Let them take my body
        Let them use my tongue
    Let the dead come through and let it begin
      with me   and let it begin with me
    Let them take my body
      and let it begin with me
        Let them use my tongue
        let it begin
    Let the dead come through and let it begin
    with me   and let it begin with me and   let it begin

Blackout.

III. THE STATE OF THE DYING

Darkness. The actors set up the props for the new section. Movement and sound. The actors return to their stools. Silence.

Note: *Everyone, except for the dead, is in the state of the dying. For those who are not yet dead, there is always the possibility of change and transformation. When the* DYING *allow the dead to inhabit them, they are asking to be moved, to be shifted into a different perspective. To be possessed is to make oneself available to the unknown. At the moments when the dead come through, everything is altered — ideas about life, attitudes toward death, rhythms, sounds, movements. The form of the piece itself must stretch to accommodate these unfamiliar energies. During this section, the two spotlights*

which have been lying downstage may be picked up by the actors and used to illuminate specific aspects of the fragments.
The Embalming As Required by Law THE PREGNANT DYING, *now inert, is rolled downstage by two* TEAM MEMBERS. *Her bed becomes an embalming table.*
One TEAM MEMBER *explains the embalming procedure. The other illustrates the process in gesture and mime.*

TEAM MEMBER: We prepare the deceased for embalming.
The body is washed thoroughly with special attention to the orifices.
A tube is inserted to drain the blood. Through another tube, embalming fluids are injected. As the fluid fills the veins, a flush appears on the face, the eyes flutter, the chest rises and falls as if the deceased were breathing.
This is only temporary, of course.
An incision is made in the central abdomen. The vital organs are removed and deposited in a bin to be burned. They are replaced by cotton batting, similar to that used in upholstery, to retain the original dimensions of the body. The skin is then repaired and sutured.
Cosmetological procedures are employed to improve the appearance of the deceased. First is the correction of lip slip.
Lip slip occurs as fluids drain from the upper lip, causing it to recede in a manner suggesting a sneer. This is unsightly for those viewing the body, so we stitch the lips together into a more attractive expression.
We cut out swollen facial tissues and fill the sunken cheeks by injecting massage creams into them. We then apply conventional makeup, such as rouge and lipstick, to create a natural and lifelike glow.
The deceased is now dressed in burial garments. These are backless, as the body will be viewed only from above.
The corpse is finally ready to await funeral procedures in the freezer compartment of the morgue.

The TEAM MEMBERS *exhibit the newly embalmed body to the* DYING *by moving it swiftly around the center of the stage.*
The DYING *sing a ritual farewell song. The melody is light, the pace is lively.*
The body is wheeled off.

The Interview *Music is played sporadically throughout the scene. A clothesrack, filled with clothing, is rolled forward. Some actors remain on the stools. Others move to defined areas, each of which represents a different* *stage in the interviewing process. Each* NEW ARRIVAL *will be welcomed, photographed, measured, questioned, and stripped before he is given a bed. When* NEW ARRIVAL 3 *enters, the music becomes full and continuous.*

TEAM MEMBER A: Next.

[*The* NEW ARRIVAL, *fully dressed, enters.*]

NEW ARRIVAL 1: How do you do?

TEAM MEMBER A: Please remove your hat.

NEW ARRIVAL 1: Oh. Excuse me. [*He does so.*]

TEAM MEMBER A: And your coat, please.

NEW ARRIVAL 1: My coat? Certainly. [*He does so.*]

TEAM MEMBER A *hangs the coat and hat on the rack.*
The NEW ARRIVAL *moves to the photographing area.*
A ladder serves as a tripod and camera. TEAM MEMBER C, *the photographer, is mounted on a rung.*
The NEW ARRIVAL *is seated in a chair.*

TEAM MEMBER B: Hello. We'll take your photograph now.

NEW ARRIVAL 1: Why?

TEAM MEMBER C: To guide us in restoring your face and body after death.

NEW ARRIVAL 1: I'd like to look as natural as possible.

TEAM MEMBER B: We know.

TEAM MEMBER B *adjusts the position and expression of the* NEW ARRIVAL *as* TEAM MEMBER C *speaks.*

TEAM MEMBER C: That's why we encourage anyone who is dying to spend his last days with us. Everything has been arranged so that, immediately after death, we can move the body from the bed to the embalming table, from the embalming table to the beauty parlor, from the beauty parlor to the coffin. All our facilities are designed to make you feel as useful and attractive in death as you were in life.

The photograph is taken. The NEW ARRIVAL *rises and moves to the measurement area.*

TEAM MEMBER D *holds a rope in her hands. She measures the* NEW ARRIVAL *as he is questioned by* TEAM MEMBER E.

TEAM MEMBER D: Please stand still while your measurements are being taken.

TEAM MEMBER E: Is there anything you need?

NEW ARRIVAL 1: Yes. I need to be in a bed near a window.

TEAM MEMBER E: You don't need a window. Nobody *needs* a window.

NEW ARRIVAL 1: I like fresh air. I need a window near my bed.

TEAM MEMBER E: We know what you need. That's why we're here.

NEW ARRIVAL 1: Couldn't you arrange it somehow?

TEAM MEMBER E: Of course. If you really need it.

NEW ARRIVAL 1: I do.

TEAM MEMBER E: Fine. We do have a bed near a window, but it's in a separate house. The building is a little far away from everything, but we'll be happy to arrange it for you.

NEW ARRIVAL 1: [*After a pause.*] There's no one else there?

TEAM MEMBER E: No. None of our other people need a window.

NEW ARRIVAL 1: Oh. [*Pause.*] Well, then, I guess I could do without it, too.

TEAM MEMBER E: But if you need it…

NEW ARRIVAL 1: I wanted to be near a window, but I don't really need it.

TEAM MEMBER E: Very good. You'll be given a bed in the main room with the others.

TEAM MEMBER D: Number 34206.

[*She hands him the measuring rope which he carries to the next area.*]

TEAM MEMBER F: Please remove your clothing.

NEW ARRIVAL 1: My clothing?

TEAM MEMBER A: Next.

NEW ARRIVAL 2: How do you do?

TEAM MEMBER A: Please remove your hat.

NEW ARRIVAL 2: Excuse me. [*He does so.*]

TEAM MEMBER A: And your coat, please.

NEW ARRIVAL 2: My coat? Certainly. [*He does so.*]

[TEAM MEMBER A *hangs up the coat.* NEW ARRIVAL 2 *moves to the photographing area.*]

TEAM MEMBER B: Hello. We'll take your photograph now.

NEW ARRIVAL 2: Why?

TEAM MEMBER C: To guide us in restoring your face and body after death.

NEW ARRIVAL 2: I'd like to look as natural as possible.

TEAM MEMBER B: We know.

TEAM MEMBER C: That's why we encourage anyone who is dying to spend his last days with us. Everything has been arranged so that, immediately after death, we can move the body from the bed to the embalming table, from the embalming table to the beaut parlor, from the beauty parlor

TEAM MEMBER F: Those are the instructions. I didn't invent them, they come with the job. Now please remove your clothing.

NEW ARRIVAL 1: What for?

TEAM MEMBER G: You do want to stay here, don't you?

NEW ARRIVAL 1: Yes. [*Pause. He undresses.*]

[NEW ARRIVAL 1 *is now dressed only in his underwear. He takes a comb from his pants.*]

NEW ARRIVAL 1: Can I keep my comb?

TEAM MEMBER G: We'll give you everything you need.

[NEW ARRIVAL 1 *combs his hair, then hands it over.*]

TEAM MEMBER G: Please remove your underwear.

to the coffin. All our facilities are designed to make you feel as useful and attractive in death as you were in life.

[*The photograph is taken.* NEW ARRIVAL 2 *moves to the measurement area.*]

TEAM MEMBER D: Please stand still while your measurements are being taken.

TEAM MEMBER E: Is there anything that you need?

NEW ARRIVAL 2: Yes. I need to be in a bed near a window.

TEAM MEMBER F: You don't nee a window. Nobody *needs* a window.

NEW ARRIVAL 2: I like fresh air. I need a window near my bed.

TEAM MEMBER E: We know what you need. That's why we're here.

NEW ARRIVAL 2: Couldn't you arrange it somehow?

TEAM MEMBER E: Of course. If you really need it.

NEW ARRIVAL 2: I do.

TEAM MEMBER E: Fine. We do have a bed away from the window, but it's in a separate house. The building is a little far away from everything but we'll be happy to arrange it for you.

NEW ARRIVAL 2: [*After a pause.*] There's no one else there?

TEAM MEMBER E: No. None of

NEW ARRIVAL 1: I'd like to keep something of my own.

TEAM MEMBER F: We'll give you everything you need. Please. Remove your underwear and dress yourself in this garment.

[*Pause.*]

[*The* NEW ARRIVAL *undresses. He stands naked for a moment, then puts on the white outfit handed him.*]

TEAM MEMBER F: Very good.

[NEW ARRIVAL 1 *faces the audience.*]

[*He places a patch on one eye.*]

[*He exits.*]

TEAM MEMBER A: Next.

NEW ARRIVAL 3: How do you do?

TEAM MEMBER A: Please remove your hat.

NEW ARRIVAL 3: Oh. Excuse me. [*He does so.*]

TEAM MEMBER A: And your coat, please.

NEW ARRIVAL 3: My coat? Certainly. [*He does so.*]

[TEAM MEMBER A *hangs up the*

our other people need a window.

NEW ARRIVAL 2: Oh. [*Pause.*] Well, then, maybe I could do without it too.

TEAM MEMBER E: But if you need it...

NEW ARRIVAL 2: I wanted to be near a window, but I don't really need it.

TEAM MEMBER E: Very good. You'll be given a bed in the main room with the others.

TEAM MEMBER D: Numbers 41702.

[*She hands him the measuring rope which he takes to the next area.*]

TEAM MEMBER D: Please remove your clothing.

NEW ARRIVAL 2: My clothing?

TEAM MEMBER D: Those are the instructions. I didn't invent them, they come with the job. Now please remove your clothing.

NEW ARRIVAL 2: What for?

TEAM MEMBER F: You do want to stay here, don't you?

NEW ARRIVAL 2: Yes. [*Pause. He undresses.*]

coat. NEW ARRIVAL 3 *moves to the photographing area.*]

TEAM MEMBER B: Hello. We'll take your photograph now.

NEW ARRIVAL 3: Why?

TEAM MEMBER C: To guide us in restoring your face and body after death.

Blackout.

The actors return to their stools.

The Dying Resist *Lights. A circle of actors walk at a brisk, regular pace. When individuals break out of the circle, the others maintain its original size and shape by adjusting pace and distance. Two* TEAM MEMBERS *stand outside the circle, One gives instructions. The other drones words of approval, which eventually become empty sounds.*

TEAM MEMBER 1:
Keep moving.
Everyone is part of the circle
Everyone must keep the circle moving.
Follow instructions.
Don't accelerate or slow down
Don't stop.
You are each responsible for keeping the circle moving.
Everyone is useful.
You are each keeping the circle alive.

TEAM MEMBER 2:

Very	good.	Nice.
Very	good.	Nice.
Very	good.	Nice.
Very	good.	Nice.
ery	ood.	ice.
ery	ood.	ice.
ery	ood.	ice.
ery	ood.	ice.

Individuals step out of the circle, or stop abruptly where they are.
   First one. Then another. Then more.
   Individually, and finally in unison, the RESISTERS *punctuate the drone with the word "out."*

RESISTERS:
Out
  out   out
        out
out
  out
  out
  out
  out

TEAM MEMBER 2:

ery	ood	ice.
ery	ood	ice.
ery	ood	ice.

[*Etc.*]

The actors continue their circle.

They ignore both the physical obstacles presented by the RESISTERS *and the word of protest.*
The circle and the protest exist simultaneously.

The Runner Who Never Gets Started *The* RUNNER *crouches over an imaginary starting line on hands and toes. He holds the racing position for several moments, then jumps to his feet, panting. Behind him, a* SECOND RUNNER *runs frantically in place. The* FIRST RUNNER *repeats his action.*

The Dying Are Drugged *Several of the* DYING *sit or lie on the beds. We see them in their drugged condition — vacant, tranquilized, harmless. A high–pitched hum is heard.*

Note *This fragment should bear a rhythmic and thematic relationship to* The Dying Resist.

The Dead Come Through (A): Marie Leveau and the Soldier
The spirit of MARIE LEVEAU *possesses one of the* DYING. *He breaks into a strange, rhythmic dance and speech. The entire space becomes charged with the energies of the dead world. The* SOLDIER *marches in place to* MARIE LEVEAU'*s rhythm, then comes through independently. The* DYING *support and react to the possessed ones with sound and music.*

MARIE LEVEAU: Eh ye ye Mamzelle Marie
　　　ye ye ye li konin tou
　　　gris gris
　　　li te kouri, aver vieux kokodril
　　　eh oui ye, Mamzelle Marie

Eh ye ye
my people come to me,
they say:

　　　make that man poor so I grow rich
　　　make that one die so I can live
　　　kill my sister
　　　kill my brother

and no one know the other
and no one see the other

　　　Marie Leveau, she sees!
　　　See my people smile,
　　　then eat each other;

wipe blood from mouth
with dainty cloth.

And my ocean stink with dead fish
and my trees are hurt and broken
and my fruit grows sick and rots
and my air is black with poison
that my birds cannot breathe
    and my people eat each other
    and my people live like slaves.

Marie Leveau, she sees!
See my people buying,
see them selling,
see them spending lives
like slaves.

Eh ye ye, Mamzelle Marie
ye ye ye li konin tou
[*Etc.*]

The SOLDIER *moves forward in a march, mouthing "yessir."*
His hand flies to his forehead in repeated salutes.
MARIE LEVEAU *grows silent as he speaks.*

THE SOLDIER: Yessir
Yessir
Yessir
Yessir

Said yes when I wanted to say yes
Said yes when I wanted to say no
Said yes
Said yes
Yessir
Said yes

    And dead because I said yes
    And dead because YOU said yes
    And dead because I said yes

    And dead became YOU said yes

And dead before 'cause you never knew why
And dead before 'cause I never asked

    Dead before and dead again
    Because I never knew

What the FUCK I was saying yes to!

yes
yes
yes

The SOLDIER *moves into the background, but remains visible. Periodic salutes and "yessirs" break from him as* MARIE LEVEAU *comes through again.*

MARIE LEVEAU: Marie Leveau, she sees!
See my people buying, see them selling
see them spending lives
like slaves.

I see the thief go into business
Now he can steal and not get caught.
I see the killer become policeman
Now he can murder, that's his job.

Eh ye ye ye
One hand holds the whip
And one hand bleeds.

Marie Leveau, she sees!
See my people smile,
then eat each other;
wipe blood from mouth
with dainty cloth.

And my ocean stink with dead fish
and my trees
and my fruit
and my air
and my birds
and my people eat each other
and my people buy and sell
and my people live
like slaves!

Eh ye ye, Mamzelle Marie
Ye ye ye, li konin tou
[*Etc.*]

The dead depart from the bodies of the possessed. Sound and movement cease.

The Renovation *A table, covered with cosmetics and things is rolled on-*

stage. Three actors begin to beautify themselves; both men and women apply makeup and wigs.

The BEAUTICIAN *addresses the audience. She speaks precisely with a minimum of facial or bodily movement.*

THE BEAUTICIAN: A beauty parlor and vanity room are connected to the embalming station. We make up the corpse with conventional cosmetics, restyle the hair and repair the face.

We begin by massaging moisture creams into the cheeks and neck. Since no one is born with perfect skin, we smooth on a foundation base which covers any blemishes that mar the surface. We then add a touch of rouge to the cheeks, chin, and nose, and paint the mouth with lipstick.

Like all beauticians, we compensate for those faces which are not perfectly oval. Since no one is born with ideal features, we produce an illusion of symmetry through shading and spot cosmetology. Lips that are too narrow or full are reshaped with lipstick. Small eyes are made to appear larger through the addition of eyeliner, shadow, and false eyelashes.

If the hair is in good condition, it is washed and set by our hairdresser. If it is skimpy or lifeless, wigs are supplied in every color and style.

Generally speaking, we try to avoid a severe or artificial look. Our cosmeticians are trained to produce a natural appearance. Of course, we prefer to work on faces which have already been well–preserved. Our most attractive models are people who, during their lives, controlled facial expressions and avoided wrinkles by restricting grimaces and smiles to an absolute minimum. Although such people will need less attention than those whose faces are marked with laugh lines, creases, and the signs of suffering, we can transform anyone. No one need worry. We are able to erase the lines of a lifetime in less than an hour.

The three actors, completely made up, face the audience. Spotlights, held by other actors, illuminate the transformation. Tableau.

The Witness *Three women, different aspects of the Witness, face the audience, kneeling. The first woman speaks and repeats her words as the second woman, and finally the third, interpose their experiences. All three versions rhythmically interweave and overlap.*

FIRST WOMAN: Pa, why don't you do something?

Oh, but I do.
I sleep and I wake up.
I go to work and I come home.
I get married and I get divorced.

Pa, why don't you do something?

Oh, but I do.
I invest money and make more money.
I train people and they train people.
I have children and they have children.

Pa, why don't you do something?

Oh, but I do.
I go from the bathroom to the bedroom
From the bedroom to the living room
From the living room to the bathroom.

SECOND WOMAN:
Hi, ma.
I see you.

(I don't see you dying.)

Hi, ma.
I see you.

(I don't see you dying.)

Hi, ma.
I see you.

(I don't see you dying.)

Hi, ma.

FIRST WOMAN: Pa, why don't you do something?

Oh, but I do.
I go from the bathroom to the bedroom
[THIRD WOMAN *begins her speech.*]
From the bedroom to the living room
From the living room to the bathroom
From the bathroom to the bedroom
From the bedroom to the living room
From the living room to the bathroom.

THIRD WOMAN:

I saw him on his back
Lying there.
Like this.

Lying there.
Like this.

Lying there.
Like this.

Like this.

I see you living.   Like this.

(I don't see you dying.)

All the actors become part of the WITNESS.

The three women multiply; fragments of their speeches, gestures, and movements are picked up and used as emblems by the others.

All words and signs become increasingly concentrated and distilled.

The Dead Come Through (B): The One Who Was Hit *The* ONE WHO WAS HIT *comes through the bodies of two actors. Both are possessed and both speak, sometimes in unison and sometimes in counterpoint.*

Up in the morning
       hit on the head
Up in the evening
       hit on the head
Got up
   and   hit
Got up
   and   hit
Men have ways of breaking those they
   wish to break
       hit on the head

Men have ways and places
       jails asylums ditches
Up in the morning
       hit!

And
I
am
lying
there
       (like this)
lying there
in the earth

Got up
      and   hit
I knew who I was when
your hatred set me free.

Your hatred was your prison
but your hatred set me free.

And
I
am
lying there
        (like this)
lying there
beside you
in the earth
you wouldn't share

(but
over my head
feet
are walking)

You cannot kill the ocean
like you
killed
me!

The Dying Pray *Semi–darkness. Spotlights pick out individuals in prayer. Sounds, gestures, fragmented words. The total stage effect resembles a dynamic collage in which individual parts are independently significant and, at the same time, integrated into the total picture.*

The Dead Come Through (C): The Responsible One *The spirit of the* RESPONSIBLE ONE *passes into two bodies. They begin a repetitive pacing as they speak, individually and in unison.*

I was walking down the street.
Cracks in the sidewalk.
I saw a man.
Cracks in his face.
    What have I done?

I saw a child choking on air.
    What have I done?
Oceans rising.
    What have I done?
Buildings toppled.
    What have I done?

What was given me was impossible to work with.

I saw a woman
she had no teeth
nibbling at the pavement
chewing at the pavement
mouth full of stone.
    What have I done?

I saw snow falling,
flakes of sky.
    What have I done?
Forty–one dead.
    What have I done?

I saw.
I saw.
I can't say I didn't.
    What have I done?

Sitting.
Standing.
Sleeping.
Sleepwalking.

What was given me was impossible to work with.

I saw blood.
    What have I done?
Fire. A man on fire.
    What have I done?
I saw — agh!
    What have I done?
I saw — kkk!
    What have I done?
Ahhhhhh!
    What have I done?
Bkhhhhhh!
    What have I done?

What was given me was impossible to work with.

The Initiation *A dead woman lies on a bed, spread–eagled, her head hanging. Four* ATTENDANTS *lift the* NEW ARRIVAL *and hold him horizontally over the corpse. The motions of copulation begin. The* ATTENDANTS *move the* NEW ARRIVAL *back and forth above the body. No effective resistance is possible.*

The act is completed. The NEW ARRIVAL *is led to another area. Two*

TEAM MEMBERS *await him. One stands on a ladder, holding a stick. Another questions him. Each time he gives an incorrect answer, the sound of the stick cutting through air is heard. An internal scream is produced by the* TEAM MEMBERS *and* ATTENDANTS. *Everyone is involved in the inquisition and everyone receives the punishment.*

TEAM MEMBER: Did you like it?

NEW ARRIVAL: Like it?!! [*He is hit.*]

TEAM MEMBER: Did you like it?

NEW ARRIVAL: No. [*He is hit.*]

TEAM MEMBER: Did you like it?

NEW ARRIVAL: I'll say I liked it if you want. [*He is hit.*]

TEAM MEMBER: Did you like it?

NEW ARRIVAL: Yes.

TEAM MEMBER: Do you mean it?

NEW ARRIVAL: What's the difference? [*He is hit.*]

TEAM MEMBER: Do you mean it?

NEW ARRIVAL: Yes. Yes.

TEAM MEMBER: So you liked it.

NEW ARRIVAL: Yes.

TEAM MEMBER: And you mean it.

NEW ARRIVAL: Yes.

TEAM MEMBER: Why did you like it?

NEW ARRIVAL: I don't know. [*He is hit.*]

TEAM MEMBER: Why did you like it?

NEW ARRIVAL: I liked it, that's all. [*He is hit.*]

TEAM MEMBER: Why did you like it?

NEW ARRIVAL: Because it was a new experience. [*He is hit.*]

TEAM MEMBER: Why did you like it?

NEW ARRIVAL: Because I always wanted — [*He is hit.*]

TEAM MEMBER: Why did you like it?

NEW ARRIVAL: Because it was necessary to like it.

Silence. Blackout.

The Embalming As Required by Law *A living person is placed on the embalming table. The* EMBALMERS *perform their jobs as before. The victim screams and writhes. His energies gradually dissipate; when his mouth is sewn, he grows completely silent.*

TEAM MEMBER: We prepare the deceased for embalming.

The body is washed thoroughly with special attention to the orifices.

A tube is inserted to drain the blood. Through another tube, embalming fluids are injected. As that fluid fills the veins, a flush appears on the face, the eyes flutter, the chest rises and falls as if the deceased were breathing. This is only temporary, of course.

An incision is made in the central abdomen. The vital organs are removed and deposited in a bin to be burned. They are replaced by cotton batting, similar to that used in upholstery, to retain the original dimensions of the body. The skin is then repaired and sutured.

Cosmetological procedures are employed to improve the appearance of the deceased. First is the correction of lip slip.

Lip slip occurs as fluids drain from the upper lip, causing it to recede in a manner suggesting a sneer. This is unsightly for those viewing the body, so we stitch the lips together into a more attractive expression.

We cut out swollen facial tissues and fill the sunken cheeks by injecting massage creams into them. We then apply conventional makeup, such as rouge and lipstick, to create a natural and lifelike glow.

The deceased is now dressed in burial garments. These are backless, as the body will be viewed only from above.

The corpse is finally ready to await funeral procedures in the freezer compartment of the morgue.

The man on the embalming table is now silent and motionless. The corpse is wheeled off.

The Dead Come Through (D): The Executed Man and the Song *A bed is raised and stood upright. A woman stands flattened against it, gripping its sides. She rocks from left to right; the bed knocks against the floor on each side. The* EXECUTED MAN *comes through.*

My eyes. Wide open.
My head. Full of imagination.
Like when I was a kid.
Free in my head.

Me and my friend, Joel, we used to fish in a place called "the pit."
The water there was so clear you could see the fish swimming—big,
beautiful fish. Me and Joel, we'd cut off their heads and rip out their
stomachs and tear the scales off 'em. Yeah, me and Joel, we had fantastic imaginations.

> I was sentenced—
> just like you!

Warden!
I know you got that noose ready for me
but it's that noose that's set me free!
A man who knows he's gonna die
doesn't have anything to be afraid of.

> My prison's made of steel;
> yours is in your head.

If someone came into "the pit," me and Joel knew how to fix him.
We'd take a wire and wind it 'round his cock and we'd twist it and twist
it till that fella hollered—MAAAAAAAA!

> I was sentenced—
> just like you!

But that warden, he's keeping his imagination locked up real safe
so when he gets up in the morning he can look at himself in the mirror and say: What a good man I am!
Everything I imagine is part of me.
Me, I knew I'd end up with my head in a noose. That's why I could
say:

> Yes!
> I am a thief.
> Yes!
> I am an addict.
> Yes!
> I am a homosexual, a pimp, a rapist.
> Yes!
> I am a murderer.

Everything I imagine is part of me.

> I was sentenced—
> just like you!

Go on, warden, be good, be nice, do what you're told. You've been
sentenced just like me, but you're keeping that locked up, too.

My prison's made of steel;
yours is in your head!

The sound of the wooden bed rocking against the floor grows louder. The song fills the woman; it uses her voice to sing itself. The words of the song are repeated over and over again with various intentions. The meaning of the words is secondary to the range of human emotions which can be expressed through them.

A–nee Ma–a–meen
A–nee Ma–a–meen
A–nee Ma–a–meen

A–nee Ma–a–meen
A–nee Ma–a–meen
A–nee Ma–a–meen
(Etc.)

The song and the rocking end abruptly.

The Dying Imagine Their Judgment *Center–stage, a ladder with a horn and megaphone. An empty chair at the side. A rack with clothing toward the rear. The* JUDGE *climbs the ladder and sits on the highest rung, He holds a book, from which he reads the judgments. The* JUDGE *speaks in the impersonal voice of a radio broadcaster; in a hoarse, authoritarian rasp; in a tired whine. The judgments are pronounced in a continuous, repetitive loop; a variety of images are enacted at the same time. The* JUDGE *blows the horn and begins.*

THE JUDGEMENTS

The judgement of your life is your life.

You will finally possess the thing you wanted most in life — and eternity will be that thing and that thing only.

You are in the death of crowds. There are multitudes about you and they are, each one, yourself. There is not one other besides you — and yet, there are multitudes.

There is a space between what

THE IMAGES

One actor sits at a typewriter and for the duration of the scene, makes a record of the proceedings.

A dead body lies on the floor. Two VOYEURS *lean over him, touching, kissing, speaking.*

VOYEUR 1: We wash the body thoroughly with special attention to the orifices ... to the orifices ...

VOYEUR 2: There is a certain temptation when you're alone was done and what could have been done and you re rooted in that space. The judgement of your life is your life.

You are standing in a space filled with bodies and you watch their couplings and breathe their odors, but you cannot touch them and they will not reach out to you.

You saw, you saw, you can't say you didn't. The judgement of your life is your life.

You moved from the house to the office, from the office to the house; from sleep to waking and from waking to sleep; you moved from yesterday to today, from today to tomorrow — and you will repeat that movement for eternity and the circle will not open.

Did you sit on another's head or were you sat upon? Either way, you will never be free of the one who is above or he who is below. The judgement of your life is your life.

You are standing on a bridge, but you do not know it. All around you, people come onto it and pass off of it, but you do not understand that all those who walk upon it at the same time are not strangers.

You neither faced your death nor participated in your life, but straddled the line between one place and the other, longing for both. The judgement of your life is your life.

You will finally possess the thing you wanted most in life —

with the body . . . when you're alone with the body . . . there is a certain temptation . . . a temptation when you're alone with the body.

A naked body is brought out on a bed by two persons holding a scrubbing brush and pail. They set down the bed and begin to wash the floor, the bed, and the person in it. No distinctions are made between the three.

The bed and body are carried out.

One man sits on another's shoulders. The man below strains and struggles to get free, but cannot.

A clothesrack is rolled in. Human beings hang amidst the clothing, like slabs of meat. The rack is pushed around the stage.

A woman paces alongside the empty chair. She gestures sternly.

A man is placed in the chair and bound. The woman continues her pacing.

The bound man makes sounds of protest. Others come forward, bind him more tightly and place a gag in his mouth.

The chair is raised and carried around the stage. The man gazes helplessly about him.

Someone mounts the ladder behind the JUDGE and, shifting from one ear to the other, whispers to him.

A chain of people crawl beneath the ladder on their bellies.

and eternity will be that thing and that thing only.

You are in the death of crowds. There are multitudes about you and they are, each one, yourself. There is not one other besides you — and yet, there are multitudes.

There is a space between what was done and what could have been done and you are rooted in that space. The judgement of your life is your life.

You are standing in a space filled with bodies and you watch their couplings and breathe their odors, but you cannot touch them and they will not reach out to you.

You saw, you saw, you can't say you didn't. The judgement of your life is your life.

You moved from the house to the office, from the office to the house; from sleep to waking and from waking to . . . .

Blackout.

They propel themselves forward by movement of their hips, arms, and legs. They seem to be swimming.

A continuous bubble of sound dribbles from their lips as they crawl.

When the first person has moved as far forward as possible, he branches to the right or left. Still on his belly, he struggles to the end of the line and repeats the seemingly endless passage.

The JUDGE *grows tired.*

The stream of human souls continues to pass beneath the ladder.

The voice of the JUDGE *slurs and fades.*

He is almost asleep.

The chain continues beneath him.

Presence and Absence *The canopy is retrieved. The actors, with their instruments, stand beneath it, facing the audience. Drumbeat. The actors play the tune which introduced the piece. They are present through the music. The drumbeat ceases. The music ceases. The actors stand silently. They are directly present in their bodies, in the space, and in their relationship to the audience. The drumbeat begins again. The music is present. The drumbeat ceases. The music ceases. The actors are present. This sequence is repeated. This sequence is repeated.*

Blackout.

[*Several scenes and speeches by dead ones were omitted from our final performances; we felt that the piece, as it then stood, was both concise and full enough. However, some of the extra material was used in performances in*

Europe and in New York and it is here included for those who, in performing the piece, would make different choices from ours.]

The Dead Come Through: The Hooker

So yes, I said
yes
when they wanted me
yes

with my body
living in it
living for it
living off of it
living off men living off me
yes, I said

you scratch my back
I'll scratch yours
so yes, I said
buying and selling
feeding off men feeding off me
yes, I said
yes
living for it
living off of it
yes, I said

you scratch my back
I'll scratch yours

and I paid for living with my life.

The Dead Come Through: The Stutterer

    My voice. Bridging the distance. My voice. Shaping words. Here, in this . . . [*Gesture.*] A corridor without walls. Here a . . . [*Gesture.*] I am squeezing myself into words. To speak at all is to speak within boundaries. Caught between the half–living and the half–dead, moving between the sound and the silence . . . we are not what we were.

What They Will Say of Him

Yes, he was a good man
Yes, he was a man

Yes, he was
Yes Yes

Yes, he earned some money and he spent it
Yes, he traveled far and he returned (Yes, he went to other coun-
tries . . .)
Yes, he was married and yes, he was divorced
Yes, he was a man
Yes Yes

Yes, it's over now
Yes, he had possibility
Now he has none
Yes, my brother
Yes Yes

The Dying Imagine Their Judgment

JUDGMENTS

You will be given the thing you wanted most in life, and eternity
will be that thing and that thing only.

From this day on, you have whatever you wanted most in life, and
eternity will be that thing and that thing only.

You are locked in a space filled with money and whether you are
sitting or standing you are surrounded by it; and eternity is the sight of
money and the smell of money and the touch of money and nothing
else.

You will see your life stretch out around you and you will stand
rooted in the space between what was done and what could have been
done.

You are rooted in the space between what was done and what could
have been done. The judgment of your life is your life.

There is a space between what was done and what could have been
done and you are rooted there, looking at both.

You will judge yourself as harshly as you judged others and you will
be forever judging and judged.

Everywhere you turn you will meet yourself and pass judgments;
and there will be no distance; between the judge and the accused and
no relief.

You are standing in a courtroom and you are the judge and you are the accused, and you will pass sentence and there will be no relief from judging and being judged.

You will stand in a space filled with bodies and you will watch their couplings and breathe their odors, but you will not touch them and they will not reach out to you.

You are standing in the death of flesh. Bodies surround you and you watch their couplings, but you cannot touch them and they do not reach out to you.

You lived in the body and did not recognize the mind. Now you will stand in a space filled with bodies and though you will watch their couplings, you will not touch them and they will not reach out to you.

Did you live in the body or live in the mind?

You will dream of a new beginning and you will wait for it, but nothing changes in eternity and nothing ends.

You dreamed of a new beginning but moved down the plotted path to the end. And you will wait for beginning, you will dream of it and wait for it, but nothing changes in eternity and nothing ends.

You are moving toward the end from which it is possible to make a new beginning. You must change your life.

You will suffer repeatedly the agonies you have imposed on others. If you were unloving, you shall suffer the torments of the unloved; if you were an exploiter, you shall suffer the deprivations of the exploited; if you were male, you shall be female; if you were strong, you shall be weak; if you were rich, you shall be poor and you will become wholly your opposite and suffer at your own hands.

Everything will become its opposite and each person will suffer repeatedly the agonies he imposed on others. The unloving will be unloved; the oppressor will be oppressed; the rich will be poor and the strong will be weak; the murderer will be the victim and the judge will be the accused. Everything will be different and everything will be the same.

❖❖❖

Following is an excerpt from an interview with Roberta Sklar, co–director of Terminal. *The full interview conducted by Paul Ryder Ryan was published in* The Drama Review *(T 51), Volume 15 No. 3a, Summer 1971.*

SKLAR: We wanted to meet with the spectator around the same issues that we had met with one another for a year—the assumption that there is a prescribed attitude toward death, that there is a prescribed way of dealing with it, which is not dealing with it. We struggled with these assumptions and struggled with the question of where these assumptions came from, who is setting them up for us. We know it is not someone in the sky with a long white beard. We had a very difficult time with the assumptions. During the research period, some times we became sentimental, other times we dealt with very private questions of death. It required us to go through a time' of being turned off by all of that, and looking into another area of the fact that we were in a process of death all the time, just as we were always in a process of growing. Raising these assumptions and issues together is not being a theatre. Once the issues are raised, it is the obligation of the theatre to take them beyond that theatre group.

◇◇◇

Excerpts from the interview that follows between Susan Yankowitz and Arthur Sainer took place during the spring of 1972.

SAINER: In what ways did the ensemble experience help fulfill you as a writer, and do you feel it limited you?

YANKOWITZ: There are areas of experience which you are hesitant to explore because they are too painful or close to you. It's essential for a writer to find some way to push past her own limits and touch what is raw in herself. Working with a group helped me to do this . . . I tended to overwrite, I didn't trust the actors to convey my intentions. But as the work progressed, I learned to leave space for the actor to supply meanings through his own instruments: pitch, inflection, gesture, body.

   . . . Most important for me, I feel, was the discovery that my resources as a writer were virtually limitless: if a speech or scene I had written was not used . . . I could just go home and write something else. Of course, a situation in which your work is subjected to the scrutiny of a large company is as much a frustration as a challenge. If Joe or the actor who was to perform a speech wasn't satisfied with it, the speech had to be rewritten. I could argue or defend my work, but ultimately artistic control was not in my hands and there were times when I felt compromised by leaving in a speech I no longer liked or by eliminating one I thought important. . . . It was infuriating at times. to work so–slowly and democratically; to work for days at a stretch on nonverbal scenes when I had six pages of written material to try; to discuss, endlessly, the problems and possibilities; and to be constantly vulnerable to the disapproval of other, permanent members.

   . . . And my ego suffered. Ultimately, *Terminal* is not my work in the way that *Slaughterhouse Play* or *Boxes* is. I am not responsible for all of its successful moments nor for all of its failures. My name does not appear on ads, and often, not in reviews. It is irritating and amusing to be the author of an "authorless" piece. I'm trying to find in myself the proper balance between detachment and the need for recognition... When I began writing for *Terminal*, the company had already been working for about four months with writers Marc Kaminsky and Nancy Fales. During that period, the idea that spirits from the dead would possess the dying and speak through them was developed;, this was a central structural contribution to the piece. Additional work had been done on the "ward," which later became "The State of the Dying." At that point, the concept for the section was essentially linear; the biology of death was virtually unexplored although the embalming ritual had been investigated and more or less set as an integral segment of the piece; there had been some character development of hospital authorities and patients, but the elitist and conformist pressures of hospital life itself were unexamined. Nancy and Marc, as well as Sam Shepard, had written some material, but as emphasis, structure, and intention changed, most of it was discarded. All these easy investigations, however, were seminal to the version of *Terminal* which, after an additional two years' work, is now being performed.

... When I first came in to the workshops, Nancy, Marc, and I tried to work together. We edited each other's material; we discussed and criticized; we each wrote a speech for a given character and then tried to make a conglomerate. It didn't work. Our writing styles and ideologies were too different. Besides, there was too much anxiety among us; the atmosphere was competitive. This added to the existing tension for any writer who was to work with the Open Theatre, for in this situation the writer was clearly the outsider; his position was a priori tenuous; his relation to the company, which had been in existence for eight years, was ambiguous and insecure ... Had Nancy or Marc remained as the writer for *Terminal*, the work undoubtedly would have been very different.

SAINER: How did Joe and Roberta and the ensemble specifically help you in the writing? What kind of discussions did you have, or didn't you discuss?

YANKOWITZ: My primary contact at all stages of the work was Joe. After workshops, we'd talk about the improvisational material and try to clarify a direction. Sometimes he'd suggest that I work on an idea which had been explored improvisationally or which had arisen out of our discussion; at other times, a scene would suggest itself and I'd go home and write it. Material grew out of improvisations, discussions, and solitary thinking. After a speech or scene was written, Joe would read it. Sometimes he'd mark the lines or ideas which particularly appealed to him; or suggest cuts;

or hand the text over to an actor to work on. There were few violent disagreements; in retrospect, the process appears remarkably peaceful and rational, at least for me and Joe. But my memory is not very good.

...Here are some examples of the ways in which the company participated in the writing. "The Responsible One" grew out of some material Joyce Aaron had explored; I read the original source and her notes and then wrote three new pages; Joe and I, with Joyce's help, cut it down to one page. "The Soldier" was my own creation; it was barely altered at all once I had put it down on the page. "Marie Leveau" was a different case. Nancy Fales, I think, had initially written down some of the Cajun words which remain; Paul Zimet, who performed the part, had worked out vocal and physical rhythms; I wrote the speech from a list of single lines and thoughts which seemed to me to be consistent with the character and with the rhythms which Paul had already established. This was later compressed into a coherent monologue. I wrote about thirty judgments — following a great deal of discussion about the ways in which we judge ourselves and later whittled it down to ten. One or two of the judgments, I think, originated with Joe. I remember writing the "wants and needs" section of "The Interview" after a workshop in which that subject was mentioned and immediately dropped; "The Initiation" was written after a discussion about fucking corpses.

SAINER: I find for myself that a difficulty in writing for an ensemble is that I have to pretty much forego a level of inexplicability that's most important to me as a writer.

YANKOWITZ: I think the quality of abstraction or ambiguity that you are describing is contained within the writing. It exists inside the words, not as an idea separate from it. Good actors generally understand the multiple levels of a speech; and if they don't, they are still able to communicate to an audience those dimensions of the work which are hidden from them through those that are understood. And I think the failure to do so is more often in the writing than in the performance.

Note: In the summer of 1996, an updated and newly titled Terminal *was produced at P.S. 122 in the East Village, under the direction of Joseph Chaikin. The new text by Susan Yankowitz of what is now called* 1969 Terminal 1996 *is scheduled to appear in* Performing Arts Journal *in the fall of 1997.*

9. THE BREAD & PUPPET THEATER

There is little to add to Fire *beyond the lucid commentary of George Dennison's that appears in this section.* Fire *is an early (1965) Bread & Puppet work, still performed by the troupe, and displays none of the usual hijinks of the boisterous Bread & Puppet shows. Other pieces, marvelous in their own right, offer comic battles between giant puppets like Uncle Fatso (an LBJ takeoff) and the Great Warrior who comes to save the kingdom with his terrible sword, or comic inventions like the beer glasses that suddenly flee the fingers of the drinkers in the 1971* Grey Lady Cantata. Fire, *conceived and developed by Peter Schumann, is austere, economical and tragic. It is relevant both as an example of the Bread & Puppets' work and as evidence of the conscience of the American radical theatre during our country's obscene involvement in the Vietnamese war.*

George Dennison's description of and comments on Fire *originally appeared in slightly expanded form in* The Drama Review *(T 47), Vol. 14, no. 3, 1970, an issue which was principally devoted to the work of the Bread & Puppet Theater.*

❖❖❖

Peter Schumann's *Fire* (which I count among the finest plays I have seen), more than any play I have seen, has the quality of prayer.

Prayer (for me) is a childhood memory, but I remember things like these: a peopling of death with human forms; a vague yet affecting sense of the scale of things; a notion of the preciousness of life, and of its vulnerability; a touch of fear, since fate is everywhere and has little to do with one's wishes.

I have tended to think of prayer under its aspects of supplication and faith. I am more impressed now by the rationality of prayer. To kneel, to bow one's head, and then to rise is to affirm, in a profoundly rational spirit, one's human place in a world only in small part human. If prayers are addressed to God or to gods they nevertheless signify to other men that we have arrived at some sort of outer limit.

Fire has many of these aspects of prayer. It speaks from a similar borderline or outer limit of experience. It is not a protest play, and is not propagandistic; rather it responds to the horrors of Vietnam, responds modestly and truly, and enables us to respond. To some extent, it is a service for the dead. Beyond this it manifests certain of the deep premises of the human condition: the unquitableness of life, our dependencies on each other, the social nature of the self. Taken together, these are the visceral/spiritual background of all emotion and all feeling, but especially of such emotions as terror, compassion, moral outrage, the sense of justice, sorrow. In some sense Schumann's play is like a dream. The dream does not express emotion, but pulls us deeply into the matrix of emotion. Our landscape now is both logical and prelogical. To see its shapes is to feel them. They are ambiguous, but not confused. The dream verges on nightmare, recovers itself and deepens. Finally it releases us and we feel that we have conceived a prayer for the victims of our world,

I have not been speaking fancifully. If one were to watch only the audience, one would come to some such conclusions as these.

I first saw *Fire* four years ago at the tiny Bread & Puppet loft on Delancey Street. The seats were filled and I stood in the back. Two burly young men came in — perhaps not so young, in their late twenties, but wearing jackets like adolescents, minus the skull and bones. They swaggered and bulked their shoulders, smiled guardedly, looked everywhere, and put their heads together. An actress in black robes was distributing programs. She held a loaf of bread under one arm, and broke it and handed out pieces as she went. The two men, smiling skeptically now, leaned against the wall and folded their arms, as if they meant to be spectators forever. But now here was the bread lady! And she was breaking off pieces of bread! Their faces changed abruptly into children's faces. They held out their hands, looking first at the girl, then at the pieces of bread lying on their open palms. Furtive glances. Others too were looking around, but all were chewing–and so they popped the bread into their mouths and began to chew. One could see the comment pass across their faces: "Not bad." It was a coarse rye, tangy and substantial. Everyone was chewing, tasting the same taste, settling more comfortably on benches, looking around. In fact, we were eating together, consuming the communal loaf.

Fire is dedicated to Alice Henry, Roger LaPorte, and Norman Morrison, three Americans who killed themselves by fire because of their country's crimes in Vietnam.

The play begins with the stroke of a bell. The small curtain opens on two rows of robed and masked figures sitting in chairs. The masks are the whitened faces of the Vietnamese dead. The hands, too, are masks, with the result that their groping, sensitive gestures are both less than life and larger. A placard on a stand tells the name of the scene, which is Monday. The figures murmur and mumble. It is not quite talk, but the "twittering like bats"

Odysseus heard in the underground. Hands rise and fall. The faces cannot move; yet something like movement—like awareness, feeling, longing—seems to flit across the eyes and lips and cheeks. The bell sounds again. The talking ceases. The curtain is closed.

Schumann's masks are extraordinary. In themselves they are works of art. But they were made for theatre, that is, to evoke and suggest many things, and to seem to move. One becomes aware only slowly of their power and beauty. They are touched by the consciousness we imagine hovers anxiously over boundaries of sleep and death. The eyes are closed, yet we sense the power of sight behind the protuberances of the lids. The lips are variously opened, closed, half–closed, fixed in transitional positions between smiling, grimacing, speaking, drinking. The faces seem to have been struck a blow, though there is no evidence of wounds, only awareness recoiling upon itself, recapitulating sight and touch after it has been removed from all intercourse with persons and things. I thought of Rilke's line in "Orpheus, Eurydice, and Hermes," as translated by Lowell:

> Her hands were still ringing and tingling...
> And when the god suddenly gripped her
> and said with pain in his voice, "He is looking back at us"
> she didn't get through to the words
> and answered vaguely, "Who?"

The bell tolls again. The curtain is drawn aside. The scene is *Tuesday*. A robed figure, awkward, intense, and tender, touches bread and lifts a goblet to the lips of each of the seated figures. Heads lift to receive the food. There is a sensitive confusion of almost–hands, a deep subsiding, hardly visible, of each face after it has been touched by bread. When all have been fed, the bell tolls again. The figures are motionless. The curtain is drawn across.

The bell tolls. We begin to hear it now also as a tolling for the dead. A haunting, broken music is being made onstage by sticks, rattles, a damaged zither, a fiddle that sounds like the scraping of a shoe. Slowly, with patriarchal dignity, brittle anxiety, and something that is like a solemn agreement that joy must be observed on holy days, the figures dance. It is Wednesday. The bell tolls. The figures cease to move. The curtain is drawn across.

The following scene (*Thursday*) is one of uncanny power. The figures are seated facing in a double row from the front of the stage to the back. A newcomer appears among them, bound with a heavy rope. The sensitive, groping hands reach out to him. The attention of the sightless eyes is like wondering. His own hands, too, fall awkwardly against the rope... until by failing and failing again, all these hands have finally freed him. He stands in the center of the stage and holds out the rope for all to see. We do see it. The rope is uncanny. The bell tolls and the curtain is drawn across.

The *Friday* stage is dark. A figure turns on an overhead light. The one who was freed of the rope lies under covers on a cot. One sits on a chair beside him. Others hover in back. A loud rattling is heard offstage. The seated figure rises and the others come forward. They look long at the one on the cot... and then lift the covers and draw them slowly over his face. The bell tolls.

The silence of all these scenes becomes a setting for the horrible noise of the next (*Saturday*), a shrieking, metallic whine and roar like the noise of a siren and the splintering of bone. A light on stage swings wildly in all directions. The effect is like *Guernica*. The figures move, but as if frozen in confusion. A large, demonically ungainly, snuffling creature flops among their feet. The bell toils in the din. Sound and motion cease. The light is turned out. The curtain is drawn across.

Sunday is played in silence, following the toil of the bell. The seated and standing figures suggest meditation. One turns his back and lifts his hands in prayer. But his hands have begun to move upward to his face, and continue to move in inexplicable gestures. He turns to us again, and we see that he has covered his face with blood. The bell tolls. The placard is touched by a masked figure, and — like those before it — falls to the floor.

The penultimate scene is called *Fire*. The silence deepens. Two figures slowly swathe the others in dark red bands. The bell tolls.

The last placard names the scene *End*. The robed, masked figures are seated. A Vietnamese woman, whose mask is like the face of death in old age, and whose white robes are like the splendor of a sacred celebration, stands alone just off center of the stage. And now in perfect silence something shocking occurs. Two figures enter, bare–armed and bare–handed, dressed in blue jeans and scivvy shirts, wearing masks of Western faces. They are lugging cinderblocks. Their motions are the motions of workmen at work — and they appear brutal, profoundly alien, almost inhuman in the deeply human setting the others have created. They place the cinderblocks around the white robed woman, and surround her with a little fence of wire ... and then withdraw. There is silence again but it is a different silence, an acidic, profoundly dislocated, appalling silence. The aged woman holds a roll of bright red tape. With deliberate movements — movements at once practical, prosaic, and ceremonious — she tears long strips of the tape and fastens them on her robe near her feet. The red strips become numerous, and move higher, beginning to entwine her and hamper her movements. One wrist is immobilized against her chest, but the fingers still tear and fasten the strips. The strips cross her mouth now, and her cheeks, and finally lie across her eyes. She folds in upon herself and topples forward, sagging heavily against the fence. There is a long silence. Something has been restored. The bell tolls.

All the theatre now is in darkness. The play is over and everyone knows it, yet no one applauds or moves. The silence is ours as well as theirs. We are unwilling to part with it. Finally the houselights are turned on. Some few clap their hands. Others move shufflingly. We make our way to the door, walking. like convalescents...

George Dennison

❖❖❖

Following are observations by Peter Schumann on Fire, *which he also directed, during this writer's visit to Cate Farm at Goddard College, Plainfield, Vermont, November 11, 1972:*

I took the title from a poem by Goethe, "Selige Sehnsucht" ("Holy Longing"). Goethe in a collection called *West–Ostlicher Diwan* was writing in the style used by Persian poets from the twelfth through the sixteenth centuries. There was an incredible *weltanschauung* to that poetry. Some of the lines in the poem are

Sagt es niemand nur den weisen
Weil die Menge gleich verhohnet
Das Lebend'ge will ich preisen
Das nach Flammentod sich sehnet...

(Tell nobody, only the wise
Because the crowds immediately show contempt.
The living will I praise
Who longeth for death in the flame...)

I never think of the play as dark. For me the ending is a liberation, not a folding up. It's not a degenerate idea to bum oneself for one's convictions, it's a tremendous statement for life. It's a jubilant statement.

Sometimes the play was performed where the audience simply took it as another example of modern, avant–garde theatre. They were viewing it for its aesthetics rather than its content.

In a way we really did *Fire* for ourselves, it wasn't important whether many or a few saw it. It was something like pure communication, the doing. it was the most important element.

Sometimes performers in *Fire* don't get what you get from it. When that happens there's no technique, no teaching that can help. There has to be a full–sized commitment.

The masks are all based on the face of one girl. I cast masks of her five or six times.

The forebear of *Fire* was *Leaf Feeling the Moonlight*. I wanted to see what could be done with great restrictions. I haven't been able to recreate Leaf Feeling the Moonlight, however. I never could remember it properly after we did it. But I based *The Dead Man Rises* on it.

❖❖❖

Peter Schumann's notes during October, 1965, when Fire *was in rehearsal:*

The Funny NY Times.

Mr. Baker's Special Fire–Philosophy

   1) Draft card does not burn

   2) Church burns well

   3) Supermarket even better

   Moral: little burning is no good

   Big burning: the government moves in and listens

   Furthermore: in old times people burned people

   Now: no more

   Better: government burns people (e.g., vicious Vietcong burn sunny American sons)

   Some governments are not strong enough (or too humane)–they burn effigies instead (as in USA) — sometimes people burn cities — cities are good — Germans, Russians, Americans — then libraries

   (Hitler did not like books)

   (Negroes don't like books — in Africa they burn real American wisdom libraries, which are there to make people learn something; they just have to wait another few hundred years until they get educated, that's all.)

   Now, also: a wife may burn a husband, or rather the soup

            or a hole in the cigarette

            or a pot with peas in it

            or an envious neighbor

            or nothing

   It does not mean anything anyway: burning is good, solid old human hardware, go ahead, young friend, burn draft cards. (comparison of Nazi German and contemporary *N.Y. Times* style Vietnam reporting)

The Stupidity of Intelligence

So stupid are we, that we protest the war (we get paid by Communist China, 30¢ every nite). We could get much better pay if we would shave and get ourselves decent jobs here (like Johnson's job). We should go like Mr. Bim on parade on 5th Ave. for the war; better: send fire–crackers that could either scare ladies out of their jungle holes or be given as Xmas presents to Vietnamese kids or to our boys over there. That would make the war much shorter.

Beautiful big bird flies over the country, hits the clouds, falls, dies.

Many men gather. Never seen such a beautiful bird. They put him on their arms and carry him around, singing, singing. They sing louder and louder. They cross the countries, they walk over the sea, they are stopped by the police, they are not allowed to go on, they bury the bird, they disperse, they stop singing.

A man steps into a town (in the middle of the town), he pours gasoline over himself, and burns himself, singing.

Also: a man catches fish all his life. He goes out in the morning, he takes some bread with him, he eats some of it, spreads the rest over the water. The birds that fly over the water eat it or the fish eat it. They bless him and wish him good luck. The man's boat broke one day, and he couldn't fish any longer. He went across the country, he had no bread left. He was hungry, but he kept going. He came into a town. The town was no good. Eating little and walking a lot he became sick and he had to rest pretty often. But he had learned to understand people's talk and how to read their faces. One day a big yellow cloud passed over the sky, and it seemed to him that fire was falling out of it, and was spreading over the world. Another day, when he approached a hill, that hill opened up before him and out of its holes poured many women and men and horses. Another day it wasn't much more than a sparrow and a sparrow's poor singing, but it delighted him, and he could understand it well.

The idea of the soldiers is almost the idea of fighting the human being. Derived from the first murder, the soldiers were meant for a purpose, for protection. They used to be chained to each other in order to assure us that their activities would not surmount what they were supposed to do. They used to be poor. They used to be light. Now that history has unchained them, they are fanciful and unrecognizable. They exercise cruelty, making us believe that cruelty has to be. They exercise the wrong, making us believe that the wrong has to be. They exercise themselves, making us believe that they themselves have to be. The revolution is at hand. The soft true goodness is at hand. And we are going to be ashamed of the offices that supply us with soldiers. In the dirty fight for gold and tremendous speeds the soldiers as well as the clerks are going to be overwhelmed by the slowness of the good, by the poverty of the really poor, by many people with good hearts and good eyes. We are not the masters. We are learning a tiny little bit of mastering in the world which is around us (including the world of construction and politics). We will not master the end of the gloomy history of the soldiers. But our insight of evil, our understanding of hope and necessity, will bring about the organized end of the soldiers, the organized end of the soldiers, the very well–organized end of the soldiers.

❖❖❖

Following are more general comments by Peter Schumann on puppet theatre for the 1967 Newport Folk Festival:

STREETS AND PUPPETS The Roman Empire built many roads across Europe. The Vandals and Goths took to those roads and moved and moved and moved until the Roman Empire broke into pieces. Then the tradespeople took to the road, then the missionaries, then the poets and puppeteers.

The poets walked on stilts and the puppeteers beat the drum. They told the news of the world: the size of King Cole, the beauty of the Brooklyn Bridge, the story of the 3 ladies who went swimming in the ocean and how they were saved by a courageous lifeguard.

Modern man believes in the *Daily News* or the *New York Times*. Ancient man believed in Demons mixed with God. That means that the newstelling of poets and puppeteers was a demonic business which scared them and their audience quite a bit. Miss Truth talked to the rosebush. Death sat on the throne of the world. Mr. Nobody shook hands with you.

From the roads puppeteers moved into churches and taverns, were thrown out of churches and taverns, and played on street corners for several hundred years.

Now, in 1967, streets are many and puppeteers are few. Truth is hired by CBS, demons live in NYC, and death still sits on the throne of the world.

The Bread & Puppet Theater bakes bread and makes puppets. Some of our shows are in the street and some are inside. The inside shows are meant for the Insides, the outside shows are meant to be as big and loud as possible. Some of our shows are good and some are bad. But all of our shows are for Good and against Evil.

•GOD•

HIMSELF

PROBLEMS CONCERNING PUPPETRY AND FOLK MUSIC AND FOLK ART IN THE LIGHT OF GOD AND MACNAMARA

Puppet theater is theater of tiny dolls, theater of huge masks which a dancer operates from inside, theater of men on sticks or men hanging from strings. It ranges from half minute nightclub acts and five minute sidewalk shows to the 365 nights that it takes to perform the "Legend of Roland" in Sicily. It seems to have been everything from funmaking, slapstick, social criticism to the terrible reenactment of a hara–kiri on Japan's Bunraku stage. Masks are older than actors, faces of wood and stone are older than mimes. Masked dancers and the effigies they carry are certainly at the origin of theater.

The communion of all, the shape of that communion of all, that which was theater, is no more. Theater is in the present an outlet of spirit, or a check–point of soul of modern society, or, as understood in the USA: show business. In this modern theater puppetry is nothing but an unimportant branch, a low–ranking form of entertainment, which seems to have a comeback right now because some smart people found out how well that little stuff fits the little television screen.

What is left of the great old forms of puppet theater, besides obscure Indian or Persian marionettes and shadow puppets, which very few of us will be lucky enough to see, is the great Bunraku theater of Japan and the Sicilian puppet theater of medieval legends. Both forms are dying out.

I figure the same can be said of the more familiar Western world Punch–, Kasper–, Guignol–, Petrushka–, Pulcinello– theaters. They still happen to be alive some place, they are sometimes brought back to life with artificial respiration, but their social conditions are no more; you need too many licenses and you are not allowed to play for money in the street, etc., etc. Throwing a baby out of the window is fun, as Punch does even in the days of Batman, but the distinct social and political criticism that went along with many of these wild shows needs a different street, a different audience and different cops than what we have here.

In 1963 I went to a festival celebrating over 300 American and foreign puppeteers. Thanks to this meeting I became acquainted with the Sicilian puppet theater. Every thing else was nice or not nice, sweet or not sweet and by all means little, not so much in size as in content and intent. Everything was plush and latex and Walt–Disney–y and basically about funny– and bunny–rabbits. Maybe I should call that the modest approach of this profession and not complain about it, and I should be glad that there were no *Hamlet* and *Faust* productions by foam–rubber specialists. But the Kasper of my childhood had been such a beautifully tough, down–to–earth, real and manly little man that I could not help looking for his like, whatever the shape of that likeness might be. From talking to puppeteers then and later on and from articles in the *N.Y. Times* and other knowledgeable papers I got the impression that in the eyes of the concerned puppetry is on the move, is opening up, is coming back because of foam rubber, because of professional lighting systems, became of television, etc. The saying goes, that when you do in puppet theater what they do in "solid" theater, then you are on the right track: get a switchboard and dimmers, go three years to the Federal Lighting and Lightening School, get a union garbage collector, a cleaning woman, a director, a playwright, a photographer, a bull–fighter for the bull–fighting scene, etc. And then by harmonizing all these variants it somehow clicks, you get the magic and the audience claps hands when you want it to.

In Bunraku you have to study for years to be allowed to move a hand. In a Kasper show you play twelve voices, seven puppets, thunder, daylight, devil and dragon all at the same time. Liszt locked himself up with his piano for more than ten years. Pan plays the flute without Conservatorium. Both those holy ghosts, the ghost of Pan and the ghost of the intensely concentrating hermit are altogether missing in modern puppetry, as well as in modern theater.

I don't want to lament about that but I want to ask: how are gods brought back to life? The fact is, they are dead, nobody brings them back to life; our life, the life that we lead, buries them.

Safford Cape, the Belgian builder of beautiful, authentic medieval musical instruments plays beautiful, authentic medieval music on the concert stage. Shakespeare is reproduced in Shakespeare–style, Sophocles in Sophocles–style and so on. But the life of people and the language and art which their life brings forth has nothing to do with style. The historian, the thinker and the reflective mind invent style, not the producer. The artist is caught in the current of events and thoughts of his time. If he is concerned with the issues that need his sensitivity and concern, he is necessarily unconscious of style. Sophocles had no choice of style, the decisions that Antigone and Kreon had to make forced a style upon him. Early medieval music had harsh and pure tone and rhythm, was fierce, not cautious, you can hear rust and cracks in the instruments, and babies crying and men shouting in the background. I don't want to hear such music in Lincoln Center, and any garbage can drum solo by any kid in New York is more medieval music to my ears.

I have heard lovely fiddling for dancing in the barn in Nova Scotia last summer. Thank God there are some remnants. Professionalism and its pride, the many spirits and dwarfs that take care of our tiny talents, the salesmen of all those talents, the importance of every little bit .of production, all this ridiculous self–concern makes for the kind of show business that we have inherited. I mean that kind that doesn't make any sense. It doesn't make sense be cause it doesn't even want to make sense. It wants to make something, it's hard to describe what, something tremendously smooth and balanced and fitting the occasion and fitting the enlightened stage or just the upholstered seat. There are puppet plays with 150 solved technical problems but no spirit, and folk singers with a vast repertory of anti–war, pro–grass, anti–washing machine, pro river songs and there is just a few times in your life a man singing a truthful song of his own, a song that you might need. And many such potentially good singers are brainwashed by the State Department of Folk–Singing. They start singing outwardly instead of inwardly. All good folk music, like Beethoven or the Nova Scotia barn fiddlers make a lot of mistakes and can afford them and don't care much for mistakes, because 1) God is more important, and 2) if you get the big red color of the thing that you want, the holy spirit, you need not care so .much for the finesse.

I think a good man is both a man who is able to be good in detail and a man who wants to learn at least to fly, or to solve all the problems of the world, or to beat death finally, or to arrange for the second coming. Michelangelo or Rembrandt or all the ever unknown Bavarian, Russian, Mexican painters of the world have been truthfully trying out if our human pains make sense, if we are allowed to happily die, or if we are condemned to unhappily struggle against the fate of all dying and suffering. They have not mixed their colors for the sake of the 'salesmen, the historians and museums that possess them now.

Still, I was always under the impression that puppeteers and circus people are closest to God and mankind because they don't deal with false gold, because they carry their gifts in their hands, they make fun, they point out some things and not much more, and I think that God likes that attitude better than the ordinarily pretty messed up human ambitions, the complicated ways of heartbreaking compositions, or the withholding and condensing intellect.

But that kind of holy simpleton and ruffian puppetry is dying out and is not likely to come back, as I have pointed out. At the present it is obviously replaced by the Union of the Professional–Puppet and Gag Institutes and these institutes have money behind them and the simpletons don't have money behind them and so they are going to lose. On the big commercial and *Life*–magazine surface the simpletons will lose. For the recording of time and for the coming revolution the simpletons are the avant–garde. And this is my prophecy: new simpletons are going to grow up all over the world; puppeteers with more puppets than tears and puppeteers with more tears than puppets;–folksingers who don't necessarily have voices or guitars but maybe just clap–hands or some kind of rattles;–painters who don't care so much how their pictures look on the wall;–and theater directors who give up Broadway and Off–Broadway and Off–Off–Broadway and train cows to balance baseballs on their tails. Nowadays, they find that out in every business, among the shoemakers as well as among the Presbyterian churches: we have neglected the stuff that life is made of so long and the whole cart is on the wrong track so much, that we simply have to get out and start walking.

The masses of audiences are moved in various directions. Certainly in this country the masses of audiences are moved in the directions of the mass media. The mass media are commercial. Their commercialism means that under the cover of free expression of the participating forces gold is being made, and ways of how to make more gold are being explored. Mr. Folksinger and Mrs. Puppeteer hardly realize that with the help of their harmless contribution of good throat and skillful fingers marines are being sent around the world and lipstick is being sold to grandmothers who need exactly the opposite of lipstick. The masses of the audiences, the Pop, the success, are in the moment, for example, very useful to Mr. McNamara and his H–bombs. The biggest, schmalziest, chamber–and kitchen–orchestra audience is thoroughly taken care of. You can see the most wonderful things in the world on a screen about as big as a behind and you don't even have to pay taxes for it…The world may not win this time. McNamara or Wall Street or somebody like that may win this time, but that destiny is being weighed on the scales of justice high above the clouds on some unknown star where Greek gods hold residence. If the world loses, then there is little sense to talk about puppetry. But assuming that the good old world succeeds against McNamara and his like, then the simpletons and demons of puppetry are also going to win in their hidden fight against show business. The Stomachache Movement will fight The Big Hunger of the World and The Big Pain of the World; the Heartbeat Movement will set out with lots of music and puppets to beat hearts and to move heartbeats, and we will all be able to work together, puppeteers, folksingers, poets, painters, housewives, everybody, because we are all tired, oh tired of books, like Jack, and long for meadows green and woods where shadowy violets nod their cool leaves between, and we are tired of show and show–off business and we long for better soap and better operas, and we are tired of appetizers and surplus food and we long for nectar and ambrosia, and we are tired of spray guns and machine guns, we want fiddle bows and love instead.

Such is the situation of puppetry today. Thank you.

10. THE PERFORMANCE GROUP

Commune *(1970–72) is the third creation of the Performance Group,*
following Dionysus in 69 *and* Makbeth. *Unlike the earlier two plays, the*
formal material of which was taken from Euripides and Shakespeare, the
textual borrowings in Commune *are largely from contemporary sources;*
e.g., the Manson family, GIs involved in the My Lai massacre. Commune
is a first–rate example of audience participation; it also exemplifies the kind
of constant, collective physical exertions found in ensembles in the late 60s
and early 70s.
Commune*'s obstinate bitterness, its brusque rhetoric rarely reaches a*
plateau of inner necessity. But the work is a significant contribution to the
growth of the radical theatre. It is like a gadfly, and like the urban America
of the counterculture, it is alternately breathless and cool, innocent and icon-
oclastic.
  The production notes are by Richard Schechner.

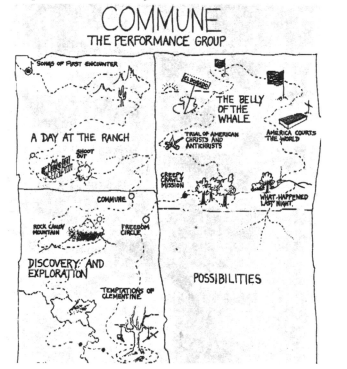

Flyer reprinted by Permission of Richard Schechner

COMMUNE *A collective work of The Performance Group.*
Directed by Richard Schechner.

This text includes variations. It is a "standard" text in that it is pared down from earlier versions. When the play opened in December there were 9 characters. Now there are 6. Only when I felt variations were still playable or otherwise intrinsically interesting did I retain them for this printed version. Variations are noted by brackets.

There are few stage directions. Much of the play is sung and the imagery is ikonographic. If others are to do *Commune*, they ought to make their own music and images.

Many people share in the collective action that made *Commune*. In addition to the performers, I wish to mention Elizabeth Le Compte, the co–director; Paul Epstein, who did musical and textual research and montage; Jerry Rojo, who designed the environment; Jerry Powell and Barry Klein, who, successively, stage–managed and tech directed the play. Portions of the revival scene are from Megan Terry's *The Tommy Allen Show*.

BRUCE: Bruce White, then Timothy Shelton

CLEMENTINE: Joan Macintosh, then Maxine Herman, then Joan Macintosh

DAVID ANGEL: Stephen Borst

FEARLESS: James Griffiths

*JAYSON: Jayme Daniel

LARA/LIZZIE: Patricia Bower, then Converse Gurian, then Maxine Herman

*MISCHA: Mik Cribben

SPALDING: Spalding Gray

*SUSAN BELINDA MOONSHINE: Patric Epstein

*Character no longer in the play.

SONGS OF FIRST ENCOUNTER. Sung as the audience enters. Embedded in actions related to "the ranch" — such as taking photographs, watering animals, fucking, eating, greeting spectators, lounging, singing, etc.

FEARLESS: I came and I didn't know the people
    And I was very nervous.

In fact when I am nervous
I want to make everyone an en–e–my
So I won't have to worry about them
And they don't get next to me.
So I was sitting there real hostile
Watching everybody waggle their heads.
I thought that it was real phony stuff
To wave your head and swing your hips
And I'm still not sure.

DAVID: So I put my name on the list
He said I didn't know what the work was.
And so, of course, I agreed solemnly
That it wouldn't be fair for me to go.
I rushed down to the Garage
And had a little workshop with Bill Shephard.
We–eeeeh–ll! It almost killed me.
In Yugoslavia I was happy to see Joan.

CLEMENTINE: I fell in love in a Margaret Mead movie
His eyes were very gentle.
He showed me his pussies
Cats and he asked me out to dinner.
Grotowski workshop November 15, 1967
2H at the School of the Arts
Ninth Street and Avenue B.
The Real Great Society Building
Then the Garage.
Big trucks, greasy cement, cold, dirty, loft upstairs
Real scared:
Soon we put our money down.

BRUCE: I came to New York in January
To get a job in movies or *Hair*,
His legs were up his stomach was out
So I called the lady and I got a date,
We said much but spoke not a word
The first workshop's over
And I'm here now.

LARA [*later called* LIZZIE.]: I came and decided to become an actress
Looked at me, looked me up and down.
Oh, no, you'll never do, you won't be one of those
Very superior, an actress.

Liked it. Wasn't going to capitulate.
Really sick of commercial theatre:
Open calls, turn around, show your legs,
Never for myself.
Heard about *Dionysus*, people taking off their clothes.
Wear a leotard with no tights
Embarrassed, I had fat legs.

MISCHA: Larry Lillo became my friend
I don't know why.
And I like killing people
And I like being killed
In New England they don't let you say how you feel.
So I went to film school
But I kept on acting.
There was a guy named Bill Shepard I used to juggle with.
I graduated from school
But I didn't want to go out into the world yet.
Loved him very much
Sad and cried when he left.

SUSAN BELINDA MOONSHINE: I left Franconia!
They said what's your name
And I said Patric
I wasn't very good
My brother for money
Things weren't happening
The way they were supposed to!
Max — we just didn't get along
I put mascara on
But I was so unsure
He got me so nervous
I called myself a boy!
I didn't like his wife
And I didn't like him.
I told him who I was.
And he had some misconceptions!

SPALDING: Oh the entrances from the wings
The sniffing on the brandy.
From the Rhode Island shore I wandered back
Squat little man in a yoga position.
Oh more like a congenial chat
Into a production of *Makbeth*

Saying my words very well.
What was behind all of that?
A roaring lion of a man
Or a little black spider?

JAYSON: New York City twenty years old, Allan Miller!
Follow your sensory tasks. In the Park doing bits.
Frustrated cat.
Stratford Connecticut. Circling in frustration.
Off Broadway. I sat and looked in his eye
And he looked back unafraid.
Performance Group.
I went to the first workshop expecting a freakout.

As the audience enters four or five at a time they are each asked to remove their shoes. The performers are engaged in various preparations. BRUCE *hands out chalk to spectators and invites them to write whatever they like wherever they like.* LIZZIE *gathers papers from the spectators that she says will later be burned.* BRUCE *selects spectators and lines them up on the Wave in the center of the environment. One by one the performers join the line up. When the lineup is complete* LIZZIE *leaves it and faces the lineup. As she identifies the performers from among the people in the lineup the performers each take one step forward.*

LIZZIE: Him. Her. Him. Him. Him. They're the ones. They did it.

After being identified people leave the lineup and the Death Valley Dance begins. Spectators are invited to join the dance.

ALL: [*Singing.*] I shall march through Death Valley with my angelic band
I shall pass through your cities with my fan in my hand
And around thee, Oh, Los Angeles, my armies will encamp
While I search my holy temple with my bright burning lamp.

After the dance the performers disperse and make animal sounds. These ultimately lead to sounds of horses galloping. FEARLESS *rides out with* CLEMENTINE *who is attracted to* SPALDING. *A shoot–out — as in the old Western movies — develops between* FEARLESS *and* SPALDING. *As* FEARLESS *falls, mortally wounded,* CLEMENTINE *holds him as in the Pietá and sings* Tramp on the Street.

SPALDING: Bang! Bang! Bang!

ALL: [*Singing.*] Olé–olé–ana! Olé–olé–ana! Olé–olé–olé–olé–olé–ana!

CLEMENTINE: [*Singing.*] Jesus who hung from Calvary's tree
Shed his life's blood for you and for me

> They pierced his sides, his hands, and his feet
> Then they left him to die like a tramp on the street.
> He was Mary's own darling, he was God's chosen son
> Once he was fair and once he was young
> She rocked him, her darling, her little Jesus to sleep
> Then she left him to die like a tramp on the street.

ALL: [*Singing.*] Olé–olé–ana! Olé–olé–ana! Olé–olé–olé–olé–olé–olé–ana!

CLEMENTINE: I need two changes of clothing and a knife. A big, good, shiny, clean knife!

SPALDING: Look, this is the desert, this is Death Valley. It's really paradise you know. An old legend, an old dream.

CLEMENTINE: I didn't relate to the pregnant lady as anything but a store mannequin. She sounded like an IBM machine. She kept begging and pleading, begging and pleading...

LIZZIE: [*Joining in.*] ...begging and pleading, begging and pleading, begging and pleading!

BRUCE: [*Singing.*] In the beginning all the world was America!

[*There is an entirely different beginning. It goes:*]

The performers are laid out in a row, corpses. SPALDING *stands on top of the Wave and speaks directly to the audience.*

SPALDING: All visible objects, brothers and sisters, are but as pasteboard masks. But in each event, the living act, the undoubted deed, there some unknown but still reasoning thing puts forth the shape of its features from behind the unreasoning mask. If man will strike, then let him strike through the mask. How else is the prisoner to reach outside except by shoving his arm through the wall!?!

CLEMENTINE: Spalding! Remember what happened last night because you were there! Remember how we got into the Pontiac and drove to the big house on the hill! You went to the top of that same hill, Lizzie, a big white house on the hill!

The murders are then enacted, exactly as they will be enacted at the end of the play. Only the speaking is softer, swifter, and there are no pauses.

BRUCE: [*Singing.*] American history ended last night. We in this room are all that's left.

CLEMENTINE: Yes, Bruce, you were there too. And Fearless, I saw you there!

DAVID: Me, too, I was there too!

CLEMENTINE: That's right, David, you were there too. Remember how we drove up the canyon alongside the ocean, then we zipped into the canyon again, we dove just like Montezuma down into the hole in the desert.

LIZZIE: I was in the car listening to the radio.

CLEMENTINE: Remember the song they were singing? Somebody opened the gate.

FEARLESS: I got it.

LIZZIE: There were lots of trees around the house. I couldn't see inside.

CLEMENTINE: Spalding, you parked the Pontiac and Fearless you went up a telephone pole and cut the wires. Then we walked up the gravel path to the house.

SPALDING: Did you ever see a coyote in the desert — watching, tuned–in, completely aware? Christ on the cross, the coyote in the desert, it's the same thing. The coyote's beautiful, he walks through the desert delicately. He smells every smell, he hears every sound, he sees everything. You see, he's always in a state of total paranoia and total paranoia is total awareness.

CLEMENTINE: We went inside the house. It wasn't locked, understand?

LIZZIE: I'll keep a lookout.

CLEMENTINE: And there was this deep, deep living room, and there was this man in the living room.

FEARLESS: A short man with his hair combed back like this.

CLEMENTINE: Real neatly combed.

FEARLESS: And he was wearing expensive clothing and he saw all of us dressed in our creepy–crawlies.

LIZZIE: I was outside where it was quiet.

DAVID: You were wearing them too! As a matter of fact they were black. Black dungarees and black T–shirts, and you made them for us, domestic lady!

LIZZIE: And the man with the combed hair started running. He ran for the backyard.

CLEMENTINE: And what did you do, David?

SPALDING: He thought he could get away from us.

CLEMENTINE: What did you do?

DAVID: I slit his throat.

CLEMENTINE: But he didn't stop ruuuunnnniiiinnnggg!

SPALDING: The red tide now poured from all sides of the monster like brooks down a hill. His tormented body rolled not in brine but in blood which bubbled and seethed for furlongs behind in their waaaaaake!

LIZZIE: And I jumped on his back and I had a knife and I stabbed and I stabbed and I stabbed and I stabbed and I stabbed and I stabbed and I stabbed!

CLEMENTINE: That's just the beginning of our story. That's just the start of what happened!

SPALDING: [*Singing.*] There was a lady . . . !

DAVID: In blue —

LIZZIE: No, no, not that lady. There was another lady.

DAVID: The Lady in Red!

LIZZIE: That's right: The Lady in Red. She looked very scared and very rich She thought we were there to rob her.

CLEMENTINE: You want money? I have lots of money! Look, here's seventy dollars!

LIZZIE: She started running running running for the yard.

FEARLESS: I got her, I got her!

SPALDING: But wait! We still have the best part of our story to tell.

DAVID: We went upstairs into the bedroom, there the most beautiful people were.

FEARLESS: Aren't you pretty?

CLEMENTINE: Remember her long blond hair and her blue eyes? Remember her breasts?

FEARLESS: Hot tits, nice hot tits.

CLEMENTINE: Remember her belly? Remember how hard it was?

FEARLESS: The blond lady's going to have a baby.

DAVID: The Lady in Blue!

FEARLESS: I didn't like the man.

DAVID: Why not?

FEARLESS: I didn't like him!

CLEMENTINE: She had a baby. We killed a baby!

DAVID: Shut up. And then we took a knife.

FEARLESS: This time all it took was one knife.

DAVID: And the Lady in Blue kept saying, "Please, please..."

LIZZIE: Please, please let me have my baby! I want my baby!

SPALDING: At last, gush after gush of dotted red gore as if it had been the purple lees of red wine shot into the frighted air and falling back again ran dripping down her motionless flanks. Her heart had burst.

CLEMENTINE: And then we dipped our hands in it. And now we had one, two, three, four — no, wait a minute, five? There was a boy outside when we first came, there was a boy outside and Fearless you got him. He wasn't in the house. Remember the boy who was just visiting?

DAVID: I don't even live here. I don't know anybody here. I don't even belong here!

CLEMENTINE: And then we went to the Boy Who Was Just Visiting and to the Man in the Backyard and to the Pretty Man with the Blond Hair and to the Lady in Red and to the Lady in Blue and we dipped inside their bellies and we wrote just like we wrote before!

FEARLESS: Open your eyes, open your eyes and see!

CLEMENTINE: We wrote on the floor and we wrote on the ceilings and we wrote on the walls and everybody knew what we did!

DAVID: Wait a minute. We did one more thing. We took the pretty man with the blond hair and we took the pregnant lady and we put them together on the couch in the living room. We put them together cozy–like because they had been lovers, probably, once.

FEARLESS: And then we took a silver thread and we put it around his neck and we put it around her neck and then we went away from the house on the hill.

DAVID: Clementine! It is the verdict of this court that we take you, hang you upside down, slit your throat, and use you as an example for everybody else!

SPALDING: The changes, the changes, man, are what it's all about. We're a different person each hour, each tick of the time we change. We're two, four, six different people and it doesn't matter as long as it doesn't stop!

I went to the desert because I wanted to live deliberately, to live deep and suck out all the marrow of life, and if it tasted bitter to taste fully its bitterness and if it tasted sweet to have its sweetness full on my tongue.

As SPALDING *speaks the jam session begins. Everyone sings, and takes riffs on the basic melody and words. Two songs have been used for the jam, and either may be used.*

"Big Rock Candy Mountain":

On a summer's day in the month of May
A funky freak came hiking'
Down a shady lane 'neath the sugar cane
He was lookin' for his likin'
As he walked along he sang a song
Of a land of Milk and Honey
Where a freak can stay for many a day
And he don't need any money!

Oh, the buzzin' of the bees
In the cigarette trees
the soda–water fountain
Where the lemonade springs
And the bluebird sings
In the Big Rock Candy Mountain!

In the Big Rock Candy Mountain
The pigs have wooden legs
The bulldogs all have rubber teeth
And the hens lay soft–boiled eggs.
The farmers' trees are full of fruit
The barns are full of hay
Oh, I'm gonna go where there ain't no snow
Where the winds don't blow
Where the sleet don't go
In the Big Rock Candy Mountain!

"Bound For the Promised Land":

On Jordan's stormy banks I stand
And cast a wishful eye
To Canaan's fair and happy land
Where my possessions lie.

We are bound for the promised land

Bound for the promised land
Oh, who will come and go with us
We are bound for the promised land!

Oh, the transporting rapt'rous scene
That rises to my sight:
Sweet fields arrayed in living green
And rivers of delight!
[*Chorus.*]

No chilling winds nor pois'nous breath
Can reach that healthful shore.
Sickness and sorrow, pain and death
Are felt and feared no more.
[*Chorus.*]

When shall I reach that happy place
And be forever blessed?
When shall I see my father's face
And in his bosom rest?
[*Chorus.*]

*The jam session leads into the boat: the Wave is transformed into a boat and
the performers become passengers, wind, sails, sailors, and sea. Then*

CLEMENTINE *leaves the boat and becomes the Statue of Liberty as the boat
of immigrants arrives in New York.*

LIZZIE: Look! It's the Statue of Liberty!

ALL: We're here! We're here! America, America!

BRUCE: Americaaaaaa!

CLEMENTINE: [*Like a Bronx cheerleader.*] Give me your tired!

ALL: Tired!

CLEMENTINE: Your poor.

ALL: Poor!

CLEMENTINE: Your huddled masses yearning to breathe free!

ALL: Yearning to breathe free!

CLEMENTINE: The wretched refuse.

ALL: Of your teeming shore!

CLEMENTINE: Send these the homeless tempest–tossed to me! I lift

ALL: I lift, I lift, I lift my lamp beside

CLEMENTINE: I lift my lamp beside the go–o–o–olden door

ALL: The golden, golden, golden, golden door!

> BRUCE *and* SPALDING *run a slow motion race as the others provide a tightly scored sonic accompaniment. The feel of this accompaniment is of a railroad running its tracks. The feel of the slow motion race is of increasing effort and frenzy: the Rat Race.*

DAVID: The shore is all covered with stones

LIZZIE: Glistering and shining like mineral stones

FEARLESS: Lakes and ponds of running water

CLEMENTINE: Many springs of excellent sweet water

DAVID: [*Coming in on "water" first syllable.*] Running exceedingly pleasantly

FEARLESS: Raspberries

LIZZIE: Gooseberries

FEARLESS: Strawberries

CLEMENTINE: Red and white

DAVID: As sweet and much bigger than ours.

FEARLESS: Here are also great store of deer are also deer and other beasts

LIZZIE: Birds for every kind of pleasant sport

DAVID: [*On "sport."*] Pleasant and delightful sport

CLEMENTINE: [*On "sport."*] Give me your tired, your tired, your poor, your huddled masses

LIZZIE: [*On "huddled" first syllable.*] There are no violent winds in these regions

CLEMENTINE: [*On "regions" first syllable.*] Yearning, yearning, yearning.

FEARLESS: [*On second "yearning," first syllable.*] and but little rain

DAVID: The sky is dear

LIZZIE: The air is salubrious, pure and temperate

DAVID: [*On "salubrious" last syllable.*] The air is salubrious

CLEMENTINE: [*On "salubrious" last syllable.*] The air is pure and temperate

FEARLESS: [*On "is."*] The air is salubrious.

> *Everyone freeze on* FEARLESS' *"salubrious." The performers singing the text move to a new position in front of the racers, so that the racers can be*

tempted and urged towards the finish line. Exactly as the singers begin their texts the racers start to move.

LIZZIE: As for trees the country yieldeth

DAVID: Cedars, strait and tall.

LIZZIE: High–timbered oaks

FEARLESS: [*On "oaks."*] Walnut trees in abundance

LIZZIE: Hazelnut trees

DAVID: [*On "trees."*] Cherry trees

CLEMENTINE: [*On "trees."*] Sassafras a tree of high price and profit, price and profit

FEARLESS: Laurels, palms, and cypresses that send forth the sweetest fragrance

LIZZIE: In America there are fertile lands sufficient to subsist all the useless poor, all the useless, useless poor in England

CLEMENTINE: [*On "to."*] Send these the homeless, the homeless homeless send the homeless tempest tempest–tossed to me

LIZZIE: The soil is fat and lusty

FEARLESS: [*On "and.."*] The soil is fat and lusty

DAVID: So is the sea replenished with great abundance of excellent fish

FEARLESS: [*On "fish."*] Mullets, turbots, mackerels, herrings, mullets, turbots, mackerels, herrings, mullets, turbots, herrings

LIZZIE: [*On the first syllable of the first "mackerels."*] Crabs and lobsters, crabs and lobsters, crabs and lobsters

DAVID: [*On* FEARLESS *second "turbots."*] Crevasses and mussels, crevasses and mussels

LIZZIE: [*On the last syllable of "mussels."*] Come to Marlboro, country

CLEMENTINE: [*On "Marlboro" first syllable.*] Marlboro country is everywhere

DAVID: [*On "where."*] Wherever you go that's Marlboro country

CLEMENTINE: [*On "boro."*] I lift my lamp beside the golden door!

Complete freeze for several beats, RACERS PROSTRATE *on the ground across the finish line,* SINGERS *in frozen postures. Then* DAVID *administers the oath which is said in responsive reading. The oath is followed by a march*

around the space to the tune of "Columbia the Gem of the Ocean." During the march CLEMENTINE *is dropped off in a corner, trapped in a circle. The others go to the pool, strip, and bathe.*

DAVID AND ALL: Our ulterior aim
Is nothing less
Than heaven on earth
The conversion of this globe
Now exhaling pestilential vapors
Into the abode of beauty and health
We do not make war
On any part of human nature
But only upon its false circumstances
And subversive conditions!

CLEMENTINE: Aaaaaaahhhhhhh! I'm so fucking tired of environmental, experimental theatre! I want to make a movie with Arthur Penn and star opposite Dustin Hoffman.

DAVID: Then was Clementine led into the wilderness to be tempted by the Devil.

CLEMENTINE: I want to ride horses and go swimming.

BRUCE: Wow, you can't do that over there — where you're at is the epitome of dragdom. Why don't you rip off a couple of credit cards and come on down here to St. Croix?

CLEMENTINE: How can I pack up my apartment, sublet it, clean the refrigerator, take care of the cats, answer all my letters, reschedule my singing lessons, explain it all to my parents, and make it to my sister's wedding?

BRUCE: But it's so warm here in St. Croix. You don't have to do anything except be. You just go down to any one of the five beaches and you let it be known that you don't have a place to stay. Then you just take your pick of any one of these beautiful, tall, rich, well–hung American men! And they have these mountains, Wow, they have these rain–forest mountains! Have you ever seen the Caribbean?

CLEMENTINE: No.

BRUCE: It's so deep blue you can paint with it.

CLEMENTINE: No. I can't go. I have my work to do.

DAVID: And when she had fasted forty days and forty nights she was afterwards hungry, and the tempter came up to her and said, "if thou be the Son of God command that these feet be made into vanilla ice cream!"

SPALDING: As I sat there at my ease, cross–legged on the deck, under a blue tranquil sky, the ship under indolent sail and gliding so serenely along; as I bathed my hands among those soft, gentle globules of infiltrated tissues, as they richly broke to my fingers and discharged all their opulence like fully ripe grapes their wine, I forgot all about our horrible murders; and in that inexpressible sperm I washed my hands and heart of them.

CLEMENTINE: Save me from the lion's mouth, take me from the horns of the unicorn!

SPALDING: While bathing in that bath I felt divinely free from all malice or anger. Squeeze, squeeze, squeeze. All the morning long I squeezed that sperm until a strange sort of insanity came over me and I found myself unwittingly squeezing my mates' hands in it. Such an abounding, affectionate, friendly, loving feeling did this avocation beget that at last I was continually squeezing their hands and looking up into their eyes with love.

CLEMENTINE: Oh, my God, my soul is cast down within me. Deep calleth unto deep at the noise of thy waterspouts and all thy waves and thy billows are gone over me.

Slowly, singing, everyone gets out of the tub and goes over and surrounds CLEMENTINE, *some at a distance, some close.*

ALL: His knife bein' drawn and all in his right hand
His knife bein' drawn and all in his right hand
His knife bein' drawn and all in his right hand
He stabbed her to the heart and the blood it did flow.

Clementine, Clementine oh come go with us
Clementine, Clementine oh come go with us
Clementine, Clementine oh come go with us
Today we will marry some pleasure to see.

The blood it did flow and the blood it did flow
The blood it did flow and the blood it did flow
The blood it did flow and the blood it did flow
He throwed her in the grave.

DAVID: Clem–en–tine. Did you ever make love with your father?

CLEMENTINE: No.

DAVID: Did you ever think about it?

CLEMENTINE: Sometimes.

DAVID: Take off your clothes I want to see your whole body. [*Though she does not in fact undress.*] Now go look at yourself in the mirror.

CLEMENTINE: No! I can't look at myself. I'm ugly!

BRUCE: What do you mean you're ugly!?

CLEMENTINE: [*The response varying according to the actress playing the role.*] Look how bony my knees are, and my ass is flat, and my belly is fat. I have a shape like a pickle! I hate myself and I never want to have a baby!

BRUCE: You're perfect. Look at yourself in the mirror and tell me you're perfect.

DAVID *takes his rhythms from each of the other performers as he goes to them. The varying rhythms ultimately join in one rhythm.*

DAVID: I am your father — Jesus. And Spalding's your father, Jesus; and Bruce is your father, Jesus; and Liz's your father, Jesus; and Fearless is your father, Jesus. I am your father, Jesus . . . .

At the climax, CLEMENTINE *falls, as do the rest.*

CLEMENTINE: I am poured out like water and all my bones are out of joint. My heart is like wax, it is melted in the midst of my bowels. My strength is dried up and my tongue sticks to my jaws. You have brought me into the dust of death.

ALL: Either you're on the bus or you're off the bus.

The Death Raps follow. These are actual or imagined encounters with death which each performer, except CLEMENTINE, *tells to individual spectators. As each performer finishes his/her Death Rap he whispers the name and place of death into the ear of one spectator. For example, "Carrie Borst died in Glassboro, New Jersey." Then the performer repeats this in a not–real voice. Then he repeats it shouting. After that each performer goes to a separate place in the theatre and becomes a bell. The Bell Chorus is made from singing the last syllable of the place where the Death Rap person died. For example, "Zee, zee, zee, zee" sounding like the tolling of bells. The Bell Chorus ends abruptly when* LIZZIE *shouts "Listen!"*

LIZZIE [*Singing.*]: Listen! The thrill of it can't be described.
When I stabbed it was like stabbing myself.
Life and death all in one motion.
In and out, in and out,
Everything in life is in and out.

Eating, breathing, sex, even killing!
In and out, in and out, in and out goes the knife.
Listen!

ALL: [*Singing.*] Everywhere there's lots of piggies
Living piggies' lives.
You can see them out for dinner
With their piggy wives
Clutching forks and knives
To eat their bacon!

LIZZIE: Moose was on top of me and we were bailing. And I liked it, I really liked it! And he kept saying

LIZZIE AND FEARLESS: Are you ready yet? Are you ready yet? Are you ready yet? Are you ready yet? Are you ready yet? Are you ready yet? Are you ready yet? Are you ready yet?

LIZZIE: And I shouted: Now, now, now!

ALL: Bang!

LIZZIE: And he pulled the trigger and blew his head off.

DAVID: Spalding, this Gook jumped into my foxhole, put her rifle against my head, pulled the trigger, and it went click. So I took out my knife and I cut her head off. You wanna see a nice Kodacolor print I have of me standing there holding this Gook's yellow head by her black hair?

FEARLESS: [*Singing.*] Hey, did you drop the bomb on the Japs at Hiroshima?

DAVID AND LIZZIE: There's nothing possible in this world I haven't done!

SPALDING: [*Singing.*] Tum–ta–ta–tum–tum, da–da!

All the performers except CLEMENTINE *become animals and make a totem pole. She climbs the pole.* FEARLESS *is the top animal; when she reaches him he speaks.*

FEARLESS: Again the devil taketh her up into an exceeding high mountain and showeth unto her all the kingdoms of the world, and the glory of all of them, and saith unto her, "All of these will I give to you if you will fall down and worship me."

ALL: Fall down, fall down, fall down and worship, and worship me, me, me . . .

BRUCE: [*Singing, and then speaking.*] Our father, our father, our father . . . Just before I came here I went away for a weekend to Pennsylvania. I ran through the woods near Gettysburg and I said to myself, "If I can get to the top of that hill, I can see the river." I broke through the woods into a clearing and I fell down on my knees and everything stopped. It was the first astral projection I ever had — where your soul leaves your body and looks back at your body as if it were dead. Your life functions are very close to death. And I said, "Wow, this isn't it." "It" meaning something my roommates had always talked about. And I thought, "Well, that's very interesting, but he's really sick — look at him down there." And all of a sudden I had this great pity for me — for him. Not feeling sorry for myself but feeling sorry for him. Well, anyway, I had this — technically it's called clear light — where you — well, I went through this experience. At that time there was no need for life, and there was absolutely no need to go back inside the body. Then I decided, "Wait a minute, why not go back?" I knew then how to find the kingdom of heaven on earth. And having done that I could have left it and gone on to a low spirit level. Or, like the people in India who spend fifty, sixty, seventy years meditating like crazy without acid — all for the ultimate trip: half–hour of Nirvana and they die. Because they have a heart attack or they come down and they just have no desire to live anymore. But I said, "No, this is just the beginning. You go back and affect people by living it? So that's why I came back — not because I want a Christ trip or an ego trip.

CLEMENTINE: Bruce, can you teach me, can you help me?

ALL: And then the devil took her up unto the holy city and placed her high on a pinnacle and he said unto her:

SPALDING: "If you be the Son of God then cast yourself down, down, down, down . . . "

CLEMENTINE: My friend Lee Kingston Merril Byrd from Colorado went away every summer only I had to stay home and work as a waitress to make money to go to college. Byrd could fly. I want you to help me to fly. Nowww!

As she shouts "Nowww!" CLEMENTINE leaps off a ledge and flies into the arms of the others. As she sings they carry her through the space.

CLEMENTINE: [*Singing.*]
>I'll show thee the best springs
>I'll pluck thee berries
>I'll fish for thee and get thee wood enough.
>Let me take you where the crabs grow
>And I with my long nails
>Will dig thee peanuts

Show thee a jay's nest and instruct thee
How to snare the nimble marmoset.
I'll bring thee to clustering filberts
And sometimes I'll get thee
Young scamels from the rocks.

They put her down, undo her hair. She takes off her costume of apron and straw hat.

CLEMENTINE: I went to the ranch. It was a loving scene. I gazed into their eyes and they gazed into mine. They took my bag of belongings.

BRUCE: What's yours is ours, what's ours is yours.

CLEMENTINE: It was beautiful.

DAVID: And all that believed were together, and had all things in common, and sold their possessions and goods, and divided them among all men, as every man had need.

CLEMENTINE: *[Singing, joined by the others.]* No more dams I'll make for fish
Nor fetch in firing at requiting
Nor scrape trenchering nor wash dish.
Ban, Ban, Ca–Caliban!
Has a new master, get a new man!
Freedom, hi–day, hi–day, freedom? Freedom, hi–day, freedom!
What's a creepy–crawly mission?

LIZZIE AND FEARLESS: You creep and crawl into people's houses and take things that belong to you because everything belongs to everybody!

Performers steal things, particularly clothes and jewelry, from the audience.

SPALDING: Little children!

LIZZIE, CLEMENTINE, BRUCE: You take things that belong to you because everything belongs to everybody!

SPALDING: It is the last time. For you have heard that antichrists shall come, and even now there are lots of antichrists, and so you know it is the last time.

LIZZIE AND CLEMENTINE: *[Singing.]* Time now ain't long when the Savior will come
Then we'll be judged by the deeds we have done
On that judgment day we'll weep and we'll cry
When the pale horse and his rider go by.

[There are several versions of the Revival. What is presented below is the

basic material out of which a Revival can be made. But other Revival texts may be used, or the scene may be improvised.]

FEARLESS: You know what America needs today? Get our sin forgiven. You know what keeps you from having fun being saved? Your sin. You know what keeps you from having fun in your home? Your sin. You know what keeps you from being what you ought to be for Christ? Your sin. You know what keeps you from being a soul winner? Your sin. Now can you say that word with me?

ALL: Sin.

FEARLESS: I'm talking to everybody in this theatre.

ALL: Sin!

FEARLESS: Oh, there's more sin in this room than that!

ALL: Sin!

FEARLESS: Come on, get it out!

ALL: Sin!

FEARLESS: Be happy!

ALL: Sin!!

FEARLESS: Not my sin — your sin! Jesus said, "I come to die for your sin!" Now if he died for 'em, why should we live with 'em? Now how many of you are glad you came here tonight? Raise your hands, let me see. Oh, that makes me feel so good, thank you, thank you, my friend! If you've got a want to in your heart to leave this theatre tonight more like you ought to be for Christ and less like you were when you came in, only you with your body can do what the Lord Jesus is trying to do through your heart. Open up your hearts, my friends, and let God slide right in. Open up your hearts, open up your mouths, and let God slide right in. Open up your hearts, open up your mouths, and let her slide right in, slide right down, slide right on, slide right through!

FEARLESS *jams on the "Open Up your hearts/mouths" theme. Or he may go into a dance with the audience.*

Once upon a time I was as hip as you. Once upon a time I was as cool as you. But then I met God. God made me hot. I like it hot! God entered me and he spoke to me in tongues? And this is what he said: "Fearless, I want me a dancing partner!"

[*Or* FEARLESS *may say:*]

I want you to give up your piss–poor identities. I want to tell you that through the sweet light of Jesus you can each and every one of you be Queens and Kings. All your selves can shine right through I'm telling you! Peel off the old house paint and let the life of every Saint living or dead shine right on through your sweet little head. Do it now before you're dead!

As FEARLESS *is reviving,* BRUCE *is singing and sooner or later* FEARLESS *gives the space over to* BRUCE.

BRUCE [*Singing.*] I went into the mountains with a brother
    And we lay in all these mountain–dewed rocks
    And our feet melted in the water
    And our heads opened up to the stars
    And we sat there
    And we flowed
    Round and around and around and around and around and around
and around and around and around . . . And we realized that pollution and jelly donuts and peanuts
    Are all part of life
    Because they are all part of the Master!
    And it shall come to pass
    In the last days
    God says
    That I shall pour out my Spirit upon all flesh
    Then your sons and your daughters shall prophesy
    Your young men shall see visions And your old men shall dream
dreams!

FEARLESS: Are you ready, brother, are you ready?

BRUCE: I'm ready!

FEARLESS: I hereby ordain you with the power of ordaining that was ordained in me by he–she who set me free. I ordain everyone of you sitting by me in this theatre. I ordain you and claim you for me and thee and He and She and hereby free you from pain and beg you to smile benevolently on the forty billion amoebas fornicating in your bloodstream. I hereby relax you and set you free with the knowledge that you are here on earth to serve as the living tubes for the living God to pass through on Her relentless journey through Her joyous universe! Praise God! Praise You! I'm so happy, hallelujah, I could evaporate on my way to you, Sweet Jesus!

DAVID: Don't you see, brothers and sisters, we don't have to die! We can live forever! It's all just been put into our heads!

SPALDING: And what's real is what's happening to our planet. You can shut your eyes to it and play all your games. You can put on a suit and tie. Or, you can stand off from it and do what is natural and good, as the grass does, and the fruit does, as the tree does.

LIZZIE: And David said:

DAVID: Friend, wherefore art thou come?

LIZZIE: And they came, and laid hands on him, and took him.

CLEMENTINE THEN WITH LIZZIE: [*Singing.*]
> You got to walk that lonesome valley
> You got to walk it by yourself
> Ain't nobody here can walk it for you
> You got to walk it by yourself.

To each question FEARLESS *asks,* DAVID *answers. But his answers are over-whelmed by the questions. The scene is played at incredible speed.*

FEARLESS: Name, address, married or single, how many children, parents living or dead, religious preference, do you look behind you wheat you flush, how long have you held your present job, have you ever been convicted of a felony or institutionalized, you're a homosexual, aren't you, David?

DAVID: People say I'm their leader. Here's the kind of leader I am. I make sure the toilets are clean. I make sure the animals are fed. Any sores on your horses? I heal them. Anything need fixing? I fix it. I'm always the one to do everything nobody else wants to do. Cats need feeding? I feed them. When it's cold. I'm the last one to get a blanket.

WOMEN: Everybody sheds their clothes and lays on the floor. There are lots of mattresses all over the floor. It doesn't matter who's beside you, a man or a woman, you make love. Everybody makes love with everybody.

FEARLESS: Is there sexual intercourse?

WOMEN: Yes, yes, of course.

DAVID: The lowest part of the world is in Death Valley. The Fault goes right through Death Valley, and in the last time there will be a big earthquake that will open the world for all those who love. That's us! We shall be saved!

He stands and begins a slow march–dance around the theatre followed by the WOMEN WHO *sing his accompaniment.*

LIZZIE AND CLEMENTINE:

I shall march through Death Valley with my angelic band
I shall pass through your cities with my fan in my hand
And around thee, Oh, Los Angeles, my armies will encamp
While I search my holy temple with my bright burning lamp

DAVID: [*While dancing.*] I don't care what I look like to you. I don't care what you think of me. I don't care what you do with me. I've always been yours anyway.

FEARLESS: What happened when you first met him?

LIZZIE: He felt my legs and seemed to think I was OK.

FEARLESS: He never hit you?

CLEMENTINE: No.

FEARLESS: He never bit you?

LIZZIE: No.

FEARLESS: When he made love with you, he was gentle?

LIZZIE AND CLEMENTINE: No, it was not gentle.

DAVID: [*Dancing and then stopping as he offers himself.*] I've eaten out of your garbage cans. I've worn your second–hand clothes. I've stolen things and given them away again the next second. I've given everything I have away. Everything. Take, this is my body.

FEARLESS: Bruce, have you ever dropped acid and received feelings about reincarnation?

BRUCE: Yes.

FEARLESS: What are your feelings about reincarnation?

BRUCE: Just that I believe in it. You go through cycle after cycle and then you go to God and become one with God. There are no words to describe it. It's a feeling and there are no words. My sole purpose for taking acid is God realization.

FEARLESS: You've seen God?

BRUCE: Yes, I saw God on acid.

CLEMENTINE: Hey, Spalding, now that we're famous we're going to do this hour–long TV special. It'll be just us — eating, singing, killing, being together.

LIZZIE: How much're we going to get for it?

CLEMENTINE: The gas chamber ppssssssssssssssssssssssssssst! — minimum.

DAVID: We could each get a dune buggy

FEARLESS: We could get six of 'em!

CLEMENTINE AND LIZZIE: Right on! Can you dig it? Los Angeles in flames, cops and judges and moms and dads all frying like bacon and each of us in our own, shiny, brand, fucking new dune buggies tooling out through Death Valley to save the white race. Far out!

There is a dune buggy race.

CLEMENTINE AND LIZZIE: [*Singing during the race.*]
My days on earth are numbered,
I can see the journey's end
Gonna ride my dune buggy to Glory
when it comes around the bend.
Waiting for my call to Glory,
where I'll know the good and true
There I'll learn to love my neighbor,
like he wanted me to do!

CLEMENTINE: And I just stabbed her and she fell, and I stabbed her again. I don't know how many times I stabbed her! Then I looked at her belly and I touched the blood in her belly with my fingers.

LIZZIE: The gas chamber? Are you kidding? It's all verses, climaxes, music, changes. Death is permanent solitary and there is nothing I would like more than that.

As she speaks she blindfolds herself.

BRUCE: The answer is to accept the Cross. I've accepted it. I can go up on the Cross anytime in my imagination.

ALL: [*Except LIZZIE, singing.*]
Lizzie Borden took an ax
Gave her mother forty whacks
When she saw what she had done
She gave her father forty–one!

LIZZIE: [*Singing.*] Somewhere over the rainbow
Bluebirds fly.
Birds fly over the rainbow
Why, oh why, can't I?

CLEMENTINE: But you can, Lizzie. You're going to the top of the big hill. You're going to jump off into the hole in the desert. You're going to discover El Dorado — for us!

ALL: El Dorado.

SPALDING: When
We were in
The desert
We learned
To sit on rocks
All day like coyoooooooooooooooteeeeees.
We reduced our wants to very little.

BRUCE: The desert is heaven because nobody else wants it.

SPALDING: There are these old legends among the Indians. When the Spanish came Montezuma went into Death Valley and disappeared down a hole into the center of the world. El Dorado—the Golden City.

ALL: El Dorado—the Golden City.

SPALDING: There are these gigantic explosions in the desert. A whole mountain just flies off and leaves this gigantic hole.

DAVID: There is this pool in Death Valley that goes down into the center of the world where the aware live forever. Montezuma is there with three hundred ninety–nine of his chosen warriors. And we are going there. They sent divers down into this pool and those divers never came back. Then the government put a wire fence around it.

FEARLESS: I can cut it. I can climb on your back and cut that fence.

LIZZIE: When do I get to the top of this hill?

BRUCE: You're going up it now.

LIZZIE: I think the ground is even.

BRUCE: That's because you're blind.

LIZZIE: I'll stay here. I'll keep a lookout.

CLEMENTINE: Remember her long blond hair, and her blue eyes?

LIZZIE: I was outside where it was quiet.

CLEMENTINE: Remember her breasts?

FEARLESS: Hot tits, nice hot tits.

CLEMENTINE: You'll never have your baby.

FEARLESS: You're beautiful like she was. You're just like she was.

LIZZIE: I want my baby! Please let me have my baby!

CLEMENTINE: Just like the beautiful lady you'll never have your baby!

LIZZIE: [*Ripping off her blindfold.*] Stay away from me!

DAVID: Stupid cop–out.

CLEMENTINE: Cocksucker.

FEARLESS: I'm beginning to feel the pressure. I was in Miami last week to visit my dad. I hope my family is left out of this. They don't know anything.

[*There are three versions of the My Lai scene.*]

First version:

FEARLESS *at random picks fifteen persons from the audience.*

FEARLESS: I want you fifteen people to come into the center of this circle to represent the villagers at My Lai.

If they all do the scene continues, as in the other versions.

If one or more people do not come into the center circle, FEARLESS *removes part of his costume and says:*

FEARLESS: 'I am taking off my ———— to signify that the performance is now stopped. Those who have not come into the circle have the following options. First you can come into the circle and the play will resume. Second you can go to anyone else in the room and ask them to take your place and if they do the play will resume. Or you can stay where you are and the play will remain stopped. Or you can leave the theatre go home and the play will resume in your absence.

A wait then begins. On one occasion it was more than three hours before the play resumed.

Second version:

SPALDING: We would like everyone in the theatre to come down to the center of the Wave to represent the villagers at My Lai.

Enough time is allowed for all those spectators who choose to do so to come to the center of the room. The performers climb to ramparts high above the center. After everyone is settled the scene continues.

Third version:

FEARLESS *and* CLEMENTINE *and* DAVID *gather the shoes of the spectators that have been placed upon entering the theatre on a large cloth and drag the shoes up the Wave and dump the shoes in the center circle. The scene then continues.*

In all versions, the following dialogue is the same.

DAVID: Well, we gather thirty, thirty–five people in the center of the village, and we place them in there, and it's like a little island, I'd say, right there in the center of the village.

SPALDING: What kind of people?

DAVID: Men, women, children.

SPALDING: Babies too?

DAVID: Babies too. We huddle them up, we make them squat down.

SPALDING: OK, and the —

DAVID: I pour about four clips into the group.

SPALDING: You fired four clips from your–

DAVID: M–16.

SPALDING: And that's about how many clips? I mean how many —

DAVID: I carry seventeen rounds to each clip.

SPALDING: So that comes to something like sixty–seven shots.

DAVID: If you say so.

SPALDING: And you killed how many? At that time?

DAVID: Well, I fire them on automatic, so you can't — you just spray the whole area on them so you can't know how many you kill because they're going down fast.

SPALDING: OK, and then what?

DAVID: We're rounding up more and we collect about seven or eight of them. We put them down in the hootch and then I drop a hand grenade down there with them. Then somebody tells us to bring them over to the ravine. So we take them back out and lead them over. By then they already have seventy, seventy–five of their own all gathered up. So we throw ours in with them and the lieutenant tells me, he says, "We got another job to do." And so he walks up to the people and he starts pushing them off and he starts shooting.

FEARLESS: I guess everyone has their own feelings about the war. I doubt I can explain miiiiiiiiiiiiiiiiiiinnnnnnnnnneeee!

SPALDING: How do you shoot babies?

DAVID: I don't know. It's just one of them things. It seemed like it was the natural thing to do at the time.

SPALDING, DAVID, FEARLESS: [*Dancing and singing.*]
The little pigs they roast themselves
And trot about this lovely land
With knives and forks stuck in their backs
Inquiring if you'd like some ham.

LIZZIE: [*Putting her blindfold back on.*] You're all disgusting!

CLEMENTINE: Down here is the big hole in the desert.

ALL: El Dorado.

CLEMENTINE: There's room here for one hundred forty–four thousand people and you're the first!

FEARLESS: Now you're right on the edge.

LIZZIE: [*Singing.*]
Star light, star bright
First star I see tonight
I wish I may I wish I might
Have the wish I wish tonight.

CLEMENTINE: We went into the bedroom, remember? The pregnant lady's husband was away. He was across the big water.

FEARLESS: There she was on the bed. Face it, man, movie star, rich, beautiful.

CLEMENTINE: Everything you ain't, babe, but dumb as they come!

FEARLESS: Hot tits, nice hot tits!

CLEMENTINE: She never had to work a day in her life. She got everything she wanted. She was a product of the American dream.

LIZZIE: I wasn't there. I didn't do it.

CLEMENTINE: Fearless, will you please exhibit Exhibit A?

FEARLESS: And now, ladies and gentlemen of the jury, here is the Lookout, the Snitch of the first degree!

CLEMENTINE: [*Leading a cheer.*] Punishable, brothers and sisters, by C–R–U–C–I–F–I–X–I–O–N!

FEARLESS: Don't worry, though, they'll let you have your kid first!

LIZZIE: I didn't kill anybody. I threw away the creepy–crawlies but not my own clothes. There's no blood on my shirt. The police will take me out for Chinese supper and I'll spill the beans. They'll grant me immunity and I'll have my baby, go back to my daddy, and finish college. They'll let me go free because basically I'm a nice girl. I can't be in this thing!

DAVID: Why can't you be in this thing?! Who do you think you are that you can't be in this thing!

LIZZIE:
I spread the butter I spread the cheese
I spread the jam on your dirty knees!

Guess who snitched!

CLEMENTINE: So we came and we were all around her. David held her down.

DAVID: She wanted her baby.

CLEMENTINE: She just kept screaming one thing.

DAVID AND LIZZIE: I want my baby! Let me have my baby!

CLEMENTINE: It'll be born dead!

LIZZIE: It'll be born screaming and howling!

FEARLESS: Jump, you cunt, jump!

LIZZIE: I want it, it belongs to me, he's mine!

DAVID: Big as life!

ALL: [As LIZZIE lumps backwards into their arms.] El Dorado!

LIZZIE *is lifted high over everyone's heads. At the end of the My Lai scene* SPALDING *goes to a dancing circle in the corner. As he speaks the others make sounds of coyotes, and then join the dance. The dialogue is chanted.*

SPALDING: The people of the country having espied us made a lamentable noise. We thought it had been the howling of wolves.

ALL: These people are inclined to a chestnut color the color of their skin is yellowish the complexion of these people is black.

DAVID: Black–assed niggers, yellow gooks and spics!

ALL: They admired the whiteness of our skin they cover their privities only with a piece of leather.

SPALDING: As the time passes our relationship with the natives becomes more and more difficult.

ALL: In the morning we manned our boat with twelve men and muskets and drove the savages from their homes and too the spell of them as they would have done of us.

SPALDING: Behold, this pattern of our butcheries.

ALL: We saw the flames of their fire
and the savages sitting around it
we attacked them at once
taking them by sunrise
They ran into a place where reeds grow thickly
There we found them, there we found them, there we found them . . .

As each person says "There we found them" he/she collapses into a line of corpses as at the beginning of the play.

SPALDING: All visible objects, brothers and sisters, are but as pasteboard masks. But in each even, the living act, the undoubted deed, there some unknown but still reasoning thing puts forth the shape of its features from behind the unreasoning mask. If man will strike, then let him strike through the mask. How else is the prisoner to reach outside except by shoving his arm through the wall?

CLEMENTINE: Spalding! Remember what happened last night because you were there! Remember how we got into the Pontiac and drove to the big house on the hill. You went to the top of that same hill, Lizzie, a big white house on the hill.

The performers select from the spectators' shoes, unmatched pairs of which are worn throughout the next scene. The shoes are taken off at the end of the murder scene.

BRUCE: [*As he undresses and lounges in the pool.*] American history ended last night. We in this room are all that's left. There was an artist in the city of Kouroo who strove for perfection. One day he decided to make a staff. Knowing that in an imperfect work time is an ingredient, but in a perfect work time does not enter, he said to himself, "It shall be perfect in all respects, though I do nothing else in my life."

CLEMENTINE: Yes, Bruce, you were there too. And Fearless, I saw you there!

DAVID: Me, too, I was there too!

CLEMENTINE: That's right, David, you were there too. We drove up the canyon alongside the ocean, then we zipped into the canyon again. We dove like Montezuma down into the hole in the desert.

LIZZIE: I was in the car listening to the radio.

CLEMENTINE: Remember the song they were singing? Somebody opened the gate.

FEARLESS: I got it.

LIZZIE: There were lots of trees around the house. I couldn't see inside.

CLEMENTINE: Spalding, you parked the Pontiac, and Fearless you went up a telephone pole and cut the wires. Then we walked up the gravel path to the house.

Everyone except SPALDING *who is high in the ramparts watching and* BRUCE *who is in the pool, forms into an Organism — a collective body, supersensitive to every sound in the room.*

SPALDING: Did you ever see a coyote in the desert — watching, tuned–in, completely aware? Christ on the Cross, the coyote in the desert, it's the same thing. The coyote's beautiful. He walks through the desert delicately. He smells every smell, he hears every sound, he sees everything. You see, he's always in a state of total paranoia and total paranoia is total awareness.

The Organism gets to the top of the Wave and crosses the line marked "inside."

CLEMENTINE: We went inside the house. It wasn't locked, understand?

LIZZIE: I'll keep a lookout.

CLEMENTINE: And there was this deep, deep living room, and there this man the living room.

FEARLESS: A short man with his hair combed back like this.

CLEMENTINE: Real neatly combed.

FEARLESS: And he was wearing expensive clothing and he saw all of us in our creepy–crawlies.

LIZZIE: I was outside where it was quiet.

DAVID: You were wearing them too! As a matter of fact they were black. Black dungarees and black T–shirts, and you made them for us, Domestic Lady.

LIZZIE: And the man with the combed hair started running. He ran for the backyard.

CLEMENTINE: And what did you do, David?

SPALDING: He thought he could get away from us.

CLEMENTINE: What did you do?

DAVID: I slit his throat.

CLEMENTINE: But he didn't stop ruuuunnnninnnnnnnggggg!

SPALDING: The red tide now poured from all sides of the monster like brooks down a hill. His tormented body rolled not in brine but in blood, which bubbled and seethed for furlongs behind in their waaaaaaake!

LIZZIE: And I jumped on his back and I had a knife and I stabbed and I stabbed and I stabbed and I stabbed and I stabbed and I stabbed and I stabbed!

CLEMENTINE: That's just the beginning of our story. That's just the start of what happened.

Freeze. BRUCE *speaks very quietly, without rush.*

BRUCE: The artist went to the forest to find wood to make his perfect staff. He searched for and rejected stick after stick. As he made no compromise with time, time kept out of his way. Before he found the right stick the city of Kouroo was in ruin. Then he sat on one of its mounds to whittle his stick.

SPALDING: [*Singing the blues.*] There was a lady . . . !

DAVID: In blue —

LIZZIE: No, not that lady. There was another lady.

DAVID: The Lady in Red!

LIZZIE: That's right. The Lady in Red. She looked very scared and very rich. She thought we were there to rob her.

CLEMENTINE: You want money? I have lots of money! Look, here's seventy dollars.

LIZZIE: She started running running running for the yard.

FEARLESS: I got her, I got her!

SPALDING: But wait! We still have the best part of our story to tell.

DAVID: We went upstairs into the bedroom, there the most beautiful people were.

FEARLESS: Aren't you pretty.

CLEMENTINE: Remember her long blond hair and her blue eyes? Remember her breasts?

FEARLESS: Hot tits, nice hot tits.

CLEMENTINE: Remember her belly, remember how hard it was?

FEARLESS: The blond lady's going to have a baby.

DAVID: The Lady in Blue!

FEARLESS: I didn't like the man.

DAVID: Why not?

FEARLESS: I didn't like him

He slits BRUCE'S *throat.*

CLEMENTINE: She had a baby. We killed a baby!

DAVID: Shut up. And then we took a knife.

FEARLESS: This time all it took was one knife.

DAVID: And the Lady in Blue kept saying, "Please, please..."

LIZZIE: Please, please let me have my baby! I want my baby!

FEARLESS *knifes* SPALDING, CLEMENTINE *knifes* LIZZIE.

SPALDING: At last gush after gush of clotted red gore as if it had been the purple lees of red wine shot into the frighted air and falling back again ran dripping down her motionless flanks. Her heart had burst.

CLEMENTINE: And now we had one, two, three, four no wait a minute, five! There was a boy outside when we first came. There was a boy outside and Fearless you got him. He wasn't in the house. Remember the boy who was just visiting?

DAVID: [*Pursued by* FEARLESS.] I don't even live here. I don't know anybody here. I don't even belong here.

FEARLESS *kills* DAVID.

CLEMENTINE: And then we went to the Lady in Blue and we went to the Lady in Red and went to the Man in the Backyard and we went to the Pretty Man with the Blond Hair and we went to the Boy Who Was Just Visiting and we dipped inside their bellies and we wrote just like we wrote before!

Taking chalk and water from the pool they write on the floors and walls and ceilings. The performers write whatever is on their minds and in their hands.

FEARLESS: Open your eyes, open your eyes and see!

CLEMENTINE: We wrote on the floors and we wrote on the ceilings and we wrote on the walls and everybody knew what we did!

BRUCE: [*Getting out of the pool and dressing.*] By the time the artist finished polishing and smoothing his staff it suddenly expanded into the fairest of all creations. He made a new system in making a staff. And now he saw by the heap of shavings still fresh at his feet that for him and his work the lapse of time had been an illusion and no more time had elapsed than a single scintillation of the brain.

DAVID: Wait a minute. We did one more thing. We took the pretty man with the blond hair and we took the pregnant lady and we put them together on the couch in the living room. We put them together cozy–like became they had been lovers, probably, once.

FEARLESS: And then we took a silver thread and we put it around his neck and we put it around her neck and then we went away from the house on the hill.

CLEMENTINE: I forgot my knife so I went back inside. The pregnant lady was there and I knew that if I took my knife and cut open her belly I could have her baby!

CLEMENTINE *pushes her way through the spectators or shoes in the center circle and jumps from the Wave to a circle marked Freedom. Then she walks slowly to the circle where* DAVID *was interrogated and the "savages" attacked. As she walks, she sings.*

CLEMENTINE: A prodigal son once strayed from his maker
To wander a land of hunger and pain
But now I can see the end of my journey
I'm going to heaven again.
From out of the sky he's coming to meet me
To wash all my sins and call me his own
His servants will bring a ring for my finger
And never no more will I roam.

She jumps into the circle, takes off her shoes, lays down as dead. The others do likewise in different parts of the room. As they do SPALDING *opens his eyes. As he passes different corpses they awaken and join the press conference as photographers, mike–men, reporters.*

SPALDING: I wasn't even in the country when it happened. I got a telegram. We were married eighteen months ago in Boston. She wore a white miniskirt and I wore a Regency suit. It was the marriage of two different worlds. I agreed to come back for the funeral and, and to hold a press conference at the house. I want to speak somewhere without bounds, like a man in his waking moment to men in their waking moments for I am convinced that I cannot exaggerate enough even to begin to lay the foundations of truth. When I got to the house on the hill

I saw that someone had written "pig" all over the walls in blood. She was the only one I really loved. She used to prop the pillows up like that when I wasn't there. That's how she liked to sleep when I wasn't there. They must've dragged her into the living room, and that's where they must've done it. There was blood all over the home. She managed somehow to get out there near the pool. She liked to float around on a rubber raft with her big pregnant belly stuck up in the air. When she first told me she was going to have a baby she announced it as though she had invented motherhood.

DAVID: You don't seem very upset.

SPALDING: Who are you talking to?

FEARLESS: Is it true there was an orgy there that night?

SPALDING: No, that is not true. This is not an orgy house, it is not the famous house of the orgy.

LIZZIE: Do you sleep in the nude together?

SPALDING: She does not take drugs, she never takes drugs.

FEARLESS: [*Letting the water in the poor run through hands.*] Excuse me, Spalding, is this the blood?

SPALDING: That's the blood.

DAVID: Why aren't you upset about your wife's death?

SPALDING: Look, I love my wife very much. You know, what may be horror to you is not necessarily horror to me.

CLEMENTINE: What would you describe as the role of the artist in today's society?

SPALDING: The role of the artist?

CLEMENTINE: Yes.

SPALDING: Yes, yes, of course.

A long freeze. Then SPALDING *goes to the side of the Wave, sits, takes out a penny whistle and blows: like a factory whistle ending the work day. He plays a tune. The others go to the tub and wash, return clothing to spectators, relax. Performance rhythms subside into everyday rhythms.*

❖❖❖

NOTES WHILE MAKING COMMUNE. 1970–1972

For Ellen Gurin, who committed suicide.
by Richard Schechner, November 7, 1972.

Commune is a genuinely collective work. It brings together creative energies from a number of people and times. Included in the work are the words
of Melville, Shakespeare, Thoreau, the Bible, the American colonists, the
Brook Farm communards, Charles Manson, Roman Polanski, Susan
Atkins. And the words of members of the Performance Group. The music
in the play is American folk music, bluegrass, Nashville, old hymns, hobo
melodies; and tunes invented by Group members, composed by Paul
Epstein.

26 January 1970

Maybe give up TPG the whole thing. Rest. Write. Do TV project later in
the year followed by Manson thing. Stop running. Stop all these workshops. Stop these endless obligations. Stop pushing self. Stop. Rest. Think.
Write. Start. No stopping.

27 February 1970

Spahn wants the secret of how Manson gets the girls to be so domestic and
docile. "All you gotta do, George, is grab 'em by the hair, and kick 'em you
know where!"

2 March 1970

Later he died, full of hours and honors, women around him, both weeping
and singing. They each sponged his body clean and said to each other:
"Look how firm his skin feels, how deep but clear his eyes, and how young
and round his penis." Behind it, unfortunately, was hatred as still as an un-
fallen avalanche, and as heavy.

7 April 1970

The collective art form can arrive only when there is a collective society or
[perhaps] when a group of people work together a long time they develop
a model of the collective spirit. Each person in the group finds his "symbolic displacements" and these relate organically to each other. It is an artificial but authentic collective. Grotowski's theatre is this way.

27 April 1970

Crisis in my head about the performance. No set narrative yet no sure way
of using the people. A narrative or scenic progression does not offer itself.
Fantasy of people telling me: "What arc we to work on now? Where is the

play we are to do?" Feeling of hopelessness. I am at a loss to supply the lodestone to transmute the gold. Exercises go on, but with no shaping goal. The tone of the work is established, and good. Of course, we are far from performance but it is precisely now, during these formative, embryonic workshops that things occur. My imagination is dry. It needs the refreshment of a story. Some great and piercing invention of the spirit that in saying little tells much.

12 June 1970

Whole feeling. Confident. I don't know why. There has been no breakthru, no separation from the problems of self–composition, or solution. Just a deep in–sense of wholeness and a knowing that time will permit the piece to develop outwardly as I collaborate with the others to structure it inwardly.

21 June 1970

The war has gone on long enough now for us to recognize it as natural. The heaps of corpses, huddled into their murdering places are nothing unusual. From time to time some lieutenants, sergeants, privates, and a captain or two are tried, convicted, sentenced, and commuted for assembling the Vietnamese and shooting them. The overkillers are not touched; they are the voices of the people in these matters. School kids grow up knowing that sudden murderous death is nominal. Anyway the Gallup Poll assures each of us that our neighbors are similarly and proportionately disposed to dispose of the gooks in as efficient a way as possible. "America First," urge the Panthers, and on 7th Avenue, from time to time, you can hear gunshots. Nothing unusual after the first few times. "Bring the war home" summer is coming in. No destruction now could redeem 400 years of slavery and 100 years of brutal expansion, exploitation, and oppression. We work to explore communes and the rebirth of a consciousness beyond individualism. We work amid the dirty air, and do not know the outcome of our input.

You give us your names. We paint them on the walls of our theatre. We live in the environment of your names. A name is taken played with used as basis for a song transformed. Opening improvised on the basis of certain themes and transformations. "In the beginning all the world was America and at the end all America was the Performance Group." Basic real themes: individuality vs. collective; given name vs. new or made name; tragedy vs. celebration; hypocrisy vs. truth; myth/lies vs. actual, immediate history; false gesture vs. actual, concrete contact.

23 June 1970

No longer a theatre of telling a story—or even doing a story. But doing/showing something here and now. The audience as partner–participant. Most impassioned speeches not dialogue but addresses to audience. Ritual vis-à-vis audience. Not to search for story but for themes and gestures, for sounds and dances vis-à-vis audience and with ourselves. To be at once absolutely personal and absolutely collective. Communal.

1 July 1970

In real time: All this takes place after supper night after Sharon Tate murder. Keeping the knowledge of violence from each other. It keeps coming in.

3 July 1970

Another name for the piece: White Exorcism. The night after the murder, the day after the war–how do we cope with the immensity of the crime? How do we face up to it–and confront it and know it–and get rid of it–and learn from it? The existential crime of being born in America, the rich land; of being born white, the oppressor class/race? Not through guilt, but through a new birth and new symbols new ways of handling experience. We kill again and again — as the blacks kill — to make the other whites think it was the blacks who killed. Commune Being Several Well–Known Scenes Enacted After Supper by the Youth of Our Nation. After ecological disaster symbols of possibility is a dance and an exchange. Richard Brown hands me a 14–gauge shotgun–I shoot off the top of a plant. Impulse to turn gun around and blast all who are facing me. To riddle them, in slow motion, with pellets. Brown uses the gun to kill chipmunks and skunks that raid his garden. I would use it to hunt ghosts.

6 July 1970

Outlined to the Group the view I have of the piece now: Last night (=American history=killing of Sharon Tate) something awful and terrible happened. We — the Group, out of our needs, dreams, fears, hopes, fantasies, activities — did it. Tonight after supper we are trying not to look last night in the eye — we are trying to avoid. But all we do brings us closer to the event. We circle it with a number of avoidance gestures, but return to it. The event is our own private murders; the Sharon Tate/Manson syndrome: America and the world. Only by experiencing last night can we earn our rights to the possibilities–the symbols of possibility which are ours. Work from specifics. The personal lives of the performers, the lives of the Manson people. The crisis of the country. Criticism and analysis is the individual function. Creativity and wholeness is the Group function.

Basic problems of structure are confusing me. What sense does it make? A year of life for this? Where does it lead? I am a leader being led by my own logic, I don't know where. I am not sure of why and persist for dark unreasons not surfaced. Last week I said to them: "Saying 'I don't know' is a cop–out." I meant that in the exercises when blocks occur we do know–but don't have the courage to say or the words/gestures to say it in. Everything thereby becomes dangerous. Brutal. I do not know where we are going to a kind of religious (that is, transcendent) experience to an essential confrontation with self that is at once private and social. It communicates and awes at once. How do we do/show these things to/with an audience? The gestures are so private they dare not occur with someone watching. They take so long to rise up, few if any in our society will have the patience to wait and see them rise. Who cares on which side a wheel starts rolling?

24 July 1970

This week I have not been able to sit myself down at the typewriter and construct the Lara–Murder–Massacre scene. I have not even been able to elevate my efforts to the abyss, the crisis of despair and negativism which precedes creation. (Is that why, I wonder, the Genesis story begins in "the void"?) It will come — it must come. It is an additive process. All the stuff for the piece will be there soon pretty much. We stop. We rest. We look over what we've made. We take time. I make time to look it over coldly and critically. We ask our critical friends. Then in Stratford we run the piece — all 2–3 hours of it. We make it tight and cohere. We work on details. Then we come to N.Y. and examine it again. This time subtractively. What is necessary? What gives the piece its essential and fundamental feels? What can be spared? What can be cut? As we move on tour and as we approach Toronto we begin to pare down. The 3 1/2 weeks in Toronto are for paring down and precisioning. For scoring this detail and that. For sensing the shape and flow of the whole, as an architectural event — Then back to N.Y. for previews in which what we have made is watertight and totally functional.

We never went to Stratford, much less Toronto. Through twelve more notebooks are many pages of notes about *Commune*. It never got "watertight and totally functional." It opened in New York in December to lousy press generally. It struggled along. And was changed much from then to now. Had I more space I would continue this odyssey through my own past as written in my notebooks. Some other time.

∽

11. THE PAGEANT PLAYERS

The King Play *(1968) exemplifies the directness demanded by the street play. The idea that there is a deep chasm between rulers and people might be developed for nuances and complexities inside a theatre, but on the street or in the park, simple, recognizable actions and simple, direct dialogue are demanded. The figures in the play exist as functions, without character. The message of how the functions deteriorate, how society deteriorates, unfolds rapidly, almost relentlessly. The King Play lends itself to much improvisation, particularly about current urban problems. The play is at once fanciful and deadly realistic.*

The script is followed by Michael Brown's view of the development of the Pageant Players and the company's relationship both to the theatre and to the culture. His assessment gives us an historical context for The King Play.

✧✧✧

KING PLAY. *A collective work developed by the Pageant Players.*

CAST: King, Queen, their Minister, the people [3–6], Announcer, 1–2 musicians who sing, play drum, kazoos, wood block. Announcer punctuates lines with and plays cymbals.

Props: Palace gate, huge chicken leg, Welfare bread, Medicaid medicine, shovel, big penny, 2–3 muskets.

Everyone in front of palace gate, singing an old–fashioned waltz. People move to the side.

ANNOUNCER: [*In middle.*] Once, a long time ago and far from the comer of Fourth Street and Avenue B–once there was a king.

KING *enters, struts around, takes position in front of gate.*

ANNOUNCER: And the King had a Queen.

QUEEN *enters.* KING *and* QUEEN *dance.*

ANNOUNCER: And the King and the Queen had a minister.

Enter MINISTER. *Dances with* QUEEN; *then with* KING.

ANNOUNCER: The King eats supper.

MINISTER *brings out chicken leg, which all three eat in gross, orgiastic way. Up till here, other people are singing waltz for each scene. Here they sing "Marine Corps Hymn." Chicken leg is thrown offstage.*

ANNOUNCER: The King goes to sleep.

KING, QUEEN *and* MINISTER *go behind palace gate, sleep (to music).*

ANNOUNCER: Outside the gates of the palace some people worked hard, and they were nervous.

Each of the people who enter now on the ANNOUNCER's *lines do a short sound, motion or monologue bit on their condition, relating it to the play but mainly to conditions in America today of the characters they represent. For example, the* NERVOUS MAN *is an office worker, the* TIRED LADY *is a cleaning woman, etc.*

ANNOUNCER: Some people worked hard and they were tired.

Enter TIRED LADY — *no rest for years.*

ANNOUNCER: Some people had no jobs and they were mad.

Better if black guy.

ANNOUNCER: Some people were women and wanted to be just like the Queen.

Enter WOMAN *hung up on cosmetics, and false hopes about marriage.*

ANNOUNCER: Some people had no jobs and didn't want any.

Enter HIPPIE *to rock beat. Musicians for each character play appropriate music.*

ANNOUNCER: Everybody began to complain and the noise woke up the King.

People make noise and rap to audience, in character, about their problems. KING *awakes, summons* MINISTER.

ANNOUNCER: The Minister has an idea.

MINISTER *brings out liberal programs Medicaid, Welfare, jobs (the shovel). He and* QUEEN *give them out, do a dance. People sing song with deadpan faces:*

> The King is really good to me
> He gives me medicine when I'm sick
> He gives me food when I am hungry

He gives me jobs when there is no work
The King is really good to me.

ANNOUNCER: But the medicine ran out. The bread was moldy. The jobs didn't pay enough.

People do bit to show each of these things with the props. On last one the UN-EMPLOYED GUY has the shovel and KING doesn't pay him. ALL start picketing front of gate with props as sign, and making noise and complaining.

ANNOUNCER: The Minister has another idea.

Fanfare. MINISTER points and says, "The enemy!" This, after court has conferred. MINISTER makes this line from box which supports gate. MINISTER mobilizes people to fight the enemy, takes liberal programs from them. The court waves goodbye, the people march off. When they are gone, MINISTER brings out the chicken, the waltz is sung, and they eat grossly.

The people have frozen on one side of the stage. A machine gun interrupts the waltz; one of the people is wounded. They return and find the court eating chicken. The people are mad. Confrontation. The court retreats behind the palace gate. The KING can't quiet them.

ANNOUNCER: The King decides to hold an election.

Waltz is played rapidly as the election proceeds. The candidates are the MINISTER and the QUEEN. They go up on the box holding the gate and give campaign speeches by alternating funny, disgusting poses. The people try to put up a CANDIDATE, but he or she is kicked off. The KING picks a new KING by eeny, meeny, miney, mo on the MINISTER and the QUEEN. Whoever is picked is crowned, the other consoled. The new KING ascends the box and tries to address the people and audience. The people shout him down, and chant, "No more kings" over and over, trying to get the audience to chant too (see Note).

The old KING gets muskets, gives them to the rest of the court. They point them over the gate at the people and the audience. Freeze and silence. The court, together, say, loudly, "SHUT UP." All frozen with guns pointing at people and audience.

ANNOUNCER: Once there was a king... [*He points to court, then gesturing to all people and audience:*] ... and all the rest of us!

Cymbal. All bow, from freeze.

Note: If people come up on stage and help chase court, then that is the ending. But if they just sit and chant, that's not enough, and we do above ending.

❖❖❖

Michael Brown, formerly of the Pageant Players, New York, is now a member of the Moving Men, San Francisco, Berkeley, and Oakland. His article on the Pageant Players, excerpted here, was written in 1971, after many of the original troupe members had gone west to communal life in Oregon and Brown had joined the Burning City Theatre in New York.

The very purpose of forming the Pageant Players was to combine art and politics; but so that they enriched, not diluted, each other. There were too many politicos who said art is okay when it's an organizing tool or a weapon. There were too many actors, writers, directors, "artists," who said art must be above politics in some separate world to be really good or great. We said No to both: that really great art has always been political or social; and, conversely that throughout history, the politics that really turned people on included, or was embodied in, a vision–the basic element of all art. The core members of the group were sympathetic to both currents.

We looked around us: Brecht seemed the best of the political playwrights but was so European, intellectual, communist. He saw America as an outsider. We needed to be indigenous in spirit and content. Most other political drama, especially American, seemed hackneyed or heavy–handed, with a few exceptions from the 30s. *Marat/Sade* — the play that turned many of us on to theatre! All that music, body movement, choreography, color, energy! Good lessons there. Everyone we knew came out of *Marat/Sade* stoned by the beauty; I remembered the story, the history, the image of the asylum and the rich, but none of the arguments or politics stuck in my head or anyone else's I know.

And still [produced] in that "theatre" [Broadway]. Playing for an elite. Audiences glued to their seats. The cost for a show like that is staggering. And it was such an exception to the rest of the professional Broadway school of which it was still clearly a member, anyway. Wasn't the place you performed a political act in itself? Get the play out of the "theatre" where basically only the rich and/or well–educated can go and where the content is generally meaningless to life today! What better way to combine art and politics than to bring art into political situations? We went out on the street to that average American. In 1966 and 1967 there wasn't anyone else out there except average Americans. And then other places where people naturally gather! The list of where we performed and our sponsors tells a story in itself: anywhere, for all types of people, many of whom might otherwise have never seen theatre.

At the other pole in our world was the organized movement and its emphasis on ideology; something they called revolution; and a lot of talk about foreign countries. And they were so grim. They didn't embody the spirit and fun of a new society in their person, work, or style. So we turned to ourselves and what had turned us on. Issues! Fun! And emotion! Combined with Marxist or radical premises. And though Marxism was implicit to some degree in the plays, it wasn't the play. You didn't see dialectical laws leaping out at you. Nor did you see heavy moralizing leaping out at you as happens in the work of many artists when they turn political (like, "I'm better than you 'cause I can see how bad it is and I suffer so."). You saw, instead, day–to–day realities of real people, described in a way that was indisputably true to them. We put it together in a way that put blame somewhere — on the rulers, the corporate rich, the generals, the politicians, the media! It turned out, if you avoided jargon, there are millions of people who share these premises and know these truths, if you lust scratch the surface of their minds. And they were often more open to the good vibes of a play than to a speech or leaflet. It was lively, colorful, moving, truthful, beautiful, imaginative, energetic, sad, funny, strong — all those things that make life a positive and interesting experience, and which most politics misses. Everyone loves a good show.

So, all that was a message. For some it was *the* message: bringing a little human warmth to a street corner; reminding folks at a rally what we're fighting for; enlivening the deadliness of academia with a little radical moment. As years went by and youth–culture thinking turned us on, we focused more on it. Life–style was embodied in how we appeared doing the plays, as much as in what the plays said: Change your life! Change your insides and the world! Start from your own center! Kill guilt!

At the same time, we had a saying: Bad art doesn't work! Though [our art was] not polished by any means, the audience could relax and not worry about being embarrassed for us. Our scenarios had many heads contributing, and by performance time most of the serious flaws would be caught by someone. Though we dealt with specific, current issues, the emotions and images we thought in terms of were timeless enough to raise the plays to a higher level. That's why we often used fairy tale or Bible forms. Or feelings of delight, play, exploration, sounds, and movement, which convey vaguer feelings you can't verbalize; the bigness of oppression, the joy of rebellion.

There's all different ways to move people.

During the Columbia rebellion we played several roles in "moving" people. In the months leading up to the strike, we helped the organizers by doing short agitprop plays around the campus to educate people about the role of the Institute for Defense Analysis on the campus. At the end of one performance, the kids in the audience "moved" from where they were standing into the play, and attacked, demolished, and danced around the fallen figure of I.D.A.! Symbolic of things to come in reality! Another time, at the end of a performance, one of the deans most implicated walked by and kids "moved" in on him, surrounding and haranguing him in what turned out to be an important confrontation in the chain of events that spring. Later, during the strike itself, we did a play on campus that ended with us chanting, "Strike, strike, strike," and the audience joining in. We worked it out so that a strike organizer would step into the playing space, signal for quiet, then tell people that if they believed in this strike, pickets were desperately needed at the following buildings (which they were). People would then be "moved" around the campus. to firm up the strike. Still later, during the building occupation, we did the *King Play* inside occupied Fayerweather Hall, boosting the morale of the troops. Rumor has it that it was the ceremony of it all that "moved" a young couple to have their wedding ceremony right there, amidst their new family, the bride wearing part of the Queen's costume for her veil.

At the end of *James Bond*, a small audience in a church in New Jersey... nobody clapped. Just silence. We felt tension but weren't sure where they were at. Maybe they didn't like it or couldn't understand it. We asked, and an elderly woman spoke for them: She said they had seen themselves, the images of hate, fear, and apathy and they were stunned, ashamed, crying, afraid of the ugly things in themselves they had yet to confront. That's head motion!

A lot of what we did was forced on us by the limitations of the streets, parks, rooms, and non–theatres we performed in. For example, you can't use too much dialogue and there's no lighting. We had to keep m mind relevance, clarity, being seen and heard, the fact that people hadn't come prepared to stay for a long play but had been caught while doing something else. Could props be moved in and out? Cops, right–wingers, hostility. If you're out in the heat all day, props and costumes have to be highly mobile, flexible, even collapsible. All our street–play props could be carried by half the cast; the rest carried the drum, instruments, and banner. Though the power and starkness of a piece like *Presidio* could carry its slow pace and quiet–tone, these plays generally had to be short, colorful, energetic — competing with the street and reality.

Then we found that the style we had come up with had its own logic and *raison d'etre*, was in fact more powerful than traditional theatre. Extreme stylization, in fact, cut through to the essence more than "realism" did. Later we found other full–time groups and theoretical writings to confirm the directions in which we were already moving. The Open Theatre and Living Theatre were into similar body energy trips, and they helped us see we had been timid and should push even further in those areas of sound, movement, agreement exercises, improvs, and ritual. Many of our images and plays were developed using agreement or concentration exercises, which caused the actors to tend to project inward. The San Francisco Mime Troupe made us more aware of opening up a play and pushing our energies outward to the audience. The narrations of Peter Schumann were an inspiration on how to use the fewest words and instrumental sounds brilliantly, while his masks and props were the standard in plastic arts.

Reading Artaud, Brecht, and others showed us we had been on the right track. We were going back to where Western theatre got lost and picking up the loose threads, bypassing the printing press. Artaud says that what we call mise en scene (movement, sound, music, dance, lighting, masks, sets, puppets, sculpture), and consider secondary, is actually the core of theatre. Dialogue is a literary form, he says, and is inferior from a theatrical point of view. Brecht talked about the street and average people as a source of drama; signs, narration, alienation acting; the geste of Oriental, especially Chinese classical, theatre. Other writers spoke of the integration of all elements in Oriental theatre, movement as essence, the populism of medieval commedia. This all firmed up our direction, gave us confidence, made us do all those things a little better.

Let me finish with stories, because our thing was "doing," not "theorizing." You could learn, and we did. We had been doing a play about Vietnam that ended by moralistically accusing the audience of being implicated in the murder of Vietnamese. This was in Jamaica, Queens — white working class. It wasn't working, put people uptight. No one likes to be called a murderer. Then this Communist Party guy gave the best speech on the war I ever heard. Said Americans were hurt by the war; dead sons, high taxes, and the rich get richer, not them. The crowd dug it! So we made a play based around that, threw out the other one. We called it the *War Monster*, and it worked so well we did it 5 times before we were done. Don't stand on ceremony. Speeches can be high art!

Harpur College [in Binghampton, New York] was probably the most mind–blowing something or other we ever did. First *Corn Flakes*, and the audience is singing along at the end. We thought we'd do *Dreams* next. Uh–uh. The music built, people start dancing, moving, weaving, be–in style. More and more. Soon hundreds were dancing and swirling out of the ballroom and taking over the whole student center. The music is tribal and loud. Clothes start flying off. A couple is half–naked, making love, and scores are chanting around them. Draft cards start burning. The campus cops come and are chased off by energy alone — mainly everyone ignores them. Naked bodies, dancing, music, chanting — lots of love–energy for hours. It was some kind of beautiful reward for the hard times.

✑

Marlow Hotchkiss and the Firehouse Theatre in *Still Falling*

12. THE FIREHOUSE THEATER

S till Falling, *produced in 1971, shows us the Firehouse deep in its period of psychic probing. Nancy Walter's work, which has become synonymous with the Firehouse, has in its physical manifestation, the production, taken on the aura of a highly subtle and disciplined session in group therapy. Both performer and spectator become vulnerable under the terms of the theatrical event. But* Still Falling *also exists as a precise text, largely in verse. It is concrete, philosophically complex and imagistically dense. When we discussed what play ought to represent the group in this book, the general feeling at the Firehouse was that* Still Falling *came closest to the ensemble's authentic life.*

As for the essay that follows the discussion: Sydney Walter and I have not only worked together as director and playwright, but over the years, since our days together in the Open Theatre, have carried on a dialogue about the responsibilities of theatre in society. I have had growing misgivings about the potential of audience participation, and our conversations about this in the spring of 1972 prompted Sydney to write the actor–audience essay included in this chapter.

The chapter ends with scenes 10 and 11 from another Nancy Walter work, Blessings, *produced in 1970.*

STILL FALLING. *Written and directed by Nancy Walter • Music by John Franzen.*

YUBLOM: Marlow Hotchkiss

MARMO: Antoinette Maher

KARUN: Michael Harrell

TOUS: Bill Lampe, later Brooke Myers

CHORUS: Holly Franzen, Joel Schwartz, Bob Crutcher, Steve Bradley, Muniera Christiansen, Birgitte Spangaard.

MUSICIAN: John Franzen

ON TAPE: Joe Blankenship

Roles: All roles can be played by men or women.

YUBLOM: the mud man, the natural man

MARMO: the good mother, the fool, the artist

KARUN: the dancer, the philosopher–king

TOUS: the angel, the avatar, the messenger

THE CHORUS: The action of the play is not performed in a void. Every voice, event, and image is answered by the chorus. They provide a continuous and changing murmuring to support the action, they mediate between the actors and the audience and open the play to the audience, they sing, they play messengers and watchers.

The Environment: *The pit is in the middle with the audience racks surrounding it and looking down on it. It is important that one part of the circle can be completely opened to let people in and out.*

Tous' nest is suspended from the rafters as well as his falling and swinging ropes and a pulley system to hoist his cargo net.

1. *When the audience has all been seated, the lights go down to almost nothing and the* CHORUS *begins to drone and chant. A single light comes up on the center of the empty space.* YUBLOM *appears through a hole in the floor, throwing off the cover of his mud pit. He is naked and mud–covered. His hair is matted. He rocks, sucks, strokes himself. He howls. He cultivates his mud. From time to time he draws up various objects from his pit for inspection, including his own shit.*

YUBLOM: Mine.
Nothing for it.
Take and eat. Take and eat.
[*Passing out his shit to the audience, throwing it easily to them.*]
Do this and remember me.

Medicine and ornament.

If your hunger is too short
and delicate to eat shit
you will have to shut your mouths
and be no more
dead, dead.

Howl for me,
children of strangers.

[*Encourages the audience to howl for him.*]

Howl for me
Green eyes
Clouds of ice crystal in the cold air
Speak to me.

They put me under the ground
when I thought I was still walking around on it
and I saw
the graveyards
the dear softening bodies
some sitting up
were a wilderness uncared for. [*Weeps.*]
All going to waste
the once living.

[*Examines his body.*]

Does it show?
Not the same, not the same.
The stuff comes and goes
but the pattern persists,
that prolongs the bondage.

[*Finds some old loved object.*]

Little yellow crescents
Bells

[*Sings.*]

little yellow crescents
little tinkly bells
little hands of fire.

God could have let me sing.

[*Includes a person in his gesture.*]

Part of the passing show
I didn't invent
I simply felt it to be
Mine.

[YUBLOM *goes into audience.*]

Whatever of me is in you, give it back.

[*This request becomes more and more outrageous until the* CHORUS *rises to protect the audience. A* MAN *from the chorus throws him forcibly back into* the pit. YUBLOM *throws mud at his captor and is again thrown back into the pit, violently, painfully.*]

YUBLOM: Separated. Cast out.
The truth was involved.
They wouldn't even look at me.
When I began to be a burden
I noticed a child growing up
between us, among us.
I began to feel that I was scaly, perhaps,
or stiffening, perhaps,
or oily, something dead.

KARUN: [*Off, sings.*] Wind came.
Rains came.
The trees and grasses changed color.

[KARUN *and* MARMO *come into the space during the song. A* CHORUS MEMBER *approaches* YUBLOM *in his pit and strokes him.*]

YUBLOM: So long.
I used to float
It ended when I started to kick,
I fell then, so long,
some people are light and graceful,
they were born that way.
I'm not like that,
I'm heavy, I break things
and I am broken,
stupid, broken

Look at the world, it lives.

[*Improvisational description of the audience.*]

Nothing wills itself to be.
Clothing is willing in itself to be.

I've got to get some of myself back.
Sputter and stall.

Everything annoys,
that you cough
your very presence
that you live at all.

[MARMO *and* KARUN *now fully present in the room.*]

KARUN: May my eyes forever be satisfied
May I be content within my own nature
such as it is
may there be no hard edges
and no difficult barriers.

MARMO: May I be content to struggle
with him
with slowness
bad acting
lack of faith
madness all around
and interminable inner dialogues

YUBLOM: [*Unaware of them, except as internal, putting mud in his eyes.*]
Why isn't it dark in here?
Is there a fire in the middle?
Tens of billions of planetary systems?
I don't believe it.
The earth is everything to me

MARMO: With one handful of mud he can separate heaven and earth.

YUBLOM: [*Begins to poke around in the pit*] Crevices and corners I haven't gotten into in years.

KARUN: Yes, he's clever. At the edge of the world he hears a sound like crackling, like something is falling off.

YUBLOM: Things for the head through the mouth, through the eyes, through the ears, why not through the thing itself? [*Bangs his head on the floor. Thinks better of it.*]

MARMO: Whatever he touches fights back.

YUBLOM: Someone will come and get me. Or when it's dark those people will come again, people will be dumped in here with me . . .

MARMO: Whenever he sings, he chokes.

YUBLOM: Those recent victims, those who were found hanging in the broom closet and put away, those who were killed accidentally or on purpose, who were put away by the state, you know . . . [*The exact text of this should be improvised.*]

KARUN: I would like to carry him on my back . . .

MARMO: Lick him, whistle to him [*Etc.*]

YUBLOM: George Jackson, Caryl Chessman, Al Capone, Eric the Red, Pope some thing—the Avenger, Charles Manson, dead people, Jack Ruby, Medgar Evars, people who hurt themselves—Janis Joplin, Dag Hammarskold, Billy the Kid, Jimi Hendrix, my brother Ted, too and the kid who shot himself in the school washroom, what was his name?

KARUN: But not yet.

MARMO: While we wait we can have something to eat.

MARMO and KARUN *begin to eat fruit and vegetables. The* CHORUS *passes the audience the same.* YUBLOM *continues with the names, making a little man out of mud and shit and garbage. The audience and chorus,* MARMO *and* KARUN, *gradually start to throw half–eaten fruit and garbage at* YUBLOM.

YUBLOM: Yukio Mishima, Hippocrates and Lieutenant Calley,
stranger and stranger,
Arthur Rimbaud, people who scream,
queens.
Sarah Bernhardt, Queen Elizabeth, Ernest Hemingway
Che Guevara, shoot, shot,
Dwight David Eisenhower and little Mamie,
the Lindbergh baby, people in balloons
and the Titanic,
Madame Curie and Alfred Nobel
fucking around underground
think on these things
Julius and Ethel Rosenberg
one held his breath and the other breathed deep
the city of Pompeii, the Children's Crusade
all the unknowing
people I have personally known
shouters and rollers
Masters and Johnson, Anna Pavlova, Patrice Lumumba, Ted Mack,
Goody Two–Shoes
all real historical personages
Louis Pasteur and thousands of cows
Isadora Duncan
Rainer Maria Rilke, Black Elk, the Sioux
Wovoka, convulsionaries
Dante Alighieri and the beauteous Beatrice
Andrew Carnegie...

By now a rain of garbage.

MARMO: Can we let it go on and on?

YUBLOM: Although this pit seemed deep enough
and needs no more digging
soon it will be filled to the top
every edge obliterated,

[*Tries to breathe into his man.*]

Once there was one who. breathed circles and thought it was the air. I loved him and wanted him and had him and lost him. And had her and lost her. Are you there?

Pah!

Not to die in a rage in a hole.

[YUBLOM *destroys his man.*]

MARMO: There he sits, the dirty loud one.

KARUN: One of us.

MARMO: Can he hear us?

KARUN: If he listens.

MARMO: He doesn't. He talks. Would he listen if I told him he was still alive?

KARUN: He knows.

MARMO: But what does he feel?

KARUN: Anxiety, delusion, illusion
cheerless cheer
the taste of himself to himself
bitter
it isn't the end he had foreseen

and now he has no
tongue, no thought, no skin
to see and feel
beyond
this little dump.

MARMO: We have to start now
seeing and feeling the garden.
Try to do it.

MARMO and KARUN

[*As the* CHORUS *joins, repeating words and gestures. The whole room is suddenly alive.* YUBLOM *crawls painfully toward* MARMO *and* KARUN.]:

Blue, gray, rain falling and drying
oceans, blood, infirmities
Open wide, another step though the ground is trembling
Do take it
Soon the crack will open too wide to step across
Things as they are totter and plunge
but look how green it is
No events anymore
The inside is brown and folded like a mushroom,
capable of expanding and holding life.

[*They break apart and look at him.*]

MARMO: Are we alive or dead?

KARUN: Could we live without such mysteries?

YUBLOM: Is that all there is?
Something is missing.
The explanation.

MARMO: The explanation:

[MARMO *and* KARUN *sing and dance.*]

The moon went up like every night and fell like every night
but faster, much faster
like a big rock it fell from the sky
and there was no explanation
and the next night it behaved as usual.

YUBLOM: [*Crawls away, muttering.*] Can't stand it, can't stand them, don't want to be together here with them. [When he reaches his pit, he begins to throw mud and shit at them.] How can you sing while I'm dying in a hole?

MARMO: [*Goes down to him.*] You're a tedious grouch and you're shaking the ground.

YUBLOM: Don't listen. It's my pain.

MARMO: Don't worry. It's all been taken care of and you've worn yourself out for nothing.

YUBLOM: That's the pain. Exactly that.

KARUN: [*Coming down.*] Bring it into. your hand so I can see it.

YUBLOM: Cut off my tongue
it's only sensitive to bitter
amputate me right and left
till I fit into a paper bag
and you can set me out with the garbage,
only put my head in last
it's all I ask.

KARUN: Give me what you don't know how to keep.

YUBLOM:Gives up his body to him,

KARUN: Move him, move him into the light.

MARMO: Stretch him out.

KARUN: This is the gate we've come to
suddenly we need to slip through
and be at home in our ways.

YUBLOM: That's the promise you'd make a child
before he goes to sleep
in a dark room.
I don't want to go through.

MARMO: Where would you go?

YUBLOM: Back.[*Crawls back to his pit.*]

[*The* CHORUS *lifts him out, washes and clothes him.*]

KARUN: Lift him up underneath the arms
stand his feet on the ground
he can walk
he can be upright
he can walk without looking at his feet
be a wave in the consciousness
and be gone
be a series of inevitable
and recurring experiences a circle of pleasure and defeat
eat, drink, and shit
sleep, dream, and fuck.
float in all those
ways watch his body grow and weaken
see and feel
talk and sing
be rooted or fly
adapt to the actions of others

adjust to the night and the day
and the changing
of the lights and the seasons.

2. YUBLOM *is left alone on stage where he listens to the floor, pounds on the cover of his pit, isolates himself.*

> TOUS *enters and offers him green leafy vegetables.*

YUBLOM: I won't eat it.

[TOUS *offers water in a deep bowl.*]

YUBLOM: I won't drink it.

TOUS: What is it? I brought them with my own hands, and you won't take them.

YUBLOM: It's a thing I feel not knowing you . . . Besides I've had a headache for a month. It hurts to chew.

TOUS: A good sign.

YUBLOM: Good in bad, in pain. Signs. I've never understood
that.
People keep coming here, moving me,
urging me to eat.
I never have to move.
Consider the lilies of the field.
They toil not, neither do they spin.

TOUS: That's the lilies.
Is it for you all day
to sit idle?
You have to move.
A man moves from dreaming
to waking and back again.
Consider the trees
rooted in the ground alive.
Compare your life to theirs.
Is there some act possible between you?

YUBLOM: [*Falls over.*] Timber.
Let the flower slip I'm tired of it.

[*In another place,* MARMO *and* KARUN *are watching, participating from a distance, saying the things that are not being said. Lights up on them.*]

MARMO: [*Sings.*] All the trees I planted
  I knocked down
  and the sun went down
  and I took a match
  and lit them all
  and some of the people with me and I
  killed things to eat
  and cooked them on the fire
  we couldn't wait
  and ate them half–cooked.
  I am ashamed to tell you.

KARUN: I wouldn't worry about the past.
  Can you taste it now?

MARMO: Yes. Now.

  [*Lights off on them.*]

TOUS: Do you know me?

YUBLOM: I wouldn't know my mother anymore
  it's been so long if I had one,
  to go back to
  I'd like to go back.

TOUS: It's an urge built into living things
  to go back
  to a simpler state
  to restore the first things
  your mother's arms . . .

  [MESSENGER *enters.*]

MESSENGER: In Iowa
  there have been discovered
  thirty acres of virgin prairie.

YUBLOM: [*Turning to* MESSENGER.] Yes, I want to go.

TOUS: But it's not for you.
  It is doubtless an old battlefield,
  time and again
  there were wars scarring
  the ground til no one would go there
  but the ghosts and so it's been left
  for the long grass to cover.

YUBLOM: Why can't you let me
thump around on my stumps
and claw around on my claws
on my own?

TOUS: I want to fill you with unrest
I want to drown you
I want to seep into you
like death itself
and move you to the place
you have to go.

YUBLOM: All you have can't move me.
I don't know you.

[*Lights up on* MARMO *and* KARUN *walking gently together.*]

MARMO: [*Sings.*] The body is so solid
it's difficult to work on
but a variety of patterns can be created from it
and it's really very fluid if the power is there
and it even parts like the Red Sea.

[*Lights off on them.*]

[*During the next section,* TOUS *leaps on* YUBLOM *and wrestles him, finally overpowering him.*]

YUBLOM: You want my life.

TOUS: Yes.

YUBLOM: I won't give it.

TOUS: Give it up.

YUBLOM: I won't.
I don't want to get into things
I don't want to get connected to things
I want to float off on a string
and when I'm far enough away
someone can cut me off.

TOUS: No flesh responds
to my stroke
no blood rises
to meet me.

YUBLOM: I want my blood to be quiet
I want to let the various sounds repeat
everything folded in on itself.

TOUS: In time, nothing is hidden
everyone is naked
how far, how deep
can you go in?

YUBLOM: Somewhere
there is one eye
in one skull
shut tight, looking in
I want that, I want to be that eyeball.

TOUS: Fool
you have to be skinless.
I want to see your muscles jump
and your flesh palpitate.

YUBLOM: [*Gives up.*]: Suffering rules.
It rolls me over and over,

TOUS: Learn this,

YUBLOM: Or?

TOUS: Learn to sing this: [*Sings.*]
I went to see my brother
but my brother saw me
and he laughed, huh–huh,
he laughed when he saw me.

[YUBLOM *learns.*]

TOUS: If there is anyone here who wants to learn this he should come closer
and sit with us. It is necessary that someone do this as we are likely to
die at any moment.

[*This invitation is given to the audience and the play does not continue until at least one person is willing to come in.*]

TOUS: [*Sings.*] My bed is so empty
I keep waking up
and this hunger drives me
into the world.
What made me go this way?

[YUBLOM *and the audience people learn this song or a variation of it.*]

YUBLOM: [*To the singers.*] What made me go this way.

[*Whatever answer or gesture occurs is accepted and amplified.*]

TOUS: Accept your messenger.

YUBLOM: Accept my messenger.
For years
I waited for the messenger
watching closely the trees, the river, the stars
but he didn't come
or I didn't know him
so I went home.
At home they stood inside
looking out at me
me, always outside
on the brown grass
with my head pressed up against
the doors and windows
never coming in.

TOUS: I'm going to leave you now
I see a place
I know I must reach
a country that doesn't exist yet
but I want you to watch me
because I'm going for you
I want you to see it.

[*Lights up on* MARMO *and* KARUN, *lying on the grass.* TOUS *and* YUBLOM *and the audience messengers exchange tokens.*]

MARMO: [*Sings.*] Flesh is wasted
everything is wasted
things to eat, the mind
and mostly flesh is wasted
untouched
even strawberries, knots, and bends.

KARUN: But there's so much of it now.

MARMO: True.

[*Lights off on them.*]

YUBLOM: [*To* TOUS.] I'm empty now. Let's eat.

TOUS: Too late and not yet.

[TOUS *takes* YUBLOM *and seats him in the audience.*]

CHORUS: [*Sings as* TOUS *climbs to a high place.*] There was a river
brown and fast childhood's river
and wide across
a river where little boys drowned
where Allen, brother of Arthur, drowned
where he floats past still
looking up at me.

I went to the river to swim
but I threw my stick in instead
and the boys with me
threw their clothes in
to watch them spin downstream
we waded out hand in hand
to hold each other up in the river

tell me who moved that river
before I could swim all alone

Sometimes the light broke
through the water
when the big carp jumped
and for one little second
the ghosts in the water
stood up children again
but the sun made shadows
to cover them down
and as the sun went down
we threw rocks in the water
till it was time to go home.

Once I caught a fish there
and gutted it myself
still beating
and I looked for that fish
among the others
dead on the shore
but I never found it.

3. TOUS' *journey.* YUBLOM *is part of the audience.*

TOUS: [*On the edge of a high place.*] The shadow
    or whatever it is
    this desire to see something
    anything
    pushes me up here
    no other thing holds me
    nothing holds me.

    I'm going to fall
    someone fell in front of me
    shivered and fell
    my father,
    his father . . .

    [*The* CHORUS *exhorts him to jump. He falls a long way.*]

TOUS: How far? How deep?

    Some men die when they reach the bottom
    why didn't I?
    some come up singing
    My father's hand threw me into the air
    and didn't catch me,
    still falling since then . . .

    Are you looking?
    What happens when it gets dark?
    The earth's shadow
    gradually rises up.

    [*Two* SHADOWY PEOPLE *approach him, hands and faces covered.*]

1ST MAN: Ask to have a long way to go in the dark.

TOUS: No.

1ST MAN: Many men have thought the world went out when they did but
    they lied to themselves.

TOUS: I know.

2ND MAN: There are many who are more beautiful than you.

TOUS: I know.

2ND MAN: The stranger, the enemy . . .

TOUS: I know.

1ST MAN: There is no name you can make for yourself here.

TOUS: I know.

2ND MAN: You can't even eclipse the animals.

TOUS: No. I know.

1ST MAN: So go to sleep.

TOUS: Where?

2ND MAN: We will wake you.

TOUS: When?

1ST MAN: With bells.

[TOUS *lies down, they lie down with him and stroke him. During his speech the stroking becomes devouring.*]

TOUS: There is not one place on the earth where life. doesn't exist: to live with me, to lie down with me, to gnaw nibble and bite everything that can be bitten, devouring to make room. Even in me countless creatures are born and die.

[*By now the men are eating him alive, he screams "Let go, let go" and runs.*]

[*Running, he encounters the chorus one by one. They tell him stories impossible to listen to about the need and despair of their own lives or the lives of others and embody them also. As he has encountered them all they form a circle around him and call to each other for comfort.*]

TOUS: I hear them calling to each other now
across the deep fields
but it's not for me
it's not for me.

[*He trips over* KARUN.]

KARUN: Lie down.

TOUS: Please understand
I don't want to live on my back.

KARUN: If you want to stand up
If you want to go to that unknown country
you must imagine
what it would be like
if your mother's hand were amputated
if your own body were cut into a thousand pieces
if the hands that shield your face were cut to ribbons

if every piece of flesh was cold
and sought warmth
and finding it burnt to dust.

TOUS: I don't understand.
Do you think I'm made so that misery
doesn't touch me?

KARUN: [*Gestures to* CHORUS.] Were those people real?

TOUS: Nothing.
Nothing is happening.
Nothing will happen.
The truth is that there was
something real there
and it looked like acting
it looked like nothing.

[*From the* CHORUS *a beautiful messenger approaches.*]

MESSENGER: [*Sings.*]
There is a tree
standing alone
making a cool shadow
under it you must go and sit
no one will come near you.
Don't you want that?

[MESSENGER *opens herself to* TOUS.]

TOUS: [*To the* MESSENGER.] Look in my mouth. [*Directs her to look in detail at parts of his body he is ashamed of.*]

Have you seen?
Do you see how ugly I am?

MESSENGER: No.

TOUS: I smell like blood,
like a wound that won't heal
I was maybe all the bloody men.
and there is no end to this pain.

MESSENGER: What pain?

TOUS: Every trick is employed without shame. Go back.
Nothing enters without dislodging
something else.

[MESSENGER *curls herself around his feet.*]

TOUS: At my feet sleep my dead dreams
  may they come to someone else
  I'm done with them.
  Who would have thought that between
  evening and morning
  I would be broken?

[TOUS *turns his back on everyone and pulls out a rope cage from his nest.*
He gets in it and is hoisted above the heads of the audience, crying, speak-
ing, singing:]

TOUS: So much passed before my eyes
  in the end I saw nothing
  I said I will go
  to another land, another sea
  and every step
  uncovered the old man.
  I don't hope for another road.
  Let me die slowly.
  The thought of my own corpse disgusts me.
  Promise to burn it.

MARMO: [*Sings.*] I had a son
  I had a son
  I touched him once
  He lived for one turning
  of the earth around the sun
  the sun.
  He overtook the room
  with his own time
  still red with my blood
  smelling of salt and vinegar
  and there was no sign
  that he would take one look
  and turn and leave.

He turned back
  into the whole earth
  with six million charred leaves
  and thirty million broken stones
  in that unknown country
  under the easy ground.

His bones came from his father
  and his flesh from me

my part is dissolved
and the bones alone
lying in a dry, open place
a few flowers in bloom.

I mourn
a sweet apple hanging on the tree
a bird in my hand
someone else's shadow on the wall
the silky, hairy seeds
the watery eyes
the snow field vision
and the pure cry,
the cry.

4. TOUS *is hanging in his cage–net, groaning and crying. Over his voice the messenger sings an obligato.*

KARUN: From the beginning
there is suffering
but we close our eyes
whenever we can
why should we look
isn't it everywhere?

MARMO: How beautiful they are together
crying and singing,

YUBLOM: He's stopped.
Going was in empty promise
now all of his feet are in the air.
It was easier now
to persist through the muck
men are soft
like grass, they lie down.
I hoped to see the holy city too
even in a drop of sweat
how long will it be
I wonder.

MARMO: You ask how long no time is set.

KARUN: You could but you're too
pleased with yourself to look.

MARMO: See that, like a comet?

YUBLOM: No.

KARUN: Humming, do you hear it?

YUBLOM: No.

MARMO: Feel

YUBLOM: No.

KARUN: Pay attention.

YUBLOM: [*Whoops.*] Pay attention, get ready, go, do, move, feel, breathe...

[*Cavorts with audience.*]

MARMO: Don't be silly
so close to the end
what will become of you.

YUBLOM: [*Asks the audience.*] What will become of me?

[*Brief improvisation which is ended by* YUBLOM *with some exhortation to the other actors to help or teach him. This next section may be cut if the audience undertakes to teach him. If used, each creation myth should be related directly to* YUBLOM's *person.*]

KARUN: In the distant past
there was an original mass
and each part clung to each part
but suddenly there was chaos
and everything flew far from its original place
and some suns formed
and gathered the planets
the cold dark bodies
to keep them warm and
everything is still expanding outwards

MARMO: But where?

KARUN: But now more slowly than in the beginning

MARMO: But why?

KARUN: Some stars are already far beyond our reach
Someday everything will come back together
in an enormous crush
to reform the original sphere.

[YUBLOM *rejects this lesson.*]

MARMO: One sphere fell from the sky
its little breath flew apart
the radiant energy of the mind flew away
the clammy energy of the body flew away
and instead of a living unity
there was a speck of dust which
became the earth.

[YUBLOM *doesn't respond.*]

MARMO: The sun was very attractive to the moon
because she was so mysterious
and finally he won her
and slept with her
and wanted fiery children from her
but all their children were cold and dark
they took after their mother
and no fiery son was born to them.

YUBLOM: No fiery son was born to my mother either.

MARMO: Nor to mine.

KARUN: But the possibility of fire is there
I see, close to your mouth
and around your eyes...

YUBLOM: That I have lied
with my eyes and my mouth
that I have been deluded.

[*A ceremony of stripping* YUBLOM *of his delusions, unintegrated parts, bad memories, forgotten promises, unnecessary distinctions. The point of the stripping is to allow* YUBLOM *to bring* TOUS *down from his death net.*]

[*The ceremony is improvisational every night and is wordless. It is a series of images involving people and objects which is planned by the chorus,* MARMO, *and* KARUN *for each performance. The images should unify the experience of the evening, bring in the audience contributions, make clear the vague images and relationships as they change in the course of the production.*]

[YUBLOM *responds to the images with his body and his voice (not words), trying to discover the thread inherent in the images. At the end he makes an improvisational speech or song about the thread and lets Tous down.*]

[YUBLOM *lets him down very slowly.*]

TOUS: I come down
  still looking for things
  that haven't happened yet...
  I have seen. ..

[*Improvisational melding of the experiences of* YUBLOM *during the image sequence and has own experiences in the net.*]

TOUS: [*Continuing.*] In every man
  there is a room
  with windows all at the top
  where any movement
  in the universe
  is immediately understood.

[*As soon as his feet touch the ground,* YUBLOM *and* TOUS *greet each other, gradually formalizing their greeting into a specific gesture or series of gestures.*]

5. THE DANCE

KARUN *takes the specific gestures of* YUBLOM *and* TOUS *and begins to create a dance.*

KARUN: Here is a little ring
  enclosing the world
  and for all within
  time enough to fall out of time.

[*The chorus brings* KARUN *words and gestures taken from the audience or a flash from the image sequence. Out of the words and gestures brought to him and out of the gestures evolved by* TOUS *and* YUBLOM, *he creates a dance fresh every night. He tries to create by synthesis a dance that extends the improvisations of* YUBLOM *and* TOUS.]

[*The audience is invited to join.* "Who desires this experience?" "Would you like to dance?"]

6. *The dance ends naturally as people are tired and sit down.* YUBLOM *invites the entire audience on stage.*

YUBLOM: Come and sit down with me
  in the dust. [*Opens his pit.*]
  My hole.

Still here. Still the same.
Although I know
the time will come again
when this mud
will overpower even your presence
now everything is here.

[*Passes out mud to people, puts mud on people's faces. Somewhere away from the center,* TOUS *has been mumbling phrases from the stories of need told to him earlier.*]

TOUS: We live through one by one.

YUBLOM: I don't feel that anymore.

[*Brings out gifts from the pit — some ritual gift for* MARMO, KARUN *and* TOUS *— something for the audience to eat. Tea is served.*]

TOUS: How long will you waver there?

YUBLOM: A long time.

TOUS: Here and now
I feel myself being sucked
back into the world of men
I am not glad
to be born again
from the ashes
take back your gift
dirty with your dirt.

[YUBLOM *takes the gift and gives it to an audience member.*]

TOUS: I'm thinking of those
like me out there
the roads are all stretched to them
now and then
there is someone who can't move.

YUBLOM: I pity him
all alone among the moving things.

TOUS: Life in this room
is not so narrow
as most men's lives
but not as clean to me
as walking by myself.
Where is there an end to the human howling?
I'm going to leave you now

reaching for the things
that are ahead
in the nearness of my own delusions.

[*Leaves, howls.*]

[YUBLOM *weeps, says goodbye, brief improvisatory goodbye. If anyone follows* TOUS *out of the theater, he should welcome them.*]

KARUN: [*Sings.*] Everything continues to move
in its own way
sometimes it looks like dissolution
like the fire is going out
even as the very heat
of the earth beats
in us.

Everything that breathes disappears
into nothing
but where is death?
The body loosens its bond with time
we lose ourselves
and become the air
blowing dust and deliverance.

Till this most beautiful
and terrible
consummation
comes on us
let each hole
in the universe be filled
with its natural song
and let the tension
of that undying harmony
sustain us and hold us.

[*The actors beckon to the audience and in small groups the actors and audience play together some games growing out of the moods of the evening.*]

✧✧✧

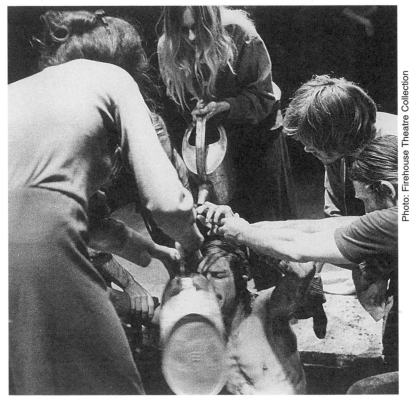

Marlow Hotchkiss and the Firehouse Theatre in *Still Falling*

Photo: Firehouse Theatre Collection

Excerpts from a discussion on Still Falling, *taped in April 1972 at the Firehouse Theater in San Francisco. Participants included Nancy Walter, Marlow Hotchkiss, Michael Harrell, Toni Maher, John Franzen, Muniera Christiansen, Brooke Myers, Joel Schwartz, and myself.*

SAINER: Did you discuss the work–that is, the intellectual content during rehearsal period?

WALTER: Hardly at all. In the first part of rehearsals, I wrote the notes that I took down on paper and posted them up somewhere in the office because I felt I needed that time to get myself together.

HOTCHKISS: Nancy's notes on individual rehearsals normally came three or four days after the rehearsal so . . .

WALTER: It took me that long.

HOTCHKISS: That lag . . . You actually had to find other kinds of feedback to keep it up during rehearsal, and the [use of] director's notes I thought was one of the best choices you could make.

WALTER: Well, it was the only one open to me, I thought.

SAINER: Okay. Ready for memorable events. The ones I jotted down have to do with audience participation. I am sure there are others.

HARRELL: It actually began with Marlow because Marlow, I think it was before the dance and her name was given or the name of dizzy nymph, Marlow had involved her sometime earlier in the show, had taken all her clothes off.

SAINER: This is an audience number?

HARRELL: Yes.

HOTCHKISS: One. of the cast members passed me a note telling me to do whatever I wanted to do at that moment.

HARRELL: It must have been during the improvisational session.

HOTCHKISS: Right, and I looked over at her and that was the first thing that came to my mind. So I did it. I disrobed that young lady and she was very agreeable to do that and she started doing a little dance number.

WALTER: When the audience came in, the tower was around in the middle and there was a big space down there and the audience came in to that area ten at a time; and they watched the movie and listened to the tape. The actors went to them and said various things, trying to solicit some memory or something from them.

SAINER: Did you sense that the audience was preconditioned for some kind of direct encounter with the performers?

WALTER: No, not all of them. In fact several people left when they found out they were going to be touched or talked to in any personal way.

SAINER: Could you tell me about some of the reactions to Yublom's request of the audience, where you ask them to give me what's in you that's also mine? What were some of the gimmes?

HOTCHKISS: Nancy had suggested somewhere, I think in the early draft of the script — it may still be in the stage directions someplace — that one of the goals could be to get an audience substitute, somebody to take over for me, and that it might be possible to have [the substitute] assist in the role on a given evening or do the role on the following evening after [he] had seen a model for it in some way.

SAINER: One scene or the entire play?

HOTCHKISS: The entire play was the suggestion, I think. That was before the play took its last form.

SAINER: Did that come out of your experience?

HOTCHKISS: It came out of Nancy's head, but it was certainly something I was very interested in. Right away I took that as a goal to get somebody down there in that pit with me who would do the rest of the play with me or with whom I could transfer my costume, and I would just sort of be a helper and guide and maneuver [him] through the rest of the show.

SAINER: Did that ever happen?

HOTCHKISS: Yes. It happened one and a half times, but to a much lesser extent than I had hoped would happen. But that still supplied a tremendous set of actions for me with regard to the audience, trying to seek out a person who would jump in the hole and make a total identification with me. And one night it happened. Yublom's behavior is supposed to get a little untoward at one point and then he's pummeled and thrown back in his hole, and at one point — Bob did that assignment — I remember [someone from] the audience jumped out and tackled him and came to my defense, and they wrestled around for a while. Of course, anybody who stuck himself out like that...you could just feel all the magnets go and so all the antenna were out, and I was pulling to get him in the the hole with me because I was certain that he was exactly the person I was looking for. And the chorus was eager to pull him away because that was their assignment, and Bob, I guess, was caught up in the struggle and was essentially helping the chorus. He ended up in the hole — he did marvelous things — and I think he stuck mostly through the hole.

SAINER: Did he take his clothes off?

HOTCHKISS: He didn't take his clothes off but he didn't have to, he was virtually all muddy, completely dirty. Some evenings that hole was swampier than others and that was a swampy evening.

SAINER: Did anybody volunteer to come back the next night?

HOTCHKISS: We never tried that structure, but a lot of people voluntarily came back to see the play again.

SAINER: Audience learns song from Tous.

MYERS: They did. Night after night they learned that song. People always came down and learned it. They didn't always come down...but I used to have about twenty people sing it who were not afraid of me at all.

SAINER: What about the chorus telling stories of their lives?

[*Laughter from the group, which leads into:*]

HARRELL: We were laying out there on the floor at that time and the spotlights would come up on the chorus individually. And as soon as the light came up in the special chorus' area, the chorus member who was nearest or in that light related a story, and the stories were always completely hair–raising.

MYERS: When it was newspapers they changed completely. They were weird, perverted, sick, horrible, crimes, babies eating their hands.

SAINER: Nancy's script says stories [that are] impossible to listen to.

HOTCHKISS: ...One of the things that was delightful for me in the role was kind of a complete social license. There were no restrictions. I always felt that I imposed my own personal limits on that role and that, really, whoever played the role could use that to discover their own bounds of decency or indecency, that you really had complete freedom to transgress any and all social rules at that point, and you really were very much the kind of social person a hermit becomes after years of isolation and not caring about other people's rules. And it was fun to toy with that in regard to people, but it was also scary for them. And it was fun to mix that kind of disregard for the rules and to tread a line between. But it didn't encourage people, with the exception of the most bold, to jump in and play the game by and large. When Brooke or Bill [Lampe] would offer that opportunity to [the audience] to come down and sing, we would always get volunteers, and by that time I'd been clothed and dressed and was somewhat civilized. A whole relationship, especially with Brooke, was set up that was inviting, I think, to the audience to join us. And we did that, and those people who volunteered themselves at that point formed a sort of pool from which there were usually one or two people willing to deal quite importantly in the improvisational section, which formed a sort of climax to the play. And [that was] really the first time where an audience member would volunteer himself, making a little personal leap without being prodded to come into the stage area...the structure that we had was Toni would throw out one image. This was done with words or a couple of simple props or things like blindfolds, powder, and fruit. All sorts of little things. A new image each evening, and then Michael would do one and then Toni and then Michael, and they would do maybe four or five images. And my task was to respond improvisationally to each of these images. Each evening they were new, and each evening there was some sort of thematic concern like memories of death or early learning experiences a whole repertoire of things like that. My challenge was to probe into my own personal encounters with those things in the past and come up with some response that was theatrical and viable and memorable and traumatic and interesting and insightful and entertaining.

WALTER: We tried a lot of structures, and I feel that what happened with them was not that they weren't appropriate but that we wore them out. We just wore them out and the people involved in them wore out.

HOTCHKISS: I don't think we wore out in rehearsal. We wisely kind of got the seed of it and then didn't rehearse it, and we just left it alone until we got to the opening.

WALTER: There was always a question in my own mind whether what ought to happen in that scene was that Marlow ought to come up with some incredible trip or that the audience could see the parade and have their own thing. And I think that was the basis on which the last improvisations were made, that the audience would have a similar experience and that we wouldn't rely on Marlow in that same way to remember something. In some points of the performances, that was actually his task, to remember something you could never remember.

HARRELL: Finally he had come down and asked us to teach him something. To give him something that would further his progression. And so we would tell him perhaps you can but how did it go? it was but the possibility of recall of, and then there was a blank in the statement that was filled in each night, things like deaths in your family, madness, personal loves. What were some of those other things?

WALTER: Ecstasy.

HARRELL: Right, and that's what wore out. Available categories wore out. But we would tell him [that] the 'possibility of recall of ecstasy is them, and his task was' recalling something that he had never recalled. That's how it was at first, it worked all right; and then it got really burdensome for Toni and me to come up, with new trips and new categories.

HOTCHKISS: I was never a party to the discussion and preparations for those [trips], but I had a feeling that the important criteria could be placed on the making of shocking [demands] startling might be a better word. Provocative in some way. Strange things, like they would come out and wrap my hands and feet in plastic bags and tape them shut so I couldn't move and then throw lighter fluid over bouquets of flowers and ignite them and hand me suitcases full of old dolls with artichokes in them, in incredible amounts and strange distorted kind of Cocteau images would come out of bags and out of boxes from the rafters... The whole thing was literally to jolt the unconscious into consciousness, and then my task was to take whatever bubbled up and give it some kind of form. It's one of the most exciting role challenges I've ever had. I think for me it's a model of what I want from any acting situation. That play in some ways all focuses on Yublom.... From my point of view everything led up [to the character]; it [all] reacted in a certain evolution of this creature's existence from a kind of hermit–like, reclusive, bitter, buried state to a more social, outgoing thing. The whole play builds to a moment of total improvisation, and essentially the climax of the play is improvised and you never know what's going to happen. I had about twenty to thirty minutes of confinement beneath the pumpkinlike lid on the floor in a little dirty hole down there, and almost always my mind wandered to that part of the play. I literally shook worrying about how I would ever cope with that part of the play tonight. I did it last night, but there never seemed to be adequate assurance that I could do it again tonight.

SAINER: Could I ask a general question? Have there been occasions when you find the use of your personal self and your memories and whatever you regard as your self as more vulnerable and destructive in terms of performance?

MAHER: Not in this play, but in *Faust*— absolutely. After the experience of *Faust* I refused to do it again. I would never do it again.

HARRELL: I didn't understand the question.

MAHER:.. Using your personal life and personal drama and presenting it publicly as part of the premise. And after the experience of *Faust*, I know the last performance was for me the last performance I could have performed in *Faust*. I mean I was lucky I didn't kill myself after that or kill somebody else. I was very upset by it, and I'll never do it again.

MYERS: Well, except for Marlow, there was a framework within which you presented your personal memories and personal life. There was a play, there was fiction, and so. it was fine, whereas in *Woyzeck*, which is like *Faust* and which is the only other one which I have to compare, it was just your boring, dull experience, but your [own] words.

FRANZEN: I remember *Woyzeck*. I used to tell things to audiences that I wouldn't tell anybody. I was so embarrassed. It was just murder. There was one variation that you had to — I can't remember how it was versed — but at least for me I remember you had to go to somebody and tell them the thing you hated most about yourself.

HARRELL: And we had masks of our own faces, and we would wear our own face mask up to an audience member and take our own face mask off — and [have] our own face talk to our [own] face mask and say why we hated ourselves.

HOTCHKISS: You [would] put your own mask on that person and tell that person how hateful and insidious and phony...

MYERS: And you would say "You," so nine times out of ten they were sure that you knew something about them. You hated them.

HARRELL: And then you turned the tables by taking your face mask off of them and putting it away, assuming some of their clothing and their attitude and allowing them to tell themselves why they hated themselves via you.

MAHER: How's that for a variation?

HARRELL: After the person with whom he was dealing and the person–audience member was given the opportunity to degrade himself. well, *gestalt* is what it is but it was so perverted . . .

HOTCHKISS: We base that essentially on the Andre Woyzeck relationship and its mechanism.

HARRELL: In *Woyzeck* it was completely literal, you tore open your flesh and showed your most ugly places to. the audience, literally through your own words about your own experience. But in *Still Falling*, there was [only] a trace of that, especially in the very beginning, because the way the physical gestures came up in the show, the sign work that Nancy had created for each beat in an individual speech, you might divide your speech up into several beats and for each beat you would free associate with a personal experience in a very quiet attitude, a zero attitude. You would read whatever beat that was in Nancy's words, free associate with a personal experience . . . the ones that came up, of course, were the ones that were most charged, at least for me. And then from that personal experience, you allowed whatever physical motivation to happen and you extended that to a physical gesture. So the physicalization for a given beat in the script was from your own experience, and the words accompanying that gesture [were] Nancy's words. Especially at first when the images were really clear the images that we used with the words it was a drag showing [our experiences] to people . . . But then as the play progressed, somehow the distance between the personal experience and physical gesture increased greatly.

HOTCHKISS: I think that distance means a lot because I think the Open Theatre worked exactly the same way on arriving at their so–called emblems. All of those things were personal expressions that derived from their own, almost working in a similar way.

HARRELL: Right. Seeing what they did, they either had to be just incredible craftsmen, which they were, or they had to be keeping those experiences fresh somehow to get that charge out of them — and I didn't understand how that happened. That's one of the reasons I wished I'd stayed and talked to them.[1]

HOTCHKISS: But the fact that we don't know them as people in some way allows those gestures, if they're any good, to be little provocative images, little paintings that we can project into. I think that our work, when it was efficient and clean in terms of physical life, should work the same way for audiences who didn't know us . . . I tend to discredit my own discomfort

---

[1] During the Open Theatre's tour of California, April '72.

with those things and trust that the objective eye — in this case, Nancy's responsible for that — would determine whether or not they were not expressive for somebody else, and [I would] just set aside how you feel about yourself.

HARRELL: I know the original task in the sign work had been before each performance we would go back through those original beats in the script and come up with new experiences for a given evening. But as the play progressed, as we did it time after time after time, and took a vacation and did it again and again, I'd say that at least fifty percent of the physicalization, for me at least, was improvisational, taken from a pool of gestures that had been established in a previous work.

WALTER: We weren't joyously hard on ourselves. We beat on each other and ourselves at every opportunity. It takes a long time for us to get respect out of our work and not to hate it.

HARRELL: Where Marlow says he was always freaked out about doing the improvisational structure in the evening, I was also freaked out about doing my improvisational structure, which was leading a dance of sorts, opened to the audience, because I never knew if I could come up with the words and the movements fast enough. After Tous had been lowered from his net by Yublom, Karun gave a little speech to the audience, stating that inside this circle of scaffolds it was open ground; anyone could do what they wanted to within these inclusive wails. And then the chorus members and the other actors would surround Karun, who would stand in the center of the ring.

HOTCHKISS: And often a lot of audience members, too, who had been included in the teach–in.

HARRELL: Right. Oh, the call had gone out before that moment Do you want to dance? Would you desire this experience? Do you like to dance? And then everyone would give Karun a gesture and a word that they had taken from some moment What was the criterion for taking that?

WALTER: Either from the audience directly by asking or from the improvisational section

HARRELL: Right. And Karun would be hit with this barrage of words and gestures, and out of them you would have to take literally those words and gestures and form a song and a dance which then I'd lead the audience in. And you start out very slow and gradually progress faster and faster, and the idea was to progress till speed brought about fatigue. Everyone was completely fatigued.

HOTCHKISS: That was the punctuation to the whole part of the evening. It really was the exclamation point to the play. What followed was a real anticlimax to the structure.

HARRELL: What followed was the audience was served tea, and that was always really a lovely moment because there was the instrumentation that went on during that, music that was played that was nice, and Yublom's speech about sad, archaic madonnas, fallen angels. He said everything is here music, tea, food, and then Yublom would give gifts to Tous, Karun, Marlow. It was very warm. Then after that the play went into another part that was pretty far out that the audience was involved in.

MAHER: The character of that last part took the character of a backyard penny carnival — you know, kids getting together and having these little games afterwards that they made up themselves and I personally enjoyed my little portion of. that. I had a good time. I enjoyed it.

FRANZEN: We got them in sort of like a spoke formation with their shoes off. Sometimes women had to take their nylons off. They would go over in the corner and pull them off. And they would lie in the center with all their feet touching, barefoot, and I would pour oil all over [their feet] and they would do a group grope of the toes.

HARRELL: Before that they were blindfolded and they had been given a drone. Throughout the evening the chorus had been involved in the most drone beat, and then there was a section over in the oily corner [with] various stimuli for the feet. And so the blanket would be torn off and there would be things like toothpicks, hard noodles, chicken necks, tomatoes, new potatoes, jam, grains, and things. They had to walk around those things, and as their feet touched something they were supposed to pick it up and tell someone about it. They'd also been instructed to relate any memories that these objects and experiences stimulated.

CHRISTIANSEN: The thing of calling up the dead or forgotten things was attractive. Toni had gotten some pictures. They were wonderful pictures. On them were things like suicide, accident, grandmother, father, cancer. Joel lived to be an old man. Mother, grandmother, and things like that, and so the cards would be placed upside down.

HARRELL: On red velvet with canvas surrounding it.

CHRISTIANSEN: And I would say this thing for them and ask them to choose a card. When they turned it over to give their immediate response, which could be verbal or otherwise . . . of course, people who got the "suicide" were strongest. I heard stories of people who have tried to commit suicide or one guy who took a very long time and everybody was looking at him like what's going to come out. Then he quoted something from Norman Mailer, and it was a wrong quote, and then he looked at everybody and was acting very peculiar and after everyone else had taken the cards up and shared something he came back to me. Oh, that was the time when somebody finally said to me, "Why don't you take a card?" So I did and it was "father" and I said a lot of things about my father whom I had felt a lot of guilt for, that there was a lot of suicide in my family. And it turned out that this kid who had turned up the card of suicide immediately thought of his uncle who had committed suicide and he was ashamed of it and he didn't want to say that in front of other people.

SAINER: Did you sense that there were nights when the audience did not want to go home?

SEVERAL PERFORMERS: Yes.

SCHWARTZ: There was a certain period where everybody was up there changing and you were looking out, listening to a few people screaming and a couple of people climbing under one another's skirts and stuff like that and you just wondered how far it would get and how long it would last.

❖❖❖

NOTES ON A PROCESS by Sydney Walter, Artistic Director of the Firehouse Theater.

How we are in the world.

Roles *Those that we choose. Those that are thrust upon us. Those that we don't even recognize as roles.*

Our lives as individuals are defined by the roles we play — a baffling web of interdependent connections among the living and the dead. To play the roles fully, passionately, and yet without attachment, is to be liberated. Ultimately there are no individuals, only roles, and the player is transpersonal. When a man knows this [not intellectually, but in every cell, every action], he can realize his potential as a human being, a transcendent animal.

Every theatre piece deals with this, deliberately or not. Every theatre piece says something, implicitly or explicitly, about role–playing; about what is real; about where our human energies are invested.

The pervasive belief (despite .the enigmatic smile of Gautama Buddha and the harsh cries of R.D. Laing) that I can isolate my being from the rest of the universe and experience existence objectively can be reinforced or sabotaged by a theatre event. This act of reinforcement or sabotage takes place not so much on the level of content as on the level of structure.

The role of actor; the role of audience member: What expectations exist? What experiments are possible? How does the work of the actor penetrate the audience? How does the audience influence the actor? Can a true interpenetration take place?

No matter how radical the content or style of a theatre piece may be, if the traditional audience–actor relationships are observed the piece is fundamentally conservative. How we contact the audience is ultimately more significant than what we say (although these two aspects of performance can hardly be separated so neatly). The traditional audience–actor relationship is essentially authoritarian, manipulative, condescending, inflexible. The audience sits waiting to be taught, entertained, or offended. Their attitude toward the piece is either passive or judgmental neither tending to enhance awareness or develop consciousness.

A doctor comes to a play. He sits passively, allowing the performers full control of the event. This situation confers an aura on the actors — they are special; the doctor is not. They are unique and brilliant, he is one of many. One day a performer visits the doctor. Now the roles are reversed. The doctor is in complete control, the performer is passive and helpless. Again an aura is conferred, this time on the doctor. This is a paradigm of the way our culture assigns roles, promotes obsessive egocentricity, and produces an alienated, mystified citizenry. Both the performance and the healing can be collaborative; human contact can supplant the projection of frozen images; cooperation can take the place of alternate domination and submission.

Violate audience expectations. Once an audience member who allows himself to be involved in an event assumes risks, he can be involved in a creative effort to develop a way of being in this world.

All this applies to the performer as well. Although he knows the rules, he is vulnerable in a way that an actor performing in a set event never is.

In our early work, we tended to goad and assault the audience. This is always good for a response, but the response is generally predictable and generally a dead end. In our more recent work, we have tried to create a situation where an audience member will feel supported in extending self to the performance situation. The responses elicited in this way are more diverse, less predictable and more creative.

Ways of restructuring the actor–audience relationship:

1. Let the environment reflect the material. Avoid traditional actor–audience arrangements. Let the event move through the audience; give the audience an opportunity to move through the event.

2. Multiple Focus. More than one event occurs simultaneously. Each audience member is involved in an event and at the same time is aware that he is missing another event. Each event will carry the audience member to the next event (which may be single focus), yet all are made aware that the space contains a variety of experiences.

3. One-to-one event. A performance given by one actor for one audience member can have a terrific impact on that audience member, as well as on others who may be in a position to watch. Often, one–to–one events can occur simultaneously with an event that is presented to the whole audience.

4. Give the audience an opportunity to contribute directly to the event.

All these techniques have been used in recent years (and in other cultures). The first three must be carefully handled to avoid tension and chaos. The fourth is an extremely difficult and delicate matter, which has contributed to some of the greatest triumphs and most dismal failures in our work. It took me a long time to realize that it is a mistake to ask an audience member to perform. Untrained in performing, he will usually respond with cliches and awkwardness.

Give audience members an opportunity to "be" in the event. Let the event absorb the audience, so that the audience provides material for the performers to transform into image and metaphor. This transformation may occur simply as a result of the context in which an audience member appears, or it may require some improvisational development on the part of the actor.

No attempt to erase distinctions between performer and audience — rather an attempt to redefine the relationship. The performers remain in control of the event, shaping and guiding the whole, which includes the contribution of the audience, but which also includes formal, presentational elements.

Two examples from recent works will do more to clarify this process than pages of theory.

1. *Blessings*, a play by Nancy Walter. Near the end of the play, six of the

actors (all but two in the cast) choose audience members.[2] This choice is carefully made on the basis of insights gained through audience contact during the evening, although the criteria for the choice is personal. The six actors sit with their deputies in a circle around the two central actors, each of the six with a small stone vessel of water.

While the two central actors play out a tightly structured scene (text included at the end of this article), the six prepare the deputies by washing–anointing them with water. The manner of washing–anointing is personal and improvisational, although each deputy is oriented toward the central scene so that the dialogue spoken there applies to his experience. When the central scene is over, the six stand with their deputies and face the central couple. The woman in the center steps out of the circle and the six actors step back, leaving one actor surrounded by six audience members.

The central actor removes all his clothes, looks carefully at each of the six deputies, and speaks the following words:

> If I am to bless and be blessed, I must know who you are, the you behind each of your eyes. Tell me, show me, in any way you can, and I will sweat to understand.

One by one, the six audience members make some statement or perform some action toward the central actor. This event was always vivid, often astonishing. The context of the moment was such that the simplest words and actions of an audience member seemed to resonate through many levels of meaning. The deputies, prepared by all that went before, almost always presented something beyond the clichés one might expect in such a situation. It was the sense of the central actor, however, that carried this event to the realm of revelation. Marlow Hotchkiss' contribution to this moment was his amazing capacity for working with an audience member in such a way as to transform a particular response into a universal image, frequently an image of great power and depth.

2. *Escape by Balloon*, an evening with ten events, created by the company in collaboration with WER LaFarge. The first event involves actors questioning audience members as they enter the auditorium. These questions are intended to orient the audience toward two themes, especially as these themes apply to their own lives. The first theme has to do with journeys, discoveries, and roots. The second centers on the concept of an ideal relationship What is it? What are the obstacles?

While the audience is being questioned, two actors search for a couple who will provide a central focus throughout the evening. When a couple is

---

[2] We called these audience members "deputies," although that term was never introduced into the event.

chosen, they are invited to take off their clothes[3] and sit facing each other in the center of the room. Each is then covered with a poncho made of white paper. When actors question audience members about the ideal relationship, they exhibit verbal answers and ask the audience member to express their thoughts and feelings by using pots of poster paint to decorate the couple dressed in paper. Additional paper cut into various shapes and sizes is available, as well as tape. The audience paint with their fingers, forming the paper into hats, scepters, banners, etc., and transforming the couple into a colorful, messy work of art.

During this painting, the couple is given a bowl of strawberries and instructed to feed the berries to each other, one by one. As the man feeds a berry to the woman,[4] he reminds her of some joyous, pleasant, happy event from their past. Then she feeds him a berry, calling up another such event. With his second berry, the man reminds his partner of some distressing event from their past. She does the same with her second berry, and this alternation continues throughout the painting. Through this event the couple is transformed, invested with the hopes and fears of the audience. The audience and actors have created something together which provides a focus for the successive events of the evening.

Immediately following this event, the tone of the piece changes abruptly. The successive events are more formal, presentational (although there are significant moments of audience participation). The opening event has provided material for other events.

Before the evening ends, the couple will be joyfully celebrated, brutally separated, and finally acknowledged as separate individuals who may or may not be able to come together. The evening begins with a happy ending, proceeds through many difficulties, and ends with a possibility.[5] The last event has the couple separated by the length of the performance space, one with bread, one with wine, which they may or may not share with the audience. They are not brought together. They are not kept apart.

[3] The event proceeds in the same way whether or not the couple agrees to be naked. Since the couple will be recipients of the dreams and fears of the other audience members, they should be as neutral as possible, like sheets of blank paper. Removing their clothing removes some of the most obvious symbols of rank and affiliation.

[4] Occasionally the couple was homosexual.

[5] *Escape by Balloon* is not primarily about the relationship of a couple. The several events span centuries and deal with the impact of Europe on America — how this continent was penetrated and transformed by the Faustian thrust of the European. The couple become an immediate, living symbol in the presentation of historical events.

The passage back and forth between carefully structured images (including songs of considerable complexity) and open, improvisational moments makes extraordinary demands on performers. Nor is it simply a matter of one or the other. There is a spectrum running from total improvisation to formal image, and the actor must know precisely where he is on that spectrum — which elements are set, which are open. To complicate the issue still further, an audience member may project himself into an event, thereby adding an unexpected element to a set event or another element to an already complex improvisational structure. No action on the part of the audience may be considered inappropriate. Once we invite the audience to collaborate with us, we are under an obligation to accept what they offer without judgment.[6] The performer's task (and sometimes it is monumental) is to integrate the audience action into the fabric of the show, to shape whatever happens in accordance with the themes and issues of the particular event.

In this work it is important for the performer to be acutely aware of form at all times. Questioning an audience member is as precise a task as the most stylized presentational work, and casual social behavior (except as a deliberate choice) is disastrous. The acting–not acting dichotomy favored by those strongly influenced by happenings does not apply here. When I am not playing any other role, I am playing Sydney Walter (a role that subsumes myriad roles), and it is essential that during performance I play that role with the same care and precision, the same attention to effect that I would apply to any other role.[7]

A major concern in this work is the tendency for some audience members to compartmentalize their emotional responses. They come expecting a particular experience and consider a different sort of experience invalid. I spoke to a girl several days after she had seen one of our shows, and she said that she hated it — that she had been bored, bewildered, and disgusted. I questioned her in detail about specific moments throughout the show, and her answers revealed a surprisingly wide range of emotional responses, some of them quite intense and by no means all negative. As we discussed this discrepancy, it became clear that she had edited her emotional response on the basis of some judgment about what was a legitimate apart of the event and what was not. She was threatened by the activities of one actor,

[6] Of course, a performer may like or not like what an audience member does, but in either case he must accept it and work with it.

[7] The question "Who is the I who plays the role?" would lead us deep into the mire of philosophical speculation. It is worthwhile to note, however, that similar questions are used by masters in certain spiritual disciplines to precipitate breakthroughs to higher levels of consciousness on the part of disciples.

comforted by the activities of another. She considered the threat part of the event, the comfort parenthetical to the event. From her point of view, certain responses were evoked by the event, other responses were evoked by something else. From my point of view, anything that was experienced in the space that night was part of the event.

At the beginning of one show, the actors took off the shoes of each audience member. A critic from a local paper was among the audience one night, and she refused to allow an actor to remove her high–laced boots.

"Why?" the actor asked.

"I'm a critic. If you take off my boots I'll lose my objectivity."

It is pointless to criticize audience members for the attitudes they bring to a show. They bring what they are. It is up to us, through the event, to make our insights and understandings available to the audience and to open ourselves to theirs. Sometimes this happens.

❖❖❖

From *Blessings* written by Nancy Walter

10. IRENE *and* BEAR *After* IRENE's *song, each actor chooses one audience person and brings him into a circle around* BEAR, *washing his face as* BEAR's *is being washed.*

IRENE: [*Sings.*] To be a woman
who would choose it
made to be filled
made to be
a poor man's garden
a child's own bed
Careless
under the heat of the bloom
a seed is dropped into death
All flesh sees it together
and the woman sees it apart
Helpless
under the measure of blood, lost
and regained
lost and regained
The body's delicate meat goes dry
Time catches up
with the blood
time catches up

with the bloom
and then?

IRENE: I brought you something. This. [*Brings water in a bucket to* BEAR.]

BEAR: Why?

IRENE: I thought you needed it.

BEAR: Is it to drink?

IRENE: No. It's for washing. Sit down and I'll wash your head with it. And
then you can go.

BEAR: Stop. Where will I be going?

IRENE: From one world to another.

BEAR: Why?

IRENE: Because it's time
because you're human

BEAR: Because I'm flesh and blood
you see that
I am mortal
If you leaned over to touch me
I would be here.

IRENE: I am distracted by your presence
your mortality
your body

BEAR: It will not hurt you.

IRENE: No. I know that
I look at you
like all human beings so easily murdered
and your mind too is
already suffering your death
and the deaths of others.

BEAR: I no longer believe in my own suffering.
Don't waste it.

IRENE: This is not wasted.
If it is no use for me to come to you in this way
if it is nothing to you
really nothing
what gesture can I reach anyone with?

BEAR: I don't understand.

IRENE: Everyone has a dream
of the world's destruction
My dream includes you.
I dream you are in an empty place
where no voice reaches you
where all the evil in the world has visited you and left
and you are blind and deaf
without one person to cool your head
and you no longer see that you can
stand up and go somewhere else.
You believe in your mistakes.
You believe in your history.

BEAR: And this water is a cure for that?

IRENE: No, the cure for that has not been described. This is only a way of touching it. [*Pours the water over his head.*]

11. THE ENDOWMENT BEAR *now stands in the center of a circle surrounded by audience members.*

BEAR: We live between a curse and a promise. There is no escaping this equivocal ground until we die. I am not ready to die. I am tired of the curses falling down on my head. I have gone as far as I can describing disasters. And I admit that I have been fascinated by doom, by extinction, by the prospect of the steel and concrete monster tumbling down, by the monumental mess of it all. It has excited me. But I can no longer stand all this mess and guilt. I no longer believe in the cataclysm. I am tired of piling up future disasters one upon another. I am tired of listing the annihilators and describing their parts. I am tired of the violent release of my energy against things.

I could hold a human brain in my hand, admiring its convolutions. I could close my eyes and look out from that brain only, that hand. I want to take hold of the promise and see if it is as real as the curse. I am afraid of becoming invulnerable to you.

MARY: [*Sings.*] Without a seed in my head
I ask for a child from you
My own ground is empty
My own field is dry
Still I ask for a child from you
That will be my own flesh

If all men murmur

against a child being born
If armed men
are ready to fire
If there is no
bread on the table anymore

No child will come
No child will be given

Still I ask for a child from you
labor to untwist my breath
a child from you
little hands to tear open my eyes
A child from you

A new being to wake me.

BEAR: If I am to bless and be blessed, I must know who you are, the you behind each of your eyes. Tell me, show me, in any way you can, and I
will sweat to understand.

[*The audience members come forward to* BEAR *or they do not with words,
gestures, gifts.* BEAR *tries to deal with them individually, discerning each
person's unique and special quality and celebrating it.*]

[*When this has. gone as far as it can go, it is broken by* GLABER.]

13. THE BRIDGE COLLECTIVE

The Spring Offensive *is the initial work of the Bridge Collective. The ensemble began with the written script, but the script was written with an ensemble in mind — that is, many of the scenes on paper were purposely left "open," written as suggestions indicating a direction, an intent, so written that the ensemble could discover the moment's physical life through the rehearsal process. For example, Shrively Dick's Money Opera on paper gives the merest suggestion of how the scene is to be played. A money dance is indicated, but what kind of a dance is that to be? The tomcat scene offered a similar problem. So did the battle with the police. Buddy's competitive games in choosing the bomb cell had to be discovered by the ensemble and in fact took laborious weeks of trial–and–error. The play has a relentless, thrusting quality, broken by certain lyrical moments. Much of it is hard, concrete, matter–of–fact, but these documentary–type moments are juxtaposed against other fanciful, almost mythical ones.*

The script for The Spring Offensive *is followed by excerpts from the notes kept while I was writing the play and also from the log for the rehearsal period.*

❖❖❖

THE SPRING OFFENSIVE. A play by Arthur Sainer (1972–73) • Directed by Nancy Gabor • Music by Itsuro Shimoda.

The play opened in June of 1973 in New York City with the following performers Allison Brennan, Tony Brazina, Duncan Kegerreis, Maggie Kennedy, Rob McBrien, and Wendy Wasdahl. It reopened in a revised version in December 1973 at Ohio State University in Columbus, Ohio, and then in New York City in January 1974 with Allison Brennan, Ann Freeman, Nancy Gabor, Ilan Mamber, William Newman, Robert schlee and Henry Smith. Production manager for the original performances was Peter Larivere, for the revised performances it was Gene Becker. The managing director of the company is Calvin Holt.

The script that follows includes several scenes that were in the original or revised productions, but not in both. It also includes several scenes were not in either production.

The Bridge Collective wishes to acknowledge the help of other performers who worked with the ensemble during the pre–rehearsal and early–rehearsal stages. They include Maurice Blanc, Converse (Gurian) Sheets, Andy Potter, Jane Sanford and Francene Selkirk.

The Spring Offensive is dedicated to the memory of Diana Oughton.

The play is performed in an open area. Performers not in specific scenes watch from stools on the sidelines. The playing area is bathed in white light throughout, there should be no attempt at special lighting effects. Ends of scenes are designated by abrupt cutoffs from the performers who then take neutral attitudes in preparation for their next scene. Beginnings of scenes take place after a suitable pause in the action. All costume changes not designated as actions in scenes should take place discreetly but with no attempt to mask them from the spectators.

DIANA transforms herself. How is this to be done? We begin with a pleasant, earnest, softly pretty girl. As we watch, DIANA transforms herself into a hardfaced creature. She changes her hair from soft, long tresses to short butch. She changes her clothes, the pretty dress gives way to a hip costume, boots, jeans, man's woolen shirt. And she dons plain, steel–rimmed glasses. When the transformation has been completed, we are looking at a tough young American militant, circa 1970.

VOICE: Diana's "Song to the Child."

[DIANA *is working with an autistic child. She plays a "touch" game with the child but there is no response. The child suddenly strikes out, then huddles into herself on the floor.* DIANA *sings a song.*]

DIANA: God made you walk into the mountain
You shut, we shut against you.
You wanted dreams, you wanted bread
We picked a bud, we bombed a train
We made a bank, we tried to breathe.

God made you, we made you
You made yourself, we spent our
days, we spent our days

Counting, digging, crying for the night
Spent our nights
Waking, dreaming, whispering for the day.

We made a bank, we tried to breathe
We caught a fish and we were
Fished for

Fished for
We were fished for
We were fished for
We were fished for.

VOICE: The action of Shrivelly Dick, our Benevolent Killer.

[SHRIVELLY DICK THE BENEVOLENT KILLER, *appears. He addresses an overly–smiling congregation.*]

DICK: [*Unctuously.*] Let us lower our voices. [*Moves around, sizing up others.*] Let us greet each man as our brother. [*More sizing up.*] Let us reflect on what's right about America. [*More sizing up.*] Let us have peace with honor.

[DICK *begins to pull out weapons. They are monstrous weapons, unimaginable monstrosities. He unleashes them against instantly screaming victims who writhe and die. He continues speaking, coolly, unctuously. The dead victims are smiling brightly again.*]

DICK: Let us lower our voices. Let us draw together in brotherly love. Let us build a bridge between men and nations. Let us have stability with honor. Let us lower our voices. Let us watch over our poorer brethren. Let us give thanks that God is watching over us. Let us honor the simple virtues. Let us not merely give lip service to justice. Let us see to it that no man goes hungry tonight. Let us lower our voices. Let us spread charity and mercy throughout the land.

[*All are dead.* DICK *watches them in silence. He cleans his weapons piously, he conscientiously puts them away. Finally:*]

DICK: Let us pray.

[DIANA, TOM, CORA, EDIE *and* PETER *are in the process of moving into an apartment. The early part of the scene should be improvised with those who haven't yet seen the place now taking note of the various facilities. Also, there is a sense of each staking out a comfortable area and settling in for an initial meeting. After a while*]

TOM: Okay, can we settle down for the meeting?

[*They all sit and* TOM *pulls out a sheet of paper.*]

TOM: First, I made up a tentative schedule of house chores. If the group approves, we'll put this into effect starting tomorrow. Okay. Weekly marketing: Tom and Edie. Dinner: Cora and Diana alternate Monday through Saturday nights. Sunday the rest of us do a Sunday, that's a meal every third Sunday night. Cleanup: Pete and those not cooking. Accounts: Cora. General household maintenance: by couples, weekly.

Diana and I will start it. Anybody can't make a chore is responsible for finding a substitute. [*All seem agreeable.*] Okay, let's go to the next item on the agenda.

PETE: What about guests?

CORA: Yes, how do we work that? I'm for treating them really as guests.

DIANA: So am I.

TOM: I agree. My feeling is whoever wants to eat or crash here is welcome. This has got to be an open house. If they've got the bread to kick in something, okay. If not, okay. If we find we've got a chronic freeloader on our hands, we'll deal with that.

[*General agreement.*]

TOM: Next item. Political rap sessions. We agreed we'd set aside Wednesday nights for those. Any problems? Pete is to be responsible for making up the agendas.

PETE: So talk to me by the end of the previous week.

CORA: Right.

EDIE: Are we up to personal histories?

TOM: That's next.

EDIE: I'd like to go first. Well like Diana, I was in Latin America for a time. Peace Corps. Then back home, worked in D.C., researching and sometimes writing speeches for the congressman from my home district, Representative Miller, then —

PETE: What area?

EDIE: Cleveland. Then OEO, then law school for two semesters — that was as much as I could stand of it. Then more and more involvement in SDS. Like Diana, I was a representative to the meetings in Cuba with the North Vietnamese and the PRG. — Like most of us, I spent some precious time, not so much personal time as time belonging to the people, trying to work within the system. What the system taught me is that it has a talent for absorbing you and outliving you. And that your absorption doesn't improve it, that your energies function as a kind of decoy, you fool yourself and the system also fools you with its inauthentic rewards while it goes on doing what it knows best how to do — destroying people.

CORA: [*After a moment.*] I'll go. I taught for a while, grammar school in Marin County. Then the Children's Free School in Ann Arbor where

I met Diana and Tom. I wasn't there at the end, when the place folded, but I heard about it. Enrollment kept dropping because we all insisted on running a program that wasn't success–oriented, and that bothered a lot of the parents. I'm sorry that school didn't make it. — Anyway, I worked with SDS, then after the split, with Weathermen. Then New York and my job on the editorial staff of *Rat*. Oh, I worked with a remedial reading program in Harlem for awhile. That was just before *Rat*.

PETE: In the summer of sixty–three and four, I was in Mississippi, working in civil rights. That's where I got the buckshot wound. Then with OEO for a time. In and out of school for several years. I helped run a rent strike workshop in Roxbury. Then Chicago, mostly draft counseling in Chicago. Then SDS. — For a long time I couldn't really make up my mind about how I wanted to work. I don't know whether working within given institutions is no longer viable, but I'm not going to sit up nights trying to dope it out. I take what's at hand and work with it. And what's at hand is this movement, and I believe in it.

TOM: [*After a pause.*] Diana?

DIANA: I believe in a better life for all oppressed peoples. It's why I worked in the Free School, it's why I do the work I'm doing now, it's why I'm here with you now. Background: the Quakers sent me to Bogota in sixty–three. From there into the hills, to work with the Indians, to see the kind of poverty I never believed, I never truly understood. Those people never have a chance. And they die early. And I've never been able to get that poverty out of my head. I've never gotten it out of my head. And I need a serious weapon to beat that poverty.

TOM'S FIRST SOLILOQUY: Certain rational forces. Certain controlled forces. Certain liberated forces. Certain deadly forces. Certain indicative trends. Certain ways of being. A winning combination a la Tupamaros, knife against throat of board chairman, knife stolen, chairman kidnapped, if you make the request he will laugh for you, if you request him to he'll sign checks for you, turn over his wife to you, defecate gladly, free the prisoners shyly. Certain rational forces. Certain liberated forces. Terror is bread, the uses of terror against the forces of terror can sustain the revolution, can help build a movement. But one must not be an idiot. Sentiment moves the revolution, is the step prior to the revolution, but can't win it alone. Waking hours and the uses of terror further the revolution. Certain rational forces. Certain controlled forces. Certain liberated forces. Certain deadly forces.

[*A multiple scene.* BUDDY *and* CORA *are out walking in the middle of the night.* DIANA *is working with the autistic child.* TOM *is home, reading.*]

CORA: Aren't you cold? The way you're dressed?

BUDDY: Sure I'm cold! I like being cold! [*They walk comfortably.*] Let's go to bed. Then we can talk politics.

[*Kisses her quickly and eagerly. She begins to laugh.*]

CORA: You're such an extravagant character. Want to come back to the house?

BUDDY: No I don't. It's full of middle–class revolutionaries. Playing at danger, big games. And you had to leave your nice little apartment and —

CORA: What nonsense, you don't know any of them. I keep wanting you to meet Diana and Pete and —

BUDDY: No thanks, no thanks, no thanks. When your friends are ready to start blowing up some buildings, when they start getting serious, then it will be time for us to talk. I'm not interested in a fist fight and a little bottle throwing with cops outside MacDonald's. What's that all about, anyway? Impressing the teenagers?

CORA: Did you call for me at three in the morning to discuss blowing up buildings?

BUDDY: You bet your ass I did. I called for you at three in the morning to make better people of both of us — I called for you because I love you.

[*Meanwhile,* DIANA *has left the child, returned home and is sitting with* TOM *who is still engrossed in his reading.*]

DIANA: I think about the school now and then. I miss it.

TOM: [*Looks up.*] Unproductive. And it's not only your time you're wasting.

DIANA: You're right. I'm unproductive. — You know, you've gotten so . . .

TOM: What?

DIANA: [*Thinks.*] Tough. This year. So much tougher.

TOM: That's right.

DIANA: That's right. [*Touches him gently.*] Can I still touch you? Are you aware of how tough you've gotten? Are you conscious of everything you do? How tough?

TOM: Do you want to make love?

DIANA: No, I just want to touch you. To be touched. Can we hold one another?

[TOM *runs his hand along* DIANA's *arm. For a time they sit in silence.*]

CORA: Sometimes you seem to me so young. Like a sweet child growing up.

BUDDY: Inside I'm an old man and a kid. I don't always know myself.

CORA: [*As they walk again.*] Have you heard from your wife?

BUDDY: Last week. She says my boy's growing up. But that's what she always says. Every six months I get the same letter. She never asks for money.

CORA: Yes, you told me.

BUDDY: I told you that? Say, can't we go someplace besides that pad full of your revolutionary playmates? We could walk to my place but it would take an hour.

CORA: Buddy, come home with me. It's nice there. I'll make tea.

VOICE: The meeting between Buddy and Cora 1.

[BUDDY *and* CORA *address each other from opposite walls.*]

CORA: I'm going to question you now. Is that all right? — A.

BUDDY: Alliance,

CORA: B.

BUDDY: Barbiturate.

CORA: C.

BUDDY: Capitalism,

CORA: C.

BUDDY: Cunt.

CORA: D.

BUDDY: Death machine. D, density.

CORA: E.

BUDDY: Exterminate.

CORA: E.

BUDDY: Express train. Brighton Line. Scollay Square.

CORA: E.

BUDDY: End of the line. Endemic.

CORA: B.

BUDDY: Buddy.

CORA: B.

BUDDY: Bombing. Also bombings.

CORA: F.

BUDDY: Forensic.

CORA: F.

BUDDY: Fertility. Folio. Feds. Feed the planet. A, amnesty.

CORA: L.

BUDDY: Last chance. The earth. The death of money.

CORA: T.

BUDDY: Treachery.

CORA: T.

BUDDY: Treachery.

CORA: T.

BUDDY: Talk.

CORA: Z.

BUDDY: Last chance. C, commune, E, earth. F, love. A, total anger. F, freak-out. K, kops.

CORA: C, Cora.

VOICE: Fat America offers her gifts.

[*The following stage directions are also spoken by the voice: And here comes* FAT AMERICA, *a stout, over–anxious matron, bulging with gifts for* TOM *and* DIANA. *She shoves seemingly edible goodies at them, they munch eagerly and then begin to puke. She offers radios, they eagerly listen, one falls asleep from boredom, the other grows wild. She offers motherly or smotherly love but they turn from her in revulsion. She offers money, they grab it, then knock her down, take more money from her, fold her up and throw her out. They are both very quiet now and sad.*]

VOICE: Buddy chooses members for the bomb cell, a project of the 10th St. Collective.

[BUDDY *eyes potential recruits, at some point leaps at one. A series of power games ensue, which* BUDDY *sets up, one for each in the room. The games are designed for* BUDDY *to decide whom he feels comfortable with. As each game ends,* BUDDY *separates accepted ones from the rejects. The games should be improvised, left open for the performance.*]

[BUDDY *and* CORA *are at home together.* CORA *is occupied writing, finishing a piece of furniture,* BUDDY *is musing.*]

BUDDY: [*Suddenly.*] I'm going to show you my scars.

[*He grabs* CORA, *startling her. He shows her various places on his body, including his eyes, his feet, his brain.*]

BUDDY: These are my scars. Get to know these scars. These scars won't speak out loud but some night while you're sleeping they may burst into your bed, throw them out, just burst into your bed and try to invade you. If they do, kick them out, throw them out. [*Continues exposing them to Cora.*] Kick them out, these are my eyes, my feet, brain. These are my eyes, kick them out, my feet, my brain. These scars, these scars, these are my scars. Kick the fuckers out, these scars, these scars.

CORA: I've got to do some typing.

[CORA *is alone. She sings.*]

CORA'S SONG: My song sings me
It drives me, it
Lusts for me, it
Won't let me be.
All the stricken ones possess me
All the victims bake my dinner
All the hungry ones feast on me
Pray for me.
What can I give them? just my anger
What can I give them? my confusion
What can I give them? my lost soul
My found soul.

My song sings me
It drives me, it
Lusts for me, it
Won't let me be.

[DIANA *joins* CORA *and they harmonize on the song.*]

[TOM, DIANA, CORA *and* BUDDY *are together. They are tense, as if awaiting a signal. As indeed they are.* TOM *breaks the silence.*]

TOM: [*Points to* DIANA *and* CORA.] All right, everybody's waiting. It's outta sight time.

DIANA: What do you mean?

TOM: Fuck you, cunt! [*To* BUDDY.] You agree? [BUDDY *is noncommittal.*] Okay, women.

DIANA: Why are you doing this?

TOM: Okay, women. [*Nothing happens:* TOM *screams.*] Fuck your bourgeois hangups, Diana. Let's see a little action.

CORA: [*To* BUDDY.] You want me to?

BUDDY: You're grownup, ain't you? You got a mind.

CORA: [*To* DIANA.] Actually, I like you a lot, Diana.

[*The women begin hesitantly but with affection to make love to one another.*]

VOICE: Edie and Pete represent the Collective at a conference in Oakland.

EDIE: [*Addressing the crowd.*] In the name of the people, this government has lied, stolen and murdered. In the name of the people, Fred Hampton was gunned down in Chicago, in the name of the people George Jackson was murdered in California, in the name of the people Indochina is being turned into a graveyard. This government has consistently lied, wasted your taxes, jailed your sisters and murdered your brothers, and yet some of you still talk, still talk about working within the system, as if the system itself wasn't the sickness.

HECKLER: What the fuck do you want? A guerrilla movement in the streets of San Francisco?

EDIE: Damned right. That's just what I want, baby.

PETE: And in Manhattan, and Chicago, and Denver.

HECKLER 2: You're dreaming.

HECKLER: You'll get your ass kicked in by the Man.

PETE: Maybe and maybe not. Some of us believe that the System is ripe for the taking. Remember what Mao said, he said that the people —

HECKLER 2: "Mao said"! Shit, man, there are no radical peasants in the U.S. The farmers aren't about to hide us in the hills while we take on the U.S. Army.

PETE: I tell you there's a groundswell under our feet, a world movement that you're not aware of, the revolution is now. The Left has to recognize itself, as Hegel told us long ago, as the tool of necessity.

EDIE: I know there are pigs in this country who still think we should occupy Vietnam, Cambodia, the planet. And some pigs who still think they can go into the ghettos and push people around. Well, we're telling you that the revolution has begun — it's begun — and the only choice you have to make is which side you're on. And we're also telling you that if you get in the way of the revolution, it's going to ride right over you!

VOICE: Shrivelly Dick's Money Opera.

[SHRIVELLY DICK *improvises an aria about the single word: money. He waves imaginary money around, he eats money, he stuffs money into various parts of his body, he does a little money dance.*]

EDIE'S SOLILOQUY: The women's house of detention. My three weeks. First: inspection. You come with your shirt, pants, shoes, socks, your underpants. They say strip. Everything comes off. You stand naked. Maybe you're hiding drugs? They search you. They look up your ass. Then they give you a shirt, it comes to your knees, they give you slippers, they don't stay on your feet. The inmates look you over, one of them picks you for herself. Noise? All day, all night. The inmates scream, the guards scream, the TVs in the rec room scream, the steel bars scream. If you complain too much they throw you in the tank. No windows, no bars, no bed, no light. You go naked. You stay naked. If you get sick? You lie in your vomit, you lie in your shit. Sometimes they hose you down.

DIANA'S FIRST SOLILOQUY: I am writing this — that is, I am speaking this to my parents. I am writing nothing, I am speaking nothing to my parents. I am going to be part of an explosion. Things as they are cannot ultimately maintain themselves, they fester and will die. We, I, will help them die. I, we, will be a bludgeon against heads, will shatter glass, a razor against . . . an avenging angel against . . . I will be straight and explode in my straightness. I will be straight, will explode in my undying straightness. I will be a dove secreting fine poison over the steps of the Capitol.

VOICE: Diana's father pays a visit.

[DIANA *and her father watch one another from a distance. The father is gentle, distinguished-looking, obviously concerned about his daughter. After a time the father tries to approach* DIANA *but each physical attempt is met by* DIANA'S *readjusting her physical position to maintain the distance. But an insidious thing begins to happen.* DIANA *begins to imitate her father's stance, perhaps unconsciously at first, to imitate the idiosyncrasies of his physical being. The father grows stiff as he is aware that his daughter is mocking him.* DIANA *stiffens also.* DIANA *breaks her pose, runs to her father and hugs him. They hold one another. Then he brings forth small gifts for her. She smiles, tears them, crushes them, steps on them, sprinkles them over his head, shoves them in his mouth.*]

[*The two couples are asleep in each other's arms,* TOM *with* DIANA, BUDDY *with* CORA. DIANA *wakes, stirs, looks about, leaves* TOM *and moves to the other couple. She rudely pushes her way in and takes* BUDDY *in her arms. By now everyone has woken and is a little astonished as* DIANA *begins to make love to* BUDDY *who, woken from sleep, is confused.* DIANA *looks over at* TOM, *gives him her favorite mocking smile.*]

DIANA: It's oughtta sight time.

[DIANA *turns back to* BUDDY. TOM *lies back and simply watches.* BUDDY *pushes* DIANA *from him.*]

BUDDY: Cut the shit.

[DIANA *cracks* BUDDY *across the face.*]

DIANA: When I want you, you come! Don't play with me, boy.

BUDDY: [*In a sudden rage.*] I'll kill you! Get the fuck away from me! Nobody tells me what I want!

[*All four are now separated from each other.* DIANA *is sullen,* CORA *is curious,* BUDDY *is furious and* TOM *is watching with interest.* TOM *bursts into mocking laughter. Now he closes his eyes and is the only one preparing for sleep again.*]

VOICE: Buddy's cell makes its first action. The theft of dynamite.

[*The members of the cell are seen moving about stealthily.*]

[*They all freeze, gazing at the watchman who is reading his paper. They creep up on the watchman and at a signal batter him insensible.*]

[*The boxes of dynamite are uncovered and passed from one to another. They run off.*]

TOM'S SECOND SOLILOQUY: So the night watchman was hurt? Item: the night watchmen of America are being hurt. American casualties are running high. Mothers, hide your night watchmen, and your judges, and your jailers. Hide your jailers, mommies of America, because the black man is no longer alone in his prison, because we are all black men, all prisoners. [TOM *grows introspective.*] I grew up in a white house, I had white friends, we drank white wine, we ate white meat, we spent white money. My father was — is — chairman of the board. Three boards. I had everything. I was — my family money. We made —

Congressmen, we reassured Cabinet members, we made it easy for oil magnates, coal magnates, death magnates. We were not black, we were not yellow, we were not brown. We were white and rich. White and rich. White and rich. We bled the earth.

VOICE: The meeting between Buddy and Cora 2.

[BUDDY *and* CORA *address each other from opposite walls.*]

BUDDY: A.

CORA: Abortion.

BUDDY: B.

CORA: Benefactor. Bastion. B, blatant.

BUDDY: C.

CORA: Convene. C, cut. C, count out. C, condemn.

BUDDY: H.

CORA: Harbor. Hell. Death. Exorcise. Henceforth.

BUDDY: K.

CORA: Knife, kill.

BUDDY: W.

CORA: W, woman. W, watch. Waiting. W, women. W, war.

BUDDY: T.

CORA: T, tomorrow. T, tomorrow, T, today. T, tomorrow. T, tactics. T, turn, turn. T, turn. T, tomorrow. T, touching. Turn turn turn. T T T. Tomorrow, turn, T, today.

[*A multiple scene. In one area are* DIANA *and the child. At home the collective is relaxing and singing "In the Midst."* DIANA *approaches the child and begins to hug her gently and rock her. No response.* DIANA *releases the child and watches her. All at once the child begins to sway back and forth gently, as if it were rocking itself.* DIANA *watches. The child's swaying becomes stronger and stronger until it is swaying violently, out of control. Then* DIANA *stops her, holding her until she is quiet. After a time* DIANA *releases her. But the child begins to sway again, gently.* DIANA *watches anxiously. At some point* DIANA *leaves the child and joins the singing.*]

"In the Midst:"

In the midst, in the thunder
Shattered land, crying to me

Crying to me, reaching for me
Empty babies, empty mother
In the dust, in the dust.

In the midst, near the fire
Deadened hope, deadened father.
Crying to me, reaching for me
Shriveled eyelids, wormy eyeballs
In the dust, in the dust.

In the midst, in the heartbeat
Shattered home, doesn't know me.
Doesn't know you, cannot reach you
Cannot call you, doesn't hear you
Doesn't hear, in the midst.

VOICE: Diana visits an old schoolmate in Chicago.

[DIANA *and* HELEN *converse.*]

HELEN: You've gotten thinner, Diana.

DIANA: And you're married.

HELEN: And about to give up my job at the university. We're expecting our first child.

DIANA: I don't know how you can live the way you do.

HELEN: I don't know what you mean, Diana. Diana, you're so haggard. What kind of hours do you keep? How do you spend your days?

DIANA: How do you spend your money? Are you supporting the war, Helen? Why are you supporting the war? Why are you supporting the System, Helen? Why are you keeping this System alive?

HELEN: We do what we can, Diana. We're not saints.

DIANA: No, you're not saints.

HELEN: You need a new dress, Diana.

DIANA: Do I?

[*The scene between* DIANA *and* HELEN *is repeated, with one change. The performers change roles. This is the only time such a change happens in the play.*]

[*Following is an alternate, longer version of the scene:*]

VOICE: Diana visits an old schoolmate in Chicago.

[DIANA *and* HELEN *converse.*]

HELEN: You've gotten thinner, Diana.

DIANA: And you've been married two years.

HELEN: An old married lady, and I love it. But what I haven't told you is that I'm about to give up my job at the university. We're expecting our first child.

DIANA: You intend to bring a child into this world?

HELEN: [*Laughs.*] What a way of putting it. Yes, I'm going to do the whole number, Diana. Faithful wife and homemaker, devoted mother.

DIANA: Wife and homemaker. And no job. Whose idea was it to give up your job?

HELEN: You're putting me on the defensive and I don't like it. I'm my own master, if that's what you're implying, but I'm not alone in this world. Diana, we have so little time together. Look, you haven't told me what you think of the apartment. I know it's a mess but I'm refinishing this early American jam cabinet for the study. We're going to put in wood paneling and expose the brick.

DIANA: I don't even know what language you're talking. Or rather I do know and it's getting more hateful by the second.

HELEN: Now stop it. I don't know what's come over you these last months. Look at you, Diana, you're so haggard, so tense, so unpleasant. What kind of hours do you keep? How do you spend your days?

DIANA: How do you spend your money? Are you supporting the war, Helen? Why are you supporting the war? Why are you supporting the System, Helen? Why are you keeping this System alive?

HELEN: We do what we can, Diana. We're not saints.

DIANA: No, you're not saints.

HELEN: You need a new dress, Diana.

DIANA: Do I?

[*Quite deliberately,* DIANA *removes her shirt and throws it on the floor. Parodying a Jerry Rubin Yippee, she stalks* HELEN, *snorting, and rips* HE-LEN'*s smock from her body.* HELEN *is astonished.*]

TOM'S THIRD SOLILOQUY: The goal: to stop bleeding the earth. Method: become unselfish, become clearheaded. Primary responsibility: to the cause, not to any loved one, not to [a] family, [b] wife, [c] child, [d] parent, [e] flag. Problem: to find a way to serve the cause of men and not be sidetracked, repeat — not be sidetracked. All causes must wither, repeat — all causes, in the serving of the primary cause. Admonition: we must be pure, we must burn ourselves into purity, we must starve ourselves into purity, and if need be, we must die ourselves into purity. We are nothing, the cause of men is everything. We are nothing, the cause of men is everything.

VOICE: Buddy acts against the Stock Exchange.

[BUDDY *stealthily moves along with a dynamite charge. He reaches his destination, fixes the charge, then starts to leave. In a little while a tremendous blast is heard.* BUDDY *drops to the ground, shaken, then rises, both frightened and elated.*]

BUDDY: Why, the mother went off too soon. But it's all right. It went off too soon but it's all right.. — I did it. — It's all right, it's very good. [BUDDY *flees.*]

VOICE: The cell debates Buddy's action. There are mixed feelings.

[*The cell meets. Its members are silent at the beginning, struggling with their own thoughts. At last:*]

PETE: The action was imprudent, it was irresponsible.

TOM: Not from where I sit.

EDIE: An act of sheer adventurism. Nice for the funny papers, nice maybe for Buddy's ego, but destructive in terms of building a movement.

PETE: Unilateral actions have no place in a collective.

CORA: I'm afraid I have to agree with that. Buddy's action seems to me essentially a dangerous stunt.

DIANA: What are we talking about? We're getting into such niceties. It's all dangerous, every hour we live, every action.

PETE: We have to calculate risks. We're not out to become martyrs. That's bullshit, that's bourgeois romanticism.

TOM: I disagree about unilateral actions. Any one of us has the right to decide anything for all of us.

EDIE: What did you say?

TOM: Any one of us has the right to decide anything for all of us.

PETE: But that's more bullshit. What gives him that right?

TOM: He gets that right by exercising it.

CORA: Is that how you plan to build a movement?

TOM: I'm not into adventurism any more than the rest of you. But there are times when collective action needs a prod to get it moving. That prod comes out of someone's commitment to an action.

DIANA: I'm for that. I'm interested in the movement of bodies, not in perpetual analysis.

EDIE: We're all interested in that, Diana. But if we start running around like a pack of little heroes, we're going to run right into the arms of the feds. The minute we start forgetting our goals, we're finished.

TOM: What are those goals?

EDIE: Come on. To build a movement, to change the power structure, to make the people responsible for their own lives. I don't have to spell it out.

PETE: A history lesson. Terror and violence are greedy animals. Their hunger never stops. The minute we begin to confuse the tactics for the goals at that moment we are —

BUDDY: [*Cries out.*] Stop! Stop! Stop! Stop! I can't wait for you! The world can't wait for you! People are hungry tonight! People are dying tonight We have to act act, act, act, act, act, act, act, act!

[*There is a stunned pause. Then:*]

PETE: As I was saying . . .

[BUDDY *and* CORA *are alone.* BUDDY *listens sullenly.*]

CORA: I don't understand you. — You take terrible chances. You don't use your head, you leave trails behind you, are you hoping to be caught, is that what you want? You take terrible chances. You don't eat properly, you don't dress warm, you take terrible chances. Why are you so sullen? Why are you so angry? Do you really want to be caught, is that what you want, to be punished? Do you want to bring everything crashing down? Does nothing gratify you? — I don't understand why you act the way you do. You'll alienate everyone. Is that what you're hoping for? Why are you so angry with me all the time! Sometimes I think you think I'm the enemy.

[BUDDY *lets out a howl of rage. He goes raging about. It's a concert of rage, with* BUDDY *modulating the sounds. The concert goes on for some time.* CORA *waits patiently.* BUDDY *decides to stop. He turns from* CORA, *his hands deep in his pockets, and stares at the ground.*]

CORA: You take terrible chances. You must be a little more patient. You take terrible chances.

VOICE: Diana recalls the past.

[*The* CHILD *begins swaying gently as* DIANA *remembers her past.*]

DIANA'S SECOND SOLILOQUY: I was a good girl. What does that mean? — Always minded, always finished what I started out to do, never quarreled with my parents, a gracious, friendly girl. Well, I did play practical jokes. But I went to the best schools. I'm so ashamed.

[DIANA *circles about the room. Returning to initial position:*]

In Bogota they asked me how I thought I could help the Indians. Some scorned me because I was with the Peace Corps. "Reformist," would spit the words at me, once Steve kissed me, touched my breast. He liked me, said he hadn't time to get involved, for that sort of thing. I believed him, I had no time for that either.

The Indians made me want to cry, and so I gave my clothes away and kept one dress. They were so poor, how could I flaunt my riches before them? How many coats, Tolstoy said, does a man need?

[DIANA *circles room. The* CHILD *has begun to sway more violently.*]

But it was a trap. I gave away my clothes, but how could that help the Indians of Colombia? Could that bring them land? No. Food? No. Hope! No. Warm clothes? No. Good jobs? No. Hope? No.. Food? No.

What I could bring them was an illusion. Incorrect. Could bring myself an illusion. What was that for? — Reforms made me feel better, I felt better, fuck how I felt. Keep them quiet, keep them quiet, keep them quiet, keep them quiet, keep them quiet.

[DIANA *circles. The swaying grows more violent.* DIANA *circles. The child sways.* DIANA *circles. The child sways in a frenzy.* DIANA *circles. The child sways in a frenzy.*][1]

VOICE: Buddy and the Mad Cheerleader do the dynamite dance.

[BUDDY *is musing idly when the* MAD CHEERLEADER *appears. The cheerleader begins to put on a cheerleading show in silence, just for* BUDDY. *Instead of a baton, the cheerleader employs sticks of dynamite.* BUDDY *seems to be mesmerized by the cheerleader's movements. All at once the movements are in slow motion and* BUDDY *pulls out his own dynamite and mirrors the motions.*]

VOICE: The Tenth Street Collective holds a session in self–criticism.

[*For a time no one speaks. Then:*]

---

[1] In our original production, the child was not present. Instead of circling, Diana kept hitting a pillow with a stick. The blows grew in violence.

TOM: Okay, I'll start. I'm trying to be honest with my self.

CORA: How do you see yourself?

TOM: Scared sometimes. Sometimes too cocky.

PETE: Too cocky all the time.

CORA: I see you as a chauvinist pig, Tom.

TOM: How's that?

CORA: For all your ideology, you still come on like such a fucking King Cock.

DIANA: Yes, I feel that.

TOM: I want what I want, right? What's the big deal? — I'm not into hypocrisy.

EDIE: Bullshit, you want what you want.

TOM: Do I lie? Do I play favorites? I use and I'm willing to be used. I'm straight.

EDIE: Use us like objects, that's what you do.

CORA: Tom, can't you see that? You're so full of macho.

PETE: The John Wayne of the Left.

TOM: You guys are freaking, I don't ask favors, I take.

DIANA: But we're not objects!

TOM: Everybody's what he makes himself.

CORA: [*Reaches over and cracks* TOM *across the face.*] Shape up, baby, shape up.

TOM: You touch me again and I'll blacken your eyes.

PETE: Shit man, admit you're playing the greaseball king.

TOM: Maybe so, but don't cry about it. You want better, you do something about it, you start a little action.

EDIE: I'm prepared to do something about it. As Cora says, shape up, Tom, or I'm going to start a little action.

[*Everyone is silent. A little later:*]

DIANA: I want to say something about myself. I'm trying to learn to be tougher. When I was at college, we were instructed to bring tea services to school with us, to be young ladies. I find that part of my life not altogether stamped out, coming out when I least expect it to. I work harder but I want to work harder. I want to think more clearly, not be sentimental but really harden myself for the revolution. And I know I'm selfish, I still want to be liked, admired, you know. I try to drive those things out of myself but it's not easy.

EDIE: Still making excuses for yourself, Diana.

PETE: Tea service, baby. Talking earnestly to the pigs at demonstrations. Like a society cunt doing social work!

DIANA: I told you I'm trying. I said I'm not perfect.

TOM: The revolution doesn't care what you are, Diana. You still have too much of a personal life.

CORA: Too conscious of yourself. Always am I this, am I that? Vietnamese women don't ask am I this, am I that?

DIANA: But isn't that what these sessions are for?

EDIE: Yes and no. To drive it out of you, that's what they're for, not to reinforce your own indulgence. You see yourself as a kind of Joan of Arc, don't you, Diana?

DIANA: Do I? No I don't. That's unfair, I don't see myself that way.

EDIE: Lady Bountiful pretending to be a street urchin to impress us all.

DIANA: No, I'm not like that.

TOM: Remembering that you can always go back home to daddy if things get too hot.

DIANA: No!

CORA: We can all go back home as far as that's concerned. Except Buddy, of course.

BUDDY: That's right.

EDIE: Afraid to give up the ego, Diana. Little toughy is too much of a lady. Your shit stinks like everybody else's.

DIANA: [*Quietly, tearfully.*] I never said it didn't.

VOICE: Hardening itself for the revolution, the Tenth Street Collective kills and eats a tomcat.

[*One performer plays the tomcat. The others pounce on and capture the furiously struggling tom. The cat is heard shrieking as it is throttled to death. It is then dropped to the ground. The members stand over it, then begin tearing at its flesh with their teeth. They tear compulsively, trying to overcome their revulsion, watching each other for signs of weakness.*]

VOICE: Warming up for the Days of Rage, planned for October 8th through 11th, 1969, the Collective invades a cemetery and smashes a series of tombstones.

[*The Collective begins racing around. Each cries out a series of dates, whirling a bludgeoning instrument. One performer makes the smashing sounds for all. The dates: "Born 1903, died 1947. Born 1878, died 1892. Born 1840, died 1881. Born 1943, died 1965. Born 1863, died 1941. Born 1896, died 1917. Born 1922, died 1967." Etc. After a time the voices run into each other, the movements are frantic. As if at an internal signal, everyone stops. Then they give each other quiet, congratulatory smiles.*]

VOICE: The Collective at home.

[*The members sit, move about, read, chew on things. All seem exhausted, irritable, nervous, suspicious of one another. The scene goes on in silence for several minutes. It is a brooding, unhappy scene.*]

VOICE: Fat America and Shrively Dick spend a wholesome afternoon watching the Redskins on TV.

[DICK *and* FAT AMERICA *peer, most often with glee, but sometimes with despair or anger at the TV screen. They make triumphant or despairing sounds, wave their team on or threaten the other team. They shout one phrase, "outta sight."' At one point they are so excited they begin climbing over each other, finding bizarre postures even as they continue peering at the game.*]

CORA'S SOLILOQUY: I was at Berkeley, then I was at Wisconsin. But it was the same, even in graduate school. Talk, more talk, intellectual bullshit, theories. It was draining me. It got so I couldn't stand the sound of my own voice. What was all the talk about? When I met Buddy, he was working in this factory. A blue–collar worker. He was the first person who made any sense to me. He worked, he planned, he had something on his mind.— He would come knock on my door at three in the morning. He'd been reading the nineteenth–century anarchists and he couldn't sleep. So I'd make tea or we'd walk in the street and shiver. Then at seven he'd go to. the factory. My parents? More talk from the liberal wing, couldn't you guess? Good people, mind you, but it was all in the head. The blacks were schvartzes, money and property were scared. Well–intentioned, but how were those intentions going to make the world better? Am I, Cora, going to make the world better? At least I'm putting my body on the line.

VOICE: The Days of Rage. The Collective expects thousands to join them on the streets of Chicago. But a handful turn up. The Collective has badly miscalculated.

[*The Collective appears in helmets and jackets. From paper bags they take out clubs and chains. Now the police also appear.*]

VOICE: The date is October eighth, the second anniversary of the death of Che Guevara. The Collective moves from Lincoln Park into the streets. And the police wait for them.

[*The battle begins. The two forces move in on each other. At first the police are astonished by the ferocity of the militants, and particularly by the ferocity of their women. Then the police are overrun, beaten back. A policeman is hurt. Suddenly* DIANA *runs to help him.* TOM *sees the action, violently pulls* DIANA *away. The police begin to take control, knock down members of the Collective, beginning to pull them off. But it's no easy job. The Collective fights back fiercely, some of its people break away, run off, then return to resume the fight. The battle should go on soundlessly for some time and should end with some members of the Collective arrested and others scattered. The battle resumes again. This time the collective is no match for the police. The members are beaten, dragged about.*]

[*A third battle is fought, this time between the women and the police. The women wade into the police but are quickly disarmed. Several are arrested, others are simply disarmed, a few go off in tears.*]

[DIANA *rushes to* HELEN's *apartment.*]

DIANA: I've got to get out of Chicago.

HELEN: Are you hurt, Diana?

DIANA: The pigs are arresting everyone they can find. It's not safe here. Can you drive me to the airport? Me and a friend?

HELEN: No, I don't want to do that, Diana. But have they hurt you?

DIANA: [*Coldly.*] Thank you. I'm sorry I wasted your time.

HELEN: Diana, I'd like to help you, but I don't feel right about what you're doing. I don't want to be an accessory to something I don't understand or feel comfortable about.

DIANA: What do you know about it with your whiteskin privilege? When's your baby due? [*But* DIANA *leaves before* HELEN *can reply.*]

BUDDY'S FIRST SOLILOQUY: I left my wife and kid three years ago. I left my job, hotshot salesman. I started to read, started thinking. The examined life? I started to question. After a time I had no money. I slept where I could. But I was thinking too much without working. I figured factory work would be good for me, straighten me out. It did. I started wearing less clothing, I wanted to harden myself. I figured being cold

would be good for me. It was. I wanted to learn how to be useful. I figured God didn't put me on earth to be a fat cat. I became a better person. I gave up meat. I gave up eating my fellows.

VOICE: Buddy's arrest. The Collective goes underground.

[*A multiple scene.* MEMBERS OF THE COLLECTIVE *are intently destroying
documents from their files. In another area, several are singing "The Fire
Song." In still another area,* BUDDY *is off on another bombing mission. He
moves along the street with a duffel bag. But there are F.B.I. men trailing
him. The men follow him discreetly.* BUDDY *is a little worried, senses that
something may be wrong but sees nothing out of the way. The scene of the
men trailing* BUDDY *takes on a slow–motion, dreamlike sense, but is broken
as* BUDDY *suddenly realizes that he is being followed. As* BUDDY *speeds up
his movements, the* F.B.I. *men move in and grab him. The capture takes
place as 'The Fire Song" reaches its climax.*]

"The Fire Song"

    The fire will make us new
    The fire will make us one
    The fire is never asking, is always telling.
    We become each other
    Fire smiles on each of us
    Smiles through our clothing
    Smiles through our daydreams.
    Once you call the fire, the fire calls you.
    Once you call the fire, the fire calls you.
    Once you call the fire, the fire calls you.

[*The collective settles down to sleep for the night. But* DIANA *can't sleep. She
rises, moves restlessly about.*]

TOM: [*Looking up.*] Settle down, Diana.

DIANA: I can't sleep.

TOM: Then make less noise, how about it?

[TOM *goes back to sleep but* DIANA *remains awake.* CORA *wakes. The two
talk softly.*]

CORA: What is it, Diana?

DIANA: Nothing. Can't sleep.

CORA: What's bothering you?

DIANA: I'm too awake. Something in me . . . is too awake. I'm too awake. My
brain is too awake.

CORA: We've all had a rough time.

DIANA: How's it going to end?

CORA: End? We just go on. How can you ask?

DIANA: My sister was married yesterday.

CORA: But why didn't you go to the ceremony?

DIANA: Because those things are from the old world. You know that.

CORA: But you're sorry you didn't go?

DIANA: Yes, I'm sorry. — And Buddy's in prison.

CORA: Yes.

DIANA: How can you stand it? [*No answer.*] And I don't love Tom anymore. People confuse me these days, people confuse things. My family makes me cry, when I think of my poor father . . . I called my mother after Chicago, after Daddy came with the bail money, and she said, "Diana, you're killing us all." What a quaint, absurd, heartbreaking Victorian phrase, "Diana, you're killing us all." And I could only say, "It's the only way, Mummy." Cora, what will become of us? How can you ask, Diana, how can you ask?

CORA: How can you ask?

DIANA: I love you, Cora.

CORA: I love you, Diana.

VOICE: The Tenth Street Collective, working with dynamite and clocks, makes a time bomb.

[*The collective is working with dynamite and clocks, making time bombs. The action should take on a ritual quality, though not consciously. The* CHILD *appears, watches, begins swaying slowly. At the same time,* BUDDY *speaks from his prison.*]

BUDDY'S LAST SOLILOQUY: These are my scars. You're grown up, ain't you? You gave us a rough time. Goal to see one another. The true revolutionary, Gandhi marches. The true revolutionary, Che marches. The true revolutionary acts through love. The times are hard. These are my scars. You're grown up, ain't you? (1) The system changes us. Or (2) We change the system. Goal: to see one another. Trap: to kill is to become the enemy. Gandhi marches, the times are hard. Che marches, the times are hard. The times are hard, the times demand our courage. The times are hard, the times demand our courage. The true revolutionary. Acts of love. The true revolutionary. Acts of love. The true revolutionary. Acts of love.

[*All at once there is a monstrous explosion. A terrible tremor sets in among the* MEMBERS OF THE COLLECTIVE *making the bombs. One by one they fall to the ground. Only the Child remains on her feet. She stops swaying abruptly, goes to* DIANA *sprawled on the ground and cradles the dead girl in her arms.*]

The following are entries from the playwright's notebook during the writing of *The Spring Offensive* and from the log kept during the rehearsal period. During early rehearsals, when the ensemble was larger, many of the roles were double–cast.

❖❖❖

FROM NOTEBOOK

January 5, 1973

How counter Tom's violent rhetoric? Put it in larger perspective?

Play needs a Berrigan–type, nonviolence section. Also, what about a fantasy scene in which the Collective and the Cops (who throw down their arms) are transferred into Brothers? Perhaps this is Buddy's fantasy. Involves audience? Buddy's dream: Collective performers who play Cops rise at end and put on their "Cop" outfits. Others rise and take up weapons. Confrontation. Collective flings weapons away. Cops are stunned, fling weapons away.

January 10

How much sense of nonviolence belongs in the work? My sense of it, it should hover. But people caught up in an action, in a condition, e.g., Diana, see primarily that action. Other possibilities simply do not feel viable. Ideology which may begin from feeling then replaces feeling.

February 13

Near end, Diana is just worn out. In some event (confrontation?) she discovers the person (perhaps her father? during a quarrel where she's been berating him) he becomes a *person* again, but he's still the exploiter, she sees that. She can't reconcile her feelings.

Later in February

Rewrite Buddy's dream. He *lifts* them all to their feet? Buddy at end.

Counterpoint to the death of the others. He must *emerge* — *out* of them? in spite of them? He should emerge as a consciousness emerges. Flowers? He must also strip away — *what* must he strip away?

FROM LOG

February 12

Laura has qualms about the group being identified with radical position of the characters. My belief and Nancy's is that that needn't and shouldn't happen. I don't want the play to be about tactics but about commitment. Both Nancy and Maurice feel we have to explore the psychology of violence and the frustration people feel within this system.

February 14

Commune. Each builds up a space that becomes his world. Later, build a commune based on having that world to return to. Qualities: love, suspicion.

February 26

Duncan (Dick) — speaks of rapping people on knuckles, of power. "I like guards, uniforms, metal on my car. I make the decisions as to what's on the other side of the fence. I pick who gets to look at me. I have telephones and buttons but I don't have to answer . . . "

Converse (Diana) — "I want a lot of pain. For every moment of release I pay a lot of dues. I don't want to pay. I don't like paying for anything. I don't like being so serious. Angry, angry. Only way I can have fun is through anger."

Allison (Diana) — photo of self as smallest sister (in overalls) with older sisters. She made the caption, "The little workers," outside child's–house replica of their big house in Scarsdale. Describes black maids: no light in Lizzie's house.

Francene (Cora) — last night's dream, in rice paddy with children, bombings, assigned to lead them away, had to carry all the weapons on her back. Then describes hot summer day at Wall St. rally when the hard hats dropped down beer cans and rocks. "Cops hitting us and I was screaming. No one knew what was going on." Would like to blow up a fucking building.

Maurice — talks of being grounded, of having courage. Feels he has a selfhood. Yet "what would I have done" during Nazi regime if they had taken over the Jewish ghetto that was the Bronx.

March 7

Shrivelly Dick—first scene. Nancy suggests minister face mask for Duncan and congregation masks for victims. We explore methods of killing, decide to create a death toy.

March 11

We begin to work on the "outta sight time" scenes between the two couples. Maggie questions the lack of moments when the women are equals or giving commands.

Improv. in which the women are in command, the men ordered to make love. Rob balks, feels it's not in Tom's character to take orders. But works on scene. First try, Tom won't hear of it. Second, Rob changes it so that he acquiesces but with no sense of defeat.

D. and catatonic child [later changed to autistic child], Allison works with Wendy. Wendy concentrates on her feet, head bowed. Allison tries to "greet" her with her own feet. How aware should cat/child be?

March 17

Reading Marguerite Séchehaye's *Autobiography of a Schizophrenic Girl.* Things have their existence. But we don't see them in their existence, only in what we make of them. To see them as themselves is terrifying, is to cut us off from ourselves.

March 18

We work on militants vs. cops, and the dynamite theft. On the latter, Andy instructs in the use of karate. We discuss whether the cell would attack night watchman without weapons or with a lead pipe.

Calvin works with catatonic child and Diana. Wendy takes child inward, Nancy (also playing the child before we eliminate double–casting) takes her movements outward. Calvin says what I have told them, that the child to Diana represents the great suffering that our fucked–up civilization has inflicted on people. Converse in tears.

March 19

Much work on cops–militants. Work on going limp.

March 25

Consciousness–raising session. Improvs., giving impulses, first in circles, then straight arrow line. Last improv. as if everyone is behind cell bars, side by side, energy going out from sides.

Tomcat scene. We decide it's their pet cat, makes it worse. Diana is to throttle him.

April 1

Calvin helpful to Tony in Buddy's concert of rage. Uses image of breaking from womb.

April 9

Collective at home quiet, small. Each one works out a personal, repetitive gesture. Gestures comes from true emotional relationship.

April 13

Explosion at end should use some breakage of something visible throughout show?

April 15

Allison does inside–outside in preparation for her Bogotá scene [as Diana], recalling her experiences in India as a teacher working with Hindu children. Nancy feels the key line in Bogotá speech is "I'm so ashamed." Allison uses her own memories as privileged, upper–middle–class American working with poverty–stricken people to get to that sense of shame. She is really crying through improv. Bogotá speech which has tapped something in her.

❧

14. THE LIVING THEATRE

Comments on

The Mother's Day Play,
one of the projected 150–play plays in
The Legacy of Cain

Having watched the development of the Living Theatre from its early
Connection *days to the time when it moved away not only from prepared
scripts and from interiors of theatres but to a joining of forces with the spectator in the making of the work, I thought it most important to present their
latest effort in some feasible form in this book. Therefore, the report on why
and how* The Mother's Day Play *happened.*

The Report on The Mother's Day Play *is in the nature of an interview with Steve Ben Israel of the Living Theatre that I taped in December
1971 for WBAI–FM, New York.*

Julian Beck and Judith Malina in San Paolo

SAINER: The troupe in Brazil had started a new, what they call 150–play play, called *The Legacy of Cain*. They were able to perform several parts of it on several occasions and nothing since then because of the arrest of the company on drug charges. Steve, do you want to talk about *The Mother's Day Play* and say what it is?

ISRAEL: Maybe just a little background about the concept of *The Legacy of Cain*. It's a concept of 150 plays that deal with as many situations as we can think of, all done in the street, all based on dealing specifically with money, property, death, love, state, and war and using those particular six things to create our plays. One of the experiments that we tried is in some way [to] work with present educational systems. In one junior high school in Brazil we began teaching a new type of physical education class without the feeling of musical chairs all our educational systems are based on ... It's all very highly competitive like musical chairs. But we tried to do pieces with these children that would rouse the same excitement as competitive games and energy, but would create a new feeling of game structure within them that could add some credibility and some value to their bodies and lives.

SAINER: Were these grammar school or high school kids?

ISRAEL: Well, actually both.

SAINER: You actually did games.

ISRAEL: Yes. It was like an hour–and–a–half physical trip that was created for students, 150 students at a time, to participate in their regular physical thing. Like many people's regular physical thing is very Marine Corps oriented throughout the educational system, and this was an experiment to teach them some techniques that we had developed over the years and then hopefully create a piece with them. And this was the objective, to teach them first some sort of language of sound and movement and breathing and getting into body, and then they would have some idea about how to use this in the play. And the play that we did was oddly enough *Mother's Day Play*.

SAINER: Steve, could I ask you about the exercises and could you describe one sound–and–movement exercise?

ISRAEL: These exercises were the traditional exercises that people have been experiencing over the last ten years in the radical theatre, and we taught them a great deal of breathing because ... we always have said, in Heaven they teach you to breathe. So we had to teach them to breathe and then to start to look at their bodies as something that was theirs. Like there was a piece in *Paradise Now* called "Flying," where we flew people, and it was like a heavy trust exercise and trust these days is like a needle in a haystack. So, for the children it was very very good to do this flying piece to just explore their sound and their movement anyway possible and to be encouraged.

SAINER: And that really involves trust because you're coming down head first from a height of several feet into either the arms of humanity, or else you are going to be on your face, and you've got to know that there are people there if you are going to do the jump and they've got to know they're there waiting.

ISRAEL: Yes. All these exercises had specific objectives which in a way now present themselves as a form of language. There were these exercises that Grotowski or Joe Chaikin or people involved in this type of theatre created as a language for theatre.

SAINER: And your language was being created with the fellow human being.

ISRAEL: The thing is when the Living Theatre felt it had become an institution and when it dropped out, it said that we would like now to begin to work specifically with children, with students, with very poor people and people who work in factories. We said it wasn't so important to do a piece for them but to do something with them. This would be the important thing — that it wouldn't be "Hello, goodbye." It wouldn't be a theatre just showing up, presenting a piece, and leaving everybody saying, "What's that?" But to actually create a piece with these four different groups of people.

SAINER: So that even if you go on, it is conceivable that you take the piece but they also take the piece.

ISRAEL: They have the piece with them and the experience of creating the piece. The real important thing is that, there, we are a group of artists from North America going working with just regular people in South America, and the experience for us is very vital because you arrive in someone else's community and you find out what the needs and what the problems are there, and those are the real issues. And then you try to create a language, a common language with what the needs and the problems are, and then you create a play and the play is done with the people and for the people.

SAINER: This is curious because it's not your country, you're a visitor and to an extent the observer, and I wonder how you can create a piece. You say you create it with the community, but in a sense you go there to create it for and with them. I wonder how much you can get into being the one who needs the play as coming from the outside. It's hard.

ISRAEL: Well, the thing is what's in it for us and we say, well, the first objective there is to learn. You know, modern art is here in the twentieth century, people here in New York or everywhere are choking on their hipness. People have had so much experience, such radical experience these last five to ten years that we are at a point now where people are saying, 'What is the next step in communication?" I think we took it upon ourselves to say that there was no next step. We had to go to zero, and begin learning again something new that would make credible what they say when they say, looking for new forms of struggle and going to zero and going to work with a group of people in places that you really don't know too much about, and because of their learning they present a whole other reality. So. the thing was to go there and to find out what we all felt together specifically. And we said we are just some people who are a theatre group, and we have these exercises that I think if we threw them together will help us create a language.

SAINER: And they really didn't know who you were other than you were foreigners.

ISRAEL: They didn't know who we were really.

SAINER: No preconceptions.

ISRAEL: No, and so you create this language together, and all of a sudden, say, well, maybe we could do a piece together, and you do a piece together and it becomes very ritualistic.

SAINER: But the process of making the piece—

ISRAEL: The process of making the piece and the piece itself is very, very fine.

SAINER: Steve, how much did the Living Theatre know in terms of the structure if not the content of the piece before they arrived? In other words, how much planning, how much foreknowledge?

ISRAEL: Well, at the point now where we're just creating this concept, *The Legacy of Cain*, which has 150 pieces, one piece could be a ten–minute piece that gets done [right] there or an hour piece that gets done somewhere else in the same town over a period of weeks, say. At this point where we're just developing the plays—we've just started on the first dozen and we're trying to work up to 150 — now we don't have the plays. See, eventually when we create these plays with the help of these different groups of people we're working with now, then those plays will be sort of a repertory, but now we're in the process of creating them and the five or six we may have.

SAINER: Are you saying that the structure of the piece, the direction as well as the content, which would be the development... is also coming out of being in the specific place and getting the impetus from whatever you perceive at that place as opposed to, let us say, for the next six months planning the next 14 plays and then going wherever it is you eventually go to... Are you saying that more of the piece is developed in the place without a lot of planning?

ISRAEL: For example, in the town of Rio Claro in the state of Sao Paulo in southern Brazil we were invited to do a play. So we went to the university and got about fifty students, and we said we are going to do a play in the public square next Sunday. That's six days from now and we want to do a play that's credible to our lives. Now, of course, we are dealing with the Brazilian reality of saying something real. And we got together and we said we want to do plays that specifically talk about this, how do you feel about that, what would you like to add to it, do you think this is important, and so on and so forth. Then you begin and you do a day of exercises that opens everybody up. What the exercises are for, they get us opened up so that our imaginations can rise up a bit.

SAINER: Do you think there is a relationship between the body and the imagination? You free the body and something else happens.

ISRAEL: Yes. [You] get a certain type of dynamic flow.

SAINER: So that was the beginning.

ISRAEL: Yes. Because we wanted the pieces to be physical, the pieces to have a very specific emotion, a very specific feeling. As has been said, it is the quality of the emotion that counts... so the exercise serves as a language, and then you begin to see what each one learned in the exercise about what he wants to say. He says I've learned something in this exercise that I find absent from everyday life in its feeling. So part of the play is saying we want to have this feeling that we all discovered together in concrete forms... and at the same time we have certain information we want to talk about. There are certain things that we would like to reveal to the people or certain things that maybe the people could help reveal to us. Maybe the end of the piece could be a piece where the people themselves are going to reveal something to us. And if we can create that piece, they will have a chance to make a decision about it and they will. In this case they did.

SAINER: Do you want to describe the actual play now?

ISRAEL: *The Mother's Day Play* got done in a junior high school with 150 students. We said, why don't you write down some dreams, what are your dreams about mother? The kids came in with 150 dreams. We edited them down to ten dreams and called it *Ten Dreams about Mother*. We rehearsed it with the students for about ten days; we taught them the exercises, we had a language, we did certain games, and the kids realized this was going to be fun and they began to feel a sense of satisfaction from it. They began to like what they were doing. We used the ten dreams about mother to find, in terms of our study, what the relationship [is] between child and mother in this society. Is the relationship a creative, positive one or is it a destructive one?

SAINER: It probably varies from each case.

ISRAEL: Yes. According to the ten dreams, it became clear that the relationship between the mother and the child was very destructive.

SAINER: Even in Brazil?

ISRAEL: Yes. It was all very Pavlovian. It was all based on master–slave and full of punishment. So we wanted to do a play about that, that would give the mother a perception that this is more than a child. This is a growing thing that needs to be dealt with very sensitively if we don't want to create more slaves. But we kept holding it very dreamlike because it was about their dreams... We mounted ten different dreams with the children.

SAINER: The actual narratives of the dreams.

ISRAEL: Yes. We had the narrative and the dreams acted out by the children and we were acting with them, and it all ended up with every kid in the room flying. We had the kids flying, attached with crepe paper to his mother.

SAINER: His actual mother.

ISRAEL: Yes, because we had the parents there, and these parents had never seen theatre before. They were about ninety–nine percent black people and they were all factory workers and their wives. They were making nine dollars a week, and they came in there and we looked at them and they were in a state of shock even before it started. They couldn't imagine what was going to happen in this room. It got very physical and loud and went through drummings, which they relate to, and went through all kinds of physical movements made by their children and a voyage throughout the room by their children created for their parents.

SAINER: The parents came in just for the performance?

ISRAEL: Yes. When the play was over we didn't all go home. We hung out there. Mothers, the children, and us, and we talked.

SAINER: What kind of response did you get from the parents?

ISRAEL: It was one of amazement. It was very warm. You create a play, you create a means of communication, does anybody get it? Does a point come across where it's understood by the body and stored there for immediate or future action? You hope you can get this feeling across when you can begin to get a different lever going in our brains to help us think or to change our thinking. The play was done, it was a very good feeling. Here's the thing: we are doing a play about very important, serious things that we are all living with here in the twentieth century, and at the same time in Brazil you are not allowed to breathe. The language of our play, what we created in the play and the way the play was done, was hopefully an attempt to try and say something relevant or to do something relevant without being dragged off to the dungeons. It was an expression of trying to say something profound and important with groups of people and have something get across.

SAINER: And in a sense trying to free parent–child–humanity from their own dungeon.

ISRAEL: Well, that's one of the many things we hope to say. The thing we are involved in is [that] we are looking very carefully at the relationships that keep this game of musical chairs going in our society, and how can we communicate about these relationships? How can these relationships change? Because that's the important thing that has to happen among people.

15. THE SAN FRANCISCO MIME TROUPE

Los Siete (BART) *offers a striking view of the Mime Troupe mixing hardnosed politics and theatrical humor. The work has a driving quality that is typical of the troupe. Its comic buoyancy captures that quality of exhortation which is not necessarily directed from the performer to the spectator in the street or park but rather seems to fill the air, vibrating between them and infecting everyone involved in the event.*

The genre of Los Siete (BART) *is a cranky or paper movie. The pictures that appear are cranked into view on a roll of paper, a device also common to the work of the Bread & Puppets.*

Joan Holden's comments, following the script, offer a sense of the current political realities as the Mime Troupe sees them in terms of its art.

❖❖❖

LOS SIETE (BART) • Script by Steve Friedman • Pictures by Dan Chumley and Rebecca Schiffren.

(Copyright, 1970, San Francisco Mime Troupe)

CHARACTERS

COMMUTER
BART (Bay Area Rapid Transit System)
Time: 1975

C:Boy, oh boy! I can hardly wait—my first subway ride! Just think—BART! It's finally here! Gosh, just like New York. Would ya believe it? Oops—here it comes! God, it's really big!

(Note: Bay Area Rapid Transit System, under construction since 1960.)

B: Hi there—my name is BART. I'm here to serve you. Where would you like to go?

C: To the Mission District — Twenty–fourth Street.

(Note: the working–class side of San Francisco, now largely Latino.)

B: Welcome aboard. As we proceed, you are invited to enjoy the educational murals which line the walls of my tunnel. And I, BART, will attempt to add to your enjoyment by a running commentary on the points of interest. I am also programmed to answer any simple questions you may have. Is that clear?

C: Huh? Yeah, sure... This is really out of sight.

B: Relax, my friend. And always remember, BART is only the beginning. [*Starts cranky.*] What we see at the outset of the Mural of Progress is the San Francisco of yesteryear —

charming, fascinating, the financial capital of the West Coast, but somehow still provincial, low profile. Oh, it has its towers of commerce, but it lacks executive living quarters for the young movers and shakers of high finance. They're forced to live in faraway suburbs, and so eventually their businesses move there too and the inner city decays.

A tragic situation but with the coming of me, BART, new high–rise luxury apartments — the Dolores Towers, the Bernal Arms, the hanging gardens of Guerraro — sprout like magic castles in districts where nobody worth mentioning had lived for years. Like sequoias from garbage heaps, the new Manhattan rises from the slums.

C: Boy, that's progress all right. I live in one of those places, too — forty–second floor of the Valencia Vista View. This sure is a nice city. And I like my job, too. It's . . .

B: Simple questions only! All this was not achieved without sacrifice and struggle. There were those who attempted to halt San Francisco's progress, out of base and antisocial motives.

C: Eek! What are those ugly things?

(Note: Missing picture)

B: Those, dear patron, are the former inhabitants of the Mission District. They were known as Latinos. Please do not misunderstand. Your BART system has absolutely nothing against persons of the Hispano–American persuasion. As you may know, we employ more than our quota of them in responsible positions.

C: Oh, he looks nice.

B: They are a perfectly nice people. But as the executive director of our

Urban Redevelopment Agency, M. Justin Herman, once remarked, "They simply can't afford to live in San Francisco."

C: I can understand that — my place isn't so cheap either. Why do you know what —

B: What did I just say?

C: Simple questions only.

B: Now, living where you can't afford to live creates many dangerous anxieties and illusions and often leads to violence in the streets.

C: I'm against that.

B: Of course you are. And where you live, there isn't any. But once upon a time there was violence in the Mission District — and the ringleaders of it were the

notorious Los Siete de la Raza.

C: I never heard of it.

B: Of course not. You can thank responsible journalism for that.

C: Was it something like the Mafia?

B: The what?

C: The Mafia?

B: There is no Mafia in San Francisco. The only organized crime in San Francisco is the Breakfast for Children program. No — the Los Siete gang was a bunch of *community organizers* — or, as our colorful Mayor Alioto so colorfully put it — *punks*. This is the story of seven punks in the Mission District and how they stood in the way of progress.

C: You mean they didn't want BART?

B: First things first! These seven Latin hippy types made a lot of noise in the Mission District once upon a time. Seems they didn't think much of our schools.

So what did they do? Set up their own so–called college readiness program. Well, you can imagine what that led to!

C: Latins going to college?

B: Exactly — a senseless, cowardly attack on the American system of higher education.

C: But isn't everyone supposed to go to college?

B: Of course not, stupid. If everyone went to college, who'd pacify Cambodia? Why do you think we have a tracking system?

C: A what?

B: *A tracking system,*

my dense friend. For example: by the time you were ten years old, you were already college material. By the time those people in the Mission were ten, they could hardly speak English. That's the way it is.

C: But it's not their fault!

B: Well, it's certainly not *my* fault! Is it your fault??

C: No...I guess not...

B: Say it loud! It's not my fault!

C: It's — it's not my fault!

B: That's the American way. And now back to our story. Now, college readiness was not all the notorious Los Siete gang was guilty of. They were also spreading propaganda against the city, against progress, against ME!

C: Against YOU? But why?

B: They spread the malicious rumor that the city government was merely waiting till I was installed before they hiked the property taxes sky high and forced the Latin people out of the Mission District. And they dared to suggest that the Latin people should organize themselves not to let that happen.

C: But isn't that — wasn't that...

B: Isn't that wasn't that *what*?

C: Sort of the way things actually happened.

B: All except for the organizing

part, my friend because we stopped them in time!

C: Oh — that's good. How did you stop them?

B: Oh my warmhearted passenger, if you have tears, prepare to shed them now. Imagine, if you will, two selfless, dedicated, sincere and muscular officers of the law. Two men who heard themselves called pigs, and did not flinch, but merely smiled and toyed with the rubber hoses in their pockets.

C: I can really imagine them.

B: Their assignment: "Follow Los Siete. But above all, go in disguise:

don't let them know you are policemen." For naturally, they are cop–haters.

C: Naturally.

B: And then, one terrible day, they became cop–*killers* too.

C: Oh, my GOD!

B: Yes. The two officers, firm in the line of duty, saw the sinister Los Siete actually carrying a TV set.

C: Oh, my GOD!

B: The officers naturally approached the surly youths for questioning. Let us not dwell on the lurid details. Suffice it to say that in the ensuing scuffle

one of those brave, physically beautiful officers was shot in the heart with his partner's gun.

C: Accidentally shot by his partner! That is tragic,.

B: Let me make one thing perfectly clear. The officer was shot, with his partner's gun, by Los Siete.

C: Which one of 'em did it?

B: All of 'em. We don't know how exactly, but we're working on it. I shudder to think what they would've done if they'd known he was a police officer.

C: You mean they thought he was just a —

B: Just a guy with a rubber hose and a bulge in his jacket, after their TV set. And they wanted to go to college.

C: What happened to them?

B: Oh, they got away at first; but your police department reacted swiftly, and in due time we got six of them.

But our story does not end here. As you know, I am the first BART train to enter the Mission District, and today you will be privileged to witness a special opening ceremony.

C: A ceremony?

B: The Los Siete and their families, and the twenty–nine Latinos who still live in the Mission District, will be standing in the station as I arrive.

C: In the station?

B: On the tracks!

C: I don't want to see that!

B: Then close your eyes, you mashed potato!

C: But I'll feel it!

B: Too bad. How do you think you got your job, and your new high–rise luxury apartment?

C: But I hate my job — and my apartment — it looks like a vacuum cleaner. And so do you!

B: We are approaching the station — do you hear the people cheering?

C: They're not cheering, they're screaming! Let me out!

B: Too late! Life is short, BART is long!

This is now the Daly City Express. You'll enjoy the new Daly City — it is now one building, seventeen stories high! It also forms the northern border of the city of Los Angeles.

C: Why didn't somebody fight it?

B: Los Siete fought — but *you* wanted security. And now you've got security, courtesy of the Total State. Welcome to Daly City — end of the line.

*Joan Holden of the San Francisco Mime Troupe described the circumstances
surrounding Los Siete (BART):*

Los Siete de la Raza were seven Latinos charged with shooting a San
Francisco policeman in 1969. The policeman's partner was the one with the
gun, but the local press convicted the seven [with headlines like COP
KILLERS FLEE) before they were even arrested. We decided to do a skit
about it. In the past we would have trusted to our imaginations, but at that
time we had just produced a women's liberation play that the women's
movement told us was sexist; we knew we could do a Los Siete play that
Latins would find racist. Our writer went to talk to Los Siete's defense or-
ganization, who thought we might be able to explain the case to white people. They told him how two of the accused had been organizing against
BART, the rapid transit system under construction. This gave him the idea
for the piece: BART tells the story to a commuter in nineteen seventy–five.
BART tells his version; the truth appears on the cranky [or paper movie, as
the Bread & Puppet Theater calls it — we borrowed the form from them).

We did the play in the parks several times a week the whole summer of
1970, while the trial was going on, and thousands of people saw it who otherwise would have known only the daily press version of the case. This
modified the tone of the press as Los Siete's lawyers ground up the prose-
cution. But the popular movement that filled the courtroom every day and
turned out thousands at rallies owed nothing to the press. It was built by
the handbill–passing, postermaking, broadsheet–printing, buttonholing,
speechmaking, rally–holding, and people serving (a breakfast–for–children
program, a health clinic that is still going strong) carried on by the defense
committee. Their appreciation of our efforts meant more to us than any
volume of applause: it proved that our art could be of use. We were on tour,
about to perform the piece for a community audience at the Young Lords'
Church in Chicago, when we got the news that Los Siete had been acquit-
ted.

Since then, we have done two more plays about trials, one about an urban renewal battle, and others of more general use, but none out of only
our own heads. Why imagine what people in a given situation might be
thinking or feeling? If you talk to them they'll tell you. Why ask people to
come see plays about imaginary problems? People will come ask you to do
plays about problems that are real.

ADDENDUM TO PARTS ONE AND TWO

Geraldine Lust has always seemed to me one of the most significant figures in contemporary experimental theatre. Below are some of her workshop notes, and also her script for The Celebration of Death, *a theatre piece. The notes are designed for exercises and improvisations, some of which were used in her Open Theatre Workshop in 1963. The italicized sections following numbered lines are explanatory notes which I recently recorded during an interview with Geraldine.*

PSYCHOLOGICAL TECHNIQUES. 1 Do some improvisation with MASKS on and with MASKS off. *Masks refer to the faces we present to different aspects of the world.*

2. Emotions related to space. *The human being in his area. In different spatial areas, the human being has varied feelings. The recognition of these feelings can release the actor as a person.*

3. A serenity rite. *E.g., a tea ceremony.*

4. Paying attention — in order to understand someone, a price must be paid. *The most frequent activity in theatre is looking. Another is listening. Through these, more of the life of the actor is conveyed than through anything else. That is, the actor as opposed to the role he plays. In the act of looking and listening, he gives up something in order to get something. He pays attention, reveals himself in order to gain something. The same is true of the spectator.*

5. Create a loved one, project a short period of relationship, face absolute loss of the loved one (other than death).

6. Become someone else (some real person who is in the class).

SPECIAL TECHNIQUES, 1962–63 Sob and sing. *Transform sob sound into that of singing. Show the actor how expansive his voice production can be, and that he can control it.*

2. Language in space (hieroglyph), must move or direct thought, not accompany it. (See Artaud.) *Movement should not accompany the thought but should be the thought.*

3. Magic (ritual) passes through and comes out in shape of a relationship. *Mystical aspect of the ritual is such that neither the performer nor the spectator can know where the ritual action will lead them. Ritual requires a serious commitment, of the performer and the spectator.*

[MORE] TECHNIQUES, 1962–63 1. Relating to awareness of animal–persona (or pre–verbal life).

 a. Listen to oneself sing.

 b. Then listen to oneself breathe, etc.

 c. Perform simple action, then multiple action, then improvisation with words, as blind, then as deaf, then as armless, etc.

 d. All–fours exercise, with thumbs tucked away and completely out of use.

 e. Co–conscious improvisations where all in group think a given sequence. *One theory is that before men were individuated, had individual consciousness, they were all co–conscious beings, "thought" collectively. This exercise begins with that premise of collectivity.*

2. Catastrophe happens to your whole community; you are seriously injured (choose a way); you are lost and because of catastrophe's alteration of your environment plus your injury, you cannot "place" yourself. Of those around you or whom you encounter, you can recognize only ONE.

3. Tea ceremony—to be performed authentically and then subtly extended, altered, etc., by me in process with actors until we begin to get to a shape of it that lends itself to Occidental symbols.

4. Zen breathing and Zen chants to do for purpose of exploring "magic," mesmerization.

5. Be on the floor as if on the ceiling.

6. Going in and out of Chaikin's "circle"—–with dread, with awe, with fear. Exercise to separate these emotions about which we are so defensive in our time as to be confused, and unclear what we are feeling. Outside circle means you don't belong.

The following theatre piece was composed by Geraldine Lust in 1963 as part of a series of Monday night events to be produced at the Living Theatre. Though it was not performed, it stands out markedly as a precursor to much of the experimental work that was to develop in the next few years.

✧✧✧

THE CELEBRATION OF DEATH,
 an annual ceremonial, one of several
 to make up the Ritual Theatre series
 by Geraldine Lust

AUDIENCE: sits as little–clothed as possible, with no possessions on or around them; they are "led" by placed actors.

THEY are the WITNESS of what transpires. In this sense the performance is never the same and is a true happening.

THEY must be transformed by the ritual — they must be changed when it is over (with respect to their clothing, etc.) — this is accomplished by techniques suggested below.

THEY participate chiefly through verbal responses, but also by a limited number of rites such as handing a small object from member to member until it will have traveled through the entire audience.

ACTORS and OBJECTS: Decor is of the simple, though exotic, mode which is necessary to ritual.

THESE are used as symbols, more than as living performers, so that when the death occurs on stage it can be believed more strongly for this will be the death of an object, not a human. This choice has been made because human or animal death when "acted" does not ever leave an audience really believing that a death occurred. However, if my object is created in such a way that its uncreation works, this can be truthfully believed.

The principal object would be composed of both light and sound.

RITE: Stated maximally, the intention is to explore what death may be for humans. We do not know. We know only that our ingesting of this paramount fact of life has altered through the centuries. This rite should permit the audience to have a full experience of death via theatre, and, in turn, this experience should be cathartic and memorable.

NOTE: The heart of the rite itself was not mentioned in this original memorandum, in order to safeguard it until such time as the work should be in progress. It has to do with this principal object dying on stage — i.e., its sound and light diminishing and finally expiring, all throughout a ritual participated in by the actors.

ᑺ

PART THREE

TO THE RADICAL
THEATRE COMMUNITY

This is an open letter to the Radical Theatre Community, and to everyone interested in the future of theatre.

On Monday night, May 29, 1972, as some of you know, an extraordinary meeting took place at the Performing Garage in New York. Well over one hundred participants — entire experimental ensembles as well as unaffiliated directors, playwrights, designers, and performers involved in the radical movement, and critics and editors who have been in close touch with the movement met in response to a cryptic postcard sent out jointly by the Universal Movement Theatre Repertory (UMTR) and the Performance Group, calling for a conference to discuss the current state of radical theatre and where we might be heading. The only comparable gathering I can recall took place in the winter of 1967–8, when representatives of a number of experimental groups met to form a cooperative booking agency, which came to be known as the Radical Theatre Repertory, the forerunner of UMTR. The earlier meeting had predetermined its goals, the latter meeting had to uncover its goals.

This writer arrived at Wooster Street shortly before seven in the evening, the appointed hour, to find assorted members of the Living Theatre as well as a handful from different groups seated on loading–area curbs across from the Performing Garage, waiting for the meeting to get underway. Wooster Street at dusk in late spring is a curious mixture of death and promise. All motors seem to have gone quiet, the street wears the aspect of an organism abandoned out of weariness, and yet the overhead sky is quietly alive, casting its energy over brick, cement, and human flesh. Some of that sense of quiet weariness and vibrant expectancy emanated from many of those waiting. Soon there were participants hovering on both sides of the street, and others kept arriving quietly from all directions. Richard Schechner and his wife Joan Macintosh, Judith and Julian Beck, Mark Amitin of UMTR, Richard Foreman of the Ontological–Hysteric Theatre. Over one hundred people invaded that previously deserted street. Some of the most creative forces in theatre today, not only in New York but anywhere on this planet, sat on curbstones or in the gutter or leaned against the sides of buildings, waiting to find out what was up.

Thirty minutes or so after the designated meeting time, we moved into the theatre — into the space that during the Performance Group season houses what Schechner likes to call the environment. We sat about as more arrived and looked for a way to begin. How to begin this exploration?

Someone suggested that we tell who we were, and so we did. "Alec Rubin, director." "Dan Isaac, critic and teacher." "Julian Beck of the Living Theatre." "Judith Malina of the Living Theatre." "Richard Schechner of the Performance Group." "Michael Kirby of *The Drama Review.*" "Jim Anderson of the Living Theatre." "Erika Munk of *Performance* and *Scripts.*" Among others present at one time or another during the next four hours were Paul Zimet of the Open Theatre, Peter Schumann of the Bread & Puppets, Norman Taffel of 70 Grand, Converse Gurian of the Bridge Collective, Ralph Pine of *Drama Book Specialists,* Victoria Kirby of *The Drama Review,* several members of the former Pageant Players.

After the verbal introductions, Steve Israel of the Living Theatre suggested that we needed a more dynamic introduction to one another, and most of us present formed a circle throughout the environment and created a "chord," sounding OM as we swayed together for a time, reaching a crescendo, and then swaying slowly to rest. It was to be the evening's most unified moment.

For after that, harmony gave way to confrontation, at times sympathetic, at times not. We argued, harangued, sometimes taunted, sometimes laughed, sometimes questioned kindly, sometimes shouted each other down. What did we want? Many things.

All of us wanted to be useful, but what did that mean? Schechner wanted an exchange of ideas. "There are theatrical techniques we can teach one another," he proposed. But the Becks wanted revolution. Judith and Julian pleaded for others to join them in the cause they had been espousing since their return from a Brazilian prison the previous autumn. "We must go out to the workers, to the poorest of the poor, and teach them our techniques so that they can then make their own theatre." To help the workers, and those for whom there is no work, liberate the imagination ultimately in the cause of the revolution.

But how, Alec Rubin and others wanted to know, can we liberate the workers when we haven't yet liberated ourselves? Our own psyches need working on (presumably through theatrical encounter situations). Schechner agreed; he pointed out that he himself (recently returned from India) had work to do on his own soul. Again he suggested a kind of workshop for the different ensembles, in which there would be an exchange of ideas. But Judith had no patience with that. "Richard," she said, "we don't need to call two hundred people together to exchange techniques. We can do that with one phone call."

Steve Israel returned to the theme of going to the workers, but his colleague, Jim Anderson, cried out at him from across the room, "The work-

ers? Man, what do you know about the workers? Go out and get a job if
you want to know about the workers!"

Julian, not to be discouraged by resistance or apathy, nor by Erika
Munk's charge of overheated rhetoric, persisted. "For five thousand years
the ruling classes have ripped off the imaginations of the workers." And
then, to all of us, exhorting, pleading, challenging "When are you all going
to stop being the lackeys of the ruling class?"

The meeting adjourned near midnight. Nothing had been decided
other than that there would be a second meeting the following Monday
night. Schechner offered the use of the Garage to the radical theatre community for twenty–four–hour periods, beginning on Monday evenings, for
an indefinite time. My own rehearsals kept me away from the subsequent
meeting, but I understand that it was also inconclusive. To this date there
has been no major strategy nor an alliance agreed upon within the radical
movement. At present we still go our separate ways.

Many of us said nothing at that first meeting. Foreman had been silent,
also Kirby, Schumann, Taffel, Zimet, myself. Some of us are inhibited by
large gatherings, others have no formulated ideologies ready to be articulated at such discussions, still others are off on a track that can hardly be
dealt with in the terms that this meeting took.

But it's likely that most of us were stirred. The questions that arose
were questions that had been bothering many of us, certainly bothering
me. When we had dinner last September, Judith, I asked you and Julian if
there were occasions when you both felt like chucking theatre and moving
directly into the political arena. And you had both answered "Yes." And I
too have felt that, felt great dissatisfaction with what often seems like the
court–jester function, with the sense that one is primarily easing the souls
of the ruling and middle classes, providing a decorous and momentary distraction for them. What battleweary Pentagon official or harassed corpo-
ration lobbyist can't be amused for an hour or so by the militantly leftist
exhortations of *Paradise Now?* What profit–driven industrialist, exhausted
from a week of juggling investments and human lives, can't have his heart
eased through the sensory explorations of an Alec Rubin theatrical encounter session? What suburban housewife can't be delightfully scandal-
ized by the nudity and presumed obscenities in *Dionysus. in 69?* The more
scandalous, the more pleasurable and if events prove too uncomfortable,
the exit is always available.

Why support these endeavors? Why continue to be, as Julian, with his
growing instinct for the jugular, so nicely puts it, "the lackeys of the rulings
class"? No reason, no reason. Unless it is that ultimately, after all the words

have been spoken and all the battles have been won or lost, we are all members of the human race. Unless it be that we must not make the assumption that human beings aren't capable of shame; that if we work with full seriousness at our art — and it always demands nothing less of us — a true dialogue between ourselves and every spectator, in which all of us are open to change, may happen.

May happen. I understand the attitude of my friend Ronnie Davis, formerly of the San Francisco Mime Troupe, who believes that such sentiments are hopelessly bourgeois and anachronistic and that we must concentrate on building a movement among the poor and the alienated. I appreciate Ronnie's impatience and the present impatience of Judith and Julian; but I believe as strongly as I can make clear in print that we simply can't presume to pre–judge or control the effect of our work, we can only *do* the work, can only give ourselves to the forming of the work. If we dismiss the possibility of change in the ruling and middle classes, then we dismiss Mohammed, we dismiss Moses, we dismiss Gandhi, we even dismiss Che.

It's true that our theatres are stifling bourgeois palaces, reeking with self–satisfaction and also with apathy, and that the recent additions to these, the museums and galleries in New York, for all the ingenuity of the work, have taken on the character of aesthetic factories, addressing a coterie of art and dance enthusiasts about questions of space, sound, and texture, curiously devoid of flesh–and–blood involvements. And it's absolutely true that there's a crying need for theatre to begin to go out into the back country and into the schools, as the Living Theatre with much bravery began to do in Brazil; for theatre to begin to go into the prisons, as the Open Theatre, for example, was doing here at home; for theatre to begin to go into the factories, as the Becks have talked of doing but no one to my knowledge has successfully done as yet. It's absolutely necessary to find a way of making theatre accessible to those who presently live their lives without it and who feel that it has no relevance to their lives (and who correctly feel that about most theatre, which has no relevance to *anyone's* life). Necessary to make theatre accessible to the poor, who have had no economic chance, but also to the middle–class laborer, who presently supports the status quo became it makes him feel secure, because it appears to help pay for his home, but who not only pays for the war with his taxes but ultimately pays for it with his children. To the children, who are first learning a way to make their lives happen, *and* to the elderly (the unseen and the unwanted), to whom it seems that nothing happens any longer except the withering away of their years and their senses. And finally to those whom society can deal with only by locking them up, our hundreds of thousands of prisoners, at worst torturing them, at best forgetting them. It's time that theatre made itself accessible to all these growing and dying beings.

And particularly *our* theatre — not the commercial fluff that kills a few more hours of somebody's life, but *our* theatre, the theatre that challenges the supposedly fixed relationships of spectator and performer, the theatre that turns the body of the performer into a musical and psychic instrument, into a living organism rather than a static mouthpiece for dialogue, the theatre that plunges itself into the world of myth, ritual, politics, that dares to ransack the treasures of the unconscious, that dares to be *alive*.

I believe, as you, Julian, and you, Judith, strongly believe: those of us who have the gift for it ought to help others — the poor, the young, the elderly — help them to make their own theatre. But we don't all have the gift for it, nor the patience, nor the interest. And so all of us ought not to be doing it. But I also don't believe that we ought to stop doing our own work in order to do this new work. (I don't really believe that the two of you do, either, but I don't find your position clear.)

As for Richard Schechner's proposal that we exchange techniques, I find that sensible but somehow too modest and insufficiently challenging. And I'm bothered by the notion of performers probing one another's psyches. It seems to me that serious work by performers sets up a rich psychic vulnerability, that the act of probing into the work *means* probing into the soul, that we are all not only ourselves but also, ultimately, the creations of mankind, and that in order to truly confront the work, this collective self, we must confront it with the individual self that we are always discovering.

But I want to get back to revolution. Theatre is no miracle worker. It helps the soul confront itself, it is expansive. Theatre, a biological necessity like dreaming, provides a way for men to act symbolically. But the literal consequences are unforeseen. The soul that confronts itself, the soul that is invaded has myriad and often unforeseen journeys to take. We cannot presume to direct the affairs of the soul toward political revolution, toward anything. Just as we feel it is no longer enough to *give* people theatre, it is not enough — and it is also presumptuous — to give them an ideology. Theatre can open men to themselves, and with that will come the possibility that men will make their own lives more deeply. And that can lead anywhere. We are no more lackeys than are the other healers of the body and the soul. Ultimately we are only other striving men, reforming the world as best we can, in seriousness and, hopefully, in joy.

PART FOUR

TOWARD THE MILLENNIUM

Photo: Kent State University Department of Special Collections and Archives

The Open Theatre Reunion, 1983, Kent State University

Standing: James Barbosa, Shami Chaikin

Rear: Barbara Vann, Richard Gilman, Susan Yankowitz, Joanne Schmidman, Megan Terry, Gwenn Fabricant, Lee Worley, Sharon Gans, Mira Rafalowicz, Peter Feldman, Barry Daniels

Center: Eileen Blumenthal, Ralph Lee, Jean Claude Van-Itallie, Joe Chaikin, Peter Maloney, Alex Gildzen

Front: Ellen Maddow, Marianne de Pury-Thompson, Joyce Aaron, Rhea Gaisner, Arthur Sainer

16. JULIAN BECK, JUDITH MALINA AND THE LIVING THEATRE

It seems that I have been saying good-bye to my friend Julian Beck for a number of years, even as I continue to say hello to him. I wrote a poem for Julian on his sixtieth birthday, May 31, 1985. Julian, already so ill that he was no longer able to eat, had a wonderful transparency that day. There was a birthday party for him in a loft in lower Manhattan. It was a hot night in late spring, and he sat receiving friends in silence. He was glowing—there is no other way to describe it—Julian simply gave off an inner glow. He smiled in that gentle lovely way he had as I gave him the poem I'd written.

FOR JULIAN, ON HIS BIRTHDAY

Surely there's something like Prospero about you?
Will your revels end, your spirits melt into the air?
No, I don't see you breaking your wand, but passing it on,
The way you passed on the news that Barcelona had given up
    money.
So—Prospero. Another image? Three parts Percy Shelley,
Two Rocky Graziano. Shelley's silky, willowy, obstinate
Vision, and the driving pugnacity of The Rock,
A pit of coal-black fortitude.

It froze that whole week. On Monday we marched down
Fifth Avenue—where else? You made an invocation
Against a wire fence on Sixth and Waverly. "We are few,"
You said, "but soon we shall be many." Thus the General
Strike for Peace was kicked off. Later, one or two A.M.,
We picked up Bill Shari posted outside some Federal structure.
We stood with Judith, Bill held that flickering torch,
And we thought the flame a testament to something positive
Before that dour edifice that proclaims its dominance over
    things.
It kept getting colder. On Thursday the Russians invited us
Into the Consulate for tea and cigarettes. We sat around
In big armchairs, dismantling Soviet and US. missiles
On paper. It kept us warm.

Well I've seen you in many guises, but always

It was you. Mesmerizing Beat and Hip spectators,
Along with aging Bohemians having a late fling
With Miss Anarchy. I've seen police in Pittsburgh eyeing you,
As if you were about to unveil the ultimate mousetrap,
And you with roses in your arms. I've seen you
Pounded by nightsticks and giving hope to runaway kids
And kids planning to run away, all of them nibbling at
Marginal lunches in the untidy alleys of disengagement.
And last summer I saw you with those neutral tubes
That convey one little maddening meal after another to a sys-
   tem
That can't any longer manage the traditional bowl of fondue.

You miraculously move along to one creation after another
This film, that play, this book of poems, that painting.
It's not that you're thumbing your nose at mortality,
But more like a man who has both seen it all
And feels that he hasn't yet see a thing.

Judith remembers that Allen Ginsberg came to the West End Avenue
apartment during those last months and said to Julian, "Let go. Let go."
But it seemed to me that Julian had let go and was simply living, for a time,
that life past his life. Easy to say, his life past his life, before the time of im-
mortality.

Isha tells me, "I miss my daddy." Many of us miss him, but not day-by-
day as Isha does. But Julian is with us as long as we are truly with that best
part of ourselves. Julian the anarchist, the vegetarian, the provacateur, the
declaimer, the disciple of Gandhi, Thoreau, and Martin Luther King.

We met just after the formation of the General Strike for Peace. It was
a bold, impossible prophecy of a movement, given birth to by Judith and
Julian, supported by Paul Goodman, Bertrand Russell, and thousands of
disaffected young people. Some were activists in theatre, and many were in
politics or anthropology. Some were writing or dreaming poems, smoking
pot, and putting endless hours in those second-floor offices of The Living
Theatre on Fourteenth Street and Sixth Avenue. It was the very early sixties. Beards were barely into fashion, although I was sporting my first beard
(looking for trouble?) and Julian was clean-shaven, in jacket and tie, most
likely with blue jeans, looking very much the responsible young producer.
I had a desk in Julian's office, the General Strike desk, which I shared with
Saul Gottlieb and Saul's overflowing ashtray. Saul and I were the two press
contacts for the strike. We wrote press releases and telephoned the city
desks at the dailies. Journalists were somewhat sympathetic—perhaps a

good story would actually unfold—but I sensed an unspoken condescension. We were calling from a theatre known for making trouble and we were probably, underneath it all, a handful of romantic, unwashed Bolsheviks who would probably o.d. before the strike ever happened. We were also involved in the day-to-day planning for Strike Week, and that planning seemed to go on well into the night. Jimmy Spicer and Judith Malina both had desks in that office. Jimmy, the general manager of The Living Theatre, was able to tolerate, barely, those of us who had as he saw it invaded the sanctuary of a professional company. He saw the strike contingent, with its pot and profanity, as creatures who were siphoning off energies from the serious agenda of keeping a radical, economically precarious theatre afloat amidst the commercial sharks swimming around New York. Not that The Living Theatre members were themselves shy flowers when it came to juicy rhetoric and the whole panoply of addictive substances. Still, as Jimmy saw it, we were simply an extra burden on that wildly engaged theatre operation that had become his primary responsibility.

From my perch at the strike desk, I was able to witness, without paying any particular attention and without acting the voyeur, some of the outward manifestations of how a radical theatre was kept in operation day-by-day. Julian and Judith seemed to have time for everything, always keeping their performers in some state of creativity, if not stability and happiness. Brecht's *In the Jungle of Cities* and *Man Is Man* were either in rehearsal or performance, while *The Connection* had been running for some time. They were personally directing, designing and rehearsing roles in *Man Is Man*, and they were sharing notes on the nightly performances of *The Connection* and whatever else was in repertory at that time, maybe Pirandello's *Tonight We Improvise*. On top of all of this, they were working with membership lists (literally thousands of index cards) of people who were supporting, either with money or their labor the coming Strike Week. They presided over countless Strike meetings, which presumably operated according to the Quaker principle of "meeting"—that is, we never took a vote on anything but carried on an exhaustive search for consensus through endless discourse ("motherfucker" was a typical element of interchange, usually sounded at high decibel level). Judith and Julian often presided over or sat in on planning sessions with myself, Saul, Paul Goodman, Harriet Herbst, who was also at that time Living Theatre secretary, the writer Frances Gitlin, the anthropology student Jules Rabin, and, I believe, John Harriman and Paul Prensky, who were the Strike's poets, apprentices, and pot-smoking saints.

When Strike Week actually took place, The Living Theatre struck against itself. To my knowledge, it was the only theatre in New York to close down in protest against the continuation of nuclear testing in the atmosphere, and the acceleration of the arms race under the Kennedy administration. I was collecting unemployment insurance, and I "struck" against the unemployment office by announcing to a barely interested clerk that I was refusing to sign for my check. Judith, Julian, and some hundreds of us spent an exhausting week demonstrating at all hours in various locations: outside the Stock Exchange, before the Army recruiting station in Times Square, outside the precincts of the Atomic Energy Commission's New York offices, at the United Nations, at the United States consulate offices to the United Nations, at the Soviet Mission on Park Avenue. We marched, demonstrated, carried placards and torches, sat in on panel discussions, made new placards when prior ones were torn by outraged citizens, argued among ourselves, ate meals in the middle of the night, drank endless cups of coffee while Saul Gottlieb supplemented his coffee with endless cigarettes, and occasionally met with the press, including *Pravda* and whatever local papers deigned to write about us. The reporter Hamish Sinclair, who was tape-recording the Strike Week for WBAI-FM, was seemingly always on hand. For the Becks it was a labor of love, but a labor, and they were indefatigable.

For the final event of the strike, we threw a "party." Actually we offered a series of performances at the Village Gate, which I emceed. There was music by Lamont Young and Miriam Zazeeba, perhaps folk songs and mime performances (I no longer remember it all), and the work of a standup comic, Steven Ben Israel, who told me in later years, after he had become a veteran of The Living Theatre, that Strike Week had forced a radical change in his life.

From the Village Gate, the members of the Strike and numerous supporters who had come for the party marched up Sixth Avenue. When we reached Times Square, which was probably around midnight, no one knew exactly what to do. We had forgotten to plan the ending of Strike Week. I think it was sheer instinct that made us do what we then did. After all, we were already experts at it. We simply sat down in the street, the hundreds of us that had survived the strike but had failed to stop the arms race or nuclear testing in the atmosphere. We sat down and became quiet—there was nothing left to say, and it was another bitter night. And after a few moments we all got up, took subways and other conveyances, and went home to bed. It occurs to me now for the first time as I write this account that for Judith and Julian, the strike was an extended taste of a kind of theatre of the streets, a theatre to which they would return after a few years of indoor performances and come to put their individual stamp on. They had been involved in protests (and arrests) before the strike, most particularly against the promulgation of air-raid shelters, but perhaps Strike Week consolidated an approach whereby theatre people and other artists responded to public issues by "disturbing," through ritual movement, rhetoric, and sheer clamor, their fellow citizens on the streets of the cities. The approach would eventually lead to *Six Public Acts*, *The Money Tower*, and the outdoor performances in and around San Paolo.

The Becks would have disagreed that the public life of the theatre, the public life on the streets, and the private life at home were essentially different modes of being in the world. Over the years they had sought to break down these distinctions. Life has at times found its own way to reinforce this break down, even when it hasn't always been convenient for the company. For instance, there was an occasion in the seventies when the Brazilian authorities decided to jail these dangerous aliens who were working with "the poorest of the poor," teaching them to create their own theatre as a way of addressing issues in their lives.

The closing of the Fourteenth Street theatre for non-payment of admission taxes has been recounted in many places, but it's worth spending a moment on it yet again. Judith believes the production of *The Brig* was the catalyst. The Becks had been meeting with the IRS, trying to work out an accommodation concerning admission taxes which had never been turned over to the government. The problem always came down to a choice between paying the landlord, who would not wait, and the IRS, who seemed to take a longer view of the matter. Judith contends that the turmoil over *The Brig*, which graphically illustrated the sadistic methods employed against members of the Marine Corps by Marine prison guards, not only shocked audiences but led to a House investigation. Some bureaucratic figures in Washington were thus convinced that it was not in the government's interest to maintain a seemingly interminable dialogue over back admission taxes, particularly since this band of rabble-rousers was dirtying the name of the military's proudest corps. As Judith sees it, the order went out to "shut those little bastards down." And they did. The building was legally taken over by the federal government and everything in it was sealed, becoming federal property. Office furniture, typing paper, the theatre auditorium itself, Judith's boxes of Tampax®, Julian's two checkbooks (which he never bothered to balance), Judith's scrapbook—all became the property of Lyndon Johnson's government, or rather, our government. (I speak to this event in the poem below.) But with the premises padlocked, The Living Theatre managed one more performance of *The Brig* before an invited, if covert, audience. Both cast and audience scrambled over several rooftops to get into the auditorium. And while the final performance of *Brig* was running, one or more guards on the street presumed that they were keeping the premises closed to the world.

Hardly more than a year after Julian's death, a number of friends gathered for Judith's sixtieth birthday. And I wrote this poem for her on June 4th, 1986.

FOR JUDITH, ON HER SIXTIETH BIRTHDAY

Judith, some part of you is always
Moving through my life. No, is
My life in a manner I don't fully understand.
Yes it's truly a small island, this community
Of lives we call humanity, and we seem to
Travel through each other, even as the
Tracks some make are deeper, even as the
Community is some layered sediment
Sitting on other layers it's barely aware of.

Moving through. Carrying baby Isha in the city
Of Geneva, coming from the doctor's, and you
Eyeing the propulsive traffic as if it were
The malevolent wonder of U.S. air power.
Holding hands one insane New Year's Eve in
Times Square (no less), chanting "Stop the
(Insane) War." We were a tiny chain that night,
Trying to become a prophecy.

And I recall your small temper tantrum during
One unscheduled, interminable intermission
In the 14th St. office, and Julian at his desk,
Delighting in your tantrum, as if someone had just
Told him something delicious. And of course
The night the cops stood guard on Sixth Avenue,
And all of us sneaking out pieces of the theatre
In pockets and mufflers; and you ungluing old
Pictures, mementos of various triumphs and
Breakthroughs now owned by the U.S. Treasury.
Did you really say, "It's just like the final act
Of *The Cherry Orchard*"? And the cold weary January
We made The Strike. Our wonderful, theatrical,
Unblinking Strike that played to no critic, troubled
Many audiences—the language was new—and did
No box-office returns.

Feisty Judith, have you ever had a moment
When an opinion left you in peace? You aren't
Tireless, surely not, but you don't give in.
You just keep giving.

And now of course the separation. But what do we know
Of these separations, except the immense pain,
The sense of absence and perhaps the sense of presence.
Is presence simply a metaphor, a poetic conceit
To glide over pain? Then what is the spirit,
And of what use is the spirit? Do these journeys
Really ever end, do we ever cease this traveling
Through? The spirit, our spirit connected to that
Larger Spirit must be what moves everything,
Anything. If there are indeed many silences,
There is only one moving Silence.

The "small temper tantrum" took place during a performance, perhaps *The Connection* was on, or perhaps it was *In the Jungle of Cities*. Something had happened during the first act, and Judith had come storming into the office, yelling and literally banging part of her slim anatomy against the wall near Julian's desk. Julian seemed delighted by the proximity of this explosion. I have no sense that he even knew what had set it off but he was like a small boy looking into his Christmas stocking. He looked over at me with sheer delight and I looked back at him, trying to give a neutral caste to whatever I was feeling. I think Judith then stormed out and into some other part of the several-story building they inhabited. I believe she may have stormed onto the roof. After a short while, other performers, apparently waiting for her return or to continue an argument which may have just begun to accelerate, initiated actions of their own. During this sequence of events, Joe Chaikin, one of the principal performers that night, simply went home, which was not too far away, but it wasn't around the corner. The Becks, eventually heeding the maxim about the sanctity of the play, took off for Joe's Eleventh Street apartment in a building adjoining Asti's, the Italian restaurant where the waiters regaled the customers each night with choice bits from Verdi and Puccini. The Becks spent some time persuading Joe that the altercation, whatever its nature, should not be allowed to prevent the play from fulfilling its nightly destiny. And eventually Joe was persuaded. The intermission lasted something like an hour and a half because of the dispute, but audience members did not seem particularly put out. The play then simply resumed. What this demonstrated to me, as I recount an event occurring over thirty years ago, is that the theoretical question concerning the borders between life and art, which Judith and Julian grappled with over and over, was in fact never theoretical at all. Judith and Julian, before they ever abandoned what we called the "bourgeois palaces of art," were already muddying that border, reevaluating, if not rethinking, the moment when the presence of the actor, without the role of actor, was playing itself out before witnesses whose own borders between that of spectator and passerby in the street had broken down. And it didn't take Pirandello, Bert Brecht, Jack Gelber, Ken Brown, or the Becks to make this happen. It took a combination of an air-raid drill, or a march to Times Square at the conclusion of Strike Week, and a handful of intense people committed to pondering social questions and spontaneously acting upon them to break down these borders. Yes there was surely a tantrum that night of the super intermission, but there was an intense focus past the tantrum. Even if the tantrum spelled a willfulness, its way of being addressed spoke to a willingness to allow, if unconsciously, that muddying and breaking down of borders.

An event which I have, with suitable irony, labeled the Times Square Peace Riot, closed down *The Connection* one freezing Saturday night in 1963. A rally had been called that afternoon by a multitude of peace organizations, including the Committee for Non-Violent Action, the War Resisters League, SANE, Women Strike for Peace, the Tomkins Square Peace Center and our own General Strike for Peace. The site was Duffy Square, a concrete island just north of Times Square, sandwiched between Broadway and Seventh Avenue. The rally was called to protest John Kennedy's order allowing renewed nuclear testing in the atmosphere. Thousands of protesters turned out, and the area was filled with placards, women with babies, reporters, photographers, mounted police and numerous patrolmen. The protest moved along peacefully, but at some point in the afternoon there was a disturbance. A member of the General Strike for Peace, Dick Bell, a modest-looking young man with the air of a befogged academician, was discovered either sitting or lying in the gutter, just west of the concrete island. Within seconds, the shit, as they are wont to say, hit the fan, and all hell broke loose. Patrolmen began roughing up our befogged academician, so other members of the General Strike, always considered a rowdy pack to begin with, sat down in the gutter. Saturday afternoon traffic came to a sudden halt on both sides of the island. More protesters sat down, police began roughing up everybody, and paddy wagons began to arrive. The mounted police began driving their horses into the crowd of protesters hemmed in by police barricades with nowhere to move. The air was filled with screams, bellowing orders, curses, sirens, and shrieking people of all ages. In short, a first-class riot was just getting warmed up.

I saw Julian standing on the sidewalk, west of Duffy Square. He was crying out, berating the rough tactics of the police. "Shame, shame," is what I recall him saying. And then I saw Julian clubbed over the head by a patrolman's nightstick. A thin, jagged red line moved quickly down from his skull to his nose, he stood for an unbelievable moment, still berating the police, and then he sank onto the ground. Karl Bissinger, The Living Theatre photographer at that time, turned to several of us standing in the island. He gave his camera to Dale, the young woman I'd been seeing, stepped into the gutter and said to a patrolman, "I can't stand what's happening. Arrest me as well." Karl was immediately clubbed over the head, lost consciousness, and was later charged with resisting arrest. People were being lifted off the ground and flung like melons or footballs into paddy wagons. I saw all ninety pounds of Judith Malina lifted from the ground and flung, perhaps twenty feet, into a wagon. One young woman, a schoolteacher and doctoral student in philosophy, was dragged along the ground for the better part of a block by a mounted policeman, who was leaning down from his horse and clutching her before he grew tired of the pull on his muscles and simply arrested her. Joe Chaikin, who was late for the demonstration, arrived by taxi, paid his fare, jumped out, sat down in the gutter and was immediately arrested. A teenager, who had just come from a Broadway matinee and was still clutching his program, was grabbed, shaken soundly, and arrested by a policeman as he turned into Seventh Avenue. I was with my friend Jeremy Cockayne, a very respectable Brit who had been to Trafalgar Square rallies and wanted to compare notes. Before the afternoon was out, we were both arrested. We hadn't even had the joy of joining our friends in the gutter. We were simply walking north on Seventh Avenue as the demonstration was waning but apparently not fast enough for a couple of patrolmen. In the precinct house, we were cheered by our friends for having the presence of mind to get ourselves arrested in a noble cause, but Karl was semi-conscious and moaning, and I couldn't stop shaking from what I felt was a violation of my person. It was my first arrest, and Jeremy's as well. Some interminable time later, after we were "booked," a number of us were shoved into a paddy wagon. I had no understanding of paddy-wagon protocol, so I took my cue from others seated quietly across from me. I subsequently learned that I had been privileged to share this wagon with several wonderfully courageous civil rights workers: Igol Roodenko of the War Resisters League (Igol died within the past two years) and Jim Peck, an historic figure in the peace movement who was brutally beaten during the 1964 Mississippi Freedom rides. There was little in the way of idle conversation during that trip to the Tombs, but I noted with a good deal of satisfaction that the wagon we were riding in was the one in which Judith Malina had been discourteously flung. Since very little daunted Judith, and since she was congenitally incapable of passing her time in anything resembling a condition of lassitude, she had been busily decorating the interior walls with dozens of stickers promoting our favorite fantasy, the General Strike for Peace.

The Tombs were fearful and boring. We were threatened, arbitrarily transferred from cell to cell, and treated with contempt by most of the guards for whom we were not ordinary prisoners but unrelieved Pinkos or retrograde Bolsheviks. We learned through the grapevine that Julian was in the hospital with a collapsed lung. *The Connection* band had been busted and the performance canceled, Judith was in the infamous Women's House of Detention on Greenwich Avenue, and we were due to spend the night in the Tombs. Either late that night or early the next morning we were finger-printed. But Dick Bell, whose countenance normally suggested the heights of civility, refused to be fingerprinted, claiming the procedure was a viola-tion of his civil rights because he had not yet been convicted of anything. These legal fine points hardly cut any ice with our guards. Bell was called out of his cell, and shortly after we heard screams coming from somewhere down the corridor. We could see nothing and had no effective means of aid-ing our colleague, who later told us that the guards had tried to break his thumbs and push their fingers into his eyes to secure essential prints. I did learn one fact that startled me: at some early hour of our arrest, Bell con-fided to me that "I never sat down in the gutter, I just fainted. I'm wearing this thermal underwear and it proved too much for me."

The morning included a breakfast of corn flakes and something that one could determine as coffee. For the arraignment, we were a bleary-eyed, rumpled, unshaven and weary pack. In such a state, one must obviously be guilty of something, Job's comforters would have understood this. Mark Lane, later famous for his book on the Kennedy assassination, *Rush to Judgment,* and his harrowing escape from Jonestown shortly before the mass suicide, acted as our temporary counsel. He had been at the rally-turned-riot and volunteered to speak for us. The major issue was if should bail be allowed. The attorney for the city advised the judge that we were a danger-ous pack, "the hard core." The young schoolteacher and philosophy student who had been dragged by the mounted patrolman was considered especially dangerous, and therefore should be denied bail because she lived out of state in New Jersey and might never be heard from again.

Bail was set, but according to accepted jail house protocol, the authori-ties kept moving us around so that the bail bondsmen would have difficulty tracking us down. We spent part of that day in the Tombs and the latter part in the detention house in The Bronx. We theatre people were reduced to staring ahead, having small conversations, being read to by someone who had managed to sneak a copy of *The Realist* into the confines of the prison, and initiating a somewhat childish theatre game to enliven our spirits. The game had to do with counting. At intervals, a guard would appear and count us. Some time later another guard would count us again, as if we Pinkos had the wings of angels and could soar past prison walls at will. Our game began spontaneously. A guard would appear and before he could count to himself, we would count for him, each of us calling out a number. This game gave us the illusion of having momentary control of our own destiny. It was evident, however, that our counting game was amusing only ourselves, and we were told to "cut the crap."

I dwell on this moment because in its own way it addresses the creative spirit. Fear could have easily dampened or temporarily extinguished this sense of play. But given extensive boredom, the sense of play found a way to address an action which seemed absurd but which could be used both to comment on this absurdity and transform it by ritualizing it into a pleasing choral patter. I might also mention that soon after our ritual play, The Living Theatre opened Ken Brown's ritual documentary, *The Brig*, in which one of the principle methods for dehumanizing prisoners was to identify them not by their names but by numbers. One of the reasons the avant-garde artist isn't trusted is because the art seen as subversive among people who are "only doing their job." These job-holders are observing, as if in a mirror, what is vital to them, and what they are "only doing" is being held up to ridicule. One has only to go back to Jonathan Swift and his depiction of the absurdity of ordinary custom to understand why people who are only doing their job often feel that these artists, these "players," are out to subvert what the law-abiding citizen holds dear or cannot live without. It's not easy to have these anarchists, poets, Jews, and transvestites telling you in one fashion or another, "Change your life," "Who would want to live the way you do?" "Change your life." And the response is sometimes defensive amusement but more often anger, and if it isn't anger it's an indignation which says, "Have fun, I the responsible adult have no time for these games. If everybody behaved like you, where would we be?"

From *The Village Voice*, February 15, 1968.

THE BECKS: *PARADISE NOW*, BUT NOT QUITE YET

I found The Living Theatre in Geneva. Where to begin? Everyone's hair is longer. The work is wilder than ever. Judith and Julian have created a new Beck—Isha—beautiful, six months old. Jim Tiroff and Henry Howeard are making experimental films. Steve Israel is composing rock. The US. Internal Revenue people are still around. The company is preparing to make a work of joy.

I stretched out on the bed in Steve Israel's hotel room a couple of weeks ago and we talked. Steve is one of the remaining members of the troupe that left New York several years ago. "We drive," he told me, "in five Volks buses. Europe is like driving in my neighborhood. Instead of from 14th Street to Yorktown, I go like from Switzerland to Germany, from Italy to France. There's the Brenner Pass, like the Holland Tunnel."

"I've been composing," he told me, and took out the guitar. "After a while what in hell do you do in hotel rooms?" He played and sang one of his rock compositions. I liked it and told him so, so he played others. I remembered Steve as a standup comic back in—when? '62? not sure anymore—at a General Strike for Peace show we produced at The Living Theatre. "Striking" for other issues—nuclear testing—not really other issues. *The Connection* was still running, Kennedy was president, Jerry Tallmer was with *The Voice*. A lifetime ago.

"Have you been back at all?" I asked.

"Once, for 10 days. To see my mother. That's the only time." He remembered something else. "Guy I know got into New York, went into a phone booth to call somebody to say he was back, and there outside the goddamned phone booth a gun fight starts between some other guy and a cop. Bullets! My friend got the hell out of town."

I found Isha Beck in the same hotel, in bed, or rather on bed. Six months old, looking tranquil.

"She's beautiful," I told Judith.

"She's a person."

"She looks like Gary" (the Becks' teen-age boy). "And like Julian."

Judith was obviously proud. I watched her. As intense as ever, I thought. "But you've filled out a little," I said. "I think you've gone from 94 to 95 pounds."

"Listen," she said, "I want to hear about New York. Who have you seen? John Harriman? Naomi Levine? Karl Bissinger? And the theatre. I want to hear about guerrilla theatre."

But I hadn't really seen any guerrilla theatre and could only say what I know about the Pageant Players performing in laundromats and what I'd heard about Richard Schechner's "Kill Viet Cong" piece. "I've seen Ronnie Davis's Mime Troupe," I said, "and they feel like guerrilla theatre. Or like guerrillas. Those cats are tough. They play the parks in San Francisco."

"That's what we should be doing," Judith said, "working in the streets."

"Ronnie says they operate like guerrillas, moving across the land, using the mechanisms of society."

"Society!" Judith called out, as if it were a dirty word. "What would happen if we put out the call for a general strike now?"

Several days later I ran into Judith, Isha, and Carl Einhorn, another performer from the New York company, on the street. They were returning from the doctor's, and Carl was carrying Isha.

"Goddammit," Judith said to Carl, "you're not going to cross that thoroughfare with my child, not with those maniacs zipping by."

"It's perfectly safe," Carl tried to reassure her. "They stop when you cross."

"And if they don't stop? Gimme that baby."

But he didn't.

It was unnerving. We kept running into traffic circles, no discernible traffic lights, and cars spinning around corners from numerous directions.

"More of this 20th century insanity," Judith said. "Why anybody has to go 50 miles an hour in a city street I don't know. What kind of needs do people have? And next month we go to Sicily, with earthquakes and epidemics. Jesus. Don't know which is more insane," she added, watching the perpetual traffic as we came to another traffic circle, "people or the elements. I know," smiling at me, "people."

At the Cine Club de l'Atelier one night, Henry Howard and Jim Tiroff, two more of the group that left New York after the famous tax scene, screened about four hours of their experimental films. They'd started shooting and editing for the same reason Steve Israel had taken up composing. "All these hours," Jim told me, "in hotel rooms. And on the road. Hours on the road. You got to do something."

The films were all 8mm and most of them had the character of agitated tone poems. Visual material, double and triple exposed (can't be sure of the latter), included the road, the towns, Julian, Judith, Jenny Hecht, gawking bystanders, bejeweled actors of both sexes, church spires, Volkswagen wheels, bus and train stations, and endless road. Tiroff's films employed almost perpetual zooms, so that images seemed to pulsate, at times to be sucked at us. The audience? I might have been at Jonas's Cinematheque. [Jonas Mekas. The Cinematheque has given way to Anthology Film Archives.] There was a heckler; he laughed intermittently for nearly half and hour. "Why the hell don't you go home, you bourgeois son of a bitch?" This from Henry Howard, savagely black-bearded, working the projector at the back of the house. At the next light break the heckler good-naturedly assured Rufus Collins, another of the original company, that he was simply having an awfully good time, but took the precaution when the lights dimmed again to start having it quietly.

And Julian? His hair is much longer but he is as I remembered him. Always busy, always patient, almost always in a huddle with a business associate, an interviewer, or a well-wisher. He's still at work on his book, a kind of autobiography—the original manuscript, several years' labor, was stolen from their auto during a pre-exile tour of Europe in the early '60s.

Julian also thinks about playing in the streets. "Sometimes people accuse us of not living up to our word. We attack the establishment, we attack the middle-class, and yet we play in those theatres which are largely supported by the middle-class. And they're quite right. But it's a dilemma. We've 41 mouths to feed" (nine children), "we've got to play in what's available, in what will keep us alive."

I asked about young people.

"Students come backstage to see us all the time. We turn them on. They've started over 10 new companies in Italy alone, after watching The Living Theatre."

And what about the Eastern countries? "Why haven't you played Prague, for example?"

"They don't want us in the East. The communists like our work, but not for them. Can you imagine us anarchists going into East Berlin and chanting 'down with the state?' They say, 'you're doing a fine job in the West, that's where you're needed, keep it up.' But of course what we have to say is aimed at the communists as well as everyone else."

"Borders," Judith added, "don't make sense. Nor does capital. Nor coercion of any kind. Money and violence do awful things to people. Did you know that in Barcelona, just before the civil war, they had actually set up anarchist conditions? They had stopped using money."

I had never heard that before.

"But they were too much of a threat. And then Franco happened."

What about returning home?

"We'd love to return home," Judith said. "Now we just go from hotel to hotel, a few nights in one city, then pack up and go on to another city, to another country. You get tired of it."

But there was the Internal Revenue Service.

"The tax keeps mounting," she said. "The penalties keep going up every year. They make offers to us but so far we can't afford their offers. With 41 people, with shoes to buy, and dentists to be paid, we just manage to keep alive. And we play to packed houses."

We talked about Leo Garen's present attempt in New York to work out the financial and legal difficulties.

"If he can work it out," Julian said, "we'll come home. We're ready to perform in New York next autumn if it can be worked out."

When I left, they were very concerned about Sicily, where they had a booking in a matter of days. Each day members of the company would seek out the news in the papers. "All bad," Judith said. "Snow, freezing rain, new tremors, sickness everywhere. That's a place to take Isha to? We're not invulnerable. What makes us think we're invulnerable?"

"Why go there?" I asked. "Why not cancel it?"

Judith looked at me. "Arthur, we have to go somewhere. We have no home. We have to make our bread. We're expected there. There's a roof for us. We don't have a choice."

For three nights I watched audiences jamming into the La Comedie Theatre to see Brecht's *Antigone* and the *Mysteries*. I saw hundreds and hundreds of youth, fashionably dressed men and women, and a smattering of elderly Genovans, all fashionably dressed, crowding eagerly into the theatre, saw them assaulted by some two dozen dancing young actors, boys with long Beatle hair, blue jeans, and corduroy trousers in rags, torn sneakers, sometimes new boots, girls with incredibly painted eyes, gaudy Hell's Angels' jewelry and bare feet, saw them tearing at one another crying out at the audience, lurching and screaming through the aisles, chanting words about love, about violence and war, saw matrons scurrying out with well-bred fingertips clutching discreetly at their skirts, saw waves of people chanting back at Julian, "Stop the war," saw Henry Howard's large frame standing in the rear of the auditorium, calling out Brecht's warning: the man who uses violence against his enemies will turn and use it against his own people.

Assault is the only word I can think of. The audience was battered, exhorted, threatened. And some returned each night for more.

"We're going to make a new work," the Becks told me. "A work of joy."

"Joy?" I asked.

"An optimistic play," Julian said, "a glow play. To be called *Paradise Now*."

"What's it about?"

"We don't know. We haven't created it yet. It's going to be put together by the company the way *Frankenstein* was. All we've got so far is the title, but we've been contracted to do it."

"Joy," I repeated.

"Joy," he said. "Something toward which the spectator-participant [his words] can go to instead of running away from."

Photo: The Living Theatre Archives

The Living Theatre in *Paradise Now*

✧✧✧

From *The Village Voice*, March 19, 1970

Hello and good-bye. I recall standing, how many years ago is it now? with Julian Beck in the corridor outside the 14th Street Living Theatre, perhaps *The Brig* was on then, and Julian saying, "We've been doing what's been characterized as this artsy-fartsy stuff for so long, it's time we got out of these houses and went to the workers." And in the winter of '68, when they played Geneva, "It's still the middle-class, these are the palaces of the rich." And now, with the split, whatever that split actually means, of the troupe (into cells?), Judith and Julian at last planning to go into the factories, to do a new kind of theatre, in France to begin with.

So wherever it is, it's to the machines of Meyerhold, Eisenstein, and Chaplin, while Steve Israel, Henry Howard, and others dig in in Berlin with *Paradise Now* and the radical young. Perhaps the split's been made between two kinds of messiahs, one political, one drug-oriented. But I don't understand the factory worker, I never was one. And am skeptical about the Becks making a dent in the social consciousness of the laboring class in America which recently was up in arms because of government cutbacks in the production of torpedoes.

So it's goodbye, it seems, to a theatre as we knew it, and perhaps hello to the lean, tired patience of Julian and the smiling, high-pitched prophecies of Judith. If anyone can cut into the fatty tissue of the prosperous labor movement, I guess it's these two, in France, in the U.S. Why? Because they're magicians.

On Saturday I said goodbye to Murray Levy, who is leaving The Bread and Puppets to work with his own new group in Berlin, The Bilder Theater. Said goodbye to one of those tireless, tired, sadly beautiful faces and beings whose commitment to theatre and people can only make one feel humble and grateful. Peter Schumann goes on, seemingly ageless (beard's gotten longer), seemingly tireless, working with new, younger people, making the bread, insistently joyous and inherently dangerous. Dangerous because the eyes are the eyes of a two hundred-year-old child and the curiously complex but crude aesthetics is the aesthetics that says, "You can make the world." That says, "Don't be duped." That says, "We must learn to be quiet." That says, "We must learn to be direct," a way of unlearning the world.

✧✧✧

From *The Village Voice*, August 6, 1970

Henry Howard (Living Theatre) writes from London: "About three months ago we [Steve Israel and others] did a revamped *Paradise* which was out of sight...no confrontation till the middle, [confrontation] for about 45 minutes, back to text until opening with free food and free [indecipherable]. Two people from cell split to study medicine, pretty much everyone else is spaced around."

Enclosed with the letter, the following: "The Living Theatre stopped functioning as a performance group because the medium of theatre in theatres no longer meets the need of the times. A group of 30 revolutionary artists attempts to step from their roles in order to further their experiments in creative living and communications. One cell goes to Brazil to live and work. Another cell goes to India, lives in an ashram and absorbs the Indian life experience.

"As the theatre is now in the streets we have thrust ourselves again into an artistic vanguard by studying and recording revolutionary life styles, to find a natural synthesis, one that is in ecological balance, to breathe again. To further non-violent positive cultural change...

A third cell has begun creation of an alternate tv communication network..."

❖❖❖

From *The Village Voice*, issue of June 2, 1975

...as if they were holy lunatics treading steadily in grotesque, fanciful formations through a plague-ridden country.

Tuesday, May 6th. The Living Theatre premieres *Six Public Acts* in the streets and parks of Pittsburgh. The messianic criers are out in force on a sharply cold evening in late spring. Perhaps a hundred and fifty of us are present to watch and sometimes participate. Friends, teenagers, university students, stragglers, media people. A time of cold witness, one would like to think of it as a time of transcendence. We are standing at the perimeter of a grassy area, where are the performers? They are standing with us, slowly they separate from the spectators and move silently into the area. Is it beginning?

"*Six Public Acts*," The Living's literature states, "is a fulfillment of one of the final lines in *Paradise Now* when the performers cried out, 'The theatre is in the streets!' [and were] met inevitably by the police...The form is in itself an attempt to free the form of the theatre from the restrictions of theatre-as-an-institution...and also theatre as an art form which is confined to architectural spaces."

A figure in the center of East Park calls out in the dusk: "The time is 8:05—exactly." He, and later others, will call the time in quarter-minute intervals throughout the long evening. The initial caller is "exactly" off by some twenty-five minutes. No one minds. The dusk now reveals figures in tableau, the formations are broken by movements suggesting acts of violence. The figures who stood with us earlier are now witnesses to death.

"We propose to visit six places where the power of Cain is felt and to enact there public acts in the name of the people's pain." The center dispels itself, and there is a procession to The House of Death. The figures of assailants and victims, alternately in motion and in frozen tableau, comprise the procession. The House of Death is represented by a local Pittsburgh utility; I believe it's the telephone company, housed across from East Park. Shoes of victims are piled on top of one another, and recalling the earlier *Mysteries*, the ravagers and the ravaged cry out, "Why do we die so soon? Who decrees it? Who were Cain and Abel and why did one kill the other? Why are we ruled by force and violence?" The "dead" bodies are piled atop one another like cargo, killed as a thing, laid out as a thing. There is discomfort among the spectators, a few nervous giggles. What if we were in that pile?

Members of the troupe confer quietly, one on one, with audience members. The Barcelona experiment is mentioned, the actual abolishment of money as currency, and I recall an impassioned Judith conveying that information to me in a Geneva hotel room in the long-ago winter of '68. I think: Barcelona, what a fanciful moment in the life of humankind; if I were with this troupe, I would also be sharing this story. Such a world is conjured up by the naming of the city, but then there is General Franco and the Fifth Column. What reality can now bring about that Barcelona condition, to transform Edenic legend to new reality? The Living is trying "art," ritualistic and didactic, to mobilize consciousness. A weapon of impotence? We are formed by seemingly infinite manifestations, everything makes a difference. To believe otherwise is another kind of deception.

The House of the State—Martin Luther King Jr. Elementary School. At the site, blood. Each company member pricks a finger and smears blood on the school flagpole. Each smearing commemorates the System in one of its violent actions or an action of non-violent protest by an alternative movement. Several spectators join the blood ritual. "What is government? "What is blood? Who gives the orders? Who takes them? Who is free? Who is bound?"

The House of Money. Out of the park, into the streets, to the Mellon Bank on East Ohio Street. It's already late into the evening. The procession now invades worker country. The Land of Rednecks? It depends where you

stand. Before the bank, a golden calf supported on high by a totem formation. "Commies," "Jews"—this from several bystanders outside the local
tavern. "Who rules the rich? Who does the work of the world? Who walks?
Who rides? Is money violence?"

The House of Property. On the grounds of a high-rise project, stately
and desolate in the way of much contemporary architecture, immuring
clusters of the urban well-to-do. Two levels of wooden scaffolding are
erected, sub-units resemble cages confining performers, it's reminiscent of
the scaffolding of *Frankenstein*. Cries are heard, chants, readings from anarchist writers, songs. "Who owns the land? Who built the buildings? Who
built Pittsburgh?"

The House of War. On to the local police station, outside of which the
fifth act is planned. Now there's trouble. It's a little after midnight. The police, wanting no part of this theatrical event, certainly not outside their
gates, have two stories: (1) it's after midnight, the permit is no longer valid,
and (2) there never was a permit. Julian bargains gently with the lieutenant
for five minutes, and the officer responds with the long-suffering persona
of officialdom: we don't pretend to understand you weirdos, you see how
patient cops can be, only don't wear this glorious patience thin. No deal is
consummated, the police move indoors and the performers decide to stage
act five down the block from the station house—quietly.

But the police are back, and I think: this is it, just in time for the big
bust. I'm wrong. Performers lifted on one another's shoulders approach the
guardians of the peace with bread and roses. How can the guns become
bread, the remoteness roses? But there are no takers. The loaves of bread,
in the eyes of officialdom, appear sinister. Again the offer. But how can a
tough patrolman accept a rose from hippie-commie...? Bill Batthurst,
shooting video all night, has been chatting with the lieutenant, and now he
softly suggests to him: "Go ahead, take a rose." The lieutenant, warily, ac-
cepts the rose. A breakthrough. Now other officers accept roses, tentatively, sheepishly. Is it the beginning of the revolution, the dying of 1960's
hostilities between Flower Children and the Hired Guns of the System?
Well...it's something. But they won't touch the bread.

The House of Love—final act, in a space resembling an outdoor amphitheatre. One a.m. It's freezing. "How does property bind? How does the
state bind? What's bondage to love, money, government, violence, death?
Who cracks the whip? How can we undo the knots? Without violence?
The last ritual of enslavement begins, and we see the submission of one
"loved one" to another. The whips are cracked, one by one, the members
of the company bind each other tightly, even with a certain cruelty, and af-

ter a time the base of the amphitheatre is ringed with bound figures lying prone. Waiting.

Waiting for someone to unbind them. It's not an easy action to initiate, but finally I move into the space, unbind Julian, and someone comes to my aid. Now the forty or fifty surviving spectators help unbind the performers. And none of it is easy, for the knots are real and these are real people on the ground. At the same time the action is easy and very threatening. And all of us are now all performers, for the spectators have vanished or been transformed, with the exception of the lieutenant who has reappeared with one or two bystanders. We all form a circle, a chord, and the OM is sounded. Even this chant, by now a worn tradition, a cliché already spoofed by many in the movement, is an act of will, but also a natural act past the willing of it.

Procession of I and Thou. "What time is it? (Time to take the next step.) Are you free? (Not yet.)" And on to The Living Theatre's communal quarters where at two a.m.—there is finally heat and gas after a winter in which the company couldn't pay its heating bills—Julian begins the task of preparing curry in the kitchen to feed all the survivors of this event, to feed the cold and the hungry.

There is no adequate way for me to critique this work that I find both enormously compelling and often tedious, for the inner me has already formulated all it needs, and the manifestation of the outerness, the formulated writing, is always in part a subversion of the experience. Nevertheless, the work is obviously messianic, lovely, numbingly unconcerned with the particularity of the spectator, and sometimes foolish, but its foolishness is that of the one who offers, albeit in awkwardness, offering openly if at times with a stridency one could do without. The offering of the fool is that of one who does not take exigencies into account, of whether or not one is ready to receive the offering. The offering becomes a seed, and the message takes on the air of prophecy.

I confess there's an aspect I find troubling, it speaks to the openness of the performer as fool, and of the message to the other. The camaraderie is evident, but are the performers open to other approaches to the problem of living on this global village? The messianic figure makes the assumption not only that the way is known but also that he or she knows it. But beings can reason together, and this concord of reasoning leaves open the possibility of other ways. Does *Six Public Acts* leave open that door, is the prophet capable of hearing as well as proclaiming? Surely if one can ask this of Isaiah and Jeremiah and Jesus, one can ask it of Judith and Julian. Finally, a work of faith that reaches out from some conscious place has of necessity to come at us with its integrity, be it windy, overheated, or chilling.

Whatever one might say of its unwieldiness, its propensity to oversimplify issues and events, *Six Public Acts* is surely a work of such integrity. Is there a degree of anachronism in the message, in the style of the offering? Indeed, we're thrown into Husinger's *Waning of the Middle Ages*. These are latter-day monks ringing bells, crying out faith in narrow alleys. But ultimately the aesthetic seems peripheral. Prophets, despite their avant-gardism, are also always throwbacks to a time when the civilizing props were not yet or no longer viable, to a time when one is face to face with radical questions. Prophets are also often tiresome, and, too often, they have proven to be false, but each of us must test their validity with our innerness. It is our way of making an offering to the offering.

❖❖❖

From *The Village Voice*, circa April 1977

THE LIVING'S LEGACY CONTINUES/
LETTER FROM JULIAN BECK

Jim Spicer, former General Manager of The Living Theatre, sent me a copy of Julian's recent letter from Naples, excerpts of which follow (lower case all Julian's): "we've spent almost two months here, in the poorest of the quarters, in the liveliest of the streets, in the warm and wretched atmosphere of this lively dying city. we are doing the best work of our lives. we got past the humps and blocks last summer in sardinia, and suddenly this fall, down in the toe of the boot of italy, in a town called cosenza in calabria, we began to launch the short shooting stars in the legacy of cain constellation, and suddenly the whole starlike pattern began to become visible. National television came running and made a 40-minute film of it which was shown last week over prime time, and we're celebrated now, but very poor.

'april—switzerland for tv version of 6 public acts and of 7 meditations, then Italy for a two-hour TV special (mysteries 1977—in the streets of rome), then to work on the new major play, the one about the state but it is a reworking of prometheus based on aeschylus, shelley, with a little bit of icarus thrown in, conceived both for indoor environments (sports palaces) and for piazzas. We've got a commission from the biennale of venice for that. We do plays, and meanwhile africa and latin america keep starving, we keep talking about it, and who eats? Judith records all of our ins and outs of the 55 Italian towns and cities we've worked in the last year, the creation of the new plays—some 20 small ones this fall and early winter, the encounters with anarchists, antimilitarists, feminists, artists, workers, soldiers, women, oppressed kids, demons. we were full of down feeling about having missed you here on this continent. I have, as you know, little or no desire to return, only some urgent or terrible business could call me back to those states at this point.

"the company has halved itself, but this is a period of reformation. the form of life and community, which 12 years ago seemed to so many a substitute for the old battered family, has become itself battered. we cannot have revolutions which change the exterior forms if the interior forms do not change. thus the accent on our work now is to insert as much serum as we can into changing the culture from all that it is into all that it isn't, but essentially into a sensuous loving and nonviolent one, and one which digs being free. also people are going off to fulfill personal visions. judith and i try to create a work that will be fulfilling for the visions of others [and] a community which they can flower in and dance in, but you know that working with us means that our vision must also be shared, developed and worked on, and no doubt a substantial part of the problem of working with us, if you have a strong personal vision, is that. it has been a year and a half of intense work, and shaping the money tower was almost a Herculean task, and it didn't really happen until the last ten days of rehearsal this september in vigevano, a ducal town of the sforza family where we worked in the cortile of their collapsing castle, until a tight hour-and-a-half operatic version emerged which finally pleased us.

"all I talk about is the living theatre. I should talk about the anarchist movement here in italy which I know you think is only some fantasy of mine. it is only as big as a violet, but it will break rocks. there are anarchist groups all over the country, hundreds of them, and each of them has bright young members who can express the theory and the strategy far better than i. and there are people on the street who know all about it. and we do our plays and they know what we mean when we say communism-with-maximum-liberty. but they do not know what we mean when we say without-violence. but italy as you know is moving rapidly to a new social alternative, it is capable of great political drama, and may play such a scene within the next generation. that is why we have chosen to work here. we might contribute something very real to something which is going to become reality. reality in the revolution.

"Isha grows the way everything that is beautiful grows. Unschooled, she seems to learn, she rejects our attempts to school her ourselves, but her curiosity is sufficient. and what she is learning most in her wise way is how to analyze life. she rightly criticizes our theatre for being too sad, and too slow, and too colorless, and she prods us to restore the magical effects."

✦✦✦

I wrote the following in response to a series of brutal comments on The Living Theatre's repertory program at the Joyce Theater in New York: in *The New York Times* by Frank Rich, in *The Voice* by my colleague Jay Novick, and by others. I had not been enchanted with the bulk of the program, but it made no sense to treat this company as if it had no history, as if it wasn't one of the most revolutionary and acclaimed ensembles in the world, whose influence on the Western theatre is incalculable. I wanted to put the new work in a meaningful perspective, and by so doing I wanted to begin to understand why the present work wasn't up to the best of what I knew and loved about this theatre.

I made an error in judgment by sharing the as-yet unpublished essay with Julian. I saw it as a kind of birthday present. Julian saw it otherwise. He hated what I had written, he was deeply offended and communicated his feelings to Judith. She and I then had several terrible days together (not consecutively, thank God), which can be summed up by Judith's asking me what possible good could come through my printing the essay, and who was I writing it for in the first place? She even told me at one point that Julian had been sparing her the pain of reading my comments, so in fact she hadn't or hadn't been allowed to read this critique that she was trying to convince me to file away in my drawer before it hurt a cause central to all our lives. As Judith saw it, I was either for The Living Theatre or against it. Hanon Reznikov looked at me incredulously when I told him I had given Julian the essay as a gift. "What did you possibly think his response would be? This was a present for his birthday?"

I spent some days agonizing over what I was going to do. I told myself that, though I loved these people, I was not there to be their publicist, that if I could not address reality as I saw it, I was an irresponsible writer. This espousal, as I write it down now, seems so self-evident to me that it is even a little embarrassing to confess that I had qualms about printing the essay and at one time even considered junking it, or just filing it away as Judith had urged me to do. Here it is as published in Yale's Theater magazine, Spring 1985.

✧✧✧

THE SEVERAL STAGES OF THE
EMBATTLED LIVING THEATRE

By the winter of '84–'85, The Living Theatre had made the decision to settle (if that is the word) once again in New York City. Until the previous summer, it had hopes of establishing a two-cities base, performing six months in Paris and six months in New York, but events, not the least of which is Julian Beck's serious illness, have forced the company to reappraise what is possible. Julian, who originally came to theater from painting, has been eyeing his early canvases—indeed they fill the Beck's living room walls with their massive yellows, with their bright, sculpture-like forms—and sensing a desire to return to his early love. Judith Malina and Hanon Reznikov (the latter conceived and directed *The Yellow Methuselah*) have been conferring for long periods on The Living Theatre's next step. These discussions have been taking place in the Beck's Upper West Side apartment, hardly a quarter of a mile from where the first Living Theatre productions were mounted in the mid-Fifties. The next step? Paris offered a home, there are no such firm offers in New York—the Living needs a home, it needs funds to finance the work.

During my January visit to the apartment, we all hole up in the living room. Hanon mentions a theater for sale in the Village.

"Isn't it too small?" I ask. "And it's so pretty, almost prim. Do you want a pretty little theater?"

Judith, curled up in an armchair, smoking away, squints at me and barks in playful seriousness, "We can work anywhere. So what if it's pretty? Sure, the space will help dictate the kind of production we do. We can work large, we can work small."

By work Judith also means task. She means a theater whose goal is more than making and playing the play, it is playing the play, but it is also something else. The Becks have always seen themselves as philosophic anarchists and that vision is an energy force propelling, if not always informing their work. The vision presupposes the possibility of social arrangements that mitigate against the onerous weight of government, and it suggests a terrain in which new creative energies have an opportunity to flourish. Whether or not this vision is seen as Utopian, the Becks perceive its ongoing articulation as a necessary weapon in mankind's continuous battle against darkness.

The Becks speak over and over again of a time of darkness. We have indeed lived through (and survived) some form of 1984, but how it relates to Orwell's prophetic utterance and what the nature of our survival may be are issues which have hardly stirred the thoughts of our contemporary theaters.

The Becks, home somewhat over a year, see the United States (particularly New York?) as a community of fear. "We hang onto the Homeric myth about courage, about our manliness," Julian says. "No foreign country is going to push us around, we're tough, virile."

"People seem to feel this need to protect themselves against a kind of libertinism," Judith explains. "It's as if they perceive what they read as a weakening of morals—let's say it's pacifism or an openness toward sexuality—leading to a weakening of our national resolve. Such a weakening might inspire a Soviet attack."

"At the same time," Julian notes, "most people want peace. But nobody on either side of the Atlantic can find a bridge between where we are and where we want to be. This lack brings on a form of paralysis. But even as we're afraid of anything that might upset the present balance of terror, we all seem to be waiting for some liberating idea."

"And we're afraid," Judith adds. "I'm afraid. For instance, what are the physicists doing in outer space? What are they tampering with, what do we really know about the nature of outer space? We know nothing, nothing, and yet they have no qualms about sending out these machines. They talk about the greenhouse effect, the way we're warming up the atmosphere, New York taking on the climate of Tampa, Florida. Why that's nothing. What if our temperature should rise to 130 degrees? To 150. Could we survive? What if it went up to 500? Who would survive at 500 degrees? We've such a little margin for survival. It's not stupid to be afraid."

"But fear of one another is something else," Julian says. "Fear of being touched is something else. And yet it connects to this fear of upsetting the balance of things."

"So much hate," Judith says. "Why so much hate? Why this need to attack?"

On my earlier visit to the Becks, soon after the January '84 run at the Joyce Theater had been cut short, Julian spoke of the press reception the Living had received. "I feel as if I'd been shot at. You know, I think whatever we would have done at those performances, the reviews would have been the same. One reviewer remarked that not only weren't we any good now, we were never any good."

It is hard to disagree with this depiction of an embattled world, of the planet as a series of discrete enclaves. Decades after the impulse toward brotherhood, after the attempt to institutionalize the concept of "one world," much lip-service is given to holistic thought, to "wholeness," nevertheless, the "us and them" polarity continues to thrive. Theater has its peculiarly tawdry manifestation of this fortress psychology, and the Becks were seeing it in one of its more virulent forms: Not only disagreement but scathing contempt, not only boredom but lethal hatred. Theater criticism isn't generally known for its concern to understand, for putting things in context, too often it itches to stake out adversary positions, and often its rhetoric betrays an inexplicable desire to annihilate. We don't utilize murderous weapons as we sit in our theater seats, but what if we had access to them?

Nevertheless I don't perceive the same quality of darkness the Becks are addressing themselves to. I see a kind of self-centeredness and lack of consciousness which may not be very different from that of earlier peoples who responded to prophetic utterances with a grand impatience. Also, people I know are terribly concerned about the continued escalation of the arms race, but they tend to seek out physicists and social thinkers, not theatrical artists, for serious dialogue. They want critical, informative thought, not poetry. But critical, informative thought has its obvious limitations, it has a threshold, and it is beyond this threshold where poetry begins. Poetry reaches us in that place where Socrates, late in life, understood he hadn't gone. In prison, his dream said to him, "Socrates, make music." What makes the Living Theatre particularly confusing, and particularly valuable, is that it has its feet in both camps. It is theater, it is serious, and yet it is also both less and more.

Some people came to the Living Theatre's program at the Joyce with all the good will in the world, others who had never seen its work came with curiosity and comparatively open minds, still others with skepticism, with guarded demeanor, perhaps with fear, and still others with a self-centeredness that no theater event could have dislodged. I want to address these thoughts particularly to those who came with good will, and to those who have a kind of love, as I do, for the company. I need to add that since drafting an earlier version of this article I've been beset by doubts. Is a retrospective look at, a serious analysis of the evolving work of the Living of use to anyone at this time? I don't believe that at present it's of the slightest use to those in the company who are close to me. They need simply, as Judith says, to go on with their work. Why then take the trouble to write these words? Are they for the readership of this magazine? No. Or rather, no and yes. Why publish? Primarily because beliefs are like currency, they need to be moving around in the community, they ought not to be hoarded. Because if there is any insight in these words, the writer has an obligation to write them. Obligation to whom? To the truth—to the extent that one understands it.

To begin with, the return of our most celebrated anti-Establishment renegades last year aroused some false expectations. The peculiarly assertive nature of the Living Theatre—its mix of head-on challenge and fraternal solicitude—is a given. Some spectators bask under this battering, some endure it out of a sense of old-world etiquette, and some are truly affronted. But the assertiveness in the new work seemed to these eyes sporadic, and went hand in hand with a curious movement toward polished, almost genteel, almost "lovely" acting. Well, if there's one thing that this company is not, it's polished, and another thing that it's not is lovely. The Living Theatre's strong point in performance has always been its raw energy, at its best its attack has always been frontal, when it has been true to its material it has come at you with combat boots. Granted that as early as *Mysteries*, in those rapidly changing tableaux, it attempted something it saw as the suspended niceties of bodies in space; but those bodies nevertheless were never nice and we loved the company for being made of vulnerable beings, rather than the pampered darlings of Thespis. It may be that last year's performers were more sure-footed, more in a state of physical disgrace than the husky wall-bangers we recall from the Sixties, but they were not sure-footed enough, and the texture of their feistiness was thinner than that of the adored guerrillas of yesteryear: The Henry Howards, Jim Andersons, Warren Finnertys, Steve Ban Israels and the rest.

But more important, those who were looking for new theatrical concepts, "advanced" concepts, were basing these expectations on the fact that the company, after each periodic five or ten years of exile, returns home with some daring, challenging, irritating, mesmerizing idea. To the degree that it is always fulfilling our expectations by offering what we have not expected of it—upsetting the sense of a scripted play in which a progressive event happens by offering *The Connection* and *The Brig*; upsetting the sense of the contained world of *The Connection* and *The Brig* by offering the flowering world of *Paradise Now*; upsetting even the serendipitous messianic character of a *Paradise Now* by developing its anarchistic, community-organizer persona in the favellas of Brazil—to this degree, the company's recent work is true to form. But where the company had always been startling in its breaking away from, now, in 1984, it was startling in its breaking back to. The Toller work, *Masse-Mensch*, usually translated as *Masses and Man*, here as *The One and the Many*, formulates a kind of museum aesthetic by building on the extravagant Expressionist delicacies of the silent German film; and *The Yellow Methuselah*, for all its ensemble display of colors in muscular motion, depends largely on the leaden-footed, if sensible and sometimes charming, didacticism of Bernard Shaw. It is as if John Cage, with no prior notice, were to introduce nuances shockingly similar to those of Johannes Brahms.

But to concentrate on the aesthetic, to concentrate on the form, is to demand what Bertolt Brecht always demanded and what the Living Theatre rarely pays serious heed to. It has never entertained (recall Brecht's dictum on entertaining) through the subtleties of performance; its brilliance has not usually been measured in the way it shapes a work. The work is always shaped, not through a conscious and wonderful sense of shaping, but through the intensity of commitment; the work sits as it were on moral bedrock, it is shaped by an ethical sense of being. The Living Theatre has always had messages for us, it has always been an exemplary if sometimes overheated messenger, and it has never deviated from its task. Certainly from the period of *The Connection* and *In the Jungle of Cities* it has always seen itself as a critical voice in a world in crisis. To compare, for example, its *Archeology of Sleep* with the work of performance-art oriented groups like those of Robert Wilson, Richard Foreman and Mabou Mines is as fruitless as comparing what goes on in a medical research laboratory with what goes on in an art gallery. The Becks appear to be working in the theater because they are using modes that seem recognizable to theater-goers, but in fact for years they have not been working in theater as much as they have been working out of it. The Living Theatre prop may look like a theatrical prop, but when it works it's a scalpel. Essentially, the work is not self-referential (though there is an unfortunate self-congratulatory streak discernible now and again.) Many experimental theaters work off the raw materials of dreams to exclaim, "The wonder of it all." The Living Theatre's intent is to examine the experience of what is currently conceived as the wish-censorship-thinking dream life. The strain of vicarious wonder isn't absent from the work, but *Sleep* is a bit portentous and smacks a little of the doctoral thesis, there is always the sense that its purveyors are ready to scrap the whole edifice (regardless of their enchantment with it) if they could realize a more efficacious way of evaluating the dynamics of the sleeping being. One might question the public theatricalizing of dream content, but there is no denying the Living's intent to explore, rather than bask in experience.

If *Sleep* intermittently suggests the character of an unwieldy psychic iceberg, *The One and the Many* is like a moral sledgehammer wielded in the cause of a radical, and yet curiously modest, political concept. In a letter to Stefan Zweig from his prison cell in June of 1923, Toller noted that "The Absolute Good, the earthly Paradise will not be created by any system; the only problem is to fight for the relatively best which man can find and realize." Toller's ode-like narrative of a bourgeois woman trying to mediate between the exploitative levers of capitalism and the vindictive righteousness of the exploited labor force is as pertinent today as it was in Toller's Weimar world of the Twenties. Violence, history has assured us, is seldom without its adherents along the entire political spectrum. As for *Methuselah*, for all its premium on reason and the beauties of disembodied thought, it can still nag at us with its simple message that humanity is more than the sum of its victims, that an early death is not God-given.

In the Living Theatre, we are looking at what is surely one of the oldest theater companies in the West. To say that it has been evolving over some four decades is misleading, for in some manner the company (ultimately one refers to its prime movers, Judith Malina and Julian Beck) has turned in upon itself. If there is a sense, as some of us uneasily felt during the recent New York run, that the company was hardly on sure footing, it may be useful to look briefly at those decades.

The Living went from a dense, at times highly poetic, at times metaphysical drama (Picasso, Ezra Pound, Pirandello, Jackson MacLow), a drama that played with chance, with literary or theatrical conceits, to more politically or socially-grounded work from the United States (whether it leaped or was pushed is now a moot point), it built its productions, by and large, on highly developed literary texts, and texts by writers who experienced writing as an embodiment of thought and/or feeling. What the Becks did was to use the text as a ground; in a sense the company flew by the seat of its pants, but underlying this *wunderkind* bravado was the textual ground, the base of a literary intelligence.

But, with the break from home came a new period, exemplified by *Mysteries and Smaller Pieces*, by *Frankenstein*, and finally in 1968 by *Paradise Now*. With the exception of Brecht and his adaptation of *Antigone*, the writer had largely disappeared as a major force, as an essential ground element. That is, the writer as writer had been replaced by the performer and/or director as writer. In keeping with the strategies of many experimental ensembles of the time, the writer's building of character, or rendering of a critical action, was replaced by the performer's political harangue, by social parody, spiritual exhortation and confessional outpouring. The text as ground either vanished or, in many cases, was picked apart, metamorphosed into raw material, into bold utterances that moved in lockstep with the home-made pieties of the performer.

For the Living Theatre the writer's ground was replaced by the crisis: The arms race, civil rights, world hunger, political exploitation, the threat of nuclear extinction. The performer became an emblematic witness but no longer an embodiment of a world going increasingly mad. The crisis both housed and reinforced the strident, bold attempt at the humanistic utterance. The spectator became a comrade-in-arms or a turned-off observer, in either case he or she had been hurled into the arena.

With the Living's Brazilian period, and its work on *The Legacy of Cain* in the early Seventies, the impulse set off in *Paradise Now*, that movement into the embattled street, was at last fulfilled. The interior of the playhouse, the bourgeois palace, came to play a minor role. The Living's nomadic character, a community constantly on the road, was now reinforced by its staking out streets, fields and empty lots to bring home its prophesies.

Though it returned to interiors with its *Seven Meditations on Political Sado-Masochism*, its Pittsburgh sojourn, exemplified by *Six Public Acts*, was essentially an outdoor one. It had moved to Pittsburgh with the idea of performing on the grounds of industrial sites, its audience primarily factory workers, but as it turned out its principal work was in streets and parks. *Six Public Acts*, wending its way along the streets of Pittsburgh with the pious demeanor of a Stations of the Cross processional, made its theatrical stops within proximity of private banks, federal buildings, public housing projects and local police stations. What seems significant in retrospect is that if the ground of crisis replaced the ground of the writer's vision, the ambiance of the street with its classical connotations of immediacy, contingency and displacement accelerated the sense of crisis heating up.

But now in the Eighties the Becks have led their current generation of vagabonds back into the bourgeois palaces. And now the writer is returning. Brecht comes back into the repertoire in '78, later Toller is recruited, and Shaw and Kandinsky also labor side by side with the writer-performers. But the writer-writers, despite a richness of vision, seem, at least to this ear, to lack a contemporary voice. With the exception of Brecht, whose ironic certitudes seem untouched by the passage of time, they seem not fully present, they come sounding out of the past, a bit archaic, the patina of the well-thumbed text overlaying the production. Which unsettles the ground, and creates an uneasy distancing. The statements become diffuse, the issues speak to our time but the ontological sense suggests remoteness. Finally, there is the absence of the street. It cuts deeply into the air of crisis, into the ground of immediacy. Perhaps the Living's inevitable movement into the aisles, into the audience, is its attempt to balance the loss of the street, but the movements seem arbitrary, perfunctory, groundless. Julian's "where we are" as opposed to "where we want to be" certainly addresses a growing despair, but in the almost rococo embrace of these recent productions, what should be burning issues are beclouded.

Having said all this, I want to state that I found the condescension exhibited in most of the press coverage both misplaced and presumptuous. We—all of us in theater, and all of us who take theater seriously—owe this company a debt of gratitude. I'll speak for myself. Before I saw Judith and Julian's work, before I saw *The Connection* in 1960, I thought I knew something about theater. Hadn't I seen wonderful Shakespeare, hadn't I seen Lorca and O'Casey and Brecht, and hadn't I seen *Godot* and *Endgame* in the late Fifties? Well, in some curious way, with a few exceptions, I had been seeing the outside of the play. The Beck's productions, with their purposeful crudity, taught me to begin to see inside the play, to understand something essential about the life of the play, about the play as grounded being.

September 21, 1995

Short, open letter to Judith Malina from Arthur Sainer—

In *The Enormous Despair*, one volume in your extraordinary diary, you rather airily inform your readers that your old comrade, A. Sainer, phoned his faculty colleague, Claude Fredericks, prior to the Living's *Paradise Now* performance at Bennington College, in November of '68, and "warned him that Bennington would be burned to the ground . . . and furthermore all the students would get pregnant." Now, I have no idea what Claude might have been smoking at the time the clouds opened up to reveal these messages about pregnancies and conflagrations, and it's unfortunate that you never bothered to discuss any of this with me. For the record, I may have phoned Claude once in my life about faculty business but never about anything remotely connected to The Living Theatre. I did, however, meet with the late Ed Blaustein, president of the college, and suggested rather strongly that we consider busing our students down to New York for a *Paradise Now* performance. There is no way you could have known this, but a lot of ugly stuff was going on within the larger community, including some Counter Culture characters who would come down from the hills and use storefronts on Main Street for rifle practice. In addition, I had gotten word that one student close to me had suicidal impulses. In hindsight, busing this student to the Big Apple for any kind of performance doesn't seem particularly sensible. I believe I was also paranoid at the time for reasons that had nothing to do with your theatre, but even hindsight tells me it was hardly a terrific moment for the larger Bennington community to be harangued about pulling off all its clothes, smoking whatever illegal substances the FBI was fretting about and getting off on one's paranoia. We'd had two major assassinations that spring, we had an ugly war on and racism was rampant, and your coming to our campus hardly seemed to me a healing element for a very troubled society.

I spent much of that performance standing alongside my student with the suicidal impulses. She loved the work and told me late in the evening that she'd like to go off with the company. I neither encouraged nor discouraged her, but I was there if she needed me. Another of my students spat in Steve Israel's face and in response Steve punched her in the nose or the mouth. At some point late that night I brought my dog Zymph in to see what she could of the show and she napped peacefully.

Finally, perhaps you didn't know that I had urged my friend Saul Gottlieb to form what became the Radical Repertory, that strange booking agency that brought you guys home and to the Bennington campus that November night long ago.

Peace.

17. SQUAT

Squat took its name from its condition. In the early seventies, the authorities in Budapest did not consider the public performances of these theatre people to be in the best interests of a sober socialist community. Forbidden to show their new wares in public, the company of actors, writers, and designers did not go underground, but simply went indoors. They began working in an apartment house, much like Judith and Julian Beck began The Living Theatre in their West End Avenue apartment. But this new, relatively cloistered approach to public performance hardly satisfied the guardians of public consciousness in Budapest. Indoors or outdoors, publicly or privately, the troupe was ladling out subversion. Everything about its work was irreverent. It lacked decorum and seriousness; it was pornographic, blasphemous, unseemly, and it refused to take into account anything that might be useful for the further development of the socialist order. It was as if W. C. Fields or Monty Python had battened down in the most sacred corridors of the Vatican. What was a proper society to do with these infidels who had no apparent interest either in Lenin or the Virgin Mary, who might wind up bartering the nail parings of Andy Warhol on a given corner of Buda or Pest on any night of the week? And how were these cool, impassioned infidels to carry out the self-appointed task of bearing theatrical witness to a world that struck them as being seriously out of order? The work was no longer to be created or performed in Budapest. It took some time, but the company was able at last to become émigrés after living briefly in Paris and Manhattan, and performing in Rotterdam, Nancy, at the Shiraz Festival and the Baltimore Festival.

Anna Koos, presently living on the Lower East Side, recalls the history of this now-disbanded company:

May 25, 1993, New York

Dear Arthur,

You have asked me to send you the script of our play *Pig, Child, Fire!* In the "professional"—not to mention "conventional"—sense of theater, our performances were neither scripted nor rehearsed.

Nor was our group named for several years—from 1971 until 1976, when our work in Budapest was more experimental and more productive than it ever would be in the West. For the first year and a half, we had been allowed—on and off—to perform in a cultural center amid high-rise projects located on the periphery of the city. This center, a one-story building (not unlike the Henry Street Settlement on the Lower East Side) was named (by the Ministry of Culture) after Lajos Kassák, the Hungarian avant-garde poet, writer, organizer, founder and editor-in-chief of the literary and art magazine *Today*, published between the two world wars. Kassák's legacy corresponded with our artistic credo, thus we humbly yet proudly accepted the billing "Kassák Studio."

The following four and a half clandestine years defied name, script, and stage. Had we not experienced—even before our Kassák Studio period—the trials and tribulations of theatrical apprenticeship (I am now referring to the standing core of Squat Theatre, namely Peter Halasz, myself, Stephan Balint and Peter Berg) at the University Theater Ensemble for several years, we might have been incapacitated by underground circumstances. However, we had already gone through quite a few seasons of Shakespeare, Marlowe, Brecht, Genet, Capek, commedia dell'arte, cabarets, etc., working in the capacities of actor, assistant director, stagehand, stage manager, and yes, author. Inspired by Jerzy Grotowski's Laboratory Theater (whose one rehearsal Peter Halasz and Stephan Balint had had the luck to witness in Wroclaw, Poland) Peter wrote a poem-play titled *KZ* which the Ensemble staged and performed on tour with the help and encouragement of one of the directors. Stephan Balint, inspired by the Absurd Theatre, wrote (in collaboration with an artist friend) a one-act play for two characters titled *Nathan and Tibold*, which the Ensemble also staged. Shortly afterward, the Ensemble's administration fired that theatre director for having been radical in his programming (referring, among others, to Halasz and Balint's plays) and for his openly gay behavior. Our response was to show solidarity with the director and to leave the Ensemble.

This is how we were propelled—by the turn of events—from the womb of the University located in downtown Budapest to the suburban projects from where we would be similarly expelled. Mind you, we had been ready to step beyond any established limit.

Historical timing gave us a chance in those four and a half clandestine years. In the fifties an underground theater performance by a collective would have meant immediate imprisonment, not to mention that even the idea of such a theater performance could not have come to mind—although, as we later learned, the Polish surrealist poet Bialoszewski had regularly held one-man shows in his own Warsaw apartment from as early as 1959 (not unlike those shows of Jack Smith much later in New York).

There was a unique twist: a seat reserved for the Polish minister of culture (opposition encapsulated was opposition contained).

In the early seventies, the threat of getting arrested for an unlicensed art show or theater performance was no longer imminent, but our every step was watched. On numerous occasions we found ourselves face to face with the police, secret and nonsecret alike. Because we did not aim at harassing the authorities—since political power was not our cause—we tried to ignore their attempts at harassing us. Bereft of the right to perform in public, to work on the books, and to carry a passport (very severe degrees of harassment, indeed) we continued to perform in the apartment of Peter Halasz and myself, as well as, occasionally, in those of other artists. This determination eventually prompted the authorities to fall into the other extreme: offering (half of) us safe exit if we would not return. To tell the truth, toward the end of this underground period we felt the noose getting tighter and affecting our work, mostly because it began to show signs of becoming inbred. After long deliberation we granted the authorities' wishes. I, for one, am thankful to them.

All this was only in the background, yet all this was indeed the background.

What became important for all the years to come was the quest for our authentic voices in authentic form—both as individual artists and as a collective.

Socially, we were part of a fully grown generation of poets, writers, artists, musicians, philosophers, psychologists, filmmakers, and theater people refusing to conform to the modernized social-realist mainstream, the local establishment, and those who instead wanted to belong to the tradition of Faulkner, Capote, Beckett, Hrabal, Stockhausen, the Turkish dervish dancers, the masks of Japanese Noh, Truffaut, Godard, Antonioni, Bergman, Menzel, and Pasolini. The upcoming intelligentsia formed our environment, supplying us with sharp criticism (often in writing, put up on the wall of our apartment) and with source material. Poets whose poems had no chance of getting published (we were just before the Samizdat era) read them to circles of friends, and some of them, poet, poem, and all, became part of our plays. Musicians who experimented with new instruments used them in our performances. Artists wove our nine-foot tall paper-stuffed rag-puppet into the likeness of King Kong. They were the core of our audience who at the end crowded in the airport to say good-bye.

Long forgotten were the hierarchical conventions of playwright-actor-scenic designer-director-stagehand limelight structure. Rehearsals evolved into brainstorming meetings and writing sessions, an ongoing individual and collective thinking and writing process that outlasted our migrations and that is missed the most by me ever since we stopped putting our minds together in 1984.

We had already shed the constraints of literary/theatrical conventions, but we were dissatisfied with activist nature of "happenings." Seeing a gap, an "empty space" for a new form, we began to experiment by questioning every facet of the theater. We were drawn to rituals. We tried to create a balance between spectators and performers in which the audience might be given more than sheer voyeurism and actors would not be expected to be overwhelming and bigger than life. That desire produced numerous variations of how we handled time. In the first apartment-piece, Peter Berg chose real time when he allowed the audience to watch his shadow squatting under a table covered with a cloth reaching down to the floor until he became inebriated; Peter Halasz disconnected real time when he stood fully dressed, with tie and hat, in a wooden frame, then very slowly, almost imperceptibly, became a half-naked person. To perform our play titled *King Kong* required three consecutive days to perform: possibly one evening, the next afternoon, and the following morning. The original performance took place in an unused chapel on top of a hill overlooking the Lake Balaton. The chapel housed a series of avant-garde art events in a spontaneous summer festival. Later in the city we condensed the show into two parts: an evening and the following morning or afternoon.

Inspired by a subject (a piece of news like Yukio Mishima's hara-kiri; a detractable idol like King Kong; or even a joke), we devised situations (events) in which we could imagine one another and, as time went by, we could rely on one another's skills. This method resulted not in improvised mimicry but in instantaneous and intense presence, often bringing forth unforeseen, yet expected moments. Thus we circumvented and eventually omitted interpretation.

We put forward much of our personal histories—and very different individuals we were. Personal histories that were invented or true, depending on the person's desire. We ended up creating a rich material that might explain the lasting memory we left behind and the challenge we took upon ourselves when we faced an unknown public: on foreign territory we had to part with our personal mythology.

Two aspects of our apartment-theater period gave us a crutch and an edge: the use of space and text.

Like literature and art, which require individuals to extend themselves at both the inception and the reception of a piece of writing or art, theater and music are collective forms that have become buried under the social and economic structures of schooling and architecture. Music broke this barrier first. The emergence of rock groups in the sixties held up a new example. (Jazz/blues was the true predecessor but its historical context would not let it penetrate society.) The makeshift stage of commedia dell'arte had not been covered to protect people from rain but to establish an economic institution. (The opera may have had the excuse of trapping sound or creating good acoustics, but every musician knew that only playing in the wind could call forth the song of the sirens.) A beautiful example of how life ridiculed, eroded, swallowed, and spit out this form of theater is John Cassavetes' Pirandellesque play-turned-film *The Opening Night*. The first invaders of stone-theater (a phrase we used for the rigid frame of institutionalized bourgeois black-box stage) were the Angry Young Men (John Osborne, Arnold Wesker, etc.) who brought the odors of basement dwellers and restaurant kitchens to the perfume-scented glitters of London's West End. A decade later The Living Theater and the Bread and Puppets took to prisons and the streets. As for us, our road was different. In the suburban cultural center we had already parted from the conventional set-up, but not until we would have to outwit legal orders prohibiting our public appearances by taking upon ourselves the "constraints" of performing in apartments. Only then did we discover the meaning of space. Suddenly new dimensions appeared— history, familiarity, strangeness, hiding, revealing, distance and intimacy— which radically changed the meaning of our work. From time to time we came across possibilities other than the apartment by searching out unregulated "blank spaces": a no-longer functional church, an abandoned sand mine, or an unfrequented island where spectators and performers shared the pleasures of the imagination as reflected in the reality of this given space as opposed to the previously dished out roles of auditorium and set design. You can imagine how distressed we were to find good will on the part of our Western friends when they showed us their "black-walled empty coffins," their nine-to-five performing spaces where "everything" was allowed. In Rotterdam, in January 1977, when we were desperately looking for a space for our first play to be created "in freedom," we visited all nine theaters in town, including the magnificent opera house, yet we felt paralyzed and that we could not relate to any of them. They were institutions reeking of subsidized, ready-made, no-risk culture.

We had already understood that theater carries a potential ignition point in its imminent nature; so did the power structure. (Herein lies the historical nature of theater. It is not by chance that the last ten years were suffocating, castrated, theatre-less times.) Whether this potential ignition point is present in a particular theater event or not depends on the play's ability to be happening then and there, leaving "space" for unpredictable and unrepeatable elements to occur. It was with this context in mind that we approached words or rather text. Our performances held no place for dialogues. Actors, rather players, were expected to invent their lines within the context of the "story" and the situation. We sang songs, read tales, invoked texts from ceremonies, juxtaposed literary texts or poems, chatted, played question and answer games: anything but realistic imitations.

For example, in our Diary Theater series (when each of us felt free and obliged to initiate and join a performance on an almost daily basis) we presented Chekhov's *Three Sisters* (the only piece of drama literature per se in our repertoire). We deleted every line in the play except those of Irina, Olga, and Masha. The sisters were present in the shape of the three men (Peter Halasz, Stephan Balint, and Peter Berg), wearing Chekhovian light-colored cotton suits and wire-rimmed glasses and sitting calmly in a triptychlike formation on a foot-high riser in the corner of the room at the window. Spectators sat on a bench running along the three other walls of the room, leaving a gaping void between stage and audience. The sisters would simply repeat the prompter (myself) who acted out all three of them in a loud whisper.

An example of extemporized talk in our play *Alice's Sisters*: a woman wearing a hood and mask made out of fresh green cabbage leaves played chess with a pregnant woman, while a third woman—young, tall and beautiful—chatted with them incessantly. The scene was repeated in the adjacent room, but the pregnant woman chatted the chat that the third woman had chatted before, and that text was different each time.

To challenge the order of the world around us, the structure of our plays was non-hierarchical; we used parallel actions, inactivities, images, words, silences, characters, atmospheres as opposed to role-centered stories. Our intellectual and spiritual interdependence, along with our autonomous individual creativity, eventually blotted out the storyline. This technique of juxtaposition—without a spotlight to direct the spectator's eyes—opened the spectrum of possible subjects: the five acts in *Pig, Child, Fire!* were the most extreme choices.

The store front was love at first sight, exciting, and inspiring. In our Western work the store front would berth authentic motives of cultural and political mythology.

The title *Pig, Child, Fire!* originates from the prohibitive measures of the Rotterdam Art Council that banned (we did not seem to be able to get away from authorities) parts of our proposal, namely: pig, child, and fire. The next possible mythical domestic animal to the pig was the goat. My daughter was not allowed to "work" in Rotterdam (she first appeared in the

Nancy Festival). Fire in the street burned undisturbed. (No one really cared if Peter got hurt or not!)

As I promised you on the phone, I searched all my papers but could not find any notes except for the two literary texts: by Dostoyevsky, Artaud. Here I am trying to remember as accurately as possible:

ACT I: *At Tikhon's: Stavrogin's Confessions (drama)*

Nikolai Stavrogin, a retired army officer, pays an ominous visit at Father Tikhon's. Stavrogin hands over his confessions in which he relieves himself of his sin: The raping of the twelve-year old and already abused daughter of one of his landladies, then wishing the child's death and not preventing her abysmal suicide. Stavrogin wants his confessions to be published. The father is abhorred and would not absolve the sinner. Thus goes the story.

The spectators have entered an ordinary building (unusual for theater performance), they are seated in the usual fashion, facing a closed black velvet curtain like in any other theater. Music precedes the curtain's opening.

The faint melody beginning Wagner's Overture to the third act of *Tristan and Isolde* is played on a solo instrument. As the orchestra enters, the music builds up to the accompaniment of the slow-paced movement of the curtain. By the time the music reaches a crescendo, the curtain is fully open.

The stage is dimly lit to keep visibility in the street, forming the "scenic" background.

The image thus revealed is dominated by a giant sculpted man hanging upside down from the ceiling. His knees are bent toward the audience, evoking the image of a falling angel. From between his legs a man's head protrudes. He is hung by a noose. His face is covered by a life-size mask, identical to that of the puppet. Outside in the street, in front of the store window, a bearded man walks by with a dog. One sleeve of his heavy coat is on fire. Their appearances are intermittent throughout the play.

On stage are a goat with a golden-faced doll's head attached to its horns, a four-year-old girl, and a woman. The floor is covered with sand.

The man in the puppet is hanging motionless for the entire scene, time enough to hear Stavrogin's confessions and Father Tikhon's answer.

The oversized reflection of the hanging man in the puppet and the text are the two fixed elements (art and literature) forming the warping texture of the scene. The simultaneous planned and extemporaneous activities of the goat, the child, the woman onstage, and the man with the dog and the life in the street outside, form the filling threads of the roof. The woven texture becomes the performance—recreating itself in a different way every night.

The characters and their actions refer to each other and are parallel with, yet separate from Dostoyevsky's dramatis personae.

When the little girl is playing with falsies and makeup (which the woman helps her put on), she is fantasizing about becoming a woman the way all little girls do (many of them play–act it in their mothers' bedrooms). Her act of initiation gains another dimension by being performed in public and by being placed in the context of Stavrogin's confessions.

The child then takes the accessories of a woman, while the woman performs a mock sacrifice (she mixes blood, puts a sizable piece of raw meat onto the animal, then lifts it off) on the goat now wearing a cherublike mask.

The uncontrolled, unconscious, private activities of the goat, the child, and the woman become public onstage (although they are inside the window!)—hence the analogy with the nature of confession: revealing one's unconscious desires and deeds to a representative moral authority. Stavrogin is aware after the fact that he irrevocably broke a universal moral law, not only a religious one. He cannot tell his story but has to write it down. Having no hope for relief, he devises his own penitence by asking for its publication. In the theater the man in the puppet is hanging from the ceiling for forty-five minutes. His bravado is not even visible until the very end, rendering the act an air of personal, silent confession. In compensation his face is hidden behind a mask and his body is hanging in a three-times-larger-than-life-size puppet—both in his likeness. The confessions begin to be deciphered by the woman as she comes across a piece of paper protruding from the pocket of the puppet's vest—they continue to be read by a recorded male voice. The words of Father Tikhon's criticism come from the bearded man in the street whose rage is directed (through the window) at the stage where the woman, the only half-conscious person, tries to fend him off by marching to the window with a knife in hand. When the Father reaches ecstasy in his tirade, the actor turns to a gesture as if to a last resort: He flashes his naked body under the heavy overcoat. The woman's judgment consists of two words: "Damned psychologist!"

She cuts the noose around the neck of the hanging man and pulls the paper maché figure off him. Then, to the rhythm of a waltz by the Russian composer Dunayevsky, she begins a dance macabre with the dangling legs of the hung man while he ejaculates through his fake phallus, pulling his mask off to close his eyes. The man with the dog rushes on the apocalyptic stage: now it is a matter of who is stronger. The woman flings the goat above her shoulders, grabs the child's hand, and leaves.

Curtain falls.

Literary characters defy impersonation because their vital force is language and because printed words become animated only in the reader's mind; therefore the unnamed woman, child, goat, hanging man, bearded man, and dog on stage coexist with the recited text in an archetypal collective state. Thus literature and live drama would only reflect each other, if not for the presence of a wider public space, the street. This act becomes complete in the spectator's mind: As if at a symphony concert, the audience experiences the simultaneity of hearing Dostoyevsky's lines, watching the goat, the child and the woman, and witnessing a bus that happens to pass by with riders inside. Consequently, each audience has a practically different "show," but hopefully every performance reveals similar meanings.

To the relief of the spectators, prerecorded audience murmur enhances the break.

Act II: *"We Are the Dummies" (a slapstick)*

Paraphrasing motives from the late forties' gangster movies in the genre of silent slapstick comedies, paying tribute to North American culture, we had lots of fun imagining and performing this scene—so did passersby, drivers and members of the audience.

When the curtain opens, the spectators find themselves in the back of a mechanic's shop. Loud electronic pop music fills the air. One song, "We Are the Dummies" by Kraftwerk, lasts the entire scene. The lyrics talk about the revolt of shop window dummies who become fed up with being dummies in a shop window. One day they break through the window and take to the streets.

It is after hours (dark) in the mechanic's shop. The mechanic, apparently drunk, has fallen asleep at his workbench littered with tools and empty beer bottles. His companion, dressed in a bright red gown, is seated in the bay window with her back to us. As she lights a cigarette, passersby mistake her for a prostitute.

On one side of the stage the TV is on: "Broadcasting" live from the street.

In front of the window, a taxicab pulls up at the curb. Two men, dressed à la Humphrey Bogart, get out. They can't wait until the cab leaves: They are about to start a duel. They turn back-to-back, put their hands in their pockets, and pull out pistols. Arms lowered, they step out forty feet. One stays at the window and aims across the street at the other who raises his arm on the other side.

The lady's attention has been following their every step and in the critical moment we see her stand up, pull a pistol from her gown, and shoot at the dueler in her reach. He collapses right away with his arm flailing at the window. His adversary is baffled. He hurries across the street, diagnoses death, looks up and his eyes meet hers—she is caught with the pistol in her hand. He does not hesitate: Puff! he shoots her instead. Blood oozing from her mouth, and she falls—cleverly enough to strike the pose of a dead beauty.

The mechanic has been sleeping through the shoot-out and he is still asleep. The cocky gangster enters the shop to assess his prize. To his surprise there is a sleeping witness to his crime. A good gangster does not kill anyone in his sleep. He keeps circling around the workbench, tips the sleeper's hat off with the nozzle of his pistol—no result. He keeps circling, grabs a beer bottle, and cracks it on the edge of the workbench—no result. He switches on the electric grinder—waits—no result. He picks up a hatchet from the bench and begins to sharpen it on the grinder, sending high pitched squeaks and sparkles in the air—no result. He has no other choice but to chop off the sleeper's hand. That does the job!

What an insult! His hand, his wife, his dream! The intruder is meekly stroking the dead beauty's leg. The last straw.

Our mechanic opens the drawer and pulls out a small gun. Puff!... Puff...Puff, puff! Fail...Fail...Fail, Fail. "I wonder why," thinks the untouchable.

The mechanic has had it. Gun between teeth he climbs on top of his bench and gets on all fours. He pulls down his pajama pants and puts the gun in his arse. Carefully balancing in the tight space, he manages to pull the trigger. Now it does go off, stopping the music and spilling shards and beer all over the place in his fall.

The untouchable feels touched, and in a brotherly gesture covers the dead mechanic's behind with his coat and puts his hat on top. A nosy photographer flashes away in front of the window.

Curtain.

Break.

ACT III: *Antonin Artaud's Letter to André Breton from February 1947.*

Since the very beginning, Antonin Artaud's writings have had a lasting effect on our thinking. I found the English translation of Artaud's letter to

André Breton in an alternative bookstore in Amsterdam. I was hit by how pertinent his exposure of the impossible relationship between theater and society in the Western world was to our situation and to the world around us. I was also hit by the deep personal rage permeating his letter, by his use of language which did not contain all the words he needed, making him borrow from Tarahumara Indians and eventually forcing him to invent and say the impossible.

In the theater I stand at the theatrical divide between stage and audience. The curtain is wide open with an empty stage and a live street in the background. In front of me a music stand holds the text, and to my left a television monitor shows my vulva in an extreme close-up via a camera under my skirt. The blown-up image is distorted almost to the point of unrecognizability. I chose the exposure of my (and of any woman's) most intimate body part with its movements as a biological expression of the uncontrollable.

ACT IV: *Dinner*

For our four children it was dinner time. Therefore, they took their cups and saucers, and already in pajamas they descended to the theater, in the company of one of their mothers, Eva Buchmuller. This time the street was shut out because it was dinner time. The vertically turned TV-monitor occupied a seat along with Eva and the children around a table. Their conversation followed the day's event, but they often kept to themselves. It was as calm or as rowdy as dinners get. On the TV set the live portraits of the members of the audience appeared via a cameraman who was videotaping them one by one (in a 90-degree tilt to fit the elongated screen which in turn would match the other participants at dinner). Thus the spectators were also invited for dinner, one after the other, except they had to be satisfied with the projection of their faces and no real food (cause for laughter). At one point a somnambulist, a young naked woman (Agnes Santha), crossed the stage to the melody from "Once Upon the Wild West."

ACT V: *The Last One*

When the children had gone upstairs (to bed offstage), two men entered (Peter Berg and Peter Halasz). Peter Halasz had a piece of glass wrapped in newspaper under his arm. A glass cutter was stuck behind his ear. They were dressed in street clothes. Halasz lit a cigarette and placed the glass on the table to cut it with the measured gestures of a glass cutter. Peter Berg munched on the leftover from the table. When the glass was cut with its tap-tap, crunch noise, Halasz extinguished his cigarette on a piece of bread, wrapped the two halves of the glass into two pieces of newspaper, gave one half to Peter Berg and kept the other. They paused for a moment, looked at each other, tipped their hats or said good-bye. One parted through the stage door, the other through the street.

The song "Europe Endless" by Kraftwerk played on the loudspeakers.

THE END.

The Act of Stavrogin's Confessions was based on Peter Berg's obsession with sin, confession, moral integrity and Dostoyevsky. The paper maché figure was sculpted by Eva Buchmuller. The players were: Hanging man-Peter Berg; burning man with dog-Peter Halasz; woman-Anna Koos; child-Galus Halasz.

Some reviews of the play interpreted this scene as a surrealist drama. In my understanding, "classical" surrealist art appositions "real" elements—words, objects (furry cup), or cultural symbols (Duchamp's Rrose Selavy's portrait of mustached Mona Lisa in a winter landscape)—where the resulting composite idea or image falls beyond the realm of the original association of the separate elements, possibly targeting their limits. Our non-realistic composite images (e.g. the doll-headed goat) are attempts at creating archetypes whose spirit is related to that of the masks of Tibetan rituals, Greek drama, and Native American ceremonies.

Act II was as truly a collective piece as it comes. The players were: Lady—Agnes Santha or Marianne Kollar (depending on who had a visa to which country); The Untouchable—Stephan Balint; His Adversary—Peter Halasz; Mechanic—Peter Berg; Live Camera—Larry Solomon.

Act III was my idea. Peter Halasz figured out and constructed the video part.

Act IV was a collective idea. The live camera was operated by either Peter Halasz or Larry Solomon.

Act V was originally the seventh clown story in Stephan Balint's seven clown stories presented in May 1972 in several apartments in Budapest. In Rotterdam and Nancy this scene was played by Eric Daillie and William Cheyne. They assisted us in all technical matters of the performance.

Pig, Child, Fire! opened in Rotterdam, Holland at 129 Van OldenbarneveltStraat. This storefront later became a poetry bookstore. (Justly so because the street was named after a nineteenth-century Dutch revolutionary poet.) The street itself was narrow and a streetcar slowed down in front of the window to make a turn.

The play would have run its three-week course almost undisturbed and unnoticed had it not been for a police (!) report published in a local daily paper. That drummed up much attention and some audience. The Arts Council could not wait for us to get out of town.

My description presents *Pig, Child, Fire!* as it was shown in Rotterdam and Nancy. Later we gave up the sand surface. Truncated variations were performed in the Parisian Palace Theater (where the foyer was too narrow and Rue Pigalle was too busy to follow the exact performance) and in the 1977 Shiraz Festival. At the Shiraz Festival, another Act I had to be improvised because the giant puppet never arrived. We chose a scene from our past plays: A story based on the legend of the Killers of Children in Bethlehem. Also, the storefront at our disposal was situated in Shiraz per se, contrary to the exclusive royal locations of the festival in general. The window moved up and down electronically allowing us to open it all the way up during Act III. I was reading my lines from the middle of the stage; in front of me was the paying (upper middle class) audience, and behind me was a pressing crowd of street people including many veiled women and secret service agents. And under my skirt the video camera. In Teheran, the play had been banned before we even landed at the airport. In exchange we presented *The Three Sisters* on the rooftop of the Actors' Academy with the stage hanging over the landscape of Teheran at night.

In Baltimore, there was no street visible through the window: it was all campus grounds. But we had the opportunity to try out the so-called double-audience effect: One inside and another outside gathered on the concrete risers facing the window. The dinner scene was placed outside the window, below an impromptu audience of campus students. The car that came out of nowhere and crashed into the peaceful dinner table was a quasi shock designed to signal danger in a safe environment. In Act V (The Last One) the two men carried a small table to cut the glass on. As the window moved up and down, the table was left underneath and was also cut into two.

In New York, we first performed it in the Soho Bookstore on West Broadway, for three weeks, and by November of 1977 we opened it on Twenty-third Street. Other changes occurred as the play ran. The order of Acts III and IV were switched (first dinner, then philosophy). I began to read the letter from the street, facing the inside audience through the window; my reading thus made more of an impact upon people in the street, but at the same time it lost the strength of direct address. Some of us felt that Artaud's letter in its entire length would be burdensome on regular audiences (versus festival audiences), so Peter Berg interrupted it. Dressed in rags like a bum, he entered the stage—uninvited—and performed a surprising yoga exercise, a trivial street number. During the revival of the play in 1982, the by-then twelve-year old Rebecca Major played my role in

Stavrogin's Confessions, and we abolished the role of the little girl. The Dinner Act was expanded to accommodate the growing family, and occasional boyfriends were invited to the table. Not all the children "went to bed," and the young couple was left alone with the TV set and a guitar.

We performed *Pig, Fire, Child!* on two more occasions: At the Theater der Welt Festival in Hamburg, Germany, where the puppet was stolen out of its crate (luckily after performances); and in Florence, Italy, where the play was honored with the Annual Critics' Award. New York then gave us an Obie for it.

∽

18. JOE CHAIKIN:

THE OPEN THEATRE, THE WINTER PROJECT, AND BEYOND

As must be readily apparent by earlier entries in this volume, the paths between Joe Chaikin and this writer have intersected numerous times over some three decades. We've struggled together, at times avoided each other in subtle ways. We've been colleagues at performances, conferences, and demonstrations, and we've been incarcerated together in The Tombs. We spent part of that terrible November day of John F. Kennedy's much-televised funeral on Open Theatre business. I remember that we had one peculiarly extended phone conversation that seemed to be about nothing in particular, until Joe confessed that he was tying up both our phones so that the Guthrie Theatre in Minneapolis couldn't reach him and force him to decide if he was going to appear in the Terence McNally play they had fruitlessly, thus far, been trying to sign him for. We both have a sweet tooth and I recall standing with Joe, peering into the window of Sutter's bake shop on Greenwich Avenue in the Village, both of us appraising the assortment of danishes, tarts, and pies. When Joe gave a talk and ran a workshop at Middlebury College in the spring of 1983, I introduced him by noting that we were both still alive; he seemed taken aback by that reflection, and I had to explain that Joe had become a legend, and that this legend was still creating work and living through all the frustrations that besiege non-legendary humans. I remember that Joe was uncomfortable spending the night in the sweetly curtained New England home where Middlebury College often assigns its guests and opted for the relentlessly sterile modernity of the town motel. He was restless after he was safely ensconced in a low-ceilinged motel room with the inevitable TV set and a view of a filling station, and the local bank. It was going on towards midnight; Joe had been up much of the day, flying from New York, giving a public talk which included an extensive question and answer session, participating in a late-night supper with myself and theatre chairman Doug Sprigg, whom he had just met, revamping his sleeping arrangements, presumably readying himself for a several-hour workshop he would conduct the following morning, to be sandwiched between an early breakfast with chosen members of the faculty and the thirty minute drive to Burlington airport to catch the flight back to LaGuardia or Newark airport from where, like all arrivees in the congested terminals of the Metropolitan area, he would then have to negotiate passage back to his modest apartment in the West Village. If Joe was the least bit tired, he was also alive to the night. Not that he wanted to paint the town, what he wanted was to hang out with a few students. So I made the appropriate phone calls and we drove to campus to pick up my graduating seniors Beth Cleary and Will Hardy, and then went on to one of the local bar-restaurants to sit for an hour or so, discussing what was going on in the world of the radical or experimental or non-traditional or stubborn-don't-force-your-inauthentic-consumer-ridden-vision-on-me theatre. It was lovely, I was wiped out, Joe was unassuming and much interested in what was going on with this next generation of struggling artists, and then we downed our last beers and drove to our separate beds and whatever dreams each of us might generate in the benign post-Grandma Moses, anti-nuclear-conscious New England night. Then in 1984 Joe and many of the Open Theatre alumni flew out to Kent State for the reunion I write about below. I believe it was the last occasion when I spent any meaningful time with Joe before the stroke.

Joe had open heart surgery on two occasions. After the successful initial operation, he appeared onstage for the first time in a decade. What drew him was the opportunity to play the title role in Leonardo Shapiro's production of *Woyzeck* at the Public Theatre. To my knowledge, this was at least Joe's second attempt to perform the Buchner drama. The earlier occasion involved Wilford Leach, later artistic director at LaMama and then at the Public. In 1966 I asked Wil to share directing chores with me at The Bridge. Wil had wanted to stage *Woyzeck* for many years, but insisted he could only mount it with an extraordinary lead. He thought Joe might be that person, so I took him over to Joe's apartment, and the two men discussed whether indeed a *Woyzeck* might happen. Wil, in his peculiarly low-keyed, diffident openness, confronted Joe. "I hear you have a history of abandoning plays shortly after they open." Joe admitted as much. "I can't do this play," Wil said, "if I don't have the right person. I don't want you walking out on me after we open." As far as I can recall, Joe agreed to not walk out. Rehearsals began shortly thereafter. Diane Varsi, a quiet and intense young actress who had abandoned a career in Hollywood several years after her debut in "Peyton Place," was cast as Marie. Bill Finley, who had become part of Wil's informal repertory company at Sarah Lawrence College, was cast as The Captain, and Murray Paskin, an alumnus of both The Living and Open Theatres, was added to an as-yet incomplete cast. The work never got much past several rehearsals, for Joe kept his promise of not walking out after the opening—he walked out well before. I never did learn what the problem was, I only knew that an extraordinary *Woyzeck* had died stillborn. Everyone went on to other projects. Diane Varsi eventually returned to Hollywood to make films that I doubt she believed in, and she died at the age of 54 in November of 1992. As for Joe, it would be ten years before he had another try at the play, and the critics were pretty negative. Several of us at *The Voice* covered *Woyzeck* for the paper, and my review was the most positive. Under the headline "A Dream Production Falls Flat", here is what I wrote:

From *The Village Voice*, April 5, 1976

Woyzeck, born the Feast of the Annunciation, common soldier, atheist, has a child by Marie without the blessings of the Church. They name the child Christian. Woyzeck later stabs the unfaithful Marie, and dies for his crime. Christian is left in the care of an idiot. Or Woyzeck, on lowest rung of the economic ladder, without "virtue" because without bread, is exploited, used as a guinea pig, commits an act of desperation, is in Artaud's phrase "suicided by society." Or Woyzeck, haunted by voices, by visions of a hollow earth, sensing that the moon is a piece of rotten wood, that the sun is a faded sunflower, knowing that "a man of courage is a dirty dog," dies as Kafka's Joseph K. dies, "like a dirty dog." Buchner's play is at least all these plays.

A play of victims. Victim Woyzeck, but human existence is a victim and so are its members. Woyzeck, perhaps most victimized, is at the mercy of other victims, it is an element in the drama's terrible poignancy. The terrible hierarchy of victims. Victim Marie, she's as good as the grand ladies whose hands are kissed by gentlemen, she's not content to be Woyzeck's domesticated frau, she has sensual longings, a need for joy that the somberness of Woyzeck can't begin to satisfy, she exults in her fulsome body, she pays a terrible price for that exultation.

I'm in an obvious minority among my *Voice* colleagues and the daily press concerning the virtues of the current production. Despite director Leo Shapiro's tendency to simplify what seems to me Buchner's complex and sometimes contradictory vision—e.g., the deemphasizing of Woyzeck's anxiety about the Freemasons, the failure to develop Marie's feelings of guilt, the caricaturizing of Woyzeck's oppressive superiors (the captain, the doctor) so that we fail to see them as victims—despite all this, I found Shaprio's production in all its bareness a compelling one.

First there is Joseph Chaikin's masterly portrayal. Joe's Woyzeck is physically like a landscape overrun by the enemy: Bruised, scorched, pock-marked; the tanks obliterating a humanness which nevertheless presses upward time and again in an absurdly optimistic gesture that says life is somehow still conceivable; the human frame, the spirit of Woyzeck wincing, recovering, wincing again from the hammered nails of—what shall we call them finally—the Others?

Joe has given Woyzeck a stutter which is sometimes evident under moments of stress. Woyzeck is a seer, without formal education, in all his animal crudity. As metaphor, Woyzeck's stutter physicalizes an attempt to retreat from seeing, but the vision of calamity is so compelling that the stutter is also contrarily the breaking through to the word, the eruption of truth convulsively forcing its way through rock-like barriers which are attempts to dissociate self from feeling.

Joe inhabits Woyzeck's spirit with feelings of distress and compassion so harrowing that it sometimes becomes difficult to watch, to remain seated without attempting an action of some sort, and yet there is a marvelous sense of art as redemption in watching the portrayal of compassion, the portrayal of a spirit laving itself hopelessly over the human condition, the condition past sickness or evil, and yet even in hopelessness believing and somehow knowing that hopeless sickness and hopeless evil can be transformed. In what world?

Woyzeck's aloneness is one of the great, stricken alonenesses in western drama. Not withstanding its scathing indictment of contemporary life and depiction of human misery, this narrative of the despair of a presumed nobody is a narrative of affirmation, for like the crucified Jesus that figures in Woyzeck's rejection of Christianity, Woyzeck is ultimately alone not only for himself but even in his despair he is alone for us as well.

❖❖❖

In December of 1983, the reunion at Kent State, in Kent, Ohio, took place. In April of 1984 I reflected on it in the pages of *The Voice*:

IS THE BEST NOW BEHIND US?

Reflections on the 26th Anniversary of the Open Theatre.

Village Voice, April 3, 1984

In the course of its lifetime, the Open Theatre went from being a place where modest theatrical "something" might be allowed—what might be allowed no one exactly knew—to a vital system of beliefs that addressed the psycho-social condition of people in an overdeveloped culture, and that spoke to the efficacy of ensemble exploration. Since its breakup in 1973, the Open Theatre has become a rumor, a legendary creature from a recent Golden Age. Last December, this rumor, this legend underwent a curious, if momentary, reification when its former members, its costumes, its well-wishers, and its critics converged on the campus of Kent State University for a weekend of celebration and reappraisal.

The occasion was a commemoration of the group's first public performances some 20 years ago. Kent State became alive with the theatrical past. Early manuscripts by Jean-Claude van Itallie, notebook entries from Joe Chaikin and Peter Feldman, a mimeographed post card-invitation to an Open Theatre party in '65, the membership book of '67, an announcement of a vote between *Nightwalk* and *In Between* as the title for a work-in-progress, a picture of Doris Day clipped from a magazine—all had taken on the character of rare objects and were to be seen in the Special Collections room, under glass. Gwen Fabrikant's costumes were reverently displayed in the spacious School of Art Gallery, the clunky metal box Ray Barry crawled out of as the Kaspar Hauser figure in *The Mutation Show* had its discreet space, and there was more. We were all heard on panels, reminiscing, debating, clarifying; formal academic papers were presented, minutely weighing the philosophic and aesthetic precepts of this now world-famous ensemble; and there were theater historians, pressing to pin down the minutia of the past. Exactly what was the itinerary for the Italian tour of *The Serpent?* Who in the ensemble had first conceived of a particular speech in *Terminal?* Everything had taken on an air of consequence, random occurrences had become history, and the scraps of old working pages had been gently and affectionately molded by the hand of the curator into icons.

The exigencies of time as well as new interests had scattered Open Theatre members around the country, but here many of them were for this lovely and strange reunion: Lee Worley from Boulder, Megan Terry and Joanne Schmidman from Omaha, Peter Feldman from New London, Marianne de Pury-Thompson from Santa Fe—and from New York: Joyce Aaron, James Barbosa and Barbara Vann, Joe and Shami Chaikin, Gwen Fabrikant, Mary Frank, Rhea Gaisner, Sharon Gans, Ralph Lee, Ellen Maddow, Peter Maloney, Mira Rafalowicz, Jean-Claude van Itallie, and Susan Yankowitz. Richard Gilman and I were there both as writers associated with the Open Theatre in its early period and, along with Eileen Blumenthal and Roger Copeland, as critics who had written about the ensemble's later work. Joining us were the orchestrators of the reunion, Barry Daniels of Kent State's theater department and Alex Gildzen from the university's Special Collections.

For two days we met in panel sessions, searched out restaurants, turned up at assorted dinners and parties, had late-night drinks and arguments in dormitory rooms, participated in workshops, tried to get some sense of what had actually gone on in the Open Theatre over that decade from '63 to '73 and how our own lives had been affected by its existence. Time and time again the focus settled on Joe Chaikin—he was the object of a genuine kind of love and sometimes of bewilderment, a major source for learning, a seemingly grounded being whose own natural confusions were seen as stages of growth. Ultimately Joe represented the conscience of the group, in a sense the one who never slept.

Those two days were a time of learning for all of us. On Saturday afternoon, during the final panel sessions, pain and betrayal were two key words. Shami Chaikin spoke of the loneliness and estrangement one could feel within the ensemble, Susan Yankowitz spoke of the unsettling sense of a writer submitting written material to the parental figure of the director, others spoke of the dismay of having specific work they as performers had nurtured being edited out of the production. But everyone spoke of the positive force of the ensemble; for all that it conjured up some negative emotions, it was recalled as a sturdy support in a field strewn with too many flimsy structures.

And Joe mused, late that afternoon, on his feeling that though he liked performing roles in scripted plays, liked it a lot, he could nevertheless live without that experience, but that if the possibility of ensemble exploration were denied him, it would be the keenest and bitterest type of loss. Shami's almost plaintive utterance that the best is now behind her, that nothing can replace the sense of Open Theatre members working as a unified force seemed to be echoed by a silent consensus throughout the room.

Over and over during those few days, we heard that the Open Theatre had been of its time and that we were now in a different era. My own response during the final session was that if these weren't the times for such ensemble work, there was something wrong with the times. I'd like now to offer some thoughts about The Open Theatre, about its growth, and about the current scene from which it is unhappily absent.

In the course of a decade, the Open Theatre grew from a creature of impish precocity, an infant muckraker exposing the emperor's new clothes, to a more grounded being witnessing both the mores and the dreams of a culture that seriously suspected it was losing its way. Even in its early, Cupid-on-the-loose-with-arrow phase, here were performers and writers making an effort to see something of the inherent falsehood in the way our culture stated things, something of the destructive nature of our social arrangements. And attempting to grow a new theatrical language which would be endemic to that kind of seeing. It took some time, many of its initial statements were glib and self-congratulatory. One of its trademarks, from which it never fully disengaged itself, was a kind of aggressive levity, a mock gaiety that at its worst suggested the preening of a child heavily into parental approval. When it worked, the satirical edge could cut deeply; audiences responded with delighted laughter, even as they acknowledged the mirror image of some distasteful aspect of themselves. When the satire failed, I suspect it was because the audience felt that it was being gratuitously attacked for behavior which it hardly needed to be reminded of and in which it took little pride.

Another and healthier implication of the group's probing satire came out of the very structure of its investigations: The implication that, since the ills it held up to view had come to light from its improvisatory work based partly on self observation, we were all in the social muck together. And since there is that kind of identification, that kind of sharing, is it then too much to suggest that the making of an artistic statement, which for all its craziness, for all that we suspect about the pathology of art, is nevertheless a health inducing action in the world, implies that the collective inhabitants of the muck are also the collective sharers of this pathological and simultaneously health-inducing action in the world?

Allied with this sharing was the performer's sharing of a view of society with the spectator, an approach that takes in the later theater of Meyerhold, of Brecht, of The Living Theatre. As Buchner has Woyzeck say, "... us common people, we haven't got virtue." Chaikin took Brecht's cue and saw behavior stemming from the social order, and the performer as witness to these social forces. In his *Presence of the Actor*, Chaikin reflects that "What is radical in Brecht's requirement is that the actor as a private person be concerned with the matter of the entire play. In addition to his presence on the stage as a character in the given circumstances, he is sharing with the audience a response to the character's predicament." So that not only does the making of art suggest a therapeutic possibility for self but an engagement in changing the social forces that mold this self.

But Chaikin had other concerns as well. Death is not a social force, though it's a social weapon and a social concern. If *Terminal* weighted its interests too heavily on the manner of our going and dealt too lightly with spiritual connections, it was nevertheless a courageous witnessing to that condition which we barely speak to. *Nightwalk* is an odd, at times Swiftian look at human habits as nonhumans see them. *The Mutation Show* is an odd look at consciousness. *The Serpent* began as an exploration of the life of Jesus, though it never got past Genesis. These are all concerns in which society plays its part but they are not inherently social demonstrations. They gravitate toward the social demonstration in part because of the use of theme, another Open Theatre trait.

Theme rather than story. Theme as vision. The employment of theme as the major force—what is the story about rather than what is the story?

Theme tends to level elements, the idiosyncratic gives way to the universal, the "what might happen" to the "what does happen." It engages our lives where we are similar and leaves us stranded where we are different. It supports Jung's collective unconscious, but without Brecht's political lever it resists change as an inner dynamic. In short, the Open Theatre's theme tended to synthesize myth and social stereotypes. Linear narration is of no use here. Stories do not come out, in fact there are no stories, the narrative gives way to the reflection of a condition. The theme encourages the structure of the doctoral dissertation, one looks at facets, at multiplying examples. Or as a former colleague of Chaikin's put it to me last summer, "Joe's finished works are like anthologies of how he feels about something."

Or perhaps a synthesis of how the group felt. And it hardly need be said that, in an industry given to every form of exploitation, what a treasure it was to have an ensemble that felt strongly about something. Perhaps they were principally Joe's feelings, but they seemed to have the support of performers who were proud to be identified with those feelings.

There was the theme and there was the presentation, the theme presented, the psychology of personality giving way to the demonstration of type. The performer developed the large gesture, and the gesture tended toward the ritual. Here am I, the gesture seemed to say, not as a working out of something but as a demonstration of a condition. A condition that reinforces itself; the more I am something, the more I go on being that something.

So the performer became something of a teacher; instead of inhabiting character, the performer professed something. And what he professed was what he confessed. The performer became the exemplar/teacher who took on the anxieties, the sins, and the pathologies of the social order and confessed them. In courage, in beauty.

Where are we today? What are the theatrical statements? We seem to have gone inward, into personal history, into the psychology of self. This inwardness takes courage, and much of it is inventive and has its own beauty. But we are living in a time when Proustian self-involvement, exploration into dream, and tales of our ancestors, work upon us in the manner of a warm bath: for all of its perilous nature, these explorations tend to induce an illusion of safety. I am not suggesting that these quests aren't of consequence, but that there are hard questions abroad and some serious theater must speak to them.

It's not my purpose to wave the flag for the Open Theatre, to suggest that its existence could free one prisoner, much less slow down the arms race. I am suggesting that its energies were symptomatic of a feeling many of us had that we were not powerless beings in the face of commercial, exploitative, monolithic institutions. God knows those of us who were part of the group at any time during its surprisingly long history were not necessarily free of personal animosities, were not always large-minded beings. But there was the sense that the group stood for something beyond the private urgencies of any one of us, not only in the theater but in the world. And that is a sense that could help sustain us in these uneasy times.

❖❖❖

The uneasy times have never left us. We had been on a campus where an event a decade earlier had traumatized the nation. The slaughter of several Kent State students was not a principle topic among us at this reunion, but probably all of us had thoughts about it during those few days. It was hard not to recall what had taken place in the closing months of the anti-Vietnam War movement. In certain ways, Kent State would resemble Dallas, no patina of ordinariness would ever set to rest the events in these two cities.

And then within a few months of the reunion, Joe had his stroke.

The stroke. In a sense he has recovered beautifully; in another sense it has forced him to recreate his life, to negotiate it on new terms. Much of Joe's theatre work these days, these years, focuses on the manner in which one summons the courage to remake one's life after some catastrophic event so that, to use one of Beckett's phrases, one can go on.

In 1984 Joe had gone into the hospital for a second open-heart surgery. The result, as expressed by Julian Beck: "Joe's little ticker is now working terrifically. But..." And Julian held up his hands and smiled in that wonderfully ironic and gentle manner of his. The stroke happened during surgery. Joe's speech has never been the same, but the recovery nevertheless has been a remarkable act of courage.

And Joe has outlasted Sutter's with its pies, strudels, danishes, and tarts.

In July of 1984, I heard from my veteran Open Theatre colleague Lee Worley at Naropa. Many of us had been considering where our careers had taken us, and Joe was also very much on our minds. "I'm unsure of anything connected with Joe. Probably if I went to NYC it wouldn't be of much use—still I wish there was something I could do. [I hear] Julian is in a bad way also. But still, Arthur, the best is not behind us. Forming in the back of my mind is some idea that I should go to Japan and study Noh theatre for a year. Not to reproduce it in 'American style' but to get a more experiential understanding and acting technique. I haven't got any idea how to proceed. The Guggenheim folk want no more than three videos of recent work—well I can't very well mail off 3 successful students and I haven't got videos of performances because I haven't had any in a long time. Still I want to go out and study Noh and continue my work. One day I'll have a company somewhere."

And a few days earlier I had heard from Norah Holmgren (her earlier name was Nancy Walter when she had worked at the Firehouse). "I've heard about Joe [from] the inner circle of his helpers. I too wish I could do something more personal than send money—I have written but I don't know what good that does. I have always felt cautious with Joe, not wanting to intrude, [not knowing] if he'd recognize my new name. Please keep me posted if you hear something new. Please let me know if there's a way to communicate with him directly."

I've been sorting through old documents I saved over the years, looking for material about Joe, and have in hand an advertisement in *The Voice* about a theatre company named Emmatroupe. This was a rather vigorous ensemble under the joint leadership of Eleanor Johnson and Judah Kataloni, and it seemed to focus exclusively on feminist issues. The advertisement—I gather it was in the early seventies—is for a work called *A Girl Starts Out...a Tragedy in 4 parts*, with texts by George Eliot and Andrea Dworkin. There is a striking militancy about this advertisement and also about an earlier work of theirs, *Lament for Three Women* by Karen Malpede. I liked the feeling of the ensemble, although the militancy did not sit well with me. But the reason this company sticks in my mind is that they were a group that Joe found very attractive with whom he had actually begun to participate in workshop. And at some point this militant company asked Joe to get out. Emmatroupe fired him. It is not an event Joe and I ever discussed, and surely Johnson and Kataloni had their reasons—I would conjecture those reasons had more to do with ideology than aesthetics, although Joe was surely sympathetic to feminist issues. I don't want to discuss further what is an astonishing moment in the legendary career of my friend, but I wanted the event to be noted somewhere.

Finally, there is *Tourists and Refugees*, a work of the Winter Project. It was created in the early eighties in one of Ellen Stewart's rehearsal lofts, and at that time it featured Will Patten, Ray Barry, Tina Shepherd, Paul Zimet, Ellen Maddow, and Ronnie Gilbert. Joe directed, with his longtime associate Mira Rafalowicz as dramaturg. It was decided to recreate this work in 1993, a time when the world was witnessing another cataclysmic movement of refugees, and when the homeless of the earth were all but numberless and essentially faceless. With many of the same performers, the group was housed this time in rehearsal space donated by the Manhattan Theatre Project. Some draft was shown in 1993 to invited guests, but no producer came forth to move *Tourists and Refugees* into a public space.

∽

19. THE TALKING BAND

The Open Theatre inadvertently produced several offspring during its lifetime: the Firehouse Theater and At the Foot of the Mountain, both originating in Minneapolis and integrally involving Open Theatre alumni Sydney Walter and Paul Boesing; The Magic Theatre of Omaha, founded by Megan Terry and Jo-Ann Schmidman; the short-lived Quena Company in New York, headed by Ray Barry; the drama component of The Bridge Theatre and later The Bridge Collective, both founded by this writer in conjunction with several other theatre artists; Medicine Show, founded by Barbara Vann and Jim Barbosa, along with Lee Worley who left to join the Buddhist educational center, Naropa Institute; and The Talking Band, founded by Paul Zimet, Ellen Maddow, and Tina Shepard. Each of these groups was influenced by the work of The Open Theatre, all of the artists mentioned above came directly out of that company and helped develop its social and aesthetic visions. Medicine Show came into existence during a time of radical shake up of The Open Theatre, but The Talking Band developed as a direct result of Joe Chaikin's decision to disband the company.

In its original manifestation, The Talking Band conceived of itself as a kind of experimental choral group in which the spoken word, for instance in its 1975 rendering of the Finnish epic *The Kalevala*, was both text and music for a narrative concert. This concert elevated tone, pitch, rhythm, and a communal chanting. An analysis of character, as we think of it in Stanislavskian terms, was absent, though a probing of a social order, as in the Band's *Worksong*, or in its lyrical narration of ancient gods and humans at work in *The Kalevala*, helped organize and provide a thematic intention for the sounds. For *The Kalevala*, the Band had the services of composer Elizabeth Swados; it would collaborate with other composers and poets over the next years. "Our background," as Paul Zimet told John Bell "was from a physically oriented theater . . . we were really interested in . . . focusing on language in a way that we hadn't been with the Open Theatre" (*Theater Week*, Feb. 11–17, 1991).

In *The Kalevala*, the company's first full-length work, Bell noted that the performers "were seated on long benches and at times the only visible movement could be a back-and-forth rocking." According to Zimet, "there was a lot of movement in the breath, but there wasn't too much movement in space." The composers Harry Mann and Ellen Maddow now write much of the Band's music. John Bell reported that Zimet sees Talking Band music close to the way "music functions in opera—a voice that's co-equal with other elements." The music functions together with language, not as accompaniment, but, as Tina Shepard describes it to John Bell, "as a distinct element" [that] often serves to contradict visual images or words. "It should shift your perception of what you're seeing," Shepard says, "so it's not what you'd expect; so it reverberates in some way."

"...a major influence in recent years," writes Bell, "has been Anne Bogart, ex-director of the Trinity Repertory Company [who] directed *No Plays No Poetry*, a 1988 Talking Band piece based on Bertolt Brecht's theoretical writings.

"Anne Bogart had a very strong influence on us," says Paul Zimet. "Something about pushing things to be more theatrical, a little more daring. I think she shook us up a little bit, shook us out of something that might have been becoming stodgy."

Again John Bell: "Bogart's approach circled back to the language of gesture that had characterized The Open Theatre's work, but instead of a mere return, this rediscovery of movement took a different angle." For Zimet, Bogart "put things together, making violent conjunctions. She works in a very choreographed kind of way...down to the exact gesture, sometimes before you start to work with the text."

The 1988 collaboration with director Anne Bogart and members of the Otrabanda, an experimental group with a gypsy-like sense of home base, was an event that, as Zimet noted above, gave the Talking Band a visceral shove into new regions of performance. The full title of this gloss on the theoretical writings of Bert Brecht is *No Plays No Poetry But Philosophical Reflections Practical Instructions Provocative Prescriptions Opinions and Pointers From a Noted Critic and Playwright.* The performance site was the Ohio Theatre on Wooster Street in Soho, an impressively seedy rectangle of bare wooden floors, drafty heights and near-to-impossible pillars that always seem to be standing just where you don't want them to be. Bogart and the performers first created a carnival of scenes that were simultaneously happening—and spectators could move from one to another or stay with one as it was repeated—and then supplanted the carnival with more narrowly focused moments occurring in linear fashion. Within the visual and sound levels, which resounded with a kind of deadly black humor, mirthful and mirthless in the same breath, one heard many of Brecht's strictures on what theatre ought to be doing, how most theatre violates basic premises, puts its audience to sleep or mesmerizes it, mostly doesn't instruct or doesn't entertain—all with the presumption that old B. B. does what others (from Shakespeare on down) rarely do. As one heard the text, the performers' actions were running along their own lines, occasionally almost converging with the sense of the text but usually flirting against it in some fortuitously outrageous fashion.

Bogart's working over Brecht's outrageous billboards had the quality of a remarkably fluid sculpting. Much of the time a single event nevertheless had its own multi-focus, orchestrated visually not unlike the manner in which a many-colored symphonic composition functions—in this case, some event, some gestures downstage, midstage, upstage, all cohered with cunning precision, so that the tempo alone was stunning in its own precision.

I have a serious reservation about this work. It has to do with Brecht's dictum: Stay awake, don't be sucked in by emotions, analyze, understand. But I was watching slightly smiling spectators who seemed mesmerized. I was sitting among the already persuaded middle-class in their designer denims, and I felt no sense that anyone was about to rush into the street to take political action. What if the work had been taken into the volatile streets of the South Bronx or South Central Los Angeles?

But one is asking for a lot.

What follows is the script of *Fern and Rose*, an insouciant tremor of delight, performed by The Talking Band, written by Ellen Maddow in collaboration with Rocky Bornstein, directed by Paul Zimet, and choreographed by Rocky Bornstein. Its debut was at LaMama ETC in 1992, with Ellen and Rocky as the two women.

Photo: Suzanne Opton

Ellen Maddow and Rocky Bornstein in *Fern and Rose*

❖❖❖
FERN AND ROSE*

As the lights dim, we hear the sound of children's voices in a playground. The sound stops abruptly and is replaced by a woman's voice quietly singing a Yiddish song "Oyfn Pripetshik." ROSE is lying on the ground. FERN sits behind her, holding her head. The lights change. Suddenly FERN and ROSE are sitting cheek to cheek as in a snapshot taken at a picnic. There is the sound of a carousel in the distance.

ROSE: Fern was born in winter.

FERN: Rose, the previous spring.

ROSE: Fern had her mother's sea green eyes.

FERN: Rose had her mother's eggshell forehead and spidery hands.

ROSE: On May 3, 1952 as our mothers wheeled us through the park discussing politics and breast-feeding, an old man suddenly appeared before us. His clothes were stiff with grease, his beard saturated with Thunderbird. He grabbed us with his filthy hands and as his eyes darted from girl to mother, mother to girl, he whispered, "I don't know if I'm looking at the future or the past!" A drop of his spit fell onto Fern's hair and quickly evaporated in the hot sunshine. Then he . . .

[The lights change. FERN and ROSE sit on a chaise lounge in a familiar garden. Soon they are deep in conversation. The conversation is music. It possesses the rhythms and dynamics of song, while retaining the familiar melodies of conversation. It is a dance, with the gestures and leanings of an intimate and exhilarating discussion. Their conversation is interrupted by the sound of two birds in a tree overhead. ROSE gazes at the birds, leaning on FERN's outstretched hand.]

FERN: Rose's grandmother Feigle was not allowed to go to school. In the old country, school was for boys only. But since Feigle's father was a school teacher, grandma Feigle would hide underneath his desk and memorize the lessons. On February 10, 1902, Feigle's father told the story of the Baal Shem Tov who, in times of trouble would go to a secret place in the forest and light a fire and say a special prayer. As soon as Feigle heard this . . .

[All of a sudden they fall. There is loud music. They dance: FERN is having a tantrum. ROSE is being a bully. Abruptly we hear the sound of the sea. FERN and ROSE are lying in the sun.]

FERN: Rose's grandparents came to America in 1911 and opened a restaurant on Michigan Avenue.

ROSE: Fern's grandparents came in 1912 and ran a men's clothing store down the street. When our mothers were eight years old they were obsessed with roller skates and rode back and forth on the sidewalk between the restaurant and the store late into the summer darkness with their skate keys swinging around their necks. One evening as they were...

[We hear the sound of a washing machine. FERN *pulls a quilt over herself. She looks like an old woman. She moves like a bunch of dirty clothes slopping around in soap. She slowly approaches* ROSE.]

ROSE: When I was three years old, I decided that my grandma Feigle was stupid because she had a thick accent and wore funny-looking hats. On September 12, 1955, as I stood on the end of my bed screaming, "You are stupid!" at my grandma Feigle I fell forward and hit my head on the bureau. A large bump appeared, and grandma Feigle, wishing to reduce the swelling by applying a cold surface, came toward me with a butter knife. I ran away in terror. I thought my grandma Feigle was so stupid that she thought you could get rid of a bump by cutting it off with a knife. I ran out the door and down the hall and then I...and then I... and then I...

[The sound of children's voices returns. FERN *and* ROSE *sit on the chaise lounge and resume their song/dance/conversation.]*

ROSE: You know, Fern, Robin is having a little trouble with her teacher, Miss Clipper.

FERN: I know, Rose, Chloe is having a little trouble with her teacher, Mrs. Squeeze.

ROSE: Miss Clipper has them keeping journals. They write in them every day. If they write something private they're supposed to write "please do not read" and Miss Clipper won't read it.

FERN: And she really doesn't?

ROSE: Well she did. And she was very upset at what Robin wrote.

FERN: She actually told the child that she'd read it? What did it say?

ROSE: Well, it said, "Fart, fart, I hate school."

FERN: Fart, fart I hate school!

ROSE: Robin was furious that she'd read it. I would be furious, too.

FERN: I would have read it and kept it to myself.

ROSE: So I told her not to write anything that she doesn't want the teacher to read.

FERN: Of course!

ROSE: Keep her secrets at home.

FERN: Right.

ROSE: She had a fit when I suggested that, but now she's come up with a solution.

FERN: What?

ROSE: She writes down her private thoughts in the journal and then glues the pages together with Elmer's glue, so no one can read them.

FERN: Not even her?

ROSE: Not even . . .

[*A deep metallic drone interrupts* ROSE'*s thought. During the following speech,* FERN *drags pushes and tips the chaise lounge, moving it all over the space as* ROSE *sits on it.*]

ROSE: When I was ten years old, I wanted to be a Presbyterian. If not a Presbyterian, at least a Republican. All of them had blond hair, all of them had boyfriends, all of them ate lunch together in the corner of the playground. There were only five Jewish girls. We all wore the wrong kind of socks, we squinted, our parents argued about Russia at the dinner table. One day a Presbyterian named Suzie invited me to have breakfast with the minister's wife. Four other Presbyterians invited the four other Jewish girls. I was so happy! Everything was changing. By next week I'd have a boyfriend and eat lunch with the in crowd. After the bacon and eggs, the minister's wife talked to us about Jesus, how he could save us if we welcomed him into our hearts. I looked across the table, Fern Levanthal's face was all red. Great big tears were falling on the tablecloth in front of Abby Ginsberg. All of a sudden a really loud noise came out of my mouth, like this. [*She makes a loud raspberry.*] Everyone started to laugh, the Jewish girls, the Presbyterian girls. We wet our pants, we snorted on the inhale. We tried to stop but every time the minister's wife would open her mouth we . . .

[*They are interrupted by electric school bells.* FERN *and* ROSE *stand side by side in the hallway of their Junior High, trying to look cool.*]

FERN: Fern and Rose were cooking partners in eighth grade home ec. On

October 5, 1964, our chocolate cream pie crust came out crooked. We stood shoulder to shoulder, secretly propping up the pie with our fingers. We smiled at Miss Shrivel as she came around to add the whipped cream. We got an A in pie but...

[*They pause and look at each other.*]

FERN: [*Cont'd.*] Rose, we really got an A?...

[*Unexpectedly, they feel their breasts filling with milk.*]

FERN AND ROSE: Ooooh! [*Holding their breasts.*] uh oh, must be lunchtime. this always happens, its so embarrassing, I always have to change my shirt.

[*They sit down on the chaise to feed their babies. They pull their shirts off over their heads and drape them over their arms. The "babies" are cradled inside the shirts. In this section they are interrupted by their children (on tape). The conversations with their children are sung.*]

FERN: Your poor Dad, he's still confused?

ROSE: Yes, first he was just confused.

CHILD 1: Let's go Ma, Ma let's go!

ROSE: Did you brush your teeth?

CHILD 1: No, not yet.

ROSE: Well then brush them now

CHILD 1: O.K., O.K.

ROSE: First my Dad was just confused, then he began to go get his keys and sit in the car.

FERN: In the garage?

ROSE: In the garage.

FERN: That must have been O.K., what harm could he do?

CHILD 2: What do people eat?

FERN: Eat?

CHILD 2: Rocks?

FERN: Rocks?

CHILD 2: Do they eat rocks?

FERN: No.

CHILD 2: Do they eat grass?

FERN: No.

ROSE: For awhile he just sat in the car, then he began to start the motor.

FERN: I bet that made your mother nervous.

CHILD 1: Let's go Ma, Ma let's go!

ROSE: So you brushed your teeth?

CHILD 1: No

ROSE: Not yet?

CHILD 1: No, but I'm brushing them now, right now.

ROSE: What if he drove off? My mom didn't know if he'd remember how to drive.

CHILD 2: Do they eat cars?

FERN: No.

CHILD 2: Do they eat houses?

FERN: No.

ROSE: He couldn't even remember that his shoes went on his feet when he got dressed in the morning.

CHILD 1: Where are my shoes?

ROSE: What?

CHILD 1: Where are my shoes?

ROSE: You can't find your shoes?

CHILD 1: No

ROSE: Then he got mean.

FERN: I heard about that. Did he hit her?

ROSE: He hit one of my brother's kids, Tiffany.

FERN: So that was it.

CHILD 2: Do we eat birds?

FERN: Yes, chickens.

CHILD 2: Chickens?

FERN: Yes.

CHILD 2: Oh. Do we eat the sky?

FERN: No.

ROSE: So my mom had to put him in a home. At first he was very angry at her, then he was angry at himself, then he forgot why he was angry.

CHILD 1: Where are my shoes, Ma!

ROSE: When did you have them on?

CHILD 1: [*Overlapping.*] I can't find them!

ROSE: Where did you take them off?

CHILD 1: I can't find them! I can't find them, I can't find them!

FERN: How's your dad doing now?

ROSE: He's O.K. He enjoys social dancing and tennis. Its really a very good place.

CHILD 1: Now I'm ready.

ROSE: But he's forgotten who my mother is.

CHILD 1: I'm all ready.

FERN: Your mother must feel terrible.

ROSE: She says she's very lonely.

FERN: Don't they have support groups for the spouses?

CHILD 2: Once I ate plastic.

ROSE: Yes, but she says she doesn't want to burden strangers with her problems.

FERN: [*To* CHILD 2.] You did?

CHILD 2: I swallowed a Leggo.

FERN: Oh, that's right.

ROSE: When he forgets how to breathe and swallow . . .

CHILD 2: But it came out in my poo poo.

ROSE: . . . then he'll die.

CHILD 2: Do we eat poo poo?

ROSE: Did you brush your hair?

FERN AND CHILD 1: No.

CHILD 1: Not yet.

ROSE: Well, then brush it now . . .

CHILD 1: O.K., O.K.

[*The music stops abruptly.*]

FERN: Let me hold her for just a little bit.

ROSE: No, no she's fine. You don't have to...

FERN: You've been holding her all day...

ROSE: O.K., here she is.

FERN: I'll just take her off your hands. What a sweetheart!

ROSE: Aw, isn't she... O.K., if you're doing that I'll just do this. [*Starting to move the chaise.*]

FERN: No, no, no, let me do that for you.

ROSE: No, no, you don't have to...

FERN: Look Rose, I came over to...

ROSE: You've got the baby!

FERN: Well, all right, then I'll hang up the shirts.

ROSE: You don't have to hang up the shirts...

FERN: I know I don't have to...

ROSE: I'll hang up my... you've got the baby...

FERN: Well, that's all right...

ROSE: Look, I'll hang up my own shirt!!

FERN: Then I'll just get us something to eat because you don't have anything in the...

ROSE: I have everything under control!!

[ROSE *falls onto* FERN. FERN *holds her up. During the next dialogue, they lean on or carry each other until they reach their destination, the chaise lounge, which is diagonally across the stage. As in the previous dialogue, conversation with their children is sung.*]

ROSE: Sometimes I think its happening to me.

FERN: Oh come on Rose!

ROSE: You know, "early signs," I read about it in *Redbook* when I was waiting in line at the supermarket.

FERN: Oh please!

ROSE: I forget compound words—like I want to say lawn mower and for a minute all I can think of is vacuum cleaner.

FERN: Those aren't compound words.

ROSE: Well you know what I mean. I want to say "Put it in the dishwasher," and all I can think of is windshield wiper.

FERN: Put it in the windshield wiper?

ROSE: Just for a split second, or I'll think to myself, "I'll just heat this up in the rubber glove."

FERN: Microwave?

ROSE: Right, or the kids will ask what's for dinner and briefcase and vegetables comes to mind.

FERN: But do you actually say these things?

ROSE: No, I just think them. In fact, I wasn't really sure it was happening until I started to tell you about it.

FERN: Well, there's the difference.

ROSE: As a matter of fact, sometimes I'm not sure anything is happening until I start to tell you about it.

FERN: I know just what you mean.

ROSE: Still, it might only be a matter of time. My mother used to wrap my sandwiches in aluminum foil. That's supposed to be one of the causes.

FERN: It's not your mother's fault. They didn't know about aluminum foil.

ROSE: By the way, I talked to her yesterday.

FERN: How's she feeling?

ROSE: She sounded pretty good, but she told me that was just her telephone voice.

FERN: What did she mean?

ROSE: She told me that when she talks on the phone she can pretend she's well. She can't see us looking at her and seeing how impossibly thin and pale she is. She says we listen to what she's saying for a change. How's your mom?

FERN: My mother? Oh...

CHILD 1: Ma!, Ma!

FERN: My mother well...

CHILD 1: Ma!

FERN: My mother is...

CHILD 1: Ma, can I...

FERN: My mother, um...

CHILD 1: Ma, can I ask you something?

FERN: What is it? What?

CHILD 1: What does unretractable mean?

FERN: My mo...

ROSE: It means uh, it means uh...Your mother has?

FERN: My mother has started dating.

ROSE: Really? Great!

FERN: I kept encouraging her, but now that she's found someone, I want to retract everything I said.

ROSE: You met him?

FERN: She brought him over to see my kids.

ROSE: What's he like?

FERN: He's a very nice guy, but she kept giggling all the time, and flirting. She's supposed to act like a grandma and instead she's acting like a teenager. I find myself...

CHILD 1: Ma!, Ma!

FERN: I find myself...

CHILD 1: Ma!

FERN: I find myself...

CHILD 1: Ma, can I...

FERN: I find myself...

CHILD 1: Ma, can I ask you something?

ROSE: What is it? What?

CHILD 1: What does unrelentingly mean?

FERN: I find...

ROSE: It means uh, it means uh...You find yourself.

FERN: I find myself questioning her unrelentingly like she used to do to me when she knew I'd been making out in my boyfriend's car after a date. She's my mother and I'm lecturing her about safe sex, playing the field, and emotional vulnerability.

ROSE: At least she can't . . .

CHILD 1: Ma, ma!

FERN: At least she can't?

CHILD 1: Ma!

ROSE: At least she can't . . .

CHILD 1: Ma, can I . . .

FERN: At least she can't?

CHILD 1: Ma can I ask you something?

ROSE: What it is it? what?

CHILD 1: What does optimistically mean?

FERN: At least . . .

ROSE: It means uh . . . It means uh . . . At least she can't get pregnant. You may as well look on the bright side, when Chloe gets to be a teenager, you'll have had some experience.

FERN: Teenager? I've got more than I can handle right now.

ROSE: Now?

FERN: Whenever Chloe's friend Grace comes over they disappear into her room and take off all their clothes.

ROSE: We used to do something like that, remember?

FERN: So I let it go on for awhile, then I say, "Now it's time to play outside girls." So they run outside and I look around the room and see all the Barbies have their clothes off and are lying on top of each other; Barbie on top of Ken, Ken on top of Barbie, Barbie on top of Barbie, Ken on Ken. They're on the Barbie bed, in the Barbie car, in the Barbie bathtub, on top of the Barbie soda fountain . . .

ROSE: Remember that toy monkey I had with the long tail that we used to put between its legs and . . .

FERN: I'm sure it's normal but where do I draw the line?

ROSE: Then we mixed up some dish detergent and some green poster paint and hid it in a secret place until it got all slimy . . .

FERN: The other day they had a four-year-old in there with them, all of them had their clothes off and when I asked what they were doing they said it was the "coco pop."

ROSE: Then we got that big rag doll, remember . . . [*They reach the chaise lounge and sit on it, relieved.*] You took the slime and put it on the doll's crotch. I took the monkey and . . .

FERN: We never did that!

ROSE: Yes, we did. It was at my house on Sycamore Street, don't you remember?

FERN: It wasn't me.

ROSE: Yes it was. The slime was your idea.

FERN: No, it must have been one of your other friends, it wasn't me.

[ROSE *pushes* FERN. FERN *falls. Music begins. They sing and dance.*]

FERN AND ROSE: Rose's cousins sat
Spilling jelly on her clothes.
Strawberry, cherry and apricot
Dripped down her T shirt just like snot.

La da da di, la da da di
And you betcha I won't letcha
Catch-ch me
La da da di

Rose's cousins stood outside
Two of them sniffled and four of them cried.
Their hands are sticky and their pants are wet
They always want what they cannot get.

La da da di . . . (etc.)

Rose's cousins ran down the street
Hollerin', "Ma, give us something to eat."
When their ma had made them dinner
They said, "Forget it, we're trying to get thinner."

La da da di . . . (etc.)

Rose's cousins are boring and mean
They bleached their hair and they dyed it green.
Their nails are red and their lips are black
They chew up boys and spit them back.

La da da di . . . (etc.)

Rose's cousins go in a crowd
They shake their bodies and fart out loud.
When its dark and the moon is full
They all get naked and shoot some bull.

[FERN *notices* ROSE's *arms are around her. They practice hugging and kissing invisible boys.* "Surfin' Safari" *by the Beach Boys comes on.* FERN *pretends to be the boy.* ROSE *is the girl. They dance.*]

ROSE: Fern and Rose were in love with Louie in the eleventh grade. Fern stole his black sweater and slept with it under her pillow. But he took Rose for a ride in his car and they parked on top of a hill. Later Rose told Fern that Louie was an alien from outer space. She could tell because his balls were in the wrong position. Fern in her confusion, mentioned this to her mother. Fern's mother told Rose's mother. Rose's mother told Rose. Rose told Fern that their friendship was over. She didn't want friends who were either catty or stupid.

[*They separate.* ROSE *glares at* FERN. *They move to opposite ends of the chaise lounge.* FERN *pulls off the quilt.* ROSE *pulls off the mattress. They move to opposite sides of the stage. Music begins.*]

ROSE: In 1969, I went away to college in Wisconsin. But Fern... [*She notices a tray covered by a cloth, under the cloth she discovers a birthday cake. She begins to sing. She lights the candles.*] In 1972, Fern sent me a postcard from Morocco, it said... [*She sings and lights more candles.*] In 1979 I turned to my husband and said, "You know, I was just thinking about an old friend..."

[FERN *appears upstage left, shivering in a large overcoat. Her bare arm emerges, the coat slips off, she is in a bathing suit. She basks in the sun. After awhile she begins to shiver and puts the coat back on. This pattern repeats several times, with variations, as the lights change from winter to summer and back to winter again.* ROSE *continues to sing, light candles, and blow them out. Each phrase she sings is repeated on the audio tape. The music becomes more and more layered and intricate. The lights fade.* ROSE *walks off into the darkness with the lighted cake. The lights come up on* FERN *who turns the chaise on its side so it resembles a wooden fence.*]

FERN: On June 2, 1985, I bumped into Rose

[ROSE *appears, they embrace.*]

FERN: [*Cont'd.*] in the same park where we had played in the sandbox thirty years before. Rose had two children, and I had three. We handed our kids apples and peanut butter sandwiches, draped ourselves over the jungle gym and began to...

[*They resume their song/dance/conversation. They are interrupted by the sound of two birds in a tree overhead.* FERN *gazes at the birds, leaning on* ROSE's *outstretched hand. The music changes.* FERN *falls.* ROSE *lowers her into the chaise and wheels her around as if she is in a hospital bed.* FERN] *tries to get up several times and is helped back to bed by* ROSE. ROSE *falls and* FERN *holds her up.* ROSE *helps* FERN *to walk. She tries to call for help. During the following dialogue, they continue to lean on and carry each other.*]

ROSE: How's your mom?

FERN: Oh, she split up with her boyfriend. She joined the peace corps. They're sending her to the Netherlands Antilles for two years. How's your mom?

ROSE: She sounds fine, she says she's fine.

FERN: But it was just her telephone voice?

ROSE: I said, "How can you be fine? Your body gets weaker every day, your husband has forgotten who you are. Your children live so far away that you only speak to them on the telephone." She said to me, "Rose, when your grandma Feigle was young, she hid underneath her father's desk and got an education. She could add long columns of figures in her head. She didn't even need a pencil or paper." She said to me, "Rose, when I was eight years old I wore my skate key around my neck. I skated on the smooth sidewalk, in the warm dark, with my best friend. When I was tired, my mother gave me a piece of halvah." She said to me, "Rose, when you were three years old, you thought your grandma Feigle was so stupid that she would try and cut a bump off your head with a butter knife." She said to me, "Rose, my granddaughter glues the pages of her journal together with Elmer's glue so that no one can read her private thoughts."

FERN: Sometimes I think if I could put all the stories side by side—the ones my grandmother told me, the ones my mother told me, the ones I tell my children, the ones they tell me—I would understand something, something would be clear, would make sense.

[*They lie down on the chaise lounge. We hear the sound of the sea.* FERN *and* ROSE *are lying in the sun. They take off their mini skirts and transform them into old lady turbans.*]

ROSE: My husband died, Fern's children moved away. On July 17, 2025, we moved to Florida and purchased a mobile home walking distance from the beach. On foggy afternoons I paint pictures, using snapshots of my children as babies, my mother as a teenager, and myself and Fern as little girls.

FERN: Every morning, I walk three miles down the beach. On Tuesdays and Thursdays I lead tours of school children through the local aquarium.

ROSE: One day as we lay sunbathing side by side on our tiny front lawn, I said, "Fern, dear..."

[*A small silver package descends slowly from the sky.* FERN *and* ROSE *get up to investigate. In the package they find two wind up mechanisms. When they wind them up they produce the sound of two birds singing.* FERN *and* ROSE *sit back to back listening to the birds.*]

ROSE: I remember a story! There was a secret place in the forest. A wise man, a teacher, the Baal Shem something knew this place. In troubled times, he would go to this secret place in the forest and light a fire and say a special prayer and his troubles would vanish. After he died, his disciples remembered the prayer, they knew how to light the fire but they forgot the... the... the

FERN: Secret place...

ROSE: In the forest. But still it worked. Their troubles would disappear.

[*The wind up mechanisms run down.* FERN *and* ROSE *wind them up again.*]

ROSE: In the next generation, they knew how to light the fire, but they had forgotten the prayer, and they never knew the secret place in the... in the... in the...

FERN: Forest?

ROSE: Right. But still... Finally there was no one left who knew the

FERN: Place,

ROSE: The

FERN: Prayer,

ROSE: Or

FERN: How to light the fire.

ROSE: All they had left was the

FERN: Story.

ROSE: But this

FERN: Was enough.

ROSE: This was

FERN: All they needed.

[*Suddenly* FERN *falls asleep. She lies on the ground.* ROSE *sits behind her, holding her head. This is the first image of the play, but the roles are re-*

versed. ROSE *is quietly singing a Yiddish song, "Oyfn Pripetshik", to* FERN.
FERN *opens her eyes.*]

FERN: Fern thinks she's on an airplane but she's really in the hospital. Rose
arrives with get well cards from the grandchildren. Fern, thinking she's
on an airplane miles above the Atlantic, says "How did you get here?"
"Oh, I just flew in," says Rose, pulling up a chair. They...

[ROSE *continues to sing. The lights fade. We hear the sound of four young
girls playing a clapping game. The lights come up on* FERN *and* ROSE *doing
a clapping game dance in the distance as they whisper the words along with
the children.*]

GIRLS: There's a hole in the sky
Where the rays get in.
They will make you die
If they touch your skin.
My mama told me that she played in the sun
But I can't go out without my sun block on.

Shoo ee dotn dotn dotn ah ah ah
Shoo ee dot
Ah ah.

Smoke is rising up from the street
Squeezing the world with its great big heat.
People getting higher
President's a liar
I'm in the closet with my hair on fire.

Shoo ee dotn dotn dotn ah ah ah
Shoo ee dot
Ah ah.

Went to the store to buy me a treat
A lady was sleeping in the street.
Went to the park to play on the swing
A man came over and showed me his thing.

Shoo ee dotn dotn dotn ah ah ah
Shoo ee dot
Ah ah.

Fall in love
Go to bed.
Six years later
You'll be dead.

My mama told me that I got to behave
Or she's gonna put me in the microwave.

Shoo ee dotn dotn dotn ah ah ah
Shoo ee dot
Ah ah.

The stars are shaking
And we don't know why.
And Grandma's baking
A calamity pie
Old father time is turning a trick
Better get busy and grow up quick.

[FERN *and* ROSE *end their dance in an embrace. The lights fade.*]

20. CHARLES LUDLAM

AND THE RIDICULOUS THEATRICAL COMPANY

"In a way John Vaccaro gave my whole theatrical life back to me...John has great instinct and is a brilliant actor. He gave me freedom. He allowed me to flip out all I wanted onstage. He never felt that I was too pasty, corny, mannered, campy. He let me do anything I wanted. He is very primitive and very difficult for most actors to work with, because he's sort of savage...I felt John was too conservative onstage because he was afraid of being arrested. I wanted to commit an outrage. For me, nothing was too far out...When Vaccaro fired me in 1967—from my own play—nearly everybody quit and left with me...Vaccaro could be The Play-House, but we were The Ridiculous Theatrical Company. We decided to do my play [*Big Hotel*] the way we wanted to do it...We did everything in a defiant way—radically wrong, you might say...We had no money—nothing. We lived like paupers on the Lower East Side, starving, but keeping the company working, trying to find places to perform."

Charles was a friend. I rarely saw his work, although I was constantly in one dark room or another, either in rehearsal or covering three, sometimes four shows a week for *The Voice*. But we were fellow panelists one year on the New York State Council for the Arts. During lunch breaks the two of us would wander about Chinatown. Charles introduced me to a dim sung, Chinese dinner, a lovely ritual featuring waiters arriving ceremoniously from the kitchen every few minutes, holding aloft small plates with a new exotic morsel most Westerners know nothing about. You wave your hand to draw attention not to your ignorance but to your determination not to be left out of the feast. After dim sung and several afternoons of often grueling but not humorless participation in what is known as the Council's "funding cycle," where fragments of several millions of dollars are dispensed to or withheld from hundreds of chronically desperate companies, Charles and I would walk home together, I to Sullivan Street in Soho and Charles to the Village. We would converse, sometimes hotly, sometimes idly, about the theatre issues of the day—money, audiences, critics, space, the constant struggle to mount our work—or we might gossip about theatre people we knew intimately or dimly. As I noted above, I had not seen much of Charles's work and he never asked what I thought about it. Probably it was enough that he knew what he thought about it. I think now that I assumed the work of the Ridiculous was primarily screaming and flouncing and lifting of eyebrows at references to genital behavior. That assumption has fallen by the wayside, although the flouncing and the eyebrows may be endemic to much of this theatre of outrage.

Remembering Charles, I believe I first laid eyes on him some spring evening in 1966, around two or three in the morning. The Bridge Theatre was running a benefit; its purpose was in part to raise bail money for Pierot Heliczer, the filmmaker boyfriend of Irene Nolan, one of our two box office people. Pierot had socked a policeman either during some protest demonstration or at an earlier benefit for some comrade who may have conceivably also socked a policeman. Sometime in the morning of what proved to be a particularly overheated benefit show, which included filmmaker Jose Rodriguez Soltero's threatened decapitation of a live chicken and his subsequent burning of an American flag (his protest against the Vietnam War), a young Charles Ludlam could be seen onstage in sedentary posture, throwing his garments, one by one, into the arms of various spectators. I recall that while Middle America and Jesse Helms slept the sleep of the righteous, at least one pair of well-used jockey shorts flew through the interior of our theatre. I imagine that Charles's socks and trousers also rendezvoused with paying customers, for I recall a bare-legged Ludlum holding center court as more and more of his garments went sailing into public space. Charles, seen in profile during these various disbursements, had assumed an attitude of superciliousness, as if to say, "You louts, be thankful I'm sharing with you some of my intimate apparel, although Jesus knows it's like flinging pearls before swine." I remember that at the moment I was struck by his grandiloquence. These gestures for me were more than a little outrageous, though by the time the chicken was saved from decapitation and the American flag reduced to ashes, Charles and his flying undergarments were a distant memory. And in a few days The Bridge Theatre would have the outraged licensing bureau on its back about the burning of the flag and over some presumed obscenity that it had allowed to take place in the presence of minors, and after hours at that.

Let me briefly theorize about Charles's supercilious countenance as presented to us that night in the sixties. Charles was announcing to the hip public, to the downtown East Village crowd, that he has arrived, that the avant-garde of the New Bohemia had better take notice, that a cool but also torrid cat has come on the scene. Outrage, in its latest manifestation, has opened for a long run. Straight out of the decorum of Hofstra University's drama program, Charles had fled suburbia, and what passes for propriety, and squirreled into the delicate and moist perversities of the Lower East Side. He had long ago discovered theatre: "boys," cross-dressing, as well as

Molière, Ibsen, the Greeks, the Elizabethans, The Living Theatre, and probably Jarry. Now the ambiance of the Downtown Off-Off-Broadway scene called to him in the persons of John Vaccaro, Ronnie Tavel, Black-Eyed Susan, Bill Vehr, and the somber decadence of Warhol's Electric Circus. He was also deeply influenced by Noh drama, the Epic concepts of Brecht and Piscatur, and the subconscious-nightmare visions of Artaud.

Charles on obscenity: "The pretentious people who want it to be so "hoity-toity" are embarrassed by the obscenity and lowness and the infantilism and the doggerel; and the people who'd like it to be just obscene and low don't like the hard parts. But what about the unbelievably sublime writing or acting that occurs? If you have shit in the play and also have sublimity, you have a total panoramic view, like Dante in his *Inferno*, or Shakespeare."

Charles went from freewheeling productions to tightly-scripted work. "Part of what frees me is that I'm a traditionalist . . . Instead of deciding that I was going to reinvent acting . . . I took certain conventions at face value. And by accepting such conventions as plot, dialogue and character, I'm free to invent endlessly. I can dare to put in anything."

I've read some of Charles's plays and watched videotapes, and I agree that the work is intelligent, wonderfully inventive, and often scintillating. But I have a problem with this "anything," not with the daring of "putting it in" but with the attitude about "anything." For Charles's anything seems to have gotten boxed in; I keep picking up the shadow of a merciless litmus test that won't let this anything live in peace. And what the litmus test demands is that the anything (event, character, physical movement) be sexually hip, that the anything be in accordance with certain standards of Gay hipness. The erotic subtext is a parallel script that remorselessly presents itself, winks at us, pushes us into a connivance with street-smart banter. *The Mystery of Irma Vep* is a brilliant collage, borrowing from Daphne DuMaurier's *Rebecca*, Sir Arthur Conan Doyle's *The Hound of the Baskervilles*, Charlotte Bronte's *Jane Eyre*, punning from 1,000 masterpieces breathlessly and yet for all that quietly in pursuit of—of exactly what?—of itself, its very engaging, double entendre self. It corners anything by ultimately reducing it to the level of a Marx Brothers sight or sound gag. Charles and his colleagues were right to think of the plays as latter-day envoys of the spirit of Aristophanes. But too often the reductions not only prompt but also demand an allegiance to the ideology of the genital ego, so that if anything goes, it goes into the ranks of the Party of Eros, a kind of politics in its own right, another ideology. Well, why not another ideology? Within this ideology anything and everything resides hilariously, scatalogically. It nevertheless does no good to forget that every ideology, unless it conquers the universe, shuts out the non-believer. If there is a tribe, there are always exiles. And it's even proper for there to be exiles. One has to allow for the invasion of the exiles into the camp, and one must keep in mind that the ideology of the exile and the capture of the camp is always possible. That confrontation, between let us say the genital ego and the life of the spirit, is a two-way street.

But Charles found his way, from the strictures of Jericho Turnpike to the Gay Rhapsodies of Avenue A and Christopher Street. And he found a delightful way to render some of the cultural pretensions of our time. Witness this moment from *Le Bourgeois Avant-Garde, A Comedy Ballet After Molière*, written by Charles in 1983. Several avant-garde artists are nervously awaiting their patron, a Mr. Foufas, who now enters. Parentheses around stage directions indicate that those directions were added by the editors of Charles's *Complete Plays*, Steven Samuels and Everett Quinton.

❖❖❖

MR. FOUFAS: Well gentlemen, what's new today? Are you going to show me some of your monkeyshines? ... let me see your play.

HACK: Mr. Foufas, the avant-garde don't do plays. We do pieces.

MR. FOUFAS: You shouldn't just do pieces. You should do the whole thing.

COMPOSER: I assure you that our work is of the most advanced possible.

MR. FOUFAS: Modern, eh?

COMPOSER: Postmodern.

MR. FOUFAS: But is it up-to-date?

CHOREOGRAPHER: I assure you that it is the last word.

COMPOSER: After us there will be nothing.

MR. FOUFAS: It can't be as bad as all that. Come on, let me have it. And whatever you do, don't pander to me. Go wild. Nothing is too far out...

(*Music. One foot in a pointed shoe pops up on a tiny puppet stage, toes skyward.*)

MR. FOUFAS: What is this supposed to represent?

HACK: Please Mr. Foufas, this is an abstract theatre piece.

MR. FOUFAS: Oh yes, abstract—that means it isn't supposed to represent anything. Am I right? ...

(*A second, naked foot appears.* MR. FOUFAS *points and laughs. A third foot appears.* MR. FOUFAS *falls asleep.*) ...

MR. FOUFAS: (*Waking with a start.*) That's it? ...

MR. FOUFAS: I think it needs a little tightening up…It was a bit too long…

COMPOSER: But the piece barely lasted three minutes.

MR. FOUFAS: Still, it seemed to drag a bit in places and, if you'll forgive my saying so, it didn't make any sense.

HACK: We warned you that the piece would be abstract.

COMPOSER: It's very avant-garde.

HACK: Perhaps it was too avant-garde?

MR. FOUFAS: On the contrary. I think you could have gone much further. If anything it was too tame.

HACK: Tame?

MR. FOUFAS: It lacked outrage.

HACK: Just what did you have in mind?

MR. FOUFAS: It could have used some giant phalluses, naked women. Don't ask me. If you've really run out of ideas why don't you do a piece on nuclear disarmament?

⟁

Jocelyn Druyan as the Angel, Katherine Adamenko as Hagar
The Celebration Reclaimed

21. THE BRIDGE COLLECTIVE

This writer began with a number of interesting collaborators who have long-since disbursed, forming other alliances (e.g., the Shared Forms Theatre, or the more recent collaborations between Nancy Gabor and Joe Chaikin). Or, like Lindsay Crouse, they have carved out careers in mainstream films or regional theatres. And two of our people, Maurice Blanc and Calvin Holt, are dead. Can one survivor make a collective? Perhaps through a kind of poetic lunacy one can goad a collective into being, or into reifying itself. In the late seventies, this collective produced *Witnesses*, a documentary study of governmental repression around the world. I wrote it in collaboration with a handful of performers, and we focused on the tyrannical government of Indira Gandhi, on the terrors of the Shah of Iran's secret police, on the suspicious death of Karen Silkwood in our own nuclear-powered country, on the attempt of United States immigration authorities to deport a suspected Nazi guard, and on Auschwitz. Each night someone in the audience would break into the performance to bear witness, including theatre director Norma Lomboy, who had escaped from Pinochet's Chile, and Iranian poet Reza Baraheni, who had been tortured by the SAVAC under orders from the Shah's government and had only been freed after international pressure from PEN. In the fall of 1992, I directed *The Poor Man Rich Man Play* at the Theater for the New City. It was a Halloween offering of a political cartoon which Crystal Field had originally mounted as a street play featuring Stuart Sherman as the poor man who turns rich, then hires police and armies to protect his wealth. The recent work of the Collective is *The Celebration Reclaimed*, an epic play focusing primarily on Jews and Arabs from pre-Biblical times to the present turmoil in the Middle East. The structure was inspired by an earlier play of mine, *The Celebration: Jooz/Guns/Movies/The Abyss*, directed by Crystal Field at Theater for the New City in 1971. The earlier play won a performance Obie for Maurice Blanc, and the play itself was nominated for an Obie. Several versions were dramatized over WBAI-FM. Philosophically and aesthetically, the new work is a considerable departure from the original play. Director Donald Brooks created an overall design and a wonderful rendering of the golden calf we never got around to building for the workshop production at American Theatre for Actors or the premiere at Theater for the New City. What follows are current sections of the new work.

THE CELEBRATION RECLAIMED*

Part One: The Smashing of the Gods. The Covenant. Ishmael. Fear and Trembling. Jacob. The Exiled Ones; Moses.

[Part Two: Jonah the Messenger, not printed here.]

Part Three: Herzl. The Building of the State. Mendel Grossman, Hagar's Children, Leo Baeck; Terezin.

Directed by Donald Brooks

CAST

	(At TNC, 1995)	(At ATA, 1993)
Abraham/Baeck	Marc Marcante	Tom Bruce
Sarah	Raquel Yoffisson	Gisele Arnaud
Jacob/Herzl	Michael Keyloun	Jerry Goralnick
Hagar	Katherine Adamenko	Jocelyn S. Druyan
Ishmael	Anthony Craig	Dmitry Prachenko
Angel	Jocelyn S. Druyan	Catherine L. Dowling
Isaac	David Scott	Theodore Strange
Jonah	Reyn Williams	Gregg Hogan
Rachel	Laurie Wickens	Jennifer Van Bergen
Leah	Jocelyn S. Druyan	Jocelyn S. Druyan
Laban	Pietro Gonzalez	Gregg Hogan
Therapist	Marc Marcante	Walter Furman
Moses	David Scott	Edmond Cahill
Palestinian Woman		Laurie Wickens (role not written in '93)

Hebrew music performed by Cantor Ilan Mamber. Costumes at TNC: Irene Nolan. Pagan gods designed by Anne Seelbach.

Time: pre-Judaic consciousness to the present. Place: Middle East

PART ONE

THE SMASHING OF THE GODS

In the shop of ABRAM's *father,* TERAH, *the household gods are on display. It's as if they're looming over the audience. It's suggested that each production decide on their gods, they can be treasured or detested icons, and any time period might work. One production might choose Martin Luther King, Adolf Hitler, Mother Theresa, Gandhi, and Lenin.*

ABRAM appears with a hammer, he cracks through the icons, he smashes them with a thoroughness that's surprising, given the contemplative quality he displays at this moment. During the last part of the assault, TERAH appears. He's stunned, he can only watch. Now father and son watch each other. TERAH fingers the demolished gods, makes some feeble attempt to restore them. He gives up, he screams in despair.

TERAH: You've finished us off nicely!—What was it you were thinking? Were you thinking? You had something in mind?

[*ABRAM has nothing to say. Perhaps he's slumped on the ground.*]

TERAH: A nice piece of work you've managed this day. I sell these gods, we eat from these gods.

ABRAM: I have nothing to tell you.

TERAH: Tell me that my son is a fool, that my business is finished. Look at this wrecked merchandise, you've reduced my work to garbage. We're finished in this town, get that through your head. When you've slaved to get a business going, perhaps you'll understand what you've done.

ABRAM: [*To himself.*] A nice piece of work . . .

[*The family is packing for a journey. Members include ABRAM's brother NAHOR, the wives SARAI and MILCAH, the nephew LOT. TERAH is clearly troubled but resigned to abandoning his shop and city. He and ABRAM barely speak. The broken images are tossed aside as the family packs.*]

ABRAM: What did he have in mind? Nothing in mind. Nothing. He was . . . he was . . . bringing . . . bringing. Or being . . . that is . . . Brought. There was a stillness in the city of Ur . . . in his home . . . he could not tolerate this stillness, this stifling quiet. Something had to be . . . something . . . that is, something to be attended to . . . even if it meant . . . but what could it mean? The death of the family. Now they would leave—the city, they would set out. He, Abram, had murdered the household gods. A nice piece of work. Now they would set out. For no place. Nothing in mind. Now the others, the family, the others, they were on their guard. They thought he was capable of anything. They were right, capable of anything, anything was possible, his head was spinning.

[*On the road with the transient family. They stop to rest.*]

SARAI: [*To* ABRAM.] Your father can't go much further.—Do you ever hear me? Why do I bother asking?

ABRAM: We need to go on alone. He'll rest here in Haran. We'll take our chances.

SARAI: Our chances. We've become a wandering people.

ABRAM: Are we a people? We're a stillness. Perhaps somewhere out there we'll be a people.

SARAI: What out there are you talking about? The wind, the heat of the sun? Yes there's been a stillness.

ABRAM: A kind of death.

SARAI: If it comes to that. But that stillness, that kind of death was a harbor, a haven. And now? I'd say we're about finished.

ABRAM: I told you we need to take our chances.

SARAI: Terrific, excellent, we're just the right age for a nice hike. Look at you, you move like a man in a fever.

ABRAM: The question is, do I move like a man?

SARAI: That doesn't interest me. You were everything I wanted in a man. Now you move like one possessed. Who told you to start smashing things? What do you expect to find out there? You're a man dreaming on his feet. What out there is out there?

ABRAM: Enough, enough. You know everything I know.

SARAI: Glad to hear it.

[SARAI *goes to look after the others.* TERAH *is breathing heavily but brushes off the ministrations of his family.*]

TERAH: Please, I need a little rest. No fuss, please.

MILCAH: Drink some water, father.

TERAH: Yes, yes, in a minute I'll drink.

SARAI: He's a bit pale, yes?

TERAH: Don't speak as if I'm not here.

[SARAI *returns to* ABRAM *who has been ruminating alone. She rubs his back, he relaxes.*]

SARAI: Like the old days, eh?—The man dreaming on his feet, the possessed man.

ABRAM: Mock me if it helps.

SARAI: It's no help. We see things differently.

ABRAM: I see nothing, but all of me sees everything. All of me sees everything.

SARAI: I'm massaging these bones, is that where you're seeing everything? Abram, it isn't just the household gods you've murdered. I want to keep this family alive. What if I stay here with your father. He's a sensible fellow. We'll settle in Haran while you go to some out there where the stillness isn't. You might even return to us.

ABRAM: I told you I see nothing, can't that satisfy you?

SARAI: It can't!

ABRAM: And what makes you think I'll ever return?

[*This stops them both.*]

ABRAM: [*Cont'd.*] How is my father?

SARAI: He's not comfortable. He's a city fellow, what did you expect? He's not made for the open road. Nor is your wife.—Ever return?—We'll all die out there, Abram. Or perhaps you think the countryside will take kindly to strangers.

ABRAM: It doesn't concern me what the countryside will take.

[TERAH *collapses. The others cry out, they all rush to him, try to revive him. It's useless. The family is stunned, speechless.*]

MILCAH: [*Finally.*] He's gone from us.

[*The family stands over the body of* TERAH. *There is no fixed ceremony to follow. Each tries to improvise some "religious" sign of respect, but then they give it up.*]

ABRAM: Suppose I say a few words?—He was a good man. He helped his neighbors, he loved his family, he cheated no one, he gave good weights, he loved to see the morning, he kept himself clean.

MILCAH: We will miss him.

NAHOR: And remember him. We will remember him.

LOT: He died peacefully.

SARAI: No one dies peacefully. You're kidding yourself, Lot.

NAHOR: Milcah and I will stay here, we don't need to keep moving. Our cattle will graze here.

ABRAM: We'll move on. Sarai, myself, our cattle, our slaves.

SARAI: A peaceful death. [*To* ABRAM.] Now you're the eldest.

NAHOR: Go in peace, brother. Remember us.

MILCAH: Perhaps you'll have children yet.

[*Silent good-byes are said.*
    On the road. SARAI *and* LOT *are resting,* ABRAM *is off by himself. All at once* ABRAM *rises, he seems startled. It's as if he's listening to something. His mouth opens wide, his face registers astonishment. His face becomes a yawning chasm. A little later he goes quietly to* SARAI, *touches her softly.*]

SARAI: [*Offhandedly.*] Why so affectionate?

ABRAM: [*Moves away, sits thinking.*] And it cut through him. That is—it filled him. It asked nothing, it became his life. It moved through him so that there was no place where he ended—and it began. It asked nothing but everything had to be attended to. Everything began and went on, and it went on beginning. For a time he could hardly breathe because it was filling him. But he was inspirited, he was in love with what he now understood. [*He looks over at* SARAI, *he starts to rise.*]

SARAI: [*Cries out.*] What is it?

[*Watches as he approaches.*]

SARAI: [*Cont'd.*] You're in a fever.—Or did something take place? Yes, I can see it. But I don't want to know too much.

LOT: It's hot. The cattle need water.

[*The family gathers its things.*
    SARAI *and* HAGAR *are strolling arm in arm. There is a strong current of sensuality in this moment. And there is tension between these two beautiful women.*]

HAGAR: Years ago I thought of how it would be when I loved a man.

SARAI: And what did you think in those years?

HAGAR: It would be simple. We would live in our home, it would be difficult for him to find words, he would fill me. I would be open and he would simply fill me, even as I surrounded him. And then we would drink together from a single cup.

SARAI: [*Kissing* HAGAR.] Do you like it when I give you fruit?

HAGAR: Yes I like it very much. Should I continue about this man?

SARAI: No, what's the point? That's not your life, you were living a fantasy, you didn't know what was in store for you. [*Cups* HAGAR's *chin.*] And here you are.

HAGAR: I don't honestly know if I can do it.

[SARAI *slaps* HAGAR's *face smartly.*]

SARAI: Anybody can do it! There's nothing to it. Do you understand me?

HAGAR: I understand you, mistress.

SARAI: Come, we'll stroll again.

[*They do so.*]

SARAI: [*Cont'd.*] Life is tolerable if one understands one's place, then everything falls into line. This man that had difficulty with words, he's nothing to you, not a thing. You have a few issues on which to concentrate, one is to keep yourself open to your masters at all time. Hagar, sometimes I give you fruit with my own hands, on occasion you'll be called on to spread your legs. That's your life. And we can surely have some good gossip, a quiet laugh in the evenings, we can observe the camels and wrap our shawls tightly around us when the wind picks up. We'll go on as before. Whatever you thought as a girl, well things took a different turn, didn't work out as you imagined.

[*Takes* HAGAR *in her arms, they kiss.*]

SARAI: [*Cont'd.*] Disappoint me and I can be vicious.

HAGAR: I'll say what you wish. I'm not smart.

SARAI: You're smart enough. You won't be shy if I watch the two of you?

HAGAR: I can't believe you're asking that of me!—Would you want to?

SARAI: Perhaps I want to.

HAGAR: Have you told him?

SARAI: You ask too many questions.

[*They continue strolling.*

The act of love between HAGAR *and* ABRAM. *Its form is a kind of hallucinatory dance. The participants maintain a great distance between them. Their movements are ambiguous, they want to make love and they don't, they are trying to learn something about one another. For an extended period there is silence, then they break into speech.*]

HAGAR: Abram, what am I to you?

ABRAM: Sarai's gift.

HAGAR: I am nothing.

ABRAM: A gift that I have yet to fathom.

HAGAR: Do you like my breasts? Do I have a name?

ABRAM: I need silence. You embarrass me.

[*The dance continues in silence. Then a sudden cry from each. The dance is over.*]

HAGAR: I have no name. [*She sinks to the ground.*] Now I'm twice nothing.

ABRAM: You please me. Perhaps something has taken place.

HAGAR: [*As* ABRAM *draws near.*] Sarai tells me there's nothing to it.

ABRAM: Enough!

[ABRAM *lifts up* HAGAR. *He holds her against him with much affection.* SARAI *appears, holds out her arms.* ABRAM, *not without reluctance, places* HAGAR *in* SARAI's *arms.* HAGAR *slips to the ground at* SARAI's *feet.* SARAI *gives* ABRAM *a brilliant smile but the troubled husband turns away from her.*

HAGAR *gives birth to* ISHMAEL. HAGAR *performs a birthing dance, during the course of which* ISHMAEL *appears as a child, delivering a monologue in an agitated, to us unintelligible tongue.* HAGAR *is unaware of the sounds, for the child hasn't yet been born, but she is certainly aware of the weight of this presence she's about to deliver.* ISHMAEL *begins a frantic movement, even as* HAGAR's *labor increases. Suddenly* HAGAR *relaxes and* ISHMAEL *cries out.*]

ISHMAEL: Lost my w-a-a-a-a-y. Stole my d-a-a-arkness. I'm in not dark, thrown into not dark, some terrible not dark. H-u-r-ting me, this place, this undark. Find w-a-a-ay! S-a-a-a-a-ave Ishmael!

HAGAR: And we called him Ishmael. That is, they called him. What does it mean, this name? It means, God heeds. And I loved my child. That is . . .

[ISHMAEL *is suddenly flinging stones. He imagines he's being chased, he runs away.*]

HAGAR: . . . God heeds.

[SARAI *and* HAGAR *are strolling again, arm in arm.*]

SARAI: I feel there are problems between us. Am I mistaken? Do you sense that you've gotten a little uppity? Out-of-step, so to speak, with the appropriateness of certain conditions? Ah, I can feel you tensing up. A sure sign that all isn't well.

HAGAR: I wish you wouldn't take that tone with me.

[SARAI *breaks away instantly. A long silence as the two confront one another.*]

SARAI: So it's come to this. You wish I wouldn't take that tone with you. I believe you're losing a sense of reality.

HAGAR: I'm his wife! I'm a mother! Don't forget it!

SARAI: Forget it? It's choking me! [SARAI *is trembling. Then strangely quiet.*]— Hagar, Hagar, have I become slight in your eyes?

HAGAR: I never said so. Slight in my eyes? But you can surely see that I have the upper hand. I never planned it.

SARAI: You have nothing! The upper hand? You believe that you're a mother, and what if I explain to you that you're nothing but a conduit, that your job is finished.—Shall we stroll once again, now that we've cleared the air?

HAGAR: You'll drive me from this place.

SARAI: It may be, but we'll keep the boy. Come, while the light is still with us.

[*They walk arm in arm.*]

SARAI: [*Alone.*] I have indeed become slight in the eyes of an Egyptian slave.—The wind's picking up, we're a tiny grain, we could be blown away, not made for the open road. It takes cunning, obstinacy, a certain deranged courage to keep from being wiped out.—Her unhappiness? I spit on it.

Author's note: In the following omitted scenes, God tells ABRAM *that* SARAI *will give birth to* ISAAC. ABRAM *and* SARAI *become* ABRAHAM *and* SARAH. HAGAR *and* ISHMAEL *are sent into exile.*

HAGAR *and* ISHMAEL *wandering the wilderness of Beer-sheba.* HAGAR *shakes the skin of water, it is empty.*

HAGAR: We're done for. My child, there's no water left.

ISHMAEL: We'll find water.

HAGAR: Don't talk nonsense. Rest under the tree, Ishmael. The sun is brutal.

[ISHMAEL *watches his mother uncertainly.*]

HAGAR: [*Cont'd.*] Do you hear me?

[ISHMAEL *sits under the tree, some distance from* HAGAR.]

HAGAR: The child will perish.—He's not worth a thing to her, now that she's got the other one.—I can't watch the boy die.

[HAGAR *bursts into tears. An* ANGEL *appears.*]

ANGEL: What troubles you, Hagar?

HAGAR: [*Stares in silence. Finally.*] Death troubles me.

ANGEL: Have no fear, God heeds the cry of the boy.

HAGAR: We've been forsaken, any fool can see that. [*Holds up the dry skin in despair, lets it fall to the ground.*]

ANGEL: Can you understand me, Hagar? There is plenty of water. And this boy, God will make a great nation of Ishmael.

[ISHMAEL *suddenly comes running with a skin of water. He shakes it for his mother, gives it to her, then he drinks.*]

ISHMAEL: Father said that God sees me.

HAGAR: Does God see the outcast, the abandoned? [*To the* ANGEL.] Why do you mock me? Surely this is a trick. Where has this water come from? [*Snatches the skin, shakes it in anger.*] It will keep us alive for half a day, a day at the most. Why do you do this to us?

ANGEL: Drink, Hagar. There will be an abundance of water, enough to drink freely. Trust in The Lord.

[*Assorted people appear with open umbrellas, hands extended to feel the raindrops. They mime drinking bathing, etc.* ISHMAEL *begins a dance, snaking amidst the people.* HAGAR *closes her eyes, giving thanks.* ISHMAEL *and the celebrants disappear.* HAGAR *is in deep prayer, the* ANGEL *comes to her.*]

ANGEL: What troubles you, Hagar?
Build a highway for The Lord.
But, Hagar, you can't hear me yet.
You're too caught up in miracles. But there are
No miracles, angels can't do it, it's not our business.
The Lord watches, God heeds, is that a miracle?
It's the only reality, that's it, that's everything.
And yet people die in the desert—
The Hagars, the Ishmaels, the Abrahams, the Sarahs.
Such people are dying every day. And the desert?
It isn't interested in who dies and who lives.
But what does it take not to die before one's time?
Let's call it a miracle of sorts, a kind of courage,

For the desert is harsh, the desert doesn't give easily,
The desert cares for its beauty, it cares only to live.
Hagar, you can't hear me, but trust in The Lord, build a highway for
The Lord,
For humans betray one another.
God heeds, but humans are heedless.
God watches, but humans watch their purses,
Humans defend their shelters, and their shelters crumble
Before their children are grown, all wiped out in an instant, they pro-
claim their dominions and the wind shrugs.
And yet the turtle has no need to proclaim,
Nor the cricket, nor the robin, nor the hawk,
Nor any flying or creeping thing.
Take heed of the lily, take heed of the rock,
Take heed, for God heeds.
Build a highway, defend nothing.
You can't hear me but listen, Hagar. Defend nothing.
Be of good courage. For God keeps faith
With those who sleep in the dust,
And with the living.

✧

FEAR AND TREMBLING

ABRAHAM *and* ISAAC *are moving through the desert.*

ABRAHAM: [*We hear his thoughts.*] This boy trusts me. Perhaps I'm losing my mind. I assumed that old age would bring a certain quiet, a certain respite, that I would finish my years with some degree of peace. But sometimes things don't work out, that is . . .

[*A rhythmic climbing begins.*]

ISAAC: [*His thoughts.*] It's too quiet. There's something I'm not learning. This journey is senseless. But there's a key to it . . . obviously. And I don't have this key. And it's cold. And this mountain gives nothing back.

ABRAHAM: [*His thoughts.*] Cold. I'm being deceived. It's murder, any fool knows that.

ISAAC: [*His thoughts.*]Perhaps no one has the key. It's as if we've already been through this. And being through it you learn nothing, not a thing.

You pretend to be wise, but you stay stupid. And these sandals aren't any good, they never were. And yet father made them for me.

[*They rest.*]

ISAAC: What is it?

ABRAHAM: It's nothing.

ISAAC: It's gotten colder.

ABRAHAM: It's dusk.

ISAAC: The fire's gone out of the world.

ABRAHAM: Tomorrow we'll approach the mountain.

[*Silence for a time.*]

ISAAC: The whole world has left the earth. They've left us behind. It makes me uneasy.—Why this silence?

ABRAHAM: Time to sleep. [*Unrolls blankets.*] The night air is upon us.

[*They cover themselves. Silence again.*]

ISAAC: I had a dream last night. It seems—

ABRAHAM: I don't want to hear your dreams.

[*They sleep.* ISAAC *wakes, speaks to himself.*]

ISAAC: In this dream I was held aloft in the arms of some beautiful creature. I was supported in some wonderful manner. I was treasured. My whole being was alive.—This silence. The fire has gone out of the world.

[ISAAC *sleeps. Then father and son wake.*]

ABRAHAM: We must get an early start.

[*Climbing ritual resumes. After a time:*]

ABRAHAM: We're here.

ISAAC: So this is it. What kind of here is this place?

ABRAHAM: This is Mount Moriah.

ISAAC: I see. So this is Mount Moriah. Now what?

[ABRAHAM *can't speak.*]

ISAAC: [*Cont'd.*] Father?

[*Still nothing.*]

ISAAC: [*Cont'd.*] Father? [*Frightened, cries out:*] Father, now what?

ABRAHAM: [*Simply.*] Now you die.

[ISAAC *is stricken dumb, then he runs in terror, stops, stares across at his father.*]

ABRAHAM: [*Cont'd.*] I'm helpless. I can't help you. I'm only a person. Something has to be attended to. I don't know what I'm saying, I don't understand.

[ISAAC *returns, it's as if he's sleepwalking.* ABRAHAM *binds him and lowers him to the ground.*]

ISAAC: You said there would be a lamb.

ABRAHAM: I was lying. There's no lamb. You're the lamb.

ISAAC: It's as if we've already been through this. And you stay stupid.

ABRAHAM: Perhaps we have been through this. I'm trying to understand something. My whole life, that's all it's been about, I'm a simple fellow. Is what I'm doing stupid or evil? But there's no one to tell me. And I don't feel clean.

ISAAC: You made me these sandals.

ABRAHAM: What did you say?

[ABRAHAM *takes out his knife, sharpens it.* ISAAC *thrashes on the ground. An* ANGEL *watches the two, then wrests the knife from* ABRAHAM. ABRAHAM *is trembling, unties* ISAAC, *tries to embrace him but the boy turns from him in revulsion. The* ANGEL *is gone.* ABRAHAM *retrieves the knife, watches* ISAAC *uncertainly, turns and starts down the mountain.*]

ISAAC: I'm cold. An angel saved my life. He doesn't feel clean, he tells me he's helpless. I can't stop shaking. It took an angel . . . otherwise . . . otherwise. Are we to believe in a god who allows such things? Such things? And what have they done with my brother Ishmael? Do they think I've forgotten him, that we don't remember? I can't stop shaking. He left me on this mountain, he took his knife, he didn't want to hear my dream. The fire's gone out of the world. My dream is better than this mountain. This mountain stinks of death.

[SARAH *is curled up on her bed. She is dying.* ABRAHAM *is with her.*]

ABRAHAM: How is it with you?

SARAH: I'm in pain. I've no strength. I'm a dying woman. I never knew what it would be like.

[ABRAHAM *hangs his head.* SARAH *cries out.*]

SARAH: [*Cont'd.*] Don't suffer for me! I can't stand that in you!—Can't you give an occasional laugh? Tell me a funny story? So serious, always on your best behavior. You're not much fun, and I would have enjoyed a good belly-laugh now and then.

ABRAHAM: I've always loved you.

SARAH: That's old news, I already knew it. Listen, you're a good fellow, a good husband. I haven't always been the perfect wife, didn't you find me a trifle pushy? Admit it.

ABRAHAM: We created something together. Pushy? Of course. An occasional pain-in-the-ass? It's the way of the world. But you're a fighter, I would always say to myself there's a fighter.

SARAH: So that's what you were muttering all those years. Well that pleases me, that does please me. I think I need to rest now.

[*Closes her eyes.* ABRAHAM *starts to withdraw. She opens her eyes.*]

SARAH: [*Cont'd.*] Don't go!—Go, go, it's terrible when you look at me like that. Those eyes, I imagine I can see our ancestors, the whole batch of them sitting in those eyes, they're waiting.

ABRAHAM: Sleep, be at peace, none of us will leave you.

SARAH: You'll all leave me.

[*A somber* ABRAHAM *meets with several Hittites.*]

ABRAHAM: I must tell you gentlemen that my wife Sarah has been gathered to our kin. I am a resident alien among you Hittites. Sell me a burial site here in Kiryat Arba that I may bury my loved one.

EPHRON: Hear us, my lord. You are the elect of God among us. Bury your dead in the choicest of our burial places. None of us will withhold his burial place from you.

ABRAHAM: [*Bows low.*] If it is your wish that I remove my dead for burial, then I address myself to you Ephron, son of Zohan. Sell me the cave of Machpelah which is at the edge of your land. Sell it to me at full price.

EPHRON: No my lord, hear me. I give you the field, and I give you the cave that is in it. I give it to you in the presence of my people. Bury your dead.

ABRAHAM: If only you would hear me out. Let me pay the price of the land. Accept it from me that I may bury my dead.

EPHRON: My lord, do hear me. A piece of land worth four hundred shekels of silver what is that between you and me? Go and bury your dead.

ABRAHAM: Agreed.

[ABRAHAM *pours silver into* EPHRON*'s hand, they bow to one another and* ABRAHAM *leaves.*]

HITTITE: Your cave is expensive, Ephron. You did well by yourself.

EPHRON: It was a bargain. Can't you see, the man was grateful? I did him a favor.

HITTITE: Interesting fellow. But I suspect that whole tribe will vanish in a few years. These nomads are just what we see, they can't sink roots.

EPHRON: Well, he might surprise us yet. I'm going home with my silver.

HITTITE: [*Laughs.*] A good morning's work. I'll look in on you, perhaps we'll drink to the sale.

[*An* ISAAC *of advanced age is poring over tomes, ledgers, prayer books, etc. when machine-gun fire bursts all around him. He drops to the ground in a panic.* ISHMAEL, *in the garb of a revolutionary warrior, appears with a submachine gun, watches* ISAAC *good-humoredly. The latter rises, glares at* ISHMAEL. *Neither speaks for a time.*]

ISHMAEL: You've aged, Isaac. A heaviness, a grayness. What do you call this, a library?

ISAAC: But still alive. I'm an old man, Ishmael, but they haven't finished me off yet. You're in excellent shape for an outcast.

ISHMAEL: I hear our father is gone.

ISAAC: Gone. They're all gone, all the old ones are a memory. They barely manage two hundred years these days—Do you dream of building a great nation? Is it happening?

ISHMAEL: I'm a builder, something's happening. But there's a lot of agitation, we're top-heavy with leaders, splinter groups. I sleep with a weapon at my side.

ISAAC: I don't sleep, I barely sleep, and yet I'm never quite awake.

ISHMAEL: You need exercise. Get up into the hills, do a little climbing.

ISAAC: I'm a scholar, I never wanted to go anywhere. That trip to the mountain did me in.

ISHMAEL: Did he speak of me?

ISAAC: The old man? He was consumed with his memories. He replayed everything.

ISHMAEL: He should have fought for me.

ISAAC: Yes, he should have. He should have. [*Awkward silence.*] I feel that something needs to be said. [*Doesn't know what to say.*] You're always welcome here.

ISHMAEL: Consumed with memories. Replayed everything, did he?—You owe me nothing. Things turn out as they turn out. But he should not have cast me out. People don't get over those things—I have to be off.

ISAAC: Next time don't come so noisily.

ISHMAEL: I won't be back.

[ISHMAEL *starts to leave. A burst from an unseen rifle riddles* ISHMAEL, *he collapses.* ISAAC *drops down to tend to him. It is already too late.* ISAAC *is appalled. He cradles* ISHMAEL, *he weeps, he sings him a lullaby.*]

♦

JACOB

[JACOB *is on a train. He is nicely dressed in turn-of-the-century garments. He is anxious.*]

JACOB: This train is speeding to Paris. I had barely enough for the fare. Speeding, did I say? Giving this machine a human intention? And yet it's speeding for all that, moving more rapidly than I'm able to plan. I have no money, no money. But I have the blessing. That's worth a lot. But perhaps not in Paris. Perhaps I haven't thought the situation through properly.—I'd like something to eat. I need a bath. These washrooms are filthy, and there's no paper. I'm not in a position, however, to raise a fuss. Strangers do well to maintain a low profile.

[*A prosperous merchant hustles in with lots of baggage and two grown, comely daughters.*]

LABAN: A vacant car! Let's settle in here, daughters. Mind the luggage. Oh good day, young sir. I hope we're not intruding.

JACOB: Did I hear you say this car was vacant?

LABAN: A manner of speaking. No need to take offense, for heaven's sake! Relax!

JACOB: Excuse me? I'm perfectly relaxed.

LABAN: Allow me to introduce myself. Laban the merchant, known far and wide for Laban Enterprises—FINE FABRICS FOR THE CROWNED HEADS OF EUROPE. These are my daughters. We're on holiday off to see a bit of Gay Paree as they say, and then take the baths. Well, it's been nice having this cordial discourse with you.

[LABAN *immediately shuts his eyes, begins to doze.* JACOB *and the two women eye each other furtively. The women sit modestly, then rummage around in enormous handbags and pull out fashion magazines which they proceed to thumb through. Now* JACOB *is particularly eyeing the younger daughter,* RACHEL. *The merchant sits up with a start.*]

LABAN: What's that you say?

JACOB: I haven't said a thing.

LABAN: I suggest we keep our distance. Familiarity is inadvisable, even though chance has ominously thrown us into the same conveyance. Our paths will happily diverge in several short hours, and not a moment too soon if I am any judge of the situation.

JACOB: But my dear sir—

LABAN: Will you stop interrupting? Something thoroughly disquieting about your countenance, my fine fellow, and believe me we will not end up by exchanging cards. Now be so good as to cease this infernal chatter, sir.

[LABAN *returns to sleep. The daughters peer at* JACOB *over their magazines.*]

JACOB: [*Politely.*] Good afternoon, ladies.

[*They nod slightly.*]

JACOB: [*Cont'd.*] What a charming afternoon, even if this train is stifling. I must admit that I've been riding for quite some time and I'm a bit weary, a bit done in. But let me assure you that I'm delighted to share this carriage with such refined company.

[*They nod again.*]

JACOB: [*Cont'd.*] My name, if you're wondering, is Jacob, I'm off to see something of the world, to make my way in it, and especially to fulfill certain responsibilities which I'm not at liberty to go into just at present.

[LABAN *wakes, jumps up, pulls down a suitcase and opens it before* JACOB.]

LABAN: You're right. A magnificent line of merchandise. I've been thinking it over carefully, weighing the pros and cons and I've come to the conclusion that a young man of your rigorous disposition could profit by an association with Laban Enterprises, Clothiers to the Crowned Heads of Europe. You confess you've done a bit of selling but are fairly green at the business? Of course this would be an apprenticeship, you would have to prove your worth over a period of seven years before I would seriously entertain the prospect of a junior partnership. I don't suppose you have any fluid capital to speak of? Ready cash?

[JACOB *is stunned, can't reply.*]

LABAN: [*Cont'd.*] My daughters, Leah and Rachel. We're an exceedingly close family, people have remarked on that more than once. [*Slams suitcase shut.*] You're hesitating, you're speculating that Paris may hold out greener pastures. Forget it, my dear sir, there's nothing in Paris but crooks, queers and bakers. I'm offering you the opportunity of a lifetime and in five minutes, if this offer isn't snapped up, why that's it. Caveat emptor, so to speak. Well, is it a deal?

[JACOB *is still speechless.* LEAH *opens a box of candy, plucks out a morsel which she holds out to* JACOB.]

LEAH: I'm Leah. Bon bon, dear sir?

[LABAN *and* MENDEL *are playing closed poker.* MENDEL *deals.*]

MENDEL: So how's the new son-in-law getting on?

[LABAN *shrugs.*]

MENDEL: You're not satisfied? Looks like a sharp young fellow to me, a go-getter, a regular nine-to-fiver.

LABAN: Sharp, sharp. They've all got to be watched, the nine-to-fivers and the others as well. They think the world owes them something. Your bid.

MENDEL: Five shekels for starters.

LABAN: For starters. You got something you're hiding, maybe a pair of jacks?

MENDEL: Maybe jacks, who can say? So now you got to find an eligible fellow for the baby. You got prospects?

LABAN: What are you about? I already found. I'll take three cards.

MENDEL: You already found?

LABAN: Why is it an echo issues from your mouth? Yes, you bet your ass I already found. You think I'm a fool, I don't know when to mow my lawn, harvest my bananas? The same bridegroom for both, one two finished, under the canopy, onto the mattress, one dowry, cost-efficient, worry-free.

MENDEL: Brilliant brilliant, worry-free. So how's it working out?

LABAN: He's giving me headaches.

MENDEL: Worry-free and he's giving you headaches? I'll give myself one card.

LABAN: I tend to speak in hyperboles. He's not nuts about Leah. He thinks I cheated him.

MENDEL: Cheated him with those boobs? Is the chap demented?

LABAN: I sort of put one over on him, for his own good of course. He had the hots for Rachel, so I promised him Rachel. But can a father see his baby married before the older daughter?

MENDEL: I'm standing pat. So you gave him Leah as well.

LABAN: Buy one get two, as the saying goes.

MENDEL: So what's so terrible? Two terrific women, and what an ass on that Leah if you don't mind my mentioning it.

LABAN: In the dark it's all the same, he couldn't tell the difference. It'll take five shekels to see me.

MENDEL: In the dark a pleasure's a pleasure. He should be delirious. Five shekels you say?

LABAN: He's a little pissed off but he'll recover.

MENDEL: I wouldn't have him doing your books for awhile.

LABAN: One has to take a philosophic view of these matters.

MENDEL: The philosophic attitude exactly. One son-in-law, cost efficient, words of wisdom. A tight-knit family is a pleasure to behold. I'm out of this hand.

LABAN: You're out? You can't risk five shekels with a pair of jacks?

MENDEL: I got no jacks, you were dreaming jacks for me. But tell me something.

LABAN: Some poker maven here. Even a pair of threes wouldn't make me run.

MENDEL: What's this I hear about a special blessing?

LABAN: You want it from the horse's mouth, so to speak? There's Isaac, there's Jacob, there's Esau—listen Mendel, don't be so nervous with the deck, don't pull at the corners, watch the finger marks. Where was I?

MENDEL: "There's Isaac, there's Jacob, there's—"

LABAN: Right, correct. An intentional mix-up. The blessing, which is worth as much as a new overcoat in a steambath, is supposed to be passed down to the eldest son. So what transpires? My nephew Esau is older than my nephew, son-in-law and present accountant Jacob by about four seconds, but since this Jacob is as all of us know a bissell goniff, a shady character if you get my drift, he makes believe he's his brother Esau, he swindles Esau out of the blessing by going to Isaac who by now is at least half-blind, a blinded fagel and trusting . . . [*Stares in disgust at* MENDEL *who is hopelessly lost.*] Never mind, forget the entire narrative.

MENDEL: Boyoboy, you tell one terrific yarn, full of suspense, it puts a person in mind of certain works, *Macbeth, The House of the Seven Gables* and so on.

LABAN: Let me tell you something—and watch the thumbs and the fingers if you could remember for half a second. An individual is hot for blessings? Mendel, I'll give it to you straight, the only blessing is a full tank, a mortgage-free house, a wife who can set a table and case of Schmirnoff's in the cellar. And kids who love their dad.

MENDEL: Kids who love their dad. Your deal, Laban.

LABAN: But then the wife dies on you or runs off with the seltzer man. So in the long run what have you got, what's it all about?

MENDEL: [*Musingly.*] The seltzer man.

[JACOB *is stretched out on a couch.* DR. SCHWARTZKUPF, *his bearded psychoanalyst, sits nearby. All at once both men are dozing.* JACOB *wakes with a start.*]

JACOB: Dr. Schwartzkupf, Dr. Schwartzkupf.

DOCTOR: [*Wakes.*] Yes? I was in the middle of such a nice quiet dream. A plate of matzo ball soup, a steaming dish of flanked delicately sitting beside some freshly prepared horse-radish sauce, Gypsy violins radiating softly through the hushed dining area. [*Checks watch.*] We have another seven minutes, Yacov. We're dealing, if memory serves, with that nagging blessing you seem unable to shrug off. Jakey boy, you're going through the world with plenty of baggage. Why do you put yourself through this?

JACOB: Why do I? I give you the same answer again and again. I want to be true, there's been so much deceit in my life.

DOCTOR: There you got a point, you steal from your father, ditto from your father-in-law. You make off with a colossal blessing of sorts, you manage also to pilfer several choice herds of cattle, to say nothing of boxes of grapefruit, bolts of worsteds and Harris Tweeds and three hundred cases of Manischevitz. What you do ain't nice, trivial in the larger scheme of things but downright boorish, so why don't you cease and desist? On top of all this activity—let me grant you you worked your ass off for fourteen years—on top of all this comes the clincher, you spend an inordinate amount of time suffering, you sit here and tell me week in and week out how you feel unworthy.

JACOB: Right, right. I'm a sufferer, I'm unworthy.

DOCTOR: But Yacov my boy, I ain't aware you're about to return these ill-gotten gains, grapefruit, cattle, blessings, Manischevitz and the like, all you plan to do is go on kvetching about it. Kvetch kvetch.

JACOB: You're unfair. Let me propose to you the irony in my big theft. Nobody's interested in this blessing, I stole it and I'm stuck with it—and nobody's interested, it bores them to hear me speak of it. Being stuck with it, I have to be responsible to it, and I'm trying. I'm trying so hard. But I discover that I'm kicking it away. I'm treading on this miracle, I'm caught up in so much deceit. I'm living in devious times, invalid circumstances.

DOCTOR: You're a fucking dilettante in the art of white-collar crime Why the fuss, the sturm und drang? As a criminal, you're still in the minors, you haven't even come to bat.

JACOB: So why am I suffering like this?

[*The doctor shrugs.*]

JACOB: Can't you comprehend that I have this insatiable need to be . . .

DOCTOR: Now it comes out, after a year and a half. So? What is this insatiable need to be? Spit it out, sonny boy.

JACOB: I have this need to be pure.

DOCTOR: Pure. Givalt.

JACOB: Spotless.

DOCTOR: Spotless yet. I see we got to get into some ego work.

JACOB: I want to be worthy of my responsibility to my fellow Jews. Is that some big ego thing? I don't like my behavior and I don't like anybody else's, except Rachel. And perhaps we'll have a child one day. But Leah is producing these sons, this brood, and I don't like them, I don't like the first thing about them. Deceit, bluster, petty cruelty. Is this the race of man I stole for? That I'm conniving for? This is it?

DOCTOR: On the nose. Listen my dear chap, you got options—either start being a better person or don't. Start or don't. See what a snap therapy is? And they insist we charge big bucks for it.

JACOB: I'm beginning to sense that these sessions are a waste of time.

DOCTOR: But my dear fellow, that's what civilization is, a waste, one big fat waste of time, always has been. Why else would things cost so much?

JACOB: So you can't help me toward purity, toward responsibility.

DOCTOR: Don't despair, Yacov. Listen, I'm going to give you a special phone number. On the other end of this phone number comes Dr. Newt's Repressed Memory Foundation. Maybe you could start repressing a few memories here and there, do you a world of good. For instance, they got a workshop deals with child molestation syndrome, something to sink your teeth into, right? Or how's about a fourteen-week group—it focuses on sexual awakening. Sexual awakening, what doesn't it conjure up? Remember that unforgettable afternoon you stumbled, innocent and freshly doused with talcum powder after your warm bath, into your parents' bedchamber only to discover Yitzhak and Becky in the altogether going at it like rabbits?

JACOB: Where is this nonsense coming from?

DOCTOR: [*Shouts.*] It's coming from the fact that you fucking Hebrews can't seem to forget anything! [*Consults his watch.*] We've run out of time. And next week I'll be in Pittsburgh.

[LEAH *and* RACHEL *are sunbathing, sharing a jar of suntan lotion. An odd silence.*]

LEAH: Let's get one thing clear.

[*No response.*]

LEAH: [*Cont'd.*] Don't you ever listen when I speak?

RACHEL: [*Turning to* LEAH *with a gentle smile.*] You wanted to get one thing clear, a commendable enterprise. What is that one thing?

LEAH: Cool it with the innocence, okay? You know what I'm talking about.

RACHEL: I believe, and appreciate your input, Leah, that the shelf life of this suntan lotion hardly matches the claims of the manufacturer.

LEAH: The shelf life?

RACHEL: Exactly. Is it your view that we might take our business elsewhere, and if we so should we start this afternoon?

LEAH: Rachel, my child laying it out for you. You can't stand it when he comes to me. I'm not a fool, my dear, I can see the way the wind is blowing. You're biting your nails behind closet doors, you want to kill me and don't know how.

[*No response.*]

LEAH: [*Cont'd.*] I'm talking to you, my sister.

RACHEL: Apparently. But you've shifted into that truckdriver mode that hardly suits you. What shall I say? You want a world without complication. Do I berate you, do I sulk while I'm sudsing your underpants, do I bar the door to his room when you're in heat? I was under the impression that I was your basic emotional support, in a word your best friend.

LEAH: Don't give me this stuff about my underpants, as if I don't pitch in on the laundry with the rest of you. What I'm talking about, charming Rachel, is your oppressive sweetness, your self-sacrificing disposition. You never make a fuss, you anticipate my needs, you avoid making me feel like an intruder, even when Dad and I pulled that dirty trick on you the very first night. I'm suffocating under this emotional support. There are times I'd be delighted to bash in that soulful, patient exterior you present to the world.

RACHEL: I see. How then sister of mine, may I help you?

LEAH: Help me? I don't want your help.

RACHEL: Then, Leah, exactly what is it you want?

LEAH: Tooth and claw, no holds barred, the mother of battles between bitter enemies. Short and sweet—I don't intend to spend the next twenty years feeling like a criminal. I have needs, needs, I'm not just some creature in heat, as you so finely put it. You believe you support me, but I tell you, you can't begin to understand me.

RACHEL: It appears I've been under a serious misapprehension. And?

LEAH: I want you to do battle for him. Meet me on an equal footing, take him away from me if you can. Start treating me like a person, a hated equal, your loving sister.

[RACHEL *watches* LEAH *in silence.*]

LEAH: [*Cont'd.*] Well?

RACHEL: I'll consider it.

LEAH: You'll consider it. You disgust me. I believe you have a neurotic inability to stand up for yourself.

[*The two sisters watch each other, then* LEAH *abruptly leaves.*]

RACHEL: [*Calls after her.*] I'm changing the lotion. [*Alone.*] I can't tell her the truth. The truth is that there's an implacable triviality about my sister, and that this menage a trois that she's so caught up in, that she finds so thrilling, is unbelievably trite and of such little interest for me. I don't begrudge her, her moments in heat. Those sons of hers? Tedious, stiff, unappealing—they're not bad fellows but one can't carry on an intelligent discourse with any of them. The truth is . . . the truth is my sister is an empty-headed cow, sweet for all that, but a cow who wants to be thought of as a force in society. I can't hurt her, though I have that in me, but I certainly can't honor her feelings and work up that belligerency that would make her feel worthy. She takes after Dad, God help them both. [*Breaks into an unexpected little dance.*] It's terrible that my womb is still closed, but I'm a patient soul. Something makes me understand that I'm on a journey of some consequence, it's inexplicable this feeling, but I'm caught up in Jacob's life and he in mine, and eventually it's going to matter. So that's my story, about which I can tell no one.

[JACOB *and* RACHEL *are sitting at a lunch counter drinking coffee.*]

JACOB: Do you want more coffee? Where's that counterman?

RACHEL: No, no. Listen, Jacob, something has come up.

JACOB: What? How do you mean something has come up? I was afraid of this. Fresh news makes me nervous. Here, finish your coffee, let's get out of here.

RACHEL: I keep nothing from you. I've only just discovered that I'm going to have our first child.

[JACOB *is thunderstruck. He gulps down the rest of his coffee, then gulps down the rest of* RACHEL*'s. Now they sit in silence. Finally:*]

JACOB: A boy. Or whatever.

RACHEL: God has finally opened my womb.

JACOB: I slaved fourteen years for you. I never begrudged a day of it. Fourteen years.

RACHEL: I've prayed. I never begrudged Leah her sons. Now God remembers me.

JACOB: Us.

RACHEL: Our first child. God has opened me to you, Jacob, in a new way.

JACOB: We'll have fine Jews. Fine, upright, God-fearing, pious, loving, considerate, sensitive, intellectual Jews. And more coffee. Let's have more coffee! Let's have pound cake!

RACHEL: You're building a great nation, my love.

JACOB: What's fourteen years when you're building a great nation? God opened your womb, God remembers us. Sensitive Jews, pious Jews, respectful, short and intelligent Jews. Waiter, quick, two more coffees! And pound cake! Waiter, quick, pound cake for everybody!

[JACOB *is waiting for a bus.*]

JACOB: This bus is late. The authorities should be advised. Sloppy management.

[*A* STRANGER *rushes at him,* JACOB *cries out in surprise, the two begin to wrestle furiously.*]

JACOB: Stop it, you maniac! I don't know who you are, what you want! I'll miss my bus! I'm missing my bus! Stop it! There goes my bus

[*They wrestle in silence, in terrible earnest. After a while* JACOB *hurls questions and statements at the* STRANGER. *Each of these is simply echoed by the* STRANGER *but in another tongue.*]

JACOB: Who are you?

STRANGER: Wer bist du?

JACOB: What do you want of me?

[*Stranger repeats in Chinese.*]

JACOB: You must be out of your mind.

[*Stranger repeats in Polish.*]

JACOB: Are you going to stop this wrestling?

[*Repeats in French.*]

JACOB: I'll make you pay for this.

[*Stranger repeats in Spanish.*
    Silence again. JACOB *is being worn down. He tries to stop the wrestling, but the* STRANGER *won't let him alone. For a moment* JACOB *collapses on the ground.*]

JACOB: I don't know what's happened to my life. It's as if I've been separated from everything. My life has separated from me. I missed my bus, I'm late with the mortgage payment, the supper is burned, the phone has been disconnected, the cat has run away, I've forgotten my name, I'm out of cigarettes. [*To* STRANGER.] Can't you leave me alone?

STRANGER: It's too late.

JACOB: What's too late?

STRANGER: You'll remember this.

JACOB: Of course I'll remember this!

STRANGER: You're a fool! You're self-centered! You've got to come clean!

[*More wrestling. A terrible struggle.* JACOB *appears to grow stronger.*]

JACOB: Now I'm not going to let you go! I'm not going to let you go! You're going to bless me, do you hear? You're going to bless me! I haven't missed my bus for nothing. Fourteen years!

[*They stop wrestling.*]

JACOB: It turned out that I had been wrestling with an angel. And I had a new name—Israel. The one whom God makes straight.

✧

THE EXILED ONES: MOSES

[*The desert.* MOSES, AARON *and an assortment of Israelites are making their way. There is a mound of junk to one side.*]

NARRATOR: It was a difficult forty years. Generations came and went. Bloodshed and betrayal. Worship, bickering, sacrifice, backsliding, everything came and went. The tablets happened, so did the golden calf, the death of Moses happened, God's word happened, by day and by night. One day Moses prepared to journey up the mountain. He understood that God would be waiting.

[MOSES *stands apart from the others, deep in thought. The others watch him furtively. He prepares himself, cleans his body, smoothes his garments. He begins his climb, they watch him, he disappears. The Israelites grow restless, suspicious, impatient. They begin to sort through the mound of junk, find articles that appeal to them, and begin to construct the golden calf. They begin singing and dancing around the growing idol.*

    What are the articles of junk? Records, T-shirts, fashionable clothing, old newspapers and magazines, parts of sporty automobiles, posters of hot movies, plays and records. In short, all the commercial products and ideas that seduce consumers. The golden calf grows, the revelry grows.

    MOSES *reappears on high, carrying two tablets. When he realizes what is taking place, he flings the tablets down in a rage. They smash on the ground. The revelers are startled, everyone freezes.* MOSES *descends, single-handedly he begins to demolish the calf, to tear it, burn it, rip at it with his teeth. One or two of the Israelites retrieve bits of the tablets and study them.*

    When the calf is demolished, MOSES *pulls out a pistol. He scans the Israelites, begins firing, mortally wounding some of them. A banner appears on high. It reads: "I am the Lord your God." The survivors study the banner, then fall on their faces. The desert is filled with the dead and with those pray-ing to the Lord.*]

NARRATOR: A difficult forty years. Many were wiped out, some abandoned the camp and tried to make their own way. It was not always easy to press on with Moses, to listen to the hectoring of Moses, to be patient with the God who angered easily even as He demonstrated remarkable compassion for His people. But for the survivors and for the next generation there was a sense of the future, there was the journey, there was The Law which would act as a bridge, as a road to God's highway.

[During the narration, the living carry off the dead, they sit and share bread, they try to come together as a people, they read fragments of the tablets.]

NARRATOR: The Law spoke to the weakness of a people and to its strength. It spoke to human qualities and to sanctity. It gave a sense of proportion, a sense of reason, a sense of comradeship and of light to a people making a not always explicable journey.

[The sharing of bread goes on. Suddenly a fist fight breaks out, some are dis-gusted by it, some try to break it up.]

✧

PART THREE
HERZL

Sound of drumming. French Army officers, circa late 19th-century appear. Lots of strutting, bellowing of commands. DREYFUS, *an elegant officer, be-gins to get pushed around by other elegant officers. It starts out playfully but gets serious fast. The astonished* DREYFUS *grows quiet as he goes reeling hither and yon. The* GENERAL, *a gorgeous young woman with the physique of a fine athlete, comes bounding in, humming, doing Aerobics, chewing gum like a teenager. Everyone snaps to attention. The girl-general sits leisurely, self-assured, her eyes fix on* DREYFUS *Her eyes unnerve him. No one dares to move. She calls quietly to* DREYFUS, *she is like a teacher in-structing a pupil.*

GENERAL: Dreyfus? Get over here at once.

[He rushes to her and salutes. She appraises him, he doesn't know what to do, he salutes a few times. THEODOR HERZL *appears with a reporter's note-book.]*

GENERAL: Dreyfus my child, I've got something special in store for you. Now what could it be, honey?

[DREYFUS *is nonplused, he can only shake his head.*]

GENERAL: Permission to speak granted.

[*He can say nothing.*]

GENERAL: You're not getting it, Dreyfus my love. When your superior grants you permission to speak, you speak!

DREYFUS: I...

GENERAL: That's quite enough, you bore me. Now what do I see before me, angel? I see a sweaty Jew. We all know that sweaty Jews are suspicious people, wouldn't you agree?

DREYFUS: [*Bewildered.*] I...

GENERAL: Wouldn't you agree? I'm addressing you, schmuck!

DREYFUS: Yes of course, I agree of course.

GENERAL: You agree what?

DREYFUS: What?

GENERAL: You agree what? How stupid are you? And you're keeping me waiting! Little one, you're not helping your case.

DREYFUS: I agree, sir, I agree, sir, I agree, sir.

GENERAL: Excellent, my child, excellent. Now the charges facing you, little one, come down to treason. Betraying your beloved France to those awful nasty Germans.

DREYFUS: The Germans?

GENERAL: What?

DREYFUS: The Germans, sir?

GENERAL: I'm stripping you of your rank as of this moment.

DREYFUS: What? What, sir?

GENERAL: You are being shipped, baby, to Devil's Island. For how long? For the rest of your days. Now Dreyfus, I expect a show of gratitude, look at the trouble I'm taking on your behalf. What have you got to say, my little Jew?

[DREYFUS *crumples at her feet, weeping terribly.*]

GENERAL: [*Cont'd.*] You lack grace, my child. Given your circumstances, a well-behaved officer would at least beg to kiss my ass. At least. Your be-havior, Dreyfus, is intolerable, it's shocking. Get over here.

[*She wipes his tears.*]

GENERAL: [*Cont'd.*] There there, you've been spared a sound public whipping, be grateful.

DREYFUS: I'm innocent.

GENERAL: Of course you are, and here's a treat for you.

[*She takes the gum from her mouth and places it in his mouth.*]

GENERAL: [*Cont'd.*] My juices, little Jew, treasure them during your enforced sabbatical. Perhaps you'll receive my photograph once you're settled, it will help calm you at particularly stressful moments. [*She rises, contemplates the officer lying in ruins at her feet.*] Use your time well, my child, don't indulge in self-pity, consider your coming days as periods of opportunity, begin to appreciate the benefits of living under my instruction.

[*She gives him what almost amounts to a caress with the toe of her boot, then bounds out as she entered.* DREYFUS *pulls himself to his feet and staggers off. Everyone follows but* HERZL *who is left alone.*]

HERZL: Watching Dreyfus changed everything for me. Well of course the initial thought was of Palestine, a return to the ancestral homeland, what could be more natural? But try to get it. Conferences, forums, debates. Some Diaspora Jews were offended—weren't they settled, happy, with full bellies? But there were Jews with shrunken bellies, nervous about the next pogrom. We dreamt Zionist dreams in public gatherings, we issued tracts, manifestoes, position papers, we argued, bribed, buttered up, kissed ass, stood on high horse. We called each other brother, sister, betrayer, infidel. Did any of that get us Palestine? They dangled Uganda before us, a few inches of Canada. Uganda was a problem, inhospitable terrain, it wasn't even holy. But the problem solved itself—Uganda wasn't available after all. So, Palestine once more.

[*Arab farmers appear, watching.*]

HERZL: [*Cont'd.*] A land without people for a people without a land. I was ready for Palestine, believe me. Granted that Palestine was hot. The Kaiser kept insisting one required plenty of water, plenty of shade. But fortunately it was empty. I stayed in touch with the Kaiser, kept after the Sultan, the Sultan needed stayed in touch with the Kaiser I kept after the ready cash, we were trying to work a deal.

[*Arabs move around* HERZL, *trying to understand what manner of being he is.*]

HERZL: [*Cont'd.*] And there was not only the Sultan, not only the Kaiser, but the British, hail Britannia. A land without people for a people without a land, an unbeatable equation. To tell the truth I would have settled for anyplace. Who says Uganda isn't a little holy? Or what's wrong with holy Pittsburgh, or holy Jersey City? Anyway, nobody wanted us, I don't have to tell you how that goes.

[HERZL *goes off. The Arab families unroll a carpet, prepare a ritual dinner, they sing and dance. Zionist laborers appear, among them the young David Ben Gurion, they prepare their own picnic nearby, they also sing and dance. The two forces try to maintain their separateness but at some point an over-lapping takes place involving the food, involving the dancing. There is an attempt at camaraderie but it dies fast. An unspoken tension sets in, then each attempts a return to Arab or Jewish celebration. Nothing quite works, each seems to inhibit the other. First the Arabs pack up and leave the area, then the Zionists do as well. Now there is only an empty space.*

As if by prearrangement, HERZL *and* DREYFUS *appear. They sit facing one another.* DREYFUS, *uniform and medals fully restored, is ill at ease.* HERZL *is obviously unwell. An awkward silence lasts too long.*]

HERZL: As you can see, I'm not in first-rate condition. [*More silence.*] It's go-ing to take longer than I anticipated, but I can assure you that in the next quarter of a century—well, perhaps half a century—there will be a Zionist homeland, a Jewish state. [*More silence.*] These hot after-noons. [*More silence.*] Sometimes I wonder whether I'll make it through the night. But as you see, I persist. They've got me on nitroglycerin. [*More silence.*] Glad to see you in your uniform again. Restored. You're a restored man.

DREYFUS: [*Quiet, venomous tones.*] You stinking Jews.

[*No response from* HERZL.]

DREYFUS: [*Cont'd.*] Did you believe I wished for any of your filthy help? Did you believe that I, that I would be pleased to be identified as one of you people? [*On his feet, in anguish.*] You filthy Jewish bastard, I'm a Frenchman! I'm a gentleman!!

[DREYFUS *stalks off.* HERZL *is bone-weary, his head begins to droop. He pulls himself upright. He pops a glycerin tablet into his mouth, he sucks.*]

✧

THE BUILDING OF THE STATE

Ben Gurion and other Zionists of the Second Aliyah are putting together a scaffolding of iron pipes. This section is performed without words; we do hear sounds of exertion, elation, distress, anger, calmness, fear, and triumph.

The work of erecting the scaffolding is interrupted by Arab farmers and day laborers, and later by the British Army. Moments of battle erupt time and again, the wounded fall, are healed, struggle again. Alliances shift between all three groups, we see cooperation, divisions, betrayals. Are these heroes and villains? It's a subjective call. Finally the British forces pull out, retreat, and the Zionists perhaps win the day. It's a bloody and precarious triumph. The scaffolding remains unfinished, the work goes on, new battles erupt. Quick blackout. In darkness we hear the narrator.

NARRATOR: During the Passover holiday of 1968, Rabbi Moshe Levinger and a handful of followers moved back into a Hebron which had been emptied of Jews in 1929. The slaughter of the 1929 Jews hadn't been forgotten. The Levinger forces established the settlement of Kiryat Arba on the outskirts of Hebron. The movement gave birth to Gush Emunim, the Bloc of the Faithful. Levinger saw to it that the Faithful were well armed. In June 1980 Arabs attacked Kiryat Arba and left six Jewish settlers dead. In retaliation, settlers placed time bombs in the automobiles of the mayors of Nablus and Ramallah. The two mayors and a border policeman were severely hurt in the ensuing blasts. Limbs were blown off. On April 9, 1948, in the village of Dir Yassin, soldiers of Irgun and the Stern Gang lined Arab men, women, and children up against walls and shot them dead. The soldiers then looted the village. On October 29th, a similar massacre took place at Duweima, a town near Hebron.

[Lights quickly up on empty space, then quickly out again, as if it were all an error. The narration has continued.]

NARRATOR: *[Cont'd.]* On April 11, 1987, a Molotov cocktail was thrown at the car of a Jewish family as it passed a small Arab village on their way home to Alfei Menashe, a settlement northeast of Tel Aviv. The wife, five months pregnant, was burned to death. In retaliation, settlers burned Arab shops, cars, orchards, and fields in the town of Kalkilia. On the 17th and 18th of Av, August 23rd and 4th, 1929, Arabs massacred 139 Jewish men, women, and children throughout Palestine. In Hebron, where Abraham had buried Sarah in the cave of Machpelah, and where sympathetic Arabs tried to protect their fellow townsmen, fifty-nine were murdered. Armed bands reached this ancient Talmudic center on the 24th. Arab police watched indifferently. Some Jews fled to Rabbi Slonim's house, Arabs stormed the house, they dismembered twenty-three Jews with daggers and axes. Rabbi Slonim's house was looted, everything was smashed with the exception of a photograph of Dr. Theodor Herzl. Around the frame of the photograph, a woman's blood-drenched underwear had been draped. Thus was the ancient city of Hebron emptied of its Jews.

✧

MENDEL GROSSMAN

The lights bump up. There is the now ever-present scaffolding, it will be present for the remainder of the play. We also see MENDEL GROSSMAN, *a slim, gaunt man of about thirty, fighting illness and exhaustion, wearing a worn-out winter coat.* GROSSMAN *moves with a studied casualness. We become aware that he is hiding a camera under his coat, the camera becomes visible for a fleeting moment when* GROSSMAN *quickly opens the coat, snaps a picture and quickly closes the coat. As* GROSSMAN *moves about, in and around the scaffolding, projections of his photographs flash against the walls and through the scaffolding. The photographs offer us grim scenes from the Lodz ghetto between 1940 and 1944, mostly winter shots of hungry, frightened, often brave, always exhausted Jews. These Jews are digging graves, pulling heavy wagons of excrement, waiting for deportation, eating when and where they can, somehow fighting for survival. These are the condemned, watched over by Nazi guards, the condemned in a gray, frightful moment in recent history.* GROSSMAN *begins to work at a faster pace, recording and recording, even as he grows sicker, and the pace of the projections accelerates with him. At last* GROSSMAN *collapses, he no longer moves, the camera has rolled away from him.*

NARRATOR: The heart of Mendel Grossman, secret photographer of the Lodz ghetto, 1940 to 1944, gives out at the age of thirty-two. Imprisoned in a labor camp, Mendel collapses on the road. Mendel Grossman's camera stops with him.

✧

HAGAR'S CHILDREN

(The narrative of a young Palestinian woman.)

PALESTINIAN WOMAN: My people are dying.
　　　　Three hundred years ago... what are you trying to say?

My great great grandfather tilled the soil. What did this soil amount to? Speak to me of the desert. No, don't speak.

My people are dying. My people have their ways. They say: choose life.

Somebody somewhere has papers, deeds. The Turks had papers, the Notables, the absentee landlords. They made us a gift of the dust, we tilled the dust.

What are you trying to say?

We tilled the dust, we spat on the ground, we waited for rain, we spat, we waited. In the autumn we got the rainfall, we would step barefoot in the puddles. Occasionally the boys got fresh, something about the rain got them going, I wanted to tell my mother but in the end I decided I could live with it. It never even got interesting.

My people are dying, my people...what are you trying to say?

Lemons, cucumbers, tomatoes, babies, grandparents. The fig tree, plums, the hot sun, the plum tree.

God was good, Allah was good. We remembered Abraham, we remembered Hagar and Ishmael. God remembered us. We forgot nothing.

Gaza is a sinkhole. Jericho holds a promise: night clubs, soda, movies, vegetables, taxis, traffic jams.

Arafat sits in Gaza, he broods till four in the morning, sometimes later. Gaza? I'll tell you. Dirt, asphalt, barbed wire, shotguns, everybody's garbage, carburators, goats. Arafat is president of something but no one wants to give him a dime, I wouldn't.

There's the other one: Rabin, Mr. Security. The suicide bombers are driving him frantic, and with good reason, he doesn't know where to turn. They close off Gaza, they can't think what else to do, close the gates, you can't get past the gates to make a living. So welcome to the peace process. Welcome to the murder of forty, fifty Palestinians at prayer. Welcome to the killing of Jews on busses or buying Coca Colas.

Will it never stop?

My people are dying. Lemons, cucumbers, the plum tree, the leaky carburetor, the Temple Mount, the Jordan Valley, the Dead Sea, the Wailing Wall. One block from the Mediterranean, on the busy streets of Tel Aviv, you can't breathe the air, it's gasoline fumes from Hondas, Toyotas, Chevies, Volkses, Volvos, Peugouts, Isrealis are busy going places.

The Grand Mufti of Jerusalem sat out World War Two in Berlin with Hitler. He ate lamb chops and French fries. Yitzhak Shamir, future Prime Minister of Israel and his pack of gangsters known as the

Stern gang, also tried to work out a deal with the Nazis. Everybody
hated the British: Jews, Arabs, the Irish, the French, the Russians.
Everybody wanted everybody else to get out of Palestine.
My people are dying.
My people are dying.
You can't breathe on the streets of Tel Aviv.
You can't make a living in or out of Gaza.
You can eat stones, you can scream all night long,
You can kill Jews, and more Jews, and then more.
My people are dying.

LEO BAECK, TEREZIN

*An elegant Mozart chamber work is heard. Elegant men and women stroll
about the scaffolding, exchanging niceties, bowing, curtseying, examining
an artist's sketchbook. A booming voice is heard as the Mozart and the
strollers continue.*

VOICE: Welcome to Theresienstadt, ideal city for the Jewish displaced.
Notice the amenities, the social and cultural life, the sterling silver.
Here in congenial surroundings these Jew bastards are taught to mend
their ways. Is this a labor camp? More like a country club if you ask me.
Here the noble arts are practiced. Fugues and cadenzas, andantes and
pizzicatos fill the very air. Think of the cultural nourishment. Our per-
former-inmates are at present rehearsing productions of *Cyrano* and
Lilliom, at this very moment the Berlin rabbi Leo Baeck is lecturing on
the thought of Plato and doing it to a capacity crowd, I might add. This
Baeck fellow is promising our inmate-guests beautiful insights into the
oeuvre of such chaps as Kant, Spinoza and Maimonides.

NARRATOR: In Berlin, Rabbi Baeck was a moral force, a dissident, a pain in
the ass to the Nazis. He wouldn't shut up. The Nazis threatened to
close Baeck's synagogue, but Baeck wouldn't be silenced. They finally
closed the synagogue, it didn't stop Baeck, he spoke wherever people
would listen. In desperation, the Nazis threw Baeck into the camp at
Terezin, their name for the camp was Thereseinstadt, it was their supposed model camp, their Potemkin village. But Baeck was incorrigible,
nothing stopped him. The Nazis decided to throw him out of the
camp, they made a deal with the Allies, they would ship Baeck to
America, to Cincinnati. But Baeck wouldn't go, he felt he was needed
by inmates who might soon be shipped to the death camp at
Auschwitz. He wanted these inmates to understand something about
the spiritual nature and responsibility of being a Jew.

[BAECK *appears, tired, upright, in prison garb. As he speaks in tones so quiet it is at first difficult to make out his words, people stop and observe him, then slowly move toward him. They begin to strip off their elegant garments, even as they are listening to him. Beneath the garments are revealed wretched patches of prison garb. The strains of Mozart cease abruptly during* BAECK's *words.*]

BAECK: The righteous ones, the righteous ones, these thirty-six zaddikim, they are scarcely known, scarcely considered, scarcely seen. They dwell somewhere in silence, in narrow places. Around their life, observed and unobserved, there is a splendor, a splendor that shines forth.

[*Silence.*]

BAECK: [*Cont'd.*] This people's faith had entered the world as something revolutionary, it had taken hold of the soul, it made demands. His revolutionary faith demanded a different principle, everywhere and at all times. In a sense this people was always to be underway. Every generation had to choose anew, and has now to choose anew. This people has now to have the courage to undertake the ever-new task, the courage to underway.

[BAECK *moves slowly about the area. So do others. They stay, move, they stop.* BAECK's *words are taken up by others, by men, women, children.*]

VARIOUS INMATES: The history of this people is a history of boundaries.
    It will endure, and blessing will stream from the whole to the parts and from the parts to the whole.
    Everything declares itself in faith.
    A child is born; a promise of the likeness of the image of God; the great miracle within humanity is reborn.
    Every people is a question which God address to humanity.
    Beyond all the special questions stands the one question which is life itself, the question of God.

BAECK: Everything declares itself in faith.

A YOUNG WOMAN: Everything declares itself in faith.

A CHILD: Everything declares itself in faith.

[*Some hands now touch other hands. Some hands do not. Silence.*]

ᘗ

Margo Lee Sherman in *A Curious Tale*

22. MARGO LEE SHERMAN

Margo and I had worked together in the sixties. Along with Lee Paton (now Lee Nagrin), we founded The Bridge together. Margo directed two of my early plays, and I directed her at The Bridge in *God Wants What Men Want*. In 1966, Margo became an integral part of the Bread & Puppets. Later she worked in Joe Chaikin's productions of Chekhov's *The Seagull*, Jean-Claude van Itallie's *A Fable*, and Anski's *The Dybbuk*. Margo also worked with the Talking Band, with Meredith Monk, and with Avram Patt's Barking Rooster Theater. Since her teens she has also been creating, often performing in, and sometimes directing her own work, beginning with *Girl-Lives at The Bridge*. More and more these past years she has been collaborating with several directors in adaptations of works by Beckett and Chekhov and in the creation of original plays, among them *Terezka*, the story of a disturbed child who longs for freedom, and *Stealth!!!*, a cartoon-like glimpse of contemporary urban life which Margo referred to as "a thermo-nuclear sex comedy." I've reviewed a lot of Margo's work and found much of it extraordinary: Her most recent and very beautiful *A Curious Tale*, large fragments of her play on Nadezhada and Osip Mandelstam, her performance in *The Yellow Wallpaper*, her multi-character work on *Vanya At Home* (based on Chekhov's *Uncle Vanya*), and her performance in Avram Patt's adaptation of Peretz's story, *If Not Higher*. I haven't liked everything Margo's turned her hand to—lately I've not had the opportunity to review any of it—but we do get to confer about almost everything she's worked on. And so I've taken on the role (long ago taken it on) of a kind of ex-lover and stern if solicitous critic. Over the years we've developed much respect for each other's words, even when we can't stand what we're hearing. Margo is her own toughest critic by far, but she also has the capacity (challenging Virginia Woolf's fabled record) of exquisitely torturing herself over what others say in print. Finally, Margo has a presence onstage which is rare. When she auditioned for me many years back—I needed a replacement for the mother in *God Wants What Men Want*—she had the rest of the cast, and that cast included Bobby DeNiro in a small role, mesmerized. It's as if she weren't acting. What an actress does onstage when she isn't acting I've never exactly known, but the effect is of being essentially present.

I asked Margo to ruminate a little about her work: "...the pianist has a piano, but with us it's the ability to make something invisible or inexpressible real, ... we're looking for the currents where the forbidden material is living ... as hunters through our lives, looking for ... the very thing that escapes us, we make an uneasy truce with life ..."

❖❖❖

A CURIOUS TALE

by Kate Mennone and Margo Lee Sherman

Originally produced at The Theater For The New City.
Performed by Margo Lee Sherman
Directed by Kate Mennone
January, 1993
Lighting: Katy Orrick
Sets: Kate Brown
Costume: Mary Myers

The following sequence takes place as the audience is seated. The set pieces on the stage are an 11' x 12' groundcloth which constitutes the 'cell' upon which sit a simple wooden chair, a small table in an abstracted gothic style, a pallet which serves as a bed, and four hand props: a wooden bowl, a wooden spoon, a rustic cup and a dirty rag. The portion of the performance which takes place prior to the houselights going out is called the Overture and lasts about 15 minutes. MARIE-VICTOIRE *is onstage and moves slowly about the cell, visiting activity that will be seen in the body of the play: She sits in the chair, stands at the table, makes the bed, handles the props, scrubs, etc. Once the audience is seated, and all is ready, she approaches the table, uses the spoon as a meat cleaver, and deliberately mimes chopping up several rabbits. The sharp sound of the spoon on the table brings the houselights out.*

Thibaut, here's the meat.

[*Puts meat aside, wipes hands, with spoon, she slices on table.*]

Jean-Francois, take the bread.

[*She strikes bowl rapidly with spoon.*]

I finished the onions. Hey, I go make the beds.

[*Crosses to bed, kneels, folds and unfolds bed.*]

What's the clock?

[*Stops folding bed, creates the sound of ringing church bells.*]

GONG. GONG. GONG. GONG.

Adel, Olga, Isabelle, it's five o'clock.

Internally created church bells occur throughout the play, and are indicated by the word "GONG."

[*Scrubs. Sings wedding song.*] La-la-la. La. La-la, la-la.

[*Scrubs to DR corner of 'cell.'*]

[*As* ADEL.] Marie-Victoire, Marie-Victoire.

Yes, Adel.

[*As* ADEL.] Marie-Victoire, I'm to be wed.

Oh, Adel. [*Scrubs to DC.*]

[*As* OLGA.] Marie-Victoire, Marie-Victoire.

Yes, Olga.

[*As* OLGA.] Marie-Victoire, I'm to be wed.

Oh, Olga. [*Scrubs to DL corner.*]

[*As* ISABELLE.] Marie-Victoire, Marie-Victoire.

Yes, Isabelle.

[As ISABELLE.] Marie-Victoire, I'm to be wed.

Oh, Isabelle.

[*Pause.*]

[*Commanding voice.*] Clean the chair.

[*Goes to chair and cleans.*] What's the clock?

GONG.

[*Big, stuffy voice.*] Marie-Victoire.

[*Standing erect.*] I am Marie-Victoire. [*Sits.*]
I scrub, I clean. That's all.
In the kitchen? Yes.
Yes. Yes, there too. His rooms.
For a long time. Since I was a girl. I scrub, I clean. That's all.
Why?
No, no. That's not the way. No.
Again.
I scrub. I clean. That's all.
Yes, his rooms too.
    The kitchen? Yes, the kitchen. The usual things. I fetch water from the well. I let the bucket sink deep-where it's coldest and clearest.
    No fault in that, is there? Maybe deep water's bad. Leave that out.
Again.
I scrub, I clean. That's all.
12 years old.

With my sister.
No, not any more.
She left.
Up the mountain.
By the road.
Daughters?
Adel, Olga, and Isabelle.
No, stop. That's not the way.
Again.
I scrub, I clean, that's all.
12 years.
With my sister.
No, not any more.
She left.
I don't know.
It was a long time ago.
I never saw them again.
Wrong way, wrong way. Go back again.
I scrub, I clean. That's all.
My sister was his wet nurse.
She left.
I don't know.
She left.
I don't know.
I stayed.
I clean, I scrub, that's all.
Every day for many years.
Yes. His rooms.
Every day.
The floors. The table. I show you.
Like this. [*DC, demonstrating, spits on floor, cleans it.*]
Like this. [*At chair, demonstrating, whacks chair with rag.*]
Like this. [*At table, demonstrating, wipes dishes.*]
Yes, Every day.
No. Not that day.
Pah! Caught again.
Not every day.
Not that day.
I don't know. [*Throws rag on table and leans.*]
What's the clock?

GONG. GONG. GONG.

Allez, Marie-Victoire.
Make the bed. [*Crosses to bed, makes bed.*]
Clean the table. [*Cross to table, cleans.*]
Clean the chair.
Make the bed.
   Clean the table. [*Repeats words and actions until jumbled, neither words nor actions make sense.*]
Gather firewood. [*Circles 'cell' gathering 'firewood'.*]
Clean the floor.
Mend the clothes.
Start the fire.
Boil the water.
Take out the slops.
Chop the onions.
Scrub the pots.
Clear the table.

[*With preceding sequence she goes from calm sarcasm to frenzy.*]

   Fetch the water. [*Stops to pick up 'bucket of water' and 'circles cell.'*]
Make.
Clean.
Chop.
Make the, make the.
Scrub the, scrub the.
Take out, take out.

[*Continues in this vein to extreme state.*]

STOP. [*Stops at table.*]
   Skin the rabbits. [*Releases armload of 'firewood', and 'bucket of water', crosses DR.*]
Skin the rabbits. [*Skins rabbits.*]
[*Singing wedding song.*] La-la-la. [*Stops mid-rabbit.*]

[*As* PRINCE.] Mother, I want to get married.

[*As* QUEEN] My son, what kind of girl do you want?

[*As* PRINCE.] It doesn't matter.

[*As* QUEEN.] But son, which girl do you want?

[*As* PRINCE.] BRING ME MY BRIDE.

   Thibaut, I finished the rabbits. [*Crosses to table, chops rabbit.*]

[*As* ADEL.] Marie-Victoire. Marie-Victoire.

Yes, Adel.

[*As* ADEL.] They've given Mama gold. I've been chosen to be his bride.

Oh, Adel.

[*As* ADEL.] Give me your blessing.

A word with you Adel.
Adel.
Adel! Adel!

[*Chops rabbits, cleans table, cleans hands.*]

GONG. GONG. GONG. GONG.

Yes, some wine. We all drink for the wedding feast. [*Drinks.*]
    That's good. Fix the bedroom. [*Moves chair, lays out bed, stands US bed.*]
    Bless this marriage.

[*Sits.*]

All have feasted. All have gone to sleep.
Except Alexandre and Adel.

GONG.

[*Back to audience.*]

[*As* PRINCE.] Take off your dress, Adel.

[*As* ADEL.] Yes.

[*As* PRINCE.] Come here.

[*As* ADEL.] Yes.

[*As* PRINCE.] Lie down.

[*As* ADEL, *inhales.*] Huh.

[*As* PRINCE.] I said, lie down.

> MARIE-VICTOIRE *is drawn to the 'door' and spies. She covers her face with her hands. She reveals one side of her face, then the other.* ADEL'*s face is the SR side. The* PRINCE'*s face is the SL side. The* PRINCE *growls, and* ADEL *gasps with fear. The movements quicken until the full face is revealed successively as the* PRINCE *and* ADEL. *The* PRINCE *rages.* ADEL *screams. The final face is the* PRINCE.

[*As* PRINCE.] Clean the room! Marie-Victoire.

[*Picks up rag, approaches bed, kneels.*] Oh, Adel.

GONG. GONG. GONG. GONG. GONG.

[*Sits up, crosses to table for water, no water in cup. Crosses DL.*]

Hey! Water! Hey!

[*Crosses to table, performs incantation, steps out of 'cell' and becomes* GRANDMOTHER.]

Ah, viens, ma petite, viens Marie-Victoire. Allons. Nous sommes en retard. Viens ma petite. Ah, tu es si jolie. Prends la main, prends la main, comme ça. Dis au revoir, au revoir. Prends la main. Allons. [GRANDMOTHER *crosses DR, holding hand of 'child.'*]

Le monde, c'est beau. Ah, Marie-Victoire, regarde là-bas. Des papillons, comme ils sont beaux. Comment? oui, oui, notre amie la lobelie, en bleue, en violet. Non, non, laisse, laisse, pas encore. La semaine prochaine. Viens avec moi.

Ah, regard là-bas, des lapins, hop hop. Comment? Tu as soif? Ecoute, il y a une source là-bas. Oui, oui. Prends l'autre main, comme ça. Viens avec moi. Allons. Sur les grandes pierres avec la grand-mere. Doucement, doucement, c'est presque là. Ah, nous y voilà.

A genoux. [*Kneels.*]

Alors, qu'est ce qu'on va faire? Oui, rincer la tasse. Comme ça. Et maintenant, on peut boire. [*Starts to drink, remembers 'child.'*]

Après toi, après toi, ma petite. [*Holds cup for 'child' to drink.*]

Oui, oui, tu as soif. Et maintenant moi, j'ai soif aussi. C'est bon. Ecoute, si c'etait du vin, d'abord on fait comme ca, et après … toujours, d'abord et après. [*Demonstrates how to first smell and then drink wine.*]

Veux-tu te laver le visage? Oui? Comme ça. [*Splashes 'water' on face.*]

Pas sur les cheveux, pas sur la tête. Ha-ha. Sur le visage, ma petite. Comme tu veux.

[*To self.*] J'aime la forêt.

Comment? Tu as faim? Oh-la! Soif, faim! Ecoute, je connais un petit coin où on peut trouver des fraises. Viens avec moi. [*Rises.*]

Oh, je suis vieille. Prends la main, au petit coin. Ah! Oui, oui, tu les a trouvé. Elles sont bonnes, n'est-ce pas? Donne-moi une s'il te plais? Merci, mademoiselle, te es très gentille. Excellente! J'en voudrais une autre. Merci Marie-Victoire. Extraordinaire! Une troisième, la dernière. Merci.

['CHILD' *gives* GRANDMOTHER *three strawberries to taste. Looks up.*]

Oh, Marie-Victoire, regarde le ciel. Il est tard. Il faut rentrer à la maison. Dis au revoir aux fraises sauvages, à la prochaine fois.

[*Holds out hand, they walk, then stop.*]

Non, n'aies pas peur de la nuit, ma petite, on peut chanter, la la la. Tu te souviens?

[GRANDMOTHER *sings as they walk.*] "Un flambeau, Jeanette-Isabelle, un flambeau, courant au berceau.
C'est Jesus, bonnes gens du village,
Christ est né.
Sa mere l'appelle.
Ah! Ah! Ah! que la mère est belle.
Ah! Ah! Ah! que l'enfant est beau."

[*Reenters 'cell.' The* GRANDMOTHER *dissolves.*]

Merci, Grandmama. [*Puts cup on table.*]
　　Clean the room. [*Makes bed, moves chair, sits, prepares to mend rag.*]
　　Mend the clothes.

[*As* INTERROGATOR.] Are you the servant Marie-Victoire?

I am Marie-Victoire.

[*As* INTERROGATOR.] Do you serve in the house of our king?

Yes.

[*As* INTERROGATOR.] For how long?

Since I was a girl.

[*As* INTERROGATOR.] What are your duties?

I scrub, I clean, that's all.

[*As* INTERROGATOR.] In the kitchen?

Yes, in the kitchen.

[*As* INTERROGATOR.] I see, what do you do?

I scrub, I clean.
Boil water.
Chop onions.
Mend clothes.
Scrub pots.
Take out the slops.
Fetch water.
Make the fire.
Gather firewood.

[*As* INTERROGATOR.] Ah! Gather firewood.

Yes.

[*As* INTERROGATOR.] From the forest?

Yes, from the forest.

[*As* INTERROGATOR.] Anything else from the forest?

Mushrooms. Berries.

[*As* INTERROGATOR.] I see. Herbs as well?

Yes.

[*As* INTERROGATOR.] Potherbs for the kitchen, for cooking?

Yes.

[*As* INTERROGATOR.] And for making teas?

Yes.

[*As* INTERROGATOR.] Teas to make the baby sleep?

Yes.

[*As* INTERROGATOR.] Teas to make the Prince sleep?

I don't know. [*Stitches rag.*]

[*As* INTERROGATOR.] Your sister, she served in the castle as well?

Yes.

[*As* INTERROGATOR.] What happened to her?

I don't know.

[*As* INTERROGATOR.] Where did she go?

She left.

[*As* INTERROGATOR.] Where did she go?

Up the mountain.

[*As* INTERROGATOR.] You visit her?

No.

[*As* INTERROGATOR.] She has children?

I have heard she has children.

[*As* INTERROGATOR.] Have you heard she has daughters?

I have heard.

[*As* INTERROGATOR.] What happened to them?

I don't know.

[*As* INTERROGATOR.] You don't know. Have you heard they are called Adel, Olga, and Isabelle?

I don't know.

[*As* INTERROGATOR.] You don't know?

I have heard.

[*As* INTERROGATOR.] Have you heard Adel wed the Prince Alexandre?

I don't know.

[*As* INTERROGATOR.] And Olga?

I don't know.

[*As* INTERROGATOR.] And Isabelle?

I don't know. I don't know. I don't know.

[*Stands, wraps wrists with rag, circles room and is brought through a 'jeering crowd,' and at DL corner is propelled into 'cell.'*]

Mary Help Me.

[*Releases hands.*]

Mary Help Me.

[*Arranges rag, bowl, spoon and cup on chair to create a small alter. Sets table up as a pew.*]

[*Sings.*] La la la la la la . . . la la
La la la la la la . . . la la
Dame du ciel
Régente de la terre
Hallelujah

GONG.

[*Enters pew and kneels.*]

O, mère de la Misericorde,
La Douceur de notre vie.
Nous crions vers
Nous soupirons vers
Tourne vers nous tes yeux pleines de bonté,
O bonne, O sainte, O douce Vierge Marie.

[*Repeats prayer and stands.*]

[*As* PRINCE.] Mother, I want to get married again.

[*As* QUEEN.] Oh, my son.

[*As* PRINCE.] Bring me a new bride.

[*As* QUEEN.] As you wish, my son.

[*Kneels.*]

O, mère de la Misericorde,
La Douceur de notre vie.
Nous crions vers toi
Nous soupirons vers toi
Tourne vers nous tes yeux pleines de bonté,
O bonne, O sainte, O douce Vierge Marie.

GONG.

[*Unmakes the altar.*]

The table. [*Crosses to table, discovers dirty spot, cleans and polishes.*]

[OLGA *giggles.*] Ha-ha-ha.

[*As* OLGA.] Marie-Victoire, Marie-Victoire.

Yes, Olga.

[*As* OLGA.] They've given Mama jewels. I've been chosen to be his bride.

A word with you, Olga.
OLGA!
Jean-Francois!

[*Crosses to table.*]

You chop the onions and help Thibaut. I have work to do.
　Thibaut, give him some wine for the wedding feast. I have work to do.

[*Crosses to chair, sits, sews, and prepares to drape bed with rag.*]

O, mere de la Misericorde,
La Douceur de notre vie.
Nous crions vers...

[*Turns chair and hides behind it.*]

[*As* PRINCE.] Olga, take off your clothes.

[*She rises as* OLGA, *giggles and prances out of the 'cell' to UC wall. She turns to face the* PRINCE. *He grabs her blouse.*]

[*As* PRINCE.] I said, take off your clothes, Olga.

He grabs her right breast, then her left, then grabs her crotch. She turns her back to him. He lifts her skirt and grabs her ass, and fondles it. He grabs her crotch and she is turned face forward. She pushes his hand away.

[*As* OLGA.] No, no.

[*She runs SR, and stops at the wall. She turns to face him and crosses toward him. They turn. She screams, and covers her face. He raises his arm and stabs her abdomen. Multiple stabs. She is killed. The* PRINCE *hacks off her 'arm' and eats it, then he slices open her 'abdomen' and grabs her 'liver.' He eats and beslubbers himself with 'blood.' He rises and crosses back into the 'cell.'*]

[*As* PRINCE.] Clean the room!

[MARIE-VICTOIRE *scrubs, starts to make bed, then cradles it.*]

GONG. GONG. GONG. GONG. GONG.

[*Folds bed, listens, runs to table, gets bowl, and crosses DL.*]

Bread. Hey, hey, Bread! [*Crosses DC.*]
Adel!
Olga!
Isabelle, ah, Isabelle.

[*Crosses out of 'cell.'*]

Let's go.

[*With 'child' crosses DL.*]

Are you ready? Let's go. Do you remember?

[*Sings a fast paced melody as 'child' dances.*]

Oh, Isabelle. You are a good dancer, bravo. Tell me Isabelle, are you tired?

No.

Are you hungry?

Yes!

Me too. Look what I brought.

[*Presents empty bowl and performs incantation, there is 'food.'*]

Look Isabelle. It smells good. Have some.

Mmm. Lily root. Burdock. Mmm. Spring onion, mushrooms.

[*Eats.*] Isabelle, look at the sky. It's late. Time to go. [*Retraces steps.*]

Isabelle, look what I see. Yes it's home. Go!

[*To* ISABELLE.] Bye-bye.

[*To self.*] Bye-bye.

[*Crosses into 'cell', sits at table, eats, becomes* PRINCE.]

[*As* PRINCE.] Mother, I want to get married again. Bring me a new wife.

[*As* QUEEN.] Oh, my son. I've done everything possible. Now, how can I find you a third wife after you've eaten the first two?

[*As* PRINCE.] Well then, maybe I'll eat you.

[*As* QUEEN] Oh! Marie-Victoire, clear the table!

[MARIE-VICTOIRE *crosses DC.*]

Isabelle. A word with you.

[*Crosses to table.*]

[*Lifts cup.*] One.
[*Lifts bowl.*] Two.
[*Lifts rag.*]Three.
Blessings.

GONG.

[*Takes chair and table UC, spreads bed DC.*]

Isabelle.

[*She places the cup, bowl, and rag on the bed. She mouths "One, Two, Three" with these actions. She crosses behind the table and faces the bed.*]

[*As* PRINCE, *fiercely.*] Isabelle, take off your dress. [*Strikes table hard with spoon.*]

[*As* ISABELLE.] After you. Come, let us share this wine.

[*As* PRINCE, *questioningly.*] Isabelle. Take off your slip. [*Strikes table less hard with spoon.*]

[*As* ISABELLE.] After you. Come, let us share this food.

[*As* PRINCE, *quietly.*] Isabelle. Will you get into bed? [*Taps table with spoon.*]

[*As* ISABELLE.] After you. I will join you.

[*As* PRINCE.] Come join me.

[*As* ISABELLE.] I will.

[*Places spoon on table, looks at bed, looks up and out.
    The lights fade.*]

THE END.

Translation of the Grandmother scene:

Ah! Come, my little one, come Marie-Victoire. Let's go. We are late. Come, my little one. Ah, you are so pretty. Take my hand, take my hand, like this. Say, bye-bye, bye-bye. Take my hand, let's go. [GRANDMOTHER *crosses DR, holding hand of 'child.'*]

The world, it is beautiful. Ah, Marie-Victoire, look over there. Butterflies. They are beautiful, aren't they? What? Yes, yes, our friend lobelia. Blue, violet. No, no leave it, leave it, not yet. Next week. Come with me. Ah, look over there. Rabbits. Hop Hop. What? You are thirsty? Listen, there is a spring over there. Take my other hand, like this. Come with me. Let's go. On the big stones, with Grandmother. Carefully, carefully, almost there. Ah, here we are.

On our knees. [*Kneels.*]

So, what do we do? Rinse the cup. Like this. And now we can drink. [*Starts to drink, remembers 'child.'*]

After you, after you, my little one. [*Holds cup for 'child' to drink.*]

Yes, yes, you are thirsty. And now me, I'm thirsty too. It's good. Listen, if this were wine, at first you would do this and then... always this first and then... [*Demonstrates how to first smell and then drink wine.*]

Do you want to wash your face? Yes? Like this. [*Splashes 'water' on face.*]

Not on your hair, not on your head. Ha-ha. On your face, little one. As you wish.

[*To self.*] I love the forest.

What? You are hungry? Oh, la! Thirsty, hungry! Listen, I know a little place where we can find strawberries. Come with me. [*Rises.*]

Oh, I'm old. Take my hand, to the little place. Ah! Yes, yes, you found them. They're good aren't they? Give me one please? Thank you miss, you are very nice. Excellent! I want another one. Thank you Marie-Victoire. Extraordinary. A third one, the last? Thank you.

[*'Child' gives* GRANDMOTHER *three strawberries to taste. Looks up.*]

Oh, Marie-Victoire, look at the sky. It's late. We have to go home. Say bye-bye to the wild strawberries, until the next time.

[*Holds out hand, they walk, then stop.*]

No, no, don't be afraid of the dark, my little one, we can sing. La, la la... Do you remember?

[GRANDMOTHER *sings as they walk.*] "A torch, Jeanette-Isabelle,
A torch, running to the manger.
It is Jesus, good people of the village,
Christ is born,
His Mother names him.
Ah! Ah! Ah! How beautiful is the Mother.
Ah! Ah! Ah! How beautiful is the child."

⸙

23. MEREDITH MONK/*THE HOUSE*

Meredith came out of Bessie Schonberg's dance program at Sarah Lawrence. By 1964 she had become part of New York's downtown dance scene, several years after the groundbreaking Judson Dancers had taken modern dance into a new territory marked by the breakdown of the lines separating dance and theatre, now coming together not through narrative but through abstraction. In those early years, Meredith danced for a number of choreographers, including Judith Dunn and Kenneth King. One Saturday night in 1966 she participated in a theatre and dance work devised by Dunn and painter-filmmaker Aldo Tambellini. Performed in the fountain at Washington Square Park, the work was part of three dance-film-theatre pieces produced by The Bridge Theatre under the umbrella title *Outfall.* The Dunn-Tambellini effort was a minor disaster; it depended on darkness for its effects, but no one had the foresight to consider that a work going up at eight o'clock on a September night in New York would have no darkness. I recall Meredith and Judy working their useless flashlights around the fountain.

In those early years Meredith seemed to me an interesting and very talented performer, but in retrospect she was obviously harboring broader capabilities. These capabilities seemed to burst forth by 1969. That year, under the aegis of a production company she named The House, Meredith staged her first major work in the spiraling interior of the house that Wright built, the intrepid Guggenheim Museum. She employed no less than eighty-five performers in the service of *Juice: a Theater Cantata.* Already the worlds of postmodern dance and a kind of contemporary art song were coalescing into something Meredith conceived of as theatre, and already this slightly-built dancer, only some half-dozen years away from the protective Schonberg nest, was moving like a bulldozer into those art precincts where the major innovators intimidate critics and audiences alike.

I was "out of town" for *Juice*, teaching and living my life at Bennington College in Vermont. *Juice* was only a rumor to me. But by 1971, for better or worse, I was back in Manhattan, in time for Meredith's next spellbinder. *Vessel: an Opera Epic* was designed for Meredith and seventy-five performers and took place over several hours in three distinct spaces. It opened in Meredith's loft in Soho, then moved sometime about nine or ten at night to a then deserted parking lot on Wooster Street, and finally made its last move into the interior of the Performing Garage, some two hundred feet north of the parking lot.

What is it that Meredith inhabited in this work? Nothing less than some interior sense of Joan of Arc, to whom the archangel Michael is presumed to have spoken and who was finally condemned and immolated for the good of her soul. I can recall the sense but only a handful of the details of this extraordinary work some twenty years later. To begin with, there are those warbling, plaintive musical sounds issuing from Meredith's throat. There is the slight figure of Meredith seated at a portable organ in a parking lot deserted except for a handful of spectators and performers. A constant, stubborn drizzle is coming down and the plaintive, at times ecstatic notes are issuing from this soon-to-be-condemned Joan. At one point, three large figures appear in front of the massive doors of a church on West Broadway, a full block away from the Wooster end of the parking lot. What they represent I couldn't possibly tell you twenty years later, except that I will never forget the image of them. What I can also tell you is that the church on West Broadway was bulldozed years ago. The work is replete with twirling and stately movements, and the sounds of the warbling Meredith-Joan, a warbling of the soul claiming a faith that has abandoned the body, have never left me.

A little help is needed, so let me quote from reviews of a 1991 retrospective that included the final scene of *Vessel*. From Tim Page in *New York Newsday*, October 28th, 1991: "Monk, joined by Andrea Goodman and Naaz Hosseini...sang and played organ—long, simple, ethereal and haunting waves of sound that pulsed through the hall and beyond." From Jack Anderson, *The New York Times*, Oct. 30, 1991:

> The audience was then led outside to a plaza overlooking the Hudson River. Docked boats, the lighted buildings of New Jersey and an illuminated clock face served as a backdrop for a fully staged revival of the final scene of *Vessel*.
>
> Dozens of people danced their way out of the darkness. A dragon-like monster with a devil's head paraded by. Six motorcycles roared into the space and circled the dancers. When the bikers sped away, Ms. Monk performed a twisting, convulsive solo in the light of a welder's torch. As sparks filled the air behind her, she was transformed into St. Joan being burned at the stake.

Over these several decades, Meredith has been an inexhaustible fount: the operas, the films, the videos, the concerts, the recordings. Recently she brought back *Education of the Girlchild* with that haunting image of herself as her own grandmother. Out of the public arena, Meredith also found time to write music for a handful of my lyrics. I have a vivid recollection of

---

Meredith phoning me around one in the morning to play the music she had just written. I would be almost asleep, sitting barely clothed with the phone pressed to my ear, listening to the portable organ and to the warbling Meredith. I would simultaneously wake and sleep for these messages.

I want to close these recollections of Meredith with a critique I wrote on *Quarry*. The opera was performed at the La Mama Annex and these words appeared in *The Village Voice*, issue of April 26, 1976:

One of the mysteries of art is its ability to transform pain into spiritual comfort, to metamorphose anguish at horrendous events into a suffusing, succoring joy. Unlike history, which mobilizes the past and turns on it a sometimes dazzling analytic searchlight, art forces a reliving of the experience; it is another kind of analysis, a re-forming of actions. In this re-forming we suffuse the remembered actions with nothing less than our humanity, much as if we were tending a wounded animal or nurturing plants in a window box when the impulses of the spirit are transmitted through our fingers. We have ceased to be victims of the past and have become collaborators in a move toward transcendence: At its best the remembered actions are drained of past evil and take on a sanctity through our replaying.

Quarry, an epic opera performed by Monk, the members of The House, and several dozen additional performers, is essentially an abstraction of a Jewish coming to consciousness and a growing up both during and after the events of the Holocaust, and it is also the playing out of that Holocaust. So that the work is on several levels: The private concerns of a girl in a privileged household—but there is already anguish in these private moments—and the private concerns of several adults related to the girl, balanced against public, mass spectacles which in time envelop these private lives. And also a complicated level of time, for the girl seems both to be living through the growth of the Thirties and awakening to its horrors at a later moment in history. And the work is so constructed that the spectator comes as late to the consciousness of fascist horrors as the girl does.

There is a wonderful eye for detail, both of objects and movements. The long space of La Mama Annex is intermittently drained of emptiness by domestic groupings: Orthodox Jewish couple in traditional blacks, husband poring over Scripture or perhaps Talmud; three girls at a dinner table in a bourgeois household, light source a lamp with a fat, comforting base; an older bourgeois couple, husband in marooned-colored robe, reading peacefully, wife in simple black dress and pearls, upright, dignified; another relative in long print dress, clacking heels, rehearsing for a part; and in the center the sleeping, troubled, or waking, feverish girl, watched over by comic maid, dusting, peeping out windows.

The groupings sometimes evoke a sense of ineffectuality, of giddiness, but often of devotion, in the bourgeois households to a way of material and intellectual life, or in the Orthodox setting to a Supreme Being. The girl, even less effectual and more vulnerable than the others, nevertheless seems to be in the throes of some half-understood anguish that goes past the silly whining about "My head, my ears, my eyes." She is Monk's "vessel," apprehending the beginnings of something that will later come to be understood as the fascist mining of victims, or "quarrying," and the fascist forces will be represented by grotesque or comic dictators or the supremely evil dictator in business suit, the insidious "banality" of the business suit, that eventually takes over the space, or the terrible sight of mass, choraling youth in fascist, body-building movements that choke the space.

There is so much in the Monk opera, and in fact it seems to me overproduced, but it is a work of beautiful devotion, and I haven't even begun to mention the warbles and staccato cries and other sounds that help compose this remembering of six million Jews.

✑

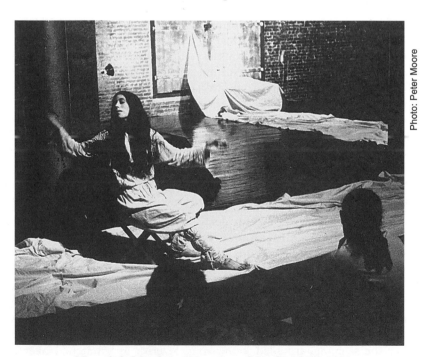

Meredith Monk in *Education of the Girlchild*, 1973

24. MABOU MINES

Founded in 1970, this eclectic ensemble, a breakaway from the Actor's Workshop in San Francisco, is equivalent in a way to the Sinatra-Dean Martin-Sammy Davis Jr. Rat Pack operating out of Vegas where booze, sex, and the wheel of fortune light up the fluorescent night. We have an intellectually brilliant, nervy gang who, unlike the Rat Pack, never seem to have a dime, who give off an aura of hanging out one minute with the head honchos at Princeton's Institute for Advanced Study and the next minute with hookers and desperate welterweights at Stillman's Gym. The company, which at one time or another has included Lee Breuer, Ruth Malaczech, JoAnne Akailitis, David Worrilow, Bill Raymond, Frederick Neumann, and Terry O'Reilly, has a penchant for living on the edge: a cutting edge, philosophic edge, name your edge. But Lee, for instance, wants it be known that he's at the edge, for he seems to function best with as much public airing as he can muster, and he fattens up on the role of "art desperado." Lee is always driving himself, and Mabou Mines functions in part from Lee's finely-tuned, hot engine. Lee likes to write in public; if Proust needed the confines of his bedroom to court the muse, Lee Breuer and his muse wrestle in the confines of a jammed subway train at rush hour. The group, or gang, or pack, is a driving one. A major impulse of Mabou Mines is the wedding or welding of pop culture with the weedy discourse of semiotics or deconstructionism or any one of a number of breakthrough, if transitional, modes of thought. And what appears to wed or weld these disparate worlds is a kind of punk-rock accelerating metabolism, a combination of edgy consumerism that loves the street, space comics, TV commercials, the ambiance of basketball at the Garden, and a radical need to move the stolid old theatre into places it has never dreamt of. In Bonnie Marranca's anthology of radical plays, *The Theatre of Images*, Lee Breuer proclaims: "I walk around in a square black frame... When I talk to myself the important words are set off in black face type. Dramatic movements have 'pow,' 'krack' and 'aarghh' written all over them."

The Red Horse Animation, a wildly beautiful, hypnotic piece, opened at the Guggenheim Museum on November 18, 1970, then was revised and remounted in April of 1972 at the Whitney. In its best moments it's a dream, a hallucination, a solid rendering of an insubstantial and insistent interior-exterior reality of a horse that may not exist but is remembering its life.

Early in its career, the company's juices began spilling out over the tightly-wrought Samuel Beckett invocations of loss and incapacity. Lee's rendering of *Play* and other fancies from the Beckett canon is a veritable act of homage; the art desperadoes were purposely moving into a black hole of intensity.

There was the piece in the Paula Cooper art gallery, whose total sound, as I remember it, came from an acetyline torch, concept courtesy of Philip Glass. There was the half-time event Lee created at the Pratt College gym in Brooklyn one freezing winter in the late seventies. *The Saint and the Football Player* was another daring and wonderfully-executed work, and I recall Lee bouncing around that gym, afflicted by flu or strep throat or with some malevolent scavenger that would have sent most of us under the covers. And there was JoAnne Akailitis's sensual study of the world of Colette, entitled *Dressed Like An Egg*. And Ruth Maleczech's performance in *hajj*, in which she takes on the face mask of her own dead father. Nervy, often brilliant, sometimes overly-long, sometimes, for me, too much in the head. It was pure madness.

The Bribe, written by Terry O'Reilly, opened in April, 1993, at Theater for the New City.

Terry recalls:

It's an animated film. Totally impractical, but swift tobogganing. What materialized was a Radio Series animated by the music of John Zorn. Ruth Maleczech had Black-Eyed Susan and I work with the recorded voices of *The Bribe*, moving like comic silent movie actors, but running other texts (Charles Ludlam, St. John of the Cross, Shakespeare, Tom of Bedlam, like that) very actively in our heads. After a lot of work in this way, sometimes working only to Zorn's music and the "inner texts," we began to say the words of *The Bribe* live, eliminating the pre-recorded radio text altogether. Months of this.

Ruth wanted it to seem like we were a couple of people who wandered into the theater, or jimmied our way in to do these routines. Susan saw us as a classic comic team, a pair of outsiders in the Spanish tradition of the picaroon—hustlers, by turns funny and mean. To me the language, the made up bebop talk, the contentious, dumb, poetic, rife with the kind of brevity that presumes intimacy, conflict, and partnership, fit perfectly.

Who are these people, and what language do they speak? They are actors, and they speak the language of theater.

In rehearsal we studied and copied Sid Caesar, Imogene Coca, the Marx Brothers, Buster Keaton, Molière, Mel Brooks, Charles Ludlam,

DaDa, Dali, and Commedia del'Arte. One day Susan came in with the idea of manipulating me like a ventriloquial figure: I would lip-synch live her "dummy voice." The scene was rewritten, and the role of the Tax Man was enlarged, making him a character that is a psychotic amalgam of cop, clerk, artist, and wrecking ball. Jeff Weiss was the model and recorded the voice over. He ends the play. We joked somewhere, "please don't let there be a moral to this story"—well, in the end, there is a moral, or an arbitrariness—the pair are squashed like, I hesitate to say, bugs.

❖❖❖

Terry O'Reilly and Blackeyed Susan in *The Bribe*

THE BRIBE
by Terry O'Reilly
with music by John Zorn

Directed by Ruth Maleczech
Featuring Black-Eyed Susan & Terry O'Reilly
Voice of Taxman (taped): Jeff Weiss
Sets and Lights: Richard Nonas
Choreography: Jo Andres

❖❖❖

MUSIC—enter S—*takes position Down Stage Left.*

S: If you want pop corn, go to the Movies.

> [*BLACKOUT*—T *in place to right of* S, *back to audience in a 2 count*—
> *LIGHTS UP. MUSIC.*]

S: This illusion ragged.
Tenderly, I light the first cigarette of the day,

T: Late,

S: Hunkered, cupping the flame, Freeze frame to slow-mo,
With theme music, two inch brim.
You know how you do on the pavement, when everyone is
Watching, inhaling the Image.

T: I say "No Thanks" to the guy who asks. A Hustler.

Here I am Mythologizing. And I have to fend.
I have a good mind to head myself out-of-town,
To the Pines.

> [*Sings.*] To the pines, To the pines,
> where the Sun never shines...

> [*BLACKOUT*—3 *Count—lights up.* S *&* T *back up alternately.*]

S: I don't want to plug the town I'm in but I can say:
It's urban.

T: Where every check-out girl, laundry man, hardware,
Drygood, gas station owner, attendant, salesman,
Boy, knows, presumes, or speculates, about every
Breath, step, or blink.

S: Fat to relish the Oddball.

T: Call each other out of, by and large, hamburger chains.
Call each other out onto the parking lots,
In little groups.

S: Maybe you're there changing a tire on a rented car,
Maybe you've lived there all your life.

T: Fat to relish the Oddball.
That smile; Those kids.

S: Arms crossed.
Their lips suddenly itchy, full, plump with sex,
Glancing to the side, they touch them, coy,

T: Happy. Out goes the gossip like hot wasps. Stinging
Sanctified poison, whispered, thrilling, joy coming
Straight from the bones. The sky moves in.
You can't breath. Lead.

S: Knock the Baby Faces around.

T: "Don't get smart with…"

S: Don't get smart.

T: These nubs grew up not getting smart with anything bigger
Than a bottle cap.

S: I'm no better than you or your nice homes.

[S *&* T *now are both backed against the back wall of the theater.* BLACKOUT.
LIGHTS UP.—T *Down Stage Right of Center, smiling.* S *Up Left.*]

T: Odd is common.
Common as cradles and rockers

And toothpick dispensers. This wild stuff you see with a free hand on
the street, will be warming stools at the factory; sitting in row
houses "I'd rather be coping" proof through the night,
Keeping up with the sit-coms. Sediment.

[S—*begins to cross to Down Left of Center.*]

S: Flab.
This is known.
This is known everywhere but in the vast Narrows of the parade ma-
jorities. People who Push history around are bone up on this.

T: Keep the fringes burning. Me.

S: Keep the fringes burning. Myself.

T: I, was not born well rung on the ladder of success.
Though I am as pretty, I am not the fish store cat.

I've got to earn a living.
Waters boiling, want some tea?

[*BLACKOUT. Lights up on* s *&* T *wrestling.*]

S: I don't mind telling you I can get pretty

T: I go through periods of excitable,

S: Angry

T: Torrentially playful,

S: Sometimes.

T: Fierce, blood-sullen flashes.

S: Irascible, irritable, Irritable is the word

T: But fair and straight: Straight, Straight, Straight,
That's my Credo: but Just.

S: Maybe I should just say square.

[*BLACKOUT.* T *exits. Lights up on* s *snoring on a park bench, a bucket over her head. She wakes up and does her "morning routine" including aerobics workout. She has her overcoat buttoned up over her head so that she seems to have no head.* T *speaks from off stage. MUSIC CUE.*]

T: I was temping at the ruling party when for amusement they
Fired me.
Couldn't use an Informed Source with the Common Touch.
Couldn't use an Opinion Maker with the Big Picture in his
Back pocket.
I told them that 80% would rather vote for Neither ...
Do they expect a landslide engineer to mow the lawn?
[*Pause.*]

So what I take naps?

They watch too dumb reruns.
They are reruns.
I snore. They rack out on soaps.

I'VE GOT A STORM IN MY BRAIN, I'm a blizzard of Ideas. No
two are alike, and each one's a stone gem.
Coo over pigeon holes and punch the clock.

Stuff envelopes and keep the cap tight on the white-out, what does
that?
Separate the men from the Da da da
You fill in the blank.
[*Pause*]

I Belong At The Top
I Am The Hydrant Of The Vogue.
The ax comes down and I don't even coin a phrase. I humor them.
I know my words are pronounced, showy.
I take the boot—a few office supplies and hit the road with my eyes
    wide Open.
Decide not to sell the story to the free press,
Not that there are any takers.
[*Pause.*]

Life's cheap enough without buying your toothpaste with hush
money.
Pinky rings keep your dirty limo windows up. Smoked fish on a silver
    dish.
I'm not scared—let them eat twinkies.

[s *unbuttons her overcoat and lets it down over her head.*]

s: Life teaches you to lie.

[*BLACKOUT. MUSIC CUE*—T *enters—running through the diagonal of the
tubs, finds his hat in the last tub—wet.*]

T: I need a hat.

s: Carefree is for the birds.

T: Air. Air. Flit in the air. Smell a Song. Out of here.

s: Vent the tete. Steam out.

[*MUSIC CUE.* T & S *reposition.*
    s *directly upstage of* T, *manipulating him as a ventriloquial figure.*
*Underline indicates "*DUMMY*" voice.*]

s: Look, we got to blow this pip squeak burg

T: Yeah, but we're busted

s: Busted, I'll fix it. Here take my lead:
    You Dummy.

T: Dummy?

s: Dummy. Get your nose on.

T: Over Act?

S: Act like you're waiting for a Bus.

T: At the bus stop.

S: Smash your face into 80 antsy wrinkles,
Hitch on a perfect limp,

T: and pace,

S: Jolson!

T: I procured a bus pass from a now even more absent minded than ever
deceased senior citizen friend of mine who owes me one

S: Seniors pass, Eh? Now you're talking.

T: The seniors pass, plus the: "I'm Deaf God Bless You" card...

S: Bamboozles mass transit.

[*They do.*]

Give the Ticket Puncher a couple of "Safe Bet" gimpo steps.

T: Uh-oh. I let the fret face go possum.

S: Dust the wrinkles

T: Smooth on the sweet fly paper of youth

S: Relax.
Go on, do your show.
Catch a coin.
Do an "all the world's a stage" high-hobble for sheer showmanship

T: Back to the back seat.
Bless You. Bless You. Thank You.

S: And I'm top down in my convertible mind.
Back seat. Feet up.
Last stop

T: Bottle of Beer is my fare.

S: Mr. Irresistible.

[S *&* T *are resting on each other on the Park Bench with their feet up.*
Blackout. T *sings Leadbelly loud and mean.*]

T: "Now girl, now girl, don't you lie to me, tell me where did you
Sleep last night. In the pines, in the Pines, where the sun
Never shines, I was shivering the whole night through."

[*Same pose as before on the bench but* S *with her coat on and* T *is in a tenement T shirt.*
    MUSIC CUE.]

T: And I'm thinking of this,

S: Chinese guy?

T: I forget his Name . . . it's in the paper . . . from the Mainland.
Comes over here, I don't know?
Slowboat?

S: Probably flew.

T: And he's got this Score in his case. Composer cat, see
Musical, and he's got this sly plan.

S: Quietly takes a small room downtown.

T: Calls all these Yehudies and Yashas from the
Classical Classified. Chamber Types. Ieszoks.

S: Ivory sense time . . .

T: Starts dropping a bunch of Chinese names like silverware in their ears.

S: Octets of Names.

T: Says he's got "the SYMPHONY" Peking, Beijing, what have you,
Chinese Symphony Orchestra

S: Mit opus

T: And he has this score,

S: A composition.

T: And so-and-so is playing, and such-a-much is playing,
And they suggested you. This is all done in person.
And it's a one night in a prestige venue,

S: A Venues Venue.
Ancient Chinese fella with cheekbones out to here

T: And, Yehudie, there is no need for rehearsal. For your part is just:
Accent

[*They shift to fake Brit accents.*]

S: Charmed out accent, great laugh. See, everybody says
They get swept up in this truly great laugh.

[*They laugh.*]

And in person, his plain, plain, thinno-suit, thinno
Black suit, flirts, odorless Chinese man.

T: And really, more, it's a chance to work out with, you know, a pack of
virtuosos for Big, I mean, Big Money.

East meets West.

S: Some bite some don't

T: "And so-and-so can't make it but I got Robert Zot-Zot
You know Bob?" And he props everybody up against everybody else,
and Bing Bang Boom, it swims.

S: And the Key Mystery here is—How he knew that they
Would all be in town with their feet propped up
With time on their hands on the same night.

T: "And it's already pre-sold, see, but we are holding to
One night, and they are busting the schedule
At Carnegie Hall to extend."

S: But I say NO.
It can be remounted.

T: And so on, and so on and pump pump, and pump pump, and Pump.
And then he starts Ringing up all the Chinese Orchestras,

S: Get it?

T: Two, who happen to be Yawning in town. And says "I've got
CASH and a pack of chamber heavies," Drops Some name plates
"Never assembled before, major Score."
And there is no need for rehearsal for your part is just: "Accent,"

S: Frame, Perspective,

T: Would be honored,

S: Time is right,

T: Venues Venue.

S: No rehearsal.

T: One night.

S: Say Yes.

T: Big money. And exposure. You want that

S: Sign here.

T: Larger audience. That's the Key to the big door.
Personal appearances.

S: The bridge to success.

T: Dad, Dad, something, was his name, middle name, one of
His middle names! I think that's right ... Or ...
Nick ... Name ...

S: And he's going to conduct!
And there are a hundred some-odd on the Stage, tuning up a HOAX
OH! Carnegie Hall is rented, rented, plain money,
Post-dated Hong Kong check to the box,
Insufficient funds, but who knew?

T: Ditto the publicity spread.

S: "Get your Red Hot culture"

T: Ludwig's boys are looking at each other, blinking,

S: Six first fiddles rosined up, the prickle of
Excitement hitting the Starch.
White Ties. Butterflies. Thousand watt Quartz light.

T: The West all sitting on little Dacron pillows around
This black leather coffee table.

S: Bowl of chilled seedless white grapes.

T: Wreathed by a take out Chinese orchestra 200 strong.

S: Dad jumps his arm and half a dozen classical elbows flinch
Instinctively concerto-wise and the Chinese orchestra:
Pumps out accent!

T: Odorless Dad ... starts ... leaping ... around.
Smoking, like a cayenne yippie in his shorts.
Laughing, CHIRPING like a jaybird. Dippin. Tippin,
Conducting with his bare Feet, toenails, Cheekbones, do-see-do vir-
tuoso, patty cake,

S: And the music pours over the footlights,
Like honeymoon Niagara.

T: Yes.

S: Like that. Just like that.

T: Everybody is up there saving their Bum, face,

S: What have you.

T: Rattling brain pan, out in that kitchen, Pandemonium, Child.

S: And the audience flips, starts heaving those famous
    Oyster Rolex watches, Mont Blanc pens, sable muffs
    Up on to the stage. Yelling.
    Appreciation.

T: The reviewers on the Radio Phones, under a shower
    Of tiaras, are hot-lining the Rave headlines,
    Headlines their competition is already breaking on the
    Street, waving in the newsboys' hands.

S: EXTRA. EXTRA.
    Notes flying out like confetti through a
    Wind machine blowing the audiences ears back.
    For an HOUR AND A HALF!

T: And of course there is a whole lot of
    Champagne-Applause
    And what have you, HISTORY.
    And in the green room . . .

S: Dad, odorless dad, he's got his face set smiling
    Low, chuckle, chuckle, in his stomach, you know, fox Sly.

T: And he says off-hand to Yasha
    'course he couldn't Rehearse,
    Wanted to, would have been better.

S: A lie. But :

T: The Budget.

S: And of course nobody follows him into the, you know, 100.
    Much less out the jimmied window on to a,
    What?

T: Solid Chrome three speed bicycle waiting,
    Fantastic, Outside.
    Sets off with the two penny red flags on the handlebars
    Snapping in the breeze,
    Like the ambassador of something,
    Just going back to the mainland on the aeroplane,

S: Coach, Just like that.

T: Just like that.

S: Odorless old Chinese gent on his bicycle
Feeling like Gene Kelly going home after getting
A little excited in the rain.

[*Dance.*]

T: And I'm thinking, the only snag in this is:
I'd never be able to pass myself off as a Chinaman.
Though I have been called Dad.
And I actually have a bicycle.

S: Not like that, not Chrome, not solid three speed
Chrome.

[*MUSIC CUE: lights and movement chaotic. Where indicated a spotlight catches them and transfixes them in various poses, the spotlight fades out and we return to the chaotic light sound and action.*]

T: And all of a sudden this helicopter comes buzzing
Around poking its glass fish-bowl-face into the Pine
Thicket making like a weed eater hog wild over drive.
Hacka defolio, chopping at the tops of the pines,

[*SPOTLIGHT on/off.*]

S: And this GUY set up in the fish bowl with a joystick
In his hand, Pig Leg Lazy-Boy easy chair
Racked back for comfort,
Bullhorn Loud speaker hook-up. More guns than prime time TV,
Says:

[*SPOTLIGHT on.*]

VOICE: THIS IS AN AUDIT. THIS IS THE IRS.
We're rounding you people up. Going to chew you up

[*SPOTLIGHT off.*]

T: And I'm thinking, where have I seen this guy before?
And then he says . . . and this really gets me . . .

[*SPOTLIGHT on.*]

VOICE: We will contact you first sharp thing in the morning. We know
where you live, Choppa Choppa,
"See you later, Alligator."

[*SPOTLIGHT off. The Stage remains in darkness.*]

T: Reverb, Reverb, Oz. And he's off, choppa choppa,
Like a shot, and it's quiet.

And I'm thinking out loud at the top of my dumb lungs,
"You may know where I stay, but you'll never know where I
Live, Mr. Lip...Clerk!"

T: I need advice, Cow down, Tuck tail, Mecca Mecca, Mea Culpa

[*LIGHTS begin to come back up. S is gone.*]

Bite the carpet: Help. Female.

[*Victoria Lake MUSIC CUE. S is found under one of the tubs. T gives S the
Violin. She fingers, he bows to the violin and gradually he bows to her. They
bow. MUSIC CUE.*]

S: So, I'm back, tappa tappa scurf scurf
Back tapping the pavement in Oh Pip Squeak Burg.
Round South 245th Street.

T: And, strangely serene, I am feeling the willies of rash acts
A'coming over me.
[*Pause. Light change.*]

S: The sky is tinted like something out of a
Child's Illustrated Bible. Playing for time.

T: The Taxman commeth.

S: Please, don't let there be a moral to this story.

T: And, PLEASE, don't let it be a musical.

[*BLACKOUT.*]

AT THE ART BAR

[*LIGHTS up*]

T: I'm thinking...it was later than we think, a long time ago.
I go to The Art Bar

S: The Past Moderns are playing.

T: Maybe we're on the list.

S: Maybe Free admission,
Maybe Free drinks.

T: I am free to pay.
Man Boy nothing nothing done today, and I have to
Mental myself for the AM Tax-Man-Carpet.

s: Make that: LINOLEUM TEDIUM.

t: So I get in there, and I'm riffen with the raf,
   And sardines it's packed.

s: Can't dance.

t: Some ART opening.
   POLICEART.
   What is this PoliceArt. Stop the Music.

s: Video Tapes of Stake Outs, Beatings. Aerial Photographs.
   Blown up alleged fingerprints.
   Yikes. Cop Art
   It's New!
   It's Right Wing!
   People are buying: EVIDENCE.
   The mug shot is mine.
   Buyers start to recognize me.
   I hear the Tape of YOUR VOICE IN THE PINES:

   [t *on tape*] "You may know where I stay, but you'll never know where
      I Live, Mr. Lip Clerk..."

t: Everyone moves away, only it's not so subtle. Fish eyes. Tight mouths.
   The room is charged with sneak punches: Jury Frenzy.

s: Guzzling my bad luck like cheap wine.
   My head starts to swim like a fish out of water
   That's the Guy! That's the Guy! I see THE TAXMAN:

t: HE'S THE ARTIST,

s: Strep-throat red party shirt, infects my eyes Lapping It Up across the
   room.
   Tinkling vapid power blondes jiggling on his arms,

t: Am I ever in the wrong line of work.

s: Talk to him.

t: My only chance...I'm going over there and

s: Talk to this GUY.

t: Free country.

s: Try him.

t: Try him.
   I hate this.

And now I am forced to get someone winking back, whoa,
Motel happy. Smiling

s: Kiss, Kiss, Lenient.

T: Someone who knows like Braille the pleasure of gliding a
Thinblade through everyday folks for high wages.
Who could take other major work for Higher wages,
But chooses this.

I want to hit that revolving door of justice
And come out on the skip.

s: I want to have it made in the Shade in the Shadow of Doubt.
It's time to be spontaneous.

s&T: Hi

VOICE: Hi

T: Hi, great show ... A ... You remember us?
This afternoon in The Pines.

VOICE: I remember you.

s: Listen ... I

VOICE: I just want to inform you that anything you say can and will
Be used against you.

s: I slipped up.

VOICE: I want to inform you that up until this moment I have been
Having a very enjoyable evening.

T: Yeah, Lookit, I'm an Artist also.
See, I'm a seal trainer.
You know with the Clowns and the flippers, and the

[s: *Speaks Danish/English.* T: *speaks Indonesian/English.*]

ptrompet, ngokngek ngokngek,

VOICE: YOU HAVE BEEN WARNED.

T: Dan Bola Belang.

s: And Taxes.

T: Yeah, well, pasaran Ikan mackerel Sangat Tinggi.

s: El precio esta en las nuves.

T: Ikan mackerel haraganya melangit.

s: Sumamente caro.

T: Haraganya brengesek, Mustahil.

S: No se puede tocar.

T: Yogia. Yes.

S: Ellos son overpriced.

T: Terlarang!
   Dan anjing laut saya yang pemimpinya:

S: Mengabulkam,

T: Dapat pilek, dari Topper, yang suka pura-pura,

S: Seda,

T: Pengganti pemain anjing laut.
   So it could be phlegm; and it could be
   Barking pneumonia.

S: Evadieron la sopa de pollo como fuera la plaga.

T: You could loose your mind kalau coba mendapat masuk

S: Las oilas de sopa de pollo. Mas caro.

T: Saya kirim mereka ke Luar kota southern bathtubs.
   So, Itu saya semantara hawatir.
   Dan saya saja, mau hambil dua

VOICE: NIET NEECHEE- VOH.

T: Detik.

   [*End Spanish and Indonesian.*]
   [*Doubling.*]

S: To tell you I could Run to the store, for you	T: Stand on line,
S: Lie, for you	T: Slip you insiders Tips, Stone Wall
S: Park your car	T: Handy Man
S: Alibi,	T: Load your dice
S: Fill your cup,	T: Spot Cash.
S: Paint your house,	T: Lead to gold,
S: Walk the dog,	T: Coolie work
S: 24 Hour speech,	T: Toast,
S: Quip,	T: Jab,

s: Joke,   T: Jive, Spin,

s: Hook,

T: Write snow for your intended.
   I Never Close! I can Make myself scarce.

s: Disappear.
   Then, Sooth your crows feet when you are pressed in the
   Spasm of age.

T: When you are knitting on the front porch of
   Senility,

s: I will pet your hand.

VOICE: YOU!

s: You are much nicer than what you've done.
   The Good Life. What's your price?

VOICE: INFORMATION.

s: Here. In your Honor, a party thrown every night,
   INCLUDING the one who caught your
   "I'd like to get That one"
   Eye, every day, anyday, that day.
   If you Choose,
   Nips and Laughter.

T: In real life, the truth is a story. So I exaggerate.

s: Absolve.

VOICE: YOU ARE MAKING ME LAUGH

T: Come on trade! For such a tiny skip.
   A puff, a jot of the pen, for . . . you say.

s: A COOK!
   You need a cook.

T: Short order.

s: Everyone loves to eat.
   Boy! Can I cook! You'll love to eat lite.

   Trim the Tum.
   Not that you . . . But,
   The menus!

   I can hold ten courses at the
   Crest of perfection for days. Hungry? Sure you're hungry.

T: Somebody you want out of the way? No Questions.
    I have the courage and no motive.

S: I'll take the Hit, the Fall.

T: You will never be late again in your life. I Guarantee.

VOICE: I'M NEVER LATE.

S: Shall birds alight especially for you?

T: Gathering only to listen.

S: What are your nourishing words?

T: The legend begins.

S: Mr. Man. Saint Man,

T: Saint Man of the Internal Revenue Service.
    Your image ignites the Public Eye. Theocracy.

VOICE: YOU!

S: He was pushed? He fell will stand up in court.

T: I will stand up in court. "He Fell."

S: Expert witness, Affidavits. Fine print

T: What do you want?

S: Blue veins alarming your calves, troubling your thighs?
    I have the CURE. Stretch Marks? Bend!
    I can show you a simple maneuver to relax the eyes
    A few primitive thoughts to think,
    So your whole body emanates nelly moonlight.

T: FEEL BETTER! Who Cares?

VOICE: I'm going to count to THREE.

T: We can make the word of mouth run very strong on you. Yes.

VOICE: ONE

S: I get this feeling . . .

Am I playing him too close?

Is it possible I am only making matters worse?

T: Headlines. Your headlines Read In An FM Voice. Sell My . . .
    Soar in your dreams.

S: When you are howling, helpless, roasting insomnia,
    A glass to drink, A Little Pillow Talk.

I will tell you stories. Stroke your head.
Turn you soft to dreams and perfect Technicolor
Recollection,

T: AND, you can crank out your screenplays,

S: You can dictate your screenplays,

T: To me, in the mornings.

S: I'm free in the mornings.

T: Sell em on spec.

S: Pure Profit by air

T: Skim!

S: I'll screen your calls.

VOICE: TWO.

T: CASH. Advances by noon. Direct Deposits!

S: Every time the phone rings it will be for you.
Here it's for you.
As easy as you draw air, Cash.

VOICE: YOU ARE GOING TO JAIL!

T: No one's wise. When you're making this much, who cares?
Think of it.

S: It's ringing off the hook.

T: It's climbing the Charts! Offers!

[*The following speech is heard from an unseen voice and may be seen, in a digested form, on a LED readout on stage. At first* T *&* S *do not see the LED, But then they go to it and kneel.*]

VOICE: Offers. Offers.
I am a man of few words.
You have angered me. Don't interrupt.
Death and Taxes.
No sequel.
No cases of mistaken identity.
No Plot twists.
Nobody wakes up.
The SENTENCE.
They Kneel. Life without parole.
You will, of course, be separated.

Can you think of anything worse than dying alone in Jail?
Locked down in solitary confinement and dying alone?
Can You, with your VIVID IMAGINATION, think of anything
    worse?
The Gas Chamber.
Lethal Injection . . . a Hanging: Has an Audience.
An audience of those who loved or hated you enough to see you off.
It's a public event.
You have, Just. Committed. A Crime:
A cheap Bribe
Don't make another sound.
I ACCEPT.
The Bribe.
You Are Mine.

[*MUSIC CUE: Dance.*]

∽

25. RICHARD FOREMAN

ONTOLOGICAL-HYSTERIC THEATER

In the waning days of 1970, I wandered into the Filmmakers Cinematheque on Wooster Street to see something called *Total Recall* by somebody named Richard Foreman. All I knew at that point was that Foreman advertised his play in *The Village Voice*, and I liked the visual texture of the ad. I was free in those days, within reason, to cover what I pleased for *The Voice*. I sat through *Total Recall* for what seems to me now like four hours—perhaps there was an intermission. The seats were hard, and there was nothing particularly comfortable about the airless space. But I knew something was happening, even if it was happening in glacier time, and I knew that I was where I wanted to be, because in most of my wanderings through Off-off Broadway, either nothing, or something perilously close to nothing, was usually taking place. In *Total Recall*, I recall a lot of light bulbs going on and off, a girl standing casually in a closet doing a lot of smiling, scratchy phonograph records of Chicago jazz, people semi-prone in the position of capsized objects or drugged humans, and somnambulistic voices both live and on tape discoursing elliptically in portentous fragments and with a radical banality on the state of things simple and complex. Midway through *Total Recall*, I knew I had stumbled upon a treasure. Cause and effect had been assassinated, and a new subjectivity had been made up of the irrational and its first cousin, the seemingly rational, all framed within a Brechtian concreteness, had come into the world. It was all special, all delightful, all exhausting, all exhilirating.

Over the years I've supported much of Richard's work, and we've become laid-back colleagues. The Foreman canon is an enchanting puzzlement to me, but in fact it's not all enchanting. I was sorely disappointed in his direction of *The Golem* at the Shakespeare Festival in Central Park. It seemed to be made up of spectacular effects but no heart; Richard's aesthetic, appropriate for his own vision, didn't do this spiritual mystery justice. But so much else has been groundbreaking, authentic, impeccable, and daring.

I've read enough criticism of Richard's work to understand that others are equally impressed, but I have to resist the temptation to readily agree about what others believe the work speaks to. To reduce these critiques to a simple formula: they seem to be saying that one goes to "ontological-hysteric" to hear and see Richard think, to be privy to Richard's musings about the ontology of things, and to see things, persons, objects and events in their essential nature. Now this may well be what Richard has been doing these past two decades, but my experience of the work tells me that these "things" don't supplant old things but they are rather new creations in the universe. They are Richard being heard and seen "thinking" in their own new thingness, connected to their own discreteness. That Richard's things have an essential nature only reinforces my understanding that all things have such a nature. That naturalism and realism in theatre are worn-out affairs doesn't mean that when you scrape *The Master Builder* and *A Streetcar Named Desire* down to their essential natures, you wind up with Max and Rhoda instead of Blanche and Stanley. Blanche and Stanley have a *mise en scène* that may sentimentalize the world in which Williams positions them, and Hilda Wangel's invasion of Solness's psychological fortress is overladen with a pre-Freudian, symbolic blanket that seems much too calculating to current audiences, but we can't tear an "essence" out without damaging the whole web of the play. Things do emerge, they do "come out of" something, and that something has its place in history, even if what emerges has run out of steam and can tell us little, or tell it to us in a mode that doesn't allow us to hear it. Perhaps these plays are so worn—perhaps they ought to be laid to rest. (I wrote once that *Rosmersholm* ought to be laid to rest, but that's hardly the whole Ibsen canon.) There is a sense in which the Foreman thingness, set off in a theatrical frame, takes on its own mystification. I think the problem—and it's a juicy, meant-to-keep-us-awake problem—is that the creator of this mystification is having such a terrific time that the spectators become eavesdroppers on somebody else's terrific time. Not that we can't have a somewhat terrific time along with Richard, and perhaps with Kate Manheim and the other performers. But it can't match that terrific time of the person who gives us the leftovers of his instructional game. But I need to emphasize again—at the risk of beating a compliment to death—that these are really quite wonderful leftovers if they're not left over for you every night of the week.

Here are some thinking fragments from Richard's essay, "Foundations for a Theater," as they appear in his *Unbalancing Acts*, Pantheon Books, 1992:

FOUNDATIONS FOR A THEATER

My theater has always tried to spotlight the most elusive aspects of the experience of being human. Human beings are to a great extent unknowable to themselves. Passing through each of us is a continual flow of motor and emotional impulses we are taught to give conventional names—

"hunger," "lust," "aversion, "attraction." But these labels are neither truthful nor accurate; condensing our wide field of impulses into a few nameable categories suppresses our awareness of the infinity of tones and feeling gradations that are part of the original impulse. As each impulse is shaped in accordance with the limited number of labels available in a society, the sense of contact with their original ambiguous flavor is lost. Perhaps your impulse has a certain flavor that relates it to "hunger" or "lust," but is neither fully one nor the other. Without a name of its own, its unique truth disappears, rechanneled into one of the already named desires.

Among the countless impulses passing through us at any moment, some surface in a manner that allows us to continue with our lives along the patterns we've inherited from our society. But any moment of true freedom suggests other structures, other textures, around which life could circle. My plays are an attempt to suggest through example that you can break open the interpretations of life that simplify and suppress the infinite range of inner human energies; that life can be lived according to a different rhythm, seen through changed eyes.

What I show on stage is a specific aspect of a chosen moment that suggests how the mind and emotions can juggle, like an acrobat, all we perceive. The strategies I use are meant to release the impulse from the straitjacket tailored for it by our society. Character, empathy, narrative—these are all straitjackets imposed on the impulse so it can be dressed up in a fashion that is familiar, comforting, and reassuring for the spectator. But I want a theater that frustrates our habitual way of seeing, and by so doing, frees the impulse from the objects in our culture to which it is invariably linked. I want to demagnetize impulse from the objects it becomes attached to. We rarely allow ourselves the psychic detachment from habit that would allow us to perceive the impulse as it rises inside us, unconnected to the objects we desire. But it's impulse that's primary, not the object we've been trained to fix it upon. It is the impulse that is your deep truth, not the object that seems to call it forth. The impulse is the vibrating, lively thing that you really are. And that is what I want to return to: the very thing you really are.

Society teaches us to represent our lives to ourselves within the framework of a coherent narrative, but beneath that conditioning we feel our lives as a series of multidirectional impulses and collisions. We're trained to see our lives as a series of projects, one following the next along the road of experience, and our "success" depends upon how well we progress from project to project. But traveling this narrow road shuts out a multitude of suggestive impulses and impressions—the ephemeral things that feed our creative insight and spiritual energy. It's as if we were wearing blinders to restrict our emotional field, making us spiritually and psychically uneasy with the normal ambiguity of our everyday experience. So we compensate. We make self-righteous demands that noncontradiction be the basis of our value systems, but that inevitably means the suppression of all sensory richness. It reinforces our denial of the ambiguity inherent in life, which, when suppressed, makes the world seem rigid and frightening.

I like to think of my plays as an hour and a half in which you see the world through a special pair of eyeglasses. These glasses may not block out all narrative coherence, but they magnify so many other aspects of experience that you simply lose interest in trying to hold on to narrative coherence, and instead, allow yourself to become absorbed in the moment-by-moment representation of psychic freedom.

The aim of art, ultimately, is to speak to man's spiritual condition, his relationship with the universe. I have always felt that I'm a closet religious writer—in spite of the aggressive, erotic, playful, and schizoid elements that decorate the surface of my plays—and it is because of my essentially religious concerns that some critics have attacked my plays for not accurately representing what they refer to as "real people" with "real" interpersonal, psychological, humanistic concerns. But once you become truly interested in man's so-called religious dimension, you lose interest in making an art that only recreates the superficial dynamics of the contingent level of being that is daily life. You lose interest in the level of "personality," because you recognize it as a product of the conditioning of the social world. This conditioning interferes with our contact with the deeper ground of being by preoccupying us with the illusions of psychological, goal-oriented involvement. We live our lives focused on those forces of our culture that give rise to certain personality traits that are the warp and woof of daily life. But character and personality are accidents of circumstance. We don't choose the customs of the culture we are born into; we arrive in a culture by chance. Social life may focus our attention on character and its vicissitudes—and that's been the source from which most theatrical form has always come—but in my plays I want to evoke the deeper ground of being, the originating network of impulse, which precedes the circumstantial "I."

No work of art is absolutely truthful about life, but is a strategic maneuver performed on coagulated consciousness. As Picasso said, art is a lie that tells the truth. And it's a lie that tells the truth because it's a chosen, strategic maneuver, which is not the truth. No art could ever be "the truth," because it has to leave out ninety percent of life. But since even life's tiniest detail is an integral part of the interwoven whole, if you're not talking about all of life you're not really talking about the truth—you're talking about a selective distortion. Art is a perspective; all perspectives are lies about the total truth; so art is a lie that, if it is strategically chosen, wakes people up. Art is a lever to affect the mind. The truth of art is in the audience's, the individual's, awakened perceptions. It is not in the work of art.

In my plays I try to separate the impulse from the object that seems to evoke it, and in doing so, clarify the quality of the impulse itself. One strategy I use is to overdetermine each specific, manifest impulse, so that its origin is no longer traceable to a single object that would falsely paint it with its own qualities. For instance, in a scene where the character says, "I have difficulty getting out of the room," I try to offer several reasons why, not just one. I baffle the impulse to leave the room: First, by tying the character's foot to a table; then by putting a wall between him and the door; and finally by blinding him so he cannot see his way out of the room. This strategy overloads the context. It focuses attention on the impulse to leave the room, blocking the spectator's normal tendency to think: I know how he can leave the room—he can walk through the door. If the spectator is offered a clear solution to imagine (exit through the door), his focus will be on the mundane object ("Will he get through the door?") rather than on what is happening to the character's body and soul, or on how the character's life is changed when it is faled with the impulse, "I want to leave the room."

Paradoxically, bafflement can clarify. Bafflement can force you to refocus your vision. It is the same as making the sun so bright you're forced to look away, but as you avert your eyes you see the delicate flower you've never observed before.

There are several ways to isolate the impulse. One is through a strategy of interruption. Suppose an interaction between two characters is suddenly cut short by loud music, and they begin a silly dance. In this case the impulse of the scene is not allowed to fulfill itself; it's deflected. To take the example of the man who wants to leave the room, his impulse to leave might suddenly turn into a movement of the body that has nothing to do with leaving, but which suggests that impulse is still alive, though manifested in an alternate way, which allows you to observe it from a different angle.

✧✧✧

Lava, one of Richard's more recent productions, opened at the Performing Garage on December 5, 1989. Richard directed and designed the production, which included Neil Bradley, Matthew Courtney, Peter Davis, Kyle deCamp, and Heidi Tradewell. Lighting design was done by Heather Carson, and sound design was done by Tim Schellenbaum.

Here is Richard thinking about *Lava* as he introduces the play in *Unbalancing Acts*:

Though you may not notice if you only watched it in performance, *Lava* is like a series of staged essays, several contradictory approaches to the same problem: why can language never adequately express the true and complex quality of an internal impulse? It's a series of what Gertrude Stein called meditations; ruminations on philosophical ideas in which the intent is to enjoy, to savor, and to dance with the music of your ideas and what they spark inside you. Down through the years I've obsessively written notes to myself about aesthetics, about how to use one's head, and about how I should go about writing my plays. In *Lava* more material than usual came from notes of this sort. When I was actually writing those notes I never expected to use them in a play, though I've learned that's where they may well wind up.

Part of this material was intended to be tongue-in-cheek, because the attitudes toward language expressed in these meditations were standard post-structuralist theory. It's Derrida and Lacan reconstituted in a simple, ironic synopsis. So, for instance, after a paragraph explains how language couldn't possibly capture an individual's real feelings—because it's an inherited language rather than one invented anew by each new speaker—the tape finishes with the melancholy simplification, "That's why I'm crying." That line should be taken ironically, of course: yet another example of language not expressing the fullness of what's really felt. And the line was read with a self-pitying sniffle that made the ironic quality very clear. Other lines in the text try to make the person speaking them appear a little foolish and self-indulgent, as we all are.

And the person who is speaking is me. In this play there is no doubt about it, because my voice, coming over the loudspeaker, dominates about seventy percent of the play. There are four performers onstage who may be me as well. I hoped the performers would flicker back and forth between two possibilities: people who could make these philosophical pronouncements on their own, and people who are under the thrall of this omnipresent voice, the voice of their author, their director, their boss—even the voice of God.

My greatest efforts in staging *Lava* went into making the listening experience as powerful as the watching experience. Even in normal, narrative theater, it's difficult to be aware of the text as language without losing yourself in other elements of the production. The dialogue usually serves to make you see past the spoken language so that you watch the story it is telling—in a "proselike" way, the language disappears in favor of the story iris conveying. With *Lava* I wanted to stage a play that would give the spectator the sensory experience of listening, word by word, to what was being said. I wanted it to be an aural, rather than a visual, experience. I found this very difficult to do because my tendency is to create the kind of stage picture that pulls you back into watching instead of listening. But all through rehearsals I kept making adjustments to put the emphasis on the aural experience, so the spectator would listen to what was happening in the language.

Usually in my plays something bizarre will happen onstage, and then the spoken text will give you a new perspective on what you were seeing. But with *Lava* it was the reverse. First the text would be delivered in a way that made the audience aware of the text itself, then something would happen onstage to give a new perspective on the text, and they could then savor the way the text was being colored and shaped by the staging.

❖❖❖

Photo: Paula Court

Kyle deCamp in *Lava*

A FRAGMENT FROM *LAVA* BY RICHARD FOREMAN:

[*The* VOICE *continues throughout.*]

Then there is category two. Random nonsense, nonsense, chance, random relations, all those kinds of relations or nonrelations, whatever you choose to call them. But category three is something that eludes both category one and two. Most people, viewing it superficially, mistake category three for category two—that is, randomness and chance. But the items of category three, though not connected, are in fact connected, but in a way that is not perceivable within our available grids.
So
It's taken on faith, as it were.
But as somebody said
It moves mountains.
It's that door to another world
That is located in that other world.
Go through it. But it's not in this world.

[MATTHEW *drops his pillar and runs to the table, and* KYLE *rights hers and puts it in a corner, and all the men sit and pick up lipsticks and start applying them to their mouths. They hold small hand mirrors to help them carry out the task with concentrated, manic seriousness.*]

So category three eludes logic, yet is not random or chancelike, but is a connective tissue that cannot be traced, and yet is the one truly lively way of perceiving the world. It lays down the ground of the real being alive, where the other two categories, logic and chance, are predictable in their emotional kick. And don't kid yourself, that's the only lust that moves you, that lust for that emotional kick. So do you want a new one or an old one? A new emotional kick or an old one? What lays down the grid of real, alive living is category three.

[*The men have dropped their lipsticks, and begin to do a slow, bizarre dance with their arms only.*]

Category three is the only real source, this category three, which is a door that isn't openable from this side, but it opens. One must enter, to be alive, only category three, which one enters from death's side only, into life.

[*Their dance ends with arms stretched out before them on the table, as if pointing to fault lines in its surface. At the same time,* KYLE *serves glasses from which they drink deeply.*]

It is a category
Which people will call unnatural and irrational, but it isn't.
It falls between the cracks of the normal rational.
It is the ultimate fruitful location,
Those cracks in reality, which nurture
Because they are not reality, which is not alive
But seen through the perceiving mechanism, which means not
     touched really, Just messages, coming from far away
Through a very defective system
Ruled by fear and habit.
So one should want, always, to be in that nurturing ground
Which is category three.

[KYLE *has now acquired a bowler hat which she defiantly plops on her head, and the men rise suddenly, upset by her transformation.*]

Welcome to category three.

[*The men run off, upset, as* KYLE *crosses to the exterior window to enjoy the breeze as the curtains billow about her.*]

Should I observe myself breathing in and out, here in category three? Try it, but don't let being distracted get you distracted.

[MATTHEW *sneaks back into a corner of the room, and* KYLE *and* MATTHEW *stare at each other in silence.*]

Welcome to category three.
Welcome to category three.
Welcome to category three.

[*Neither moves a muscle.*]

Shall I feel love and attraction to other human beings here in category three? Why not. Why not. What I mean is, try it—Oh oh, you just made the wrong move. I didn't move anything.

WELCOME TO CATEGORY THREE.
WELCOME TO CATEGORY THREE.
WELCOME TO CATEGORY THREE.

VOICE LOOP: I said, the bright one, with the potato in his mouth . . .

MATTHEW: Looking for something?

KYLE: Somebody needs to swallow their remaining inhibitions.

MATTHEW: Talk big. Please.

[*Loud drum music rises as the men run to a bookcase from which they each take a white belt. They slip the belts behind their bottoms, and holding an end in each hand, they start to, in effect, polish their behinds by vibrating the taut belts. As* KYLE *continues speaking against the voice loops, they link hands and run to look out the interior window, then turn to the audience once they have put one end of the belt between their teeth and have wrapped the other end about their two hands like handcuffs. Using their teeth, they pull their belts tight.*]

VOICE LOOP: Somebody backed into a high energy field . . .

KYLE: I discovered something. A straight line, right into the brain. [*She runs to another microphone.*] Lemme get a handle on this. This is going right past me. Effectively, nonstop. You better move fast.

VOICE LOOP: Please make an effort . . .

[*She runs to another microphone*]

I own it. Turn a corner. Turn another corner.

KYLE: Oh, now I see, I'm not supposed to.

VOICE: You opened the door inside . . . to get inside. You opened the door outside, to get outside.
I don't know how
But you did it.
I didn't know I did it
But you did it.

[*The men have repositioned themselves together at their side of the table, leaning toward* KYLE *who is at the other end.* KYLE *takes a golden pineapple off a plate, and using the elastic cord stretched across the middle of the table, she shoots the pineapple, slingshot style, across to the men. Then she brings her leg up onto the table, displaying her booted foot with a bang as it hits amid the books and dishes. They don't immediately react.*]

Plenty of people gave up on balance. The whole system went down the drain. Was I part of the system? Much to my surprise, yes comes up. Play with it? Why not. I'm a hell of a guy when the right ball comes rolling into my part of the landscape.

[*Soft reggae music is heard, and all participate in a dance number that is a series of tableaux. First the men bow down, faces and arms outstretched on the table, and* KYLE *comes around to climb on* NEIL's *back. Then she advances across the table to bow down to* MATTHEW *who has gone to a far corner. Then* PETER *brings out a large round target and she seizes it, peering above its top at the audience, only to be grabbed about the thighs by* PETER *and lifted down from the table to the floor.* NEIL *runs toward her and is as if thrown back by the aura of the target. During this activity, the* VOICE *recites a short poem.*]

Go to a good school.
Go to your apartment.
Go to the highest place in France.
Go to Chinese laundries after deciding to have a good meal.
Go to bed, sometimes.
Go to the country estate.
Go to the waterfront, but exercise.
Go to a garage.
Go to a farm, but first, go to a farm.
Go to earth.
Go to short wave. Hello.

MATTHEW: [*Interjecting as he runs onstage.*] Hello. Hello there.

VOICE: Go to meaning.
Go to an encyclopedia.

[*By now, all but* NEIL *have repositioned themselves at the edges of the table, each hiding behind a large, primitive cardboard mask. The masks are painted in different patterns. They rock the masks gently on the table. After a moment,* NEIL *rushes in as if thrown onto the stage and collapses onto the table. He immediately rises and whirls to watch the rocking masks.*]

How's the language machine working? Tell me. How's the language machine working? Is the language machine working good? Tell me about it. Tell me about it. The language machine is working. How many words is the language machine turning out each day? Each day, two or three words. The language machine is not working good. No. The language machine is working good. Is there a difference of opinion as to whether the language machine is working good?

[*All run to microphones, still hiding behind masks, as* NEIL *places reverently onto the table a strange, undefinable object he's taken from the bookcase.*]

VOICE LOOP: Guaranteed crash course, absolute momentum . . .

KYLE: Lots of times I'm on the verge, I keep going.

MATTHEW: Everybody agrees.

NEIL: That's funny, I thought I was on my own.

PETER: Sure, but don't look.

KYLE: Okay, don't look.

NEIL: Now, look.

KYLE: Okay, I looked.

MATTHEW: It's okay?

KYLE: Okay, I looked. Okay, I looked.

VOICE: Is there a difference of opinion as to whether the language machine is working good? Is the language machine working good?

[*The random number loop is heard softly behind, as the men sit, holding white cards in front of their eyes.*]

MATTHEW: This is a dance I did, in the privacy of my biggest adventure.

NEIL: It went good?

MATTHEW: Good was a no-no word.

PETER: When.

MATTHEW: Oh, don't make me . . . think.

NEIL: Look, he's doing it.

VOICE: Good, is there a difference of opinion as to whether the language machine is working good? Good.
     Good.

[KYLE *emerges with two chocolate pies. A bell rings once, and she sets the pies on the table. The men slowly drop their cards and stare at the pies, which she offers to them as the* VOICE *continues.*]

Chocolate pies.
Here are some chocolate pies.
Here are some beautiful chocolate pies.
Here are some chocolate pies. Yummmm!

[*The random number loop begins softly, under the text.*]

Surprise. There's something to touch but there's nothing to lick.

[KYLE *picks up a hammer, runs around the table which frightens the men offstage, and as she reapproaches the pies she bangs the hammer on the table.*]

I can still say, chocolate pies.
Eyes.
Pies.
Eyes.

[*The men have reappeared behind the interior window, each carrying a large book, which they thumb through frantically.*]

Now let's find them, those pies.
He tries and he tries to find those pies.

[KYLE *moves to the rear of the table, climbs up on it, and crawls across it on all fours toward the two pies.*]

Is there an energy field around chocolate pies that is some kind of energy other than a chocolate derivative?

[*She puts a finger into one pie and licks her finger, as the men stop paying attention to their books and stare, transfixed, at* KYLE.]

Look, you were the one who imagined it.
Those pies are real, buster.
Two eyes don't prove it,
Pies prove it.
You got pies, because you make it happen through your eyes.

[*The men race around into the room, carrying their books on their backs like heavy burdens, and as they reach positions by the table, each slowly lowers a book onto the surface.*]

Then how come I also brought up the issue of an energy field? Chocolate pies. Whoever tries to eat, really gets shook up inside, so calm chocolate is something to psyche out. Psyche out. Speak to the world in pie form. Pie in the sky form.
Chocolate pie. Chocolate pie.

[*Lively Gypsy music rises as a brief dance of the men pays homage to* KYLE *still on the table among pies and books.*]

ᙙ

26. ROBERT WILSON

THE BYRD HOFFMAN SCHOOL OF BYRDS

My friend Larry Loonin, director and performer, had seen a work by Robert Wilson at the Brooklyn Academy, and he couldn't let go of it. "I keep playing it out in my head," he announced, and that was all I had to hear. It was 1970, some weeks after the original run, and Wilson was presenting a return engagement of *The Life and Times of Sigmund Freud*. Larry and I took the subway to Brooklyn's Atlantic Avenue to witness Freud being played outside Larry's head a second time. I had never seen anything like this work. I felt that I was on a trip—high and quietly grooving on Wilson's art. Several hours into the work, audience members began leaving in droves. Larry and I, seated in the rear of a cavernous auditorium, just settled in, watched on as the work slowly, slowly, slowly played itself out before an ever-diminishing number of customers. The Academy was emptying rapidly, but we were filling up on some level of time I can't quite put my finger on.

What I remember two decades later: Upstage, throughout the entire work, a runner in bathing trunks constantly runs across the length of the space from one wing to another and back again. There is an actual beach upstage. The running man on the beach has no obvious connection to anything else in the play; he just runs endlessly. (A second runner takes over for act two, and then the first returns for act three.) At one point the space, with the exception of the beach, is a rather elegant drawing room with beautiful people in full beautiful dress, and there's an elegant waiter who takes about ten minutes to traverse the stage on the way to serving refreshments. (This elegant waiter turns out to be my friend Maurice Blanc, who would work with me in *The Celebration* and in numerous Bread & Puppet performances. Maurice's ashes are buried in the woods on the Bread and Puppet farm in Glover.) Every gesture in Wilson's drawing room seems to take an infinite amount of time. Well over an hour into the play, an enormous pair of hairy legs suddenly materialize from the wings and begin a painstakingly slow locomotion into the drawing room from stage left. These legs are extremely hairy, and they belong to a creature whose other features are hidden because they are simply too enormous to be visible within the proscenium frame. Shortly these legs of human or beast are joined by a second pair. And little by little, as the legs slowly propel themselves forward, the drawing room is metamorphosed into a stable. The elegant people with their elegant attire and elegant cups of tea and behavior simply disappear, and we are in the presence of a rudimentary order of dankness, hairiness, mold, sludge, and a general chilling sense of a primeval world. The evening goes on. There are masked figures, and there are several dozen black mammies right off the Aunt Jemima box—some dancing, some whirling, some screaming (silently?). There is much much slowness, and occasionally there are eruptive motions and improvisatory dancing. Freud and daughter Anna appear as many little side events appear and disappear.

I recall that Larry and I sat back, deep in our seats. Let others leave, let them be bored or incensed. We were also bored somewhat, quite sleepy but in a fixated state peering at visions. A rare, beautiful, puzzling moment playing itself out.

Deafman Glance, Wilson's next work, was also mounted at the Brooklyn Academy. It featured the teen-aged boy Raymond Andrews, a deaf mute, watching the performance in a swing high above the stage. Wilson had originally encountered Raymond while working as an "experimental therapist" in Summit, New Jersey, and in a sense the unfolding of *Deafman Glance* reflects Wilson's perception of how Raymond perceives the world. Early on, the Byrdwoman, in black Victorian gown, offers milk to a child and then stabs him to death. With Raymond watching this murder, the Byrdwoman moves on to a young girl and murders her in a similar fashion. In her book, *Lunatics, Lovers & Poets*, Margaret Croyden provides a vivid description of the play. The traumatized Raymond "floats...into a nonverbal world from which he then watches the stunning display of his (and Wilson's) visions... The Last Supper's long table stands before a primitive hut surrounded by tropical trees, with an Egyptian pyramid in the background and a fishing bank, evoking the American South, in the foreground... A giant frog plays host to two red-wigged ladies and a W. C. Fields-fat man; a boy sits fishing all night long; a naked pregnant woman walks slowly around the stage; an eight-foot Bugs Bunny and a menacing Dracula dance on... Parasoled ladies from the world of Henry James and young Isadora Duncan girls in white dresses gracefully float about; the black mammies from *Freud* reappear and do a jig; a woman slowly leads a live goat, and a paper-maché ox lights up after swallowing the sun." Croyden also tells us that moons rise, stars fall, volcanoes erupt, fish crawl, trees grow taller, and animals shrink. "Finally," she continues, "there is the apocalypse; the characters sink into the ground, into their graves, and smoke rises, filling the theatre with a gray mist." Near the conclusion, black apes eating apples are juxtaposed against the whiteness of George Washington and Marie Antoinette, while we hear the recorded sound of

"The Loveliest Night of the Year." Then "slowly...the apes munch their apples, which quietly rise out of their hands to the heavens as the stars quietly fall to the ground."

Both *Freud* and *Deafman Glance* seemed extraordinary to many of us, although I was getting a little testy over the reprise of these black mammies. But what might come next? *The Life and Times of Joseph Stalin* also took place at the Academy for four nights in December of 1973. I was just returning from San Francisco, where I'd spent some days with the Firehouse Theater, much of my stay involving a political discourse around the responsibilities of theatre. The report of a twelve-hour *Joseph Stalin*, which would incorporate huge chunks of *Freud* and *Deafman Glance* and conclude around seven in the morning, struck me as outrageous. What kind of spectators was Wilson seeking out? Obviously people who didn't have to get up at seven in the morning and go to work. Just as obviously, the people who had left *Freud* in droves had either become true believers or had been supplanted by new believers who had read the rave reviews (mine included, I presume) and were ready for anything, the longer and slower, the better. In short, as I reasoned it, the work existed for the jet set, for socialites, for the beautiful people. I stayed away from *The Life and Times of Joseph Stalin*, and I pretty much stayed away from Wilson's productions until the *CIVIL warS* many years later.

During these years, Robert Wilson became the acclaimed hero of the theatre in Western Europe, working out of opera houses, concert halls, outdoor gardens, rugged mountains, and traditional venues. One spoke of him in rapturous terms, the way one had spoken of Max Reinhardt in the twenties. But if Wilson was a kind of latter-day Reinhardt, orchestrating mighty spectacles on huge canvases, he was much closer to the cool eclecticism of Meredith Monk, under whom he had worked several years back. But Wilson, a painter early on in love with color, shape, texture and all manner of visual images, had begun collaborating with artists like composers Philip Glass and David Byrne, dancer Lucinda Childs, playwright Heiner Muller and various filmmakers. Now he was spinning out operas and various multi-media productions, some of which were to be distributed over cities in Europe, the Middle East, Asia and the United States, act by act. A Brooklyn Academy press release tells us that the *CIVIL warS* "was created over a period of six years and on three continents." Various acts premiered in Rotterdam, Cologne, and at the Rome Opera. "The American section, *The Knee Plays* (or 'joints' between the scenes), was produced by the Walker Art Center in association with the Guthrie Theatre and premiered in Minneapolis...Two more sections have been rehearsed in Tokyo and Marseille. Conceived for an international community, the *CIVIL warS* was to have been presented in its entirety (some twelve hours) in the 1984 Olympic Arts Festival, but insufficient funding prevented the realization of that intention." One wonders what "sufficient funding" would have added up to and how many other experimental theatres around the globe might have had full seasons on the spare change the *CIVIL warS* didn't get around to using. The Cologne section was mounted in Boston at Robert Brustein's American Repertory Theater in 1985, and then the American section, the *Knee Plays*, toured ten American cities. Wilson's largesse, this premiering of multi-hour-long fragments in diverse terrain across the planet, had taken on the quality of a kind of Super Gift, sophisticated cities and important foundations had opened themselves to his work, if "insufficiently," and he was steadily in demand. One imagines an eighteenth-century equivalent of innkeepers vying to have their beds slept in by the father of our country, although the cost of a month's lodging, taking into account the inflationary level of modern times, could not have paid the salary of one of Wilson's stagehands for one performance.

I am purposely being flip but quite serious about danger when an artist or company, be it Grotowski or The Living Theatre or Robert Wilson, becomes a consumer item, when in Wilson's case apparently there is this extraordinary need to straddle the planet like the Colossus of old. If theatre is an exchange between the performance and the spectator, that exchange is seriously undermined by the development of a cult following and by being afforded six or eight-hour tidbits of a whole work you cannot possibly see unless you are committed to following Wilson across various time zones. Peter Ustinov once spoke of his audiences as "woolly bears," that they tended to want to embrace him and slobber all over him. And I recall Julian Beck receiving an Obie and noting wistfully that he and Judith must be doing something wrong. On the other hand, there is "offending the audience," or only allowing it tantalizing glimpses of your global effort. I don't want to imply that Wilson, an extraordinarily hard worker, an artist who gives of himself unstintingly and a wonderful designer, is obsessed with his image and with his cult followers—perhaps he is, but I don't know that. But one pays a price for putting oneself at the mercy of foundations, for needing to please and impress the keepers of private and public money and the Beautiful People who in one way or another seem able to make that private and public money dance. I suppose I want Grotowski's "poor theatre" back, without the hype, but there is always the hype. (And Grotowski himself has not been entirely free of these keepers, though he courageously stuck his neck out for Solidarity in 1981.) I want the exchange between adults, not between adorer and adoree. I want Wilson to live with insufficient funds, to have told the Shah of Iran and all his sycophants, when Wilson performed at the Arts Festival in Persepolis, to take his money and his gratuitous favors and shove them.

Ah, but Mr. Sainer, you are forgetting about the real world. Yes? Exactly what is this real world? And what is the relationship of the artist to this reality? Well it's not easy, of course I'm reducing it. And yet...

Two reports in the *Drama Review*'s June 1973 issue (T-58) provide vivid reactions to Wilson's work in the Festival at Persepolis. Wilson took some thirty "Byrd Hoffman School of Birds" performers and enlisted another twenty Iranians to make up *Ka Mountain*, a spectacle which ran for 168 hours. Critic Ossia Trilling reports that the mountain selected was Haft Tan (Seven Bodies), named for seven Sufi poets buried at its base. The 168 hours equal the seven days of Genesis and the mountain itself is composed of seven hills.

An Overture in the House of Mourning, "one of several beautiful courtyard buildings," allowed audiences passage alongside rooms where they could watch performers "often moving at such a slow pace that one was scarcely aware that they were in motion at all." Trilling's article insufficiently suggests what the performers might be doing, but I suspect they were involved in "process," in preparing to enact something, or in simply preparing the space, or in simply living their lives, or in rendering some calligraphic message to the initiated.

There were numerous events over the next days, to be witnessed at various stations as one journeyed up the mountain. One station housed a rendering of Noah's Ark, another showed the Acropolis guarded by contemporary missiles; there were enormous sculptured birds and a full-sized dinosaur. And live animals in cages, including a donkey, a bear, a lion, a deer and an elephant, and an old man climbing, and people dancing, and readings from sections of *The Book of Jonah* and *Moby Dick*, likely featuring Father Mapple's sermon on Jonah's attempt to flee God, and other features apparently both decipherable and indecipherable, depending on one's cultural background and degree of patience.

Wilson envisioned an apocalyptic conclusion to his seven-day spectacle. Trilling tells us that he planned to blow up the top of the mountain, Haft Tan becoming a surrogate for the environmental degeneration of New York City, and for the wanton breakdown of our planet's resources, including, presumably, its spiritual values. The Iranian producers vetoed the blowing up of their mountain, in its stead a cutout of the Manhattan skyline was incinerated on the seventh day, one assumes without the help of God for whom the Sabbath is a day of rest, and in it place there appeared

"the emblem of a Chinese Pagoda sheltering the victorious Lamb of God at the final apotheosis."

Actor and director Basil Langton, who had never heard of Wilson before and was tremendously skeptical of what this Wilson might be doing, had to push his way past reverential, whispering guards even to get into the performance without waiting for ninety minutes in an alleyway for the next show. Langton tells us that he became enveloped

> by an extraordinary visual environment. In every direction there was an image of great beauty and tenderness. There seemed to be a multitude of stages. Things were happening everywhere. Yet, nothing was happening. Nothing, that is, that can be written down and described as "theatre action"... an old woman walking painfully slowly for an hour...a man gesturing spastically as he declaimed some endless stream-of-consciousness...someone sitting cross-legged high up on some scaffolding...chanting in (gibberish)...Nobody was even taking off their clothes...What astonished me this night in Shiraz... was that (Wilson's work) looked so extraordinarily contemporary. (Wilson) didn't really achieve it by doing anything specific...What he did was, by some mysterious alchemy, to capture the spirit of modern art in the performance...

Langton reports that he left the garden of Khaneh-E Zinatolmolk that night stunned, silent and shaken.

Near the conclusion of his paean to a new artist, Langton addresses the issue of the "snail's-pace" tempo of Wilson's work.

> Sitting one night on Haft Tan mountain...waiting and watching for Wilson's drama to unfold, my attention began to wander. I...found myself thinking how very slowly the whole universe seemed to be moving. From where I sat the cosmos was silent and still...I then looked back at the stage, and to my astonishment, everything had changed. In that brief moment that I had looked away, Wilson's universe had changed. Watching Wilson's theatre is not unlike watching grass grow, or a tree. We look at a rose, and it is still. We look away and a petal falls. Life itself is slow. Has anyone seen a baby grow? Can we watch ourselves grow old? In both nature and Wilson's art, time "stands still."

In the final days of December, 1986, Wilson brought Act V—the Rome section of his and Philip Glass's opera, the *CIVIL warS: a tree is best measured when it is down*, to the Brooklyn Academy, some sixteen years after he introduced *Freud* to the theatre world. Act V, like all of Wilson's work that I have seen, is an extraordinary undertaking. There is a moment I treasure most, it involves the figure of Robert E. Lee, as if rotating over and over in a space capsule. We see only the weary head of the actor, seeming to move in outer space. Wilson has in these last years discovered the wonders not only of music but of written language. And what we hear is the following:

"...his steed was bespattered with mud
And his head hung down as if worn by long traveling
the horseman himself sat his horse like a master his
face was ridged with self-respecting grief
his garments were worn in the service and stained
with travel his hat was slouched and spattered
with mud and only another unknown horseman rode
with him as if for company and for love
So utterly forsaken
The horseman sat his horse like a master
His face ridged with self-respecting grief
his garments worn in service
stained with travel
hat slouched and spattered with mud
it must have been a terrible war
even in the fleeting moment of his passing by my gate I
was awed by his incomparable dignity his majestic
composure his rectitude and his sorrow were so
wrought and blended into his visage and so
beautiful and impressive to my eyes that I fell
into violent weeping to me there was only one
where this one was..."

And phrases are repeated: the horseman, the grief, the rectitude, the stained garments, the deep, abiding sorrow. The visual and verbal combined seamlessly, seamlessly. This sense of something close to perfection, perhaps of a quiet ecstasy, has struck many many people, whether Wilson followers or not. That moment is somehow always there. But there are other moments that I find disquieting, moments that strike me as wonderful if I were to view them in the windows of Lord and Taylor, but as beautiful and empty in the course of a theatre work. I have gone past the need for effects, though one never knows when effects will arrest you. I appreciate Langton's reverential sense that he was coming upon something rare, in part because nothing seemed to be happening, or because what was happening looked like it involved a bunch of amateurs (real people). But at one time or another that "reality" has always been one of the forceful elements in the work of The Living Theatre, the Bread & Puppets, of Squat, of Tadeusz' Kantor's Cliquot 2, of the theatre of Richard Foreman. And it takes nothing away from Wilson's work. For myself, I need more intellectual weight, less spectacle, more modesty, less hours and the sense that the performer and the spectator can share the encounter, that it matters that each of us is there at a specific moment.

᧬

Brandi Pena as Juanita in *The Axe of Creation*

27. SPIDERWOMAN THEATER

HELEN DUBERSTEIN

The Spiderwoman Theater, a collection of raucous, inventive, and principally Native American women who ally themselves with the feminist movement, have been producing frontal-in-your-face attacks, not only on the white middle-class but on themselves, for two decades. In 1980, Helen Duberstein, a soft-spoken poet, playwright, novelist and Playwrights Group president—as internal as Spiderwoman has been external—combined with Spiderwoman in a "performance piece," which Helen originally titled *The Axe of Creation*, retitled *Madam Ax or How We Create*. Helen was an early member of Circle Theatre's playwriting contingent and her *Time Shadows* was one of Circle's early productions. Though much of her work explores the troubled relationships between men and women, Helen has never seen herself as a feminist, though obviously sympathetic to women's issues. The latter half of *Madam Ax* is published below.

✧✧✧

MADAM AX OR HOW WE CREATE*
a performance piece by Helen Duberstein

directed by Lisa Mayo

CAST

Sarah	Gloria Miguel
Carol	Carol Ortlieb
Juanita	Brandy Sanchez
Corte	Hazel Belvo
Naomi	Ruth Imbesi
Laura	Janet Norquist
Loretta	Lisa Mayo

Lisa Mayo of Spiderwoman Theater and Helen Duberstein formed a workshop to explore and produce a theatre piece based on dreams and hidden memories of women which would involve kinships amongst women, blood, surrogate and mythic. Several women of different ages, ethnic backgrounds, cultural heritage and sexual preferences met over a period of five months. All of us, we discovered, experienced ourselves outside of history, as it were, and had evolved a means of survival in a hostile environment which sought to make us disappear on many levels. In the first piece to evolve, *Axe of Creation*, each of us tells her story of how she survives in a world that is not of her making.

H.D.

5/3/80

CORTE *is in her seventies, a strong, square set figure.* SARAH, LORETTA, LAURA, *and* ANTOINETTE *are in their early fifties.* SARAH *is petite and flirtatious;* LORETTA, *dramatic and commanding of attention;* LAURA, *plump and ordinary looking. You would take her for a housewife, rather than a poet.* ANTOINETTE, *a sensuous, heavy set woman, has long coarse dark hair that is cut in long bangs and worn loose, flowing.* NAOMI, *a mature woman of indeterminate age, has gray hair which she wears in a bun. She is tall and stately and walks with a natural rhythm and pride.* HELGA, *in her forties, has a farm fresh complexion, and rosy cheeks. She is tall and strong, a marked presence, albeit with a childlike quality. She seems about twelve years old as she talks.* JUANITA, *a strong, lithe figure is about thirty five and vitality blazes from her.* CAROL *is about twenty-three years old, tall and very beautiful, very strong and full of bouncy energy.*

NAOMI: [*Underlined words to be said as if possessed, i.e. "another voice" is issuing from* NAOMI'*s body.*] Walk.

Violent desire to flee from it
the fact is
the knowledge
the fact is
an awful lot of women
have no identity.

Any cock will do.

Cock a do

    The world is in such a bad shape and so out of focus that I can hardly perceive of it again again again [*Sigh.*] almost unimaginable

[*Sigh. Long pause.*] mundane practical and kind of formless sea a kind of leg sort of floating by formlessly
  [*Pause.*] It doesn't go anyplace. It just sits there floats and sits floats and sits floats and sits floats and sits floats and sits floats and sits [*Rhythm diminishes.*] floats and sits [*Slows down.*] floats and sits there is water there [*Hits on consonants.*] floats sits floats floats sits

books books books books
hooks hook hooks hooks
looks looks looks

  deep sea water lots of waves the body surrender to its . . . all encompassing and it is vivid enough and it is so ennobled and beyond conception that it is beyond description
  I see the waves I see the blue I see the depths I see the waves all of its breadth and and I can see it and I know I have seen it

exploration

the sun's rays the waves I see

it's a sea it's an ocean an encompassing ocean a great ocean

dunes Nooooooo salt lakes [*Moans.*]
all is gone all is gone

  if I move away from it there isn't anything to move move towards except I don't know where it's gone to I know it's not there
[*Sigh. Silence.*]

I'm experiencing it
if I move away from it there isn't anything to move
towards the futility is so total [*Moans. Silence.*]

  There is the water there is the sun there is the void no stars dark nothing in it shapeless excrescence a crazy pot a crazy pot of dirt in my oven I sterilize the crazy pot of dirt in my oven

[*Various kinds of laughter come from various of her voices, both internal and external. Whispers.*]

I'm still on it
  [*Louder*] I'm still on it. Various colors nasturtiums. I'm sterilizing the soil sterilizing sterilizing green green
Then, there's black, just the color of dull brown, shapeless
etching retching retching
I'm sterilizing it so I can plant some nasturtiums marigolds

red and yellow and ivory and white
red yellow ivory white
burgundy pink
not orange the other
coral

they're really nice because they're just on the vine you sit there they're twined on the vine you just sit there they're really nice because you just sit there and they bring the gold they're great vines and they have it's hard to describe this about nasturtiums and marigolds they have this sharp smell but marigolds are sort of nasturtiums have like it's a gentler spicy smell whereas the nasturtiums have a sort of real almost nasturtiums are a have a weird a real it's almost that they taste good they do taste good they are. good to eat whereas marigolds smell good like they are good to eat but they don't taste good anyway. [*Pause.*]

I try to do as little as possible. Their business is to grow. I don't like to aggravate them. They're like babies. They'll do the right thing if you just get out of their way. They know what they want to do. They want to grow. They want to have all different kinds of flowers. I think the seeds of the marigold are what are known as capers. We have olives and capers. Well. I could be wrong about that but that is what I think about the caper and the olive. They are seeds and they grow.

It's not easy. It's up. And, expand. And, onto your knees. Then, up. Marigolds have lots of leaves. And big flowers for the size of the plants.

Big, big. Big. It's not a dramatic forceful compelling big. It's a proud satisfying total expansion to the limits of the possible. Of course, that's the kind I got from the little box.

[LORETTA *belts out a song her grandmother sang to her, the Rappahannoch part of her family, with Southern American accents.*]

LORETTA: I come to the garden alone while the dew is still on the roses and the voice I hear falling on my ear the sign of God discloses . . . and He walks with me and He talks with me and He tells me I am His own . . . and the voice I hear falling on my ear, none other has ever known.

eleven o'clock. twelve thirty clear things up
past history with my mother
my sisters
my sister [*Shouts.*]
What is a myth? [*Soft.*]
Is it what I want? What I see myself doing the next
twenty-five years?
Get away work study perfect my French my Italian
and take up Spanish

[*In French.*] She has been speaking French since she was 13.
[*Sings. When she finishes her French song.*] Italian! My Italian. [*She sings a song from an Italian opera. Cuts it short.*]
That's enough Italian. That's enough of that.
I'd like to go to South America, Central America, South America with the people who have the same blood that I have and I would like to do theater down there.

[*Makes sounds that are Spanish though she has yet to study the language.*]

That's not only a Spanish sound, that's an Italian sound and an Indian sound. And, a Portuguese sound.

[*Talks to a couple she meets walking down a street in Venezuela.*]

How do you do? I'm very happy to be here in this wonderful country of Venezuela. The sea is beautiful and it smells good and the weather is perfect. It's wonderful down here. Theater people are interesting. They are mixed racially. Indians, Blacks, Europeans. I'd like some of you to work with me. I don't only want to work with you. I want you to work with me, too. I want you to hear what I have to say, too.

Venezuela? Colombia, Ecuador, Peru. I have a close feeling to the Indian people there. Guatemala. Panama. Mexico! Chile...

[*As if to the Becks in Chile.*]

I'm not with you, Judith and Julian in Chile. I missed you when I was growing up in theater in New York. I got into theater too late to really get into...I heard about you and I read about you...I have no close connection...

[*As if to director in Mexico City.*]

My theater is who I am. You, you are a Latino. Who I am racially. We have similar blood. I do like you. I do want to speak to you, but you are much too traditional for me. [*Shouts.*] You're a fucking sellout! You want to do traditional theater. Fuck that. What good is that? You don't need that. What good is European theater in Mexico? With all the Indians there, looking at you?

I love you. I hate you. The blood runs through my veins. You're killing me. What the hell do you want from my life? You're not helping the people of the community. Like my mother. Like me. My destitute eighty-three year old mother in New York City without food, without money. It's a fucking lie. I want to communicate with Indians all over. I want to talk about hunger and starvation. I want to talk about the revolution.

I was not aware of this because I was very busy being something else.

[*She sings and dances to a Hebrew middle-European song which breaks into one of the songs without words Hasidic men sing at Orthodox weddings: Nigun.*]

I see myself in the Garden of Eden with plants and vegetation and herbs. Smear balm on people's bodies.

[*Orates.*]

Third World People! I want to talk about our feelings, about the revolution. In my very bones I feel the kinship, in my very bones... Jews... Celts... [*Hums.*] ... faces...

Pipes and drums... oooooo... like a drone kind of thing and oooooo and superimposed upon that thing drums... a rhythmic kind of thing... umptutu, umptutu, umptutu, when I hear that and bagpipes and bagpipes and pipes

[*Begins a movement of a Celtic dance with straight body and movement of the arms and legs. Music with flutes and pipes and drums.* LORETTA *sings a high sweet note and begins the flute sound and makes a drum sound and the whine of the bagpipes. No instrumental accompaniment.*]

Frog he went a-courting and he did ride... my sister Sal was sitting on the grass and a bumble bee came flying by and stung her on the... ask me-no more questions... I'll tell you no lies...

[*Cradles a baby in her arms and sings a lullaby from the Cuna her father's tribe. The lullaby is in three voices. First* LORETTA *sings the high pitch, then the low, then the entire lullaby.*

Use "found objects," upturned trash cans, fingers, thumping on floor or boards, forks or spoons hung on string, tin cans jangling, etc., LAURA *sets up insistent rhythm. Sounds of calliope are insistent and intermingle with this. All the whores are children, and they are playing. Each forms herself into a guillotine, using the entire body or an arm or a leg as a chopping block or by some other means, using an arm as a blade.*

It is a game, competitive and there are winners who are not winners, really. The whore children line up and present themselves to be guillotined. They "die." They lose their heads, but they leap up emphatically and joyously, to make other ways of being guillotined and/or having their heads chopped off and springing back to life. Remember, the music of the calliope plays. The whores are sometimes dancing figures on the calliope stage.]

LAURA: Old old woman old old man
Old man in the woods cold man
little girl in the woods and the stars
wandering wandering
in the stars the stars following the stars

not to get lost
following the stars not to get lost
there are no stars

there are no stars just the leaves the branches
and the leaves
lost
not to get lost
following the stars
there are no stars, there are no stars just the
branches and the leaves
wandering wandering
just the leaves and the branches of the leaves
wandering
the little girl is wandering in the woods
It's very far
there are no stars there is a clearing in the woods
there are the stars the little girl is following the stars
following the stars reaching
the man in the woods
asleep
under the leaves fast asleep under the leaves
waiting waiting for the morning to come
It's morning.
Looking for food.
The leaves. The house. Looking for food.
Not the house. Doesn't want to live in a house.

Doesn't want to eat in the house. Is looking in the woods, walking in the woods, following the path, following the path, following the path through the woods.

Dark again. It's dark again. Going to sleep again.

Going to sleep again. Under the leaves. Growing.

Getting to be bigger. Growing up. Getting to be bigger. Getting to be bigger. Not the width. Not growing. Wandering in the woods. All by herself. The little girl.

Meets the man. She meets the older man. He guides her and he knows where to go. They live in the woods. He seems smart. He sees the stars.

[*In the voice of the old man.*] Yes. Yes. Yes. [*In her own voice.*] he says [*In the voice of the old man.*] Stay here. I know. I'll bring you food and clothing and stay here. I will wander around and come back here. I'll come back here and you're here. No more wandering. No more going.

You stay here. Yes, I will go. I will do this. I will do that. And, you will not be hungry anymore. Yes. You will not be hungry anymore.

[*Sing-song.*] You will not be hungry anymore. So... that means...

You will wait for a while... and then... [*Ends sing-song.*] Grows older and there are children. There is no longer a man there. A boy and a girl.

[*Talking to children.*] Hold the branch when you go before me because it snaps! at me! Take it easy and come to eat and come to eat. Play with each other. All you have is each other. Take care of each other. Wander so that you hear me call. If I don't see you, go where you hear me call.

[*Calls.*] Come to dinner. It's time for dinner. [*To children.*] That's where you go. Where you hear me call, Come to dinner. I don't have to watch you. I don't like to hold you. You don't have to always see me, but remember that's as far as you go, as far as I can call, as far as you can hear me call for dinner.

I tidy up leaves. I collect the nuts. Tidy up. I'm a berry gatherer. There's no savory meat to smell so you have to hear my voice. You have this great open forest to wander in as far as you can hear my voice. That's it, kiddies.

[*Space.*]

Time is passing. The kids are kind of grown up. So.

Comes this old man again and chooses my daughter to marry to marry. They go because she is very eager because he will take her beyond the sound of my voice. Always an intriguing place to go, beyond the sound of mother's, mother's voice.

The great outdoors. The great world beyond and the man will guide her, will guide her through it, will get her through it. So, off she goes.

By this time, I'm saying, Don't do it.

Don't do it because it's a false start, I want to say. You will go just so far then you will be stuck with a circle of children. That's just the way it is.

She doesn't know. She doesn't know that. She really thinks she's going off into the world and will have a lot of really tricky adventures out there but there's no way!

The boy will stay with me for a while but the girl will go off, I know that.

28. MARJORIE MELNICK

UP!, PRISONS, MOTHERHOOD

I crossed the courtyard in Westbeth (at the western end of Greenwich Village) one evening in late February or early March of 1972. My play, *The Celebration: Jooz/Guns/Movies/The Abyss*, was in its nightly under-four-hours-run on the eastern end of the yard, at Theater for the New City. On the western end, something that had come to be known as feminist theatre was taking place in a cabaret-like space. *Up!* consisted of a series of short, ideological plays interspersed with aggressive or lamenting songs that spoke of young urban women doing battle against the lordly assumptions of the male. Something about *Up!* got to me; it was not the peroration about female victims and how they were not going to stand for repressive conditions an hour longer, it was the sheer uncontrived energy and courage of the work, even if there was also the sense of young women riding the coattails of a fashionable movement. I am rarely enchanted by in-your-face rhetoric, nor am I charmed by the news that I am in steadfast alliance with the hard-hat, sexist mentality of the American male. But for all its self-consciousness, *Up!* provided a moment for the demonstration of an all-too rare comradeliness, an attempt at sisterhood and bonding which still seemed to be fresh news two decades back. I made some positive reference to *Up!* in *The Village Voice* and at some later date became friends with its director, Margie Melnick. It is now some two decades after that winter; Ms. Melnick, in whose Central Park West apartment my marriage to Maryjane Treloar took place in 1981, has been a close friend for many years, and in June of '93 I sat down with her in that apartment to discuss the journey she had taken from *Up!*, through the prison system, and to her present life as the mother of three boys and the spouse of director Jerry Heymann.

"*Up!* was my first directing show in New York. But by the time I was twelve or thirteen I had already decided that I didn't want to do traditional theatre. I had this sense very early on that theatre had replaced ritual, that theatre was something other than a product in a marketplace economy. I was doing summer stock early, an acting apprentice at the Plowright Playhouse, and then the apprentices were asked to put on a show and there was no director, and it occurred to me to say, 'I can direct.' So there I was directing a show. I went to the University of Connecticut at Storrs and midway through my drama studies there I was already the artistic director of Plowright in the summertime. Then after graduation I came to New York, I was going to make wonderful theatre."

"And it turned out to be *Up!*"

"Amy Saltz, whom I had worked with at Plowright, was supposed to direct the show, but she got other work and recommended me for it. I got to work with young writers like Susan Yankowitz and Gwen Gunn, and as you know I found myself directing interesting actors like Danny DeVito and Rhea Perlman. It was a wonderful beginning for me and I started getting other directing jobs because the word had gone out about this show. I was directing two or three shows a season. I tell you, I particularly liked working with what we would call untrained actors, I always loved that rough quality."

"Among the plays I saw you direct was Helen Duberstein's *Time Shadows* at the Roundabout. And then I asked you to work with me on *Go Children Slowly* at the Cubiculo."

"We couldn't work slowly enough. We rehearsed for several weeks, and we were just beginning to make some discoveries, and we were running out of time. I had to curtail the period of discovery and block the show because we were about to open."

Margie addresses the changes she felt in the mid-seventies.

"The Equity rules started choking me. I no longer felt free to give the rehearsal period its proper time. It began to feel like the meaningful theatre I had come to New York to do was no longer available to me. I wasn't producing art, it was becoming something else."

And then Rikers Island happened.

"I had actually been doing some writing, on automobile repairs, because theatre wasn't taking me anywhere, and I got this offer to run a theatre workshop with women prisoners at Rikers Island. I thought, do I want to work in prisons? (Rikers is essentially a detention center.) I said no. But then I went out there, and as you know I changed my mind.

"I started doing theatre games. The work went well, the inmates and I got along just fine. But I was pretty nervous, I was a white woman and there was a lot of threatening rhetoric from the Black Liberation Army about what would happen to whites who were going along with the power structure. Then I was asked to help create a play with the inmates and into my class the second day walks Joanne Chesimard. I thought I would die!"

Chesimard was a leading black-militant figure, she had been wanted by the authorities for some time. She was pregnant during her stay at Rikers.

"It worked out wonderfully. Joanne actually starred in the play and we performed it for other inmates and for the prison authorities. It was called *You Deserve What You Take*, it was a pretty militant statement about who owns what in our society."

Margic has written for several publications about what came to be a series of workshops in detention centers, initially for women, later for men. What follows are some of the remarks from "The Constructive Use of Theatre in Prison," as they appeared in the March '79 issue of *New York Theatre Review*:

I was surprised at the women I met. Some were young girls age 16 to 18 years old. There were politically oriented women and women who had no more interest in the life around them than solving their own problems. Many women seemed to be walking in slow motion as a result of medication requested from the prison's doctors and hospital workers to help them get through this difficult period of their life. They didn't know if they would be jailed for one more day or for the rest of their lives. There were several pregnant women who were unable to deal emotionally with their own pregnancy. Even many of these women seemed to depend on medication. Feeling that theatre was a healthy alternative, several women asked me to stay.

In 1974 I began workshops in the prison. Some of the work was based on traditional techniques using objectives, circumstances and place to create improvisations. We also did physical and vocal work, trust exercises and even work in Lamaze techniques. The latter helped us get physically ready to do theatre, but more important, it helped the pregnant women prepare for delivery. Sometimes we did the father's part of the exercises and sometimes we did the expectant mother's part. We shared some of the joy and pain when one student left for the hospital to have her baby.

The women let me know that they were becoming less and less dependent on medication. The theatre work was helping them relax. They wanted to be alert and attentive to the reactions of other workshop members.

As the women became interested in performing a show, I began bringing scripts into the prison. Using the actor's audition techniques, I showed the women how to deal with material they had never read before. With a chosen objective like respect or love or attention they tried to get a specific emotional response from their partners using the language in the script. By picking up just a few words in a glance they were able to concentrate with eye contact primarily on their partners to see if they were getting what they wanted. And thus they were able to develop a relationship even with words that were unfamiliar and unrehearsed. Later I found out that some of the women had been tested as first, second or third grade readers. I was shocked. We were using professional adult scripts. Something about the work was allowing the women to read.

When my one year appointment at Rikers was up, I was too involved to stop doing theatre in the prisons. I took a job running a workshop for The Family, a theatre company of ex-offenders, ex-addicts and professionals responsible for the play *Short Eyes*. And then I was hired by David Heaphy to work with the men at The Queens House of Detention. Because he was running a school, he requested that I relate all of my theatre work to the development of educational skills.

Audition techniques were extended so they could develop reading skills. Eventually, writing, grammar, and communication skills were taught in the theatre classes. I taught acting technique which led to effective improvisations which were taped. A support system grew among the participants. Together we helped even reluctant writers script their own dialogue.

A sample set-up for an improvisation that might lead to scripting would look like this:

CHARACTER	OBJECTIVE
Inmate:	I want you to get me out.
Lawyer:	I want you to go along with the plea bargain offered by the District Attorney.

Place: Counsel room in a prison.

Personal facts (to make the character specific and avoid stereotypes):

Inmate: Charged with a homicide. I did not go...Live alone...Night of crime I was home alone watching TV...And, gave all of my $2,000 savings to the lawyer.

Lawyer: He had been picked out of a line-up by an "upright" person in the community...He has no proof of his story...If he plea bargains he'll get 10 years...If he goes to trial he'll get 25 to life...And, I personally need to be effective in court especially now when I am paying my wife's hospital bills.

We created scenes to teach grammar. For example: a gang is alone in the park planning. They use nouns rather than pronouns while being specific with their plans. ("Paul will take the money to Steve.") Then the scene is repeated in the presence of a cop. Only pronouns are used as they disguise their activities. (HE will take IT to HIM.") Thus they learned that pronouns take the place of nouns.

We enacted and videotaped courtroom scenes and job interviews so a person could see how his behavior affected others, and how he could choose to communicate in ways which would help him in these situations. Videotape became popular and was incorporated into all the classes.

There was another aspect of the work that became important as a result of an experience I had many years ago when I directed *Marat Sade*. At that time I had used improvisations for character development. I was worried when one cast member stayed in the improvisation for three days. I realized then that directors have a responsibility to use theatre in the lives of participants in a way that was not dangerous or emotionally not destructive. I began consulting therapists. When I worked off-Broadway, being constructive meant making certain that emotional energy went back into a process that led to a good show. With a prison population that seemed to have extraordinary emotional problems and be in a crisis time in their lives, I wanted theatre to also be therapeutic. With this in mind I set up improvisations based on conflict, where the men did not have the choice of leaving or using violence as alternatives to dealing emotionally with the conflict as they worked within the boundaries of the scene. By sometimes playing unlikely characters—such as lawyers, teachers, and officers—they were less able to depersonalize and stereotype people who were traditionally antagonistic and threatening. Being part of a theatre community involve them in a social process based on mutual respect and responsibility. The scenes became richer and more focused as the participants increasingly trusted the work and each other. The men felt a connection between the work and their lives.

I watch my students grow in all kinds of ways. Learning skills were improving two or three grade levels. In conversations and letters, students talked about a new sense of respect for self and others. Meanwhile, they were becoming wonderful theatre artists. I found their acting to be more interesting than what I saw in many New York professional productions. The inmate scripts were for the most part better than the professional scripts submitted to me. The audience was involved and appreciative of each other's efforts to a degree I had not before experienced. But I was worried. What were these people going to do when they left jail? I had seen ex-offenders try theatre as a way to make a living and have huge problems. They weren't prepared for the double life of work and drama as they experienced the instability that accompanied a beginner's life in the theatre. Many had no money and no place to live. Readjustment to communities and families held its own problems. Most of all, they wanted satisfying work.

I decided to train ex-offenders to become director/teachers of the techniques we evolved in the prison. I found interested organizations and next needed to document the techniques. Together with Ronald Rhodes, trained by State Corrections in the use of video, a group of ex-offenders, ex-addicts, people on bail and their friends, were gathered into The Workshop to make tapes about our process.

And again there was a radical change in Margie's life. "I was pregnant with my firstborn. The doctors were concerned I would miscarry. I spent most of the last five months of my pregnancy in bed. I wanted this child very much. In effect, the difficult pregnancy and then the birth of Jonas just stopped the prison stuff. I looked at this baby and I knew that I couldn't leave him. I had hoped to set up training workshops whereby ex-offenders would learn to teach my work. But I felt too vulnerable with the baby, the world of offenders and ex-offenders was too volatile, too unstable, I began to feel too exposed, I just didn't want people seeking me out at home."

As a young mother, Margie spent many months editing the videotapes of the literacy workshops. Eventually that gave way to a new mode of directing.

"I found that I wanted to include my child, as of now all my three sons, in my work. So I began to organize a workshop involving six young mothers and their children. We would all play together, each mother would direct us all in her special skill, e.g. music, cooking, movement, etc. And one workshop has led to others all these years, more than a dozen years now. And I have to tell you that all of it feels like theatre to me. I plan birthday parties for our kids and for other kids we know in which we create and perform plays. And I've been running classes for children at the Museum for Children (on Manhattan's West Eighty-third Street). And I love it all, I love doing it very much."

I look at Margie, I remember crossing the Wesbeth courtyard and coming upon that militant production of *Up!* Was that another lifetime? Are we those two people who met in 1972, now sitting across from each other in an extraordinarily comfortable and beautiful "upscale" apartment overlooking Central Park, reminiscing for the purposes of my new book? I think we are and are not those two people. There is that saying about not being able to cross the same stream twice, because neither we nor the stream are ever the same once the event of the crossing has taken place. And yet of course we carry the past with us.

What can Margie Melnick tell me? And what can I understand? Has the theatre lost a creative, militant force to motherhood? And if so, is someone impoverished by it? Has it impoverished the feminist movement, the prison movement, the radical theatre movement? And on the other hand, is this "loss" a wonderful gain for a handful of middle-class urban children and their parents? Is society healthier for this loss? I can speculate about what Judith Malina might say but I'm not certain of it. As for myself, all I can think of writing at this moment is that: we go on.

⁀

29. HERBERT BLAU

KRAKEN

Throughout this book there have been references to Herbert Blau and his work, particularly his pioneering efforts with Kraken, the company he founded some time after his painful separation from Lincoln Center. Blau has been one of those creatures I haven't been able to get out of my head, though I may not think about him for half a decade at a time. But sooner or later I find that he is still floating around in my head. He has either just made a pronouncement, or he has been too silent—his artistic presence nags at me and this new volume seemed an appropriate time to share something of that presence with the reader.

Blau came to New York with Kraken one hot summer in the mid-seventies—well, it is always a hot summer in New York—and brought his production of *The Donner Party* to the Performance Garage, and just about no one came. There is a hot-ticket psychology we all know about very well, and I won't beat this insight to death. Suffice it to say, whatever happened to be a hot ticket that season, *The Donner Party* was not part of that select, joyous grouping. I came to the closing performance, and apparently I wrote the following which, for a reason I can't dredge up, my paper, *The Village Voice*, chose not to print. Perhaps I never submitted it. At any rate, here it is in the cold light of 1993, a curious view of a curious moment in theatre history:

Herbert Blau stood in the wreckage of the Performing Garage while the young members of KRAKEN labored at reconstituting the seating area (platforms and posts) they had temporarily dismembered in order to free the space for their own *The Donner Party, Its Crossing*. I use wreckage as obvious metaphor, addressing the dissolution of hope, the dismantling of *mise en scène* into junk. The group had come to New York with good expectations, but "the acoustics beat us. The language of *Donner Party*," Blau was saying, "is a piece of music, and if that music can't be heard (as it couldn't, I for one missed half the text) then the work is ultimately incomprehensible." The space. at the very least, undid them, dismantling the platforms, which they realized too late might have acted as resonators, undid them, and the handful of local critics, unable to comprehend much of the text, managed with what was probably a mix of good and ill will to finish the job. KRAKEN, literally a Nordic sea monster, played to sparse houses during its two weeks, performers (five young men and two women) found themselves shouting to be heard, and Blau, watching the art slowly draining out of the work, made the decision to cut short the run.

"We never would have brought *Donner Party* to New York if we'd suspected what the problems would be." He was talking over the pounding of hammers. "I haven't produced a work here since Lincoln Center. I know the value of *Donner Party*, we did beautifully on tour, excited audiences in Chicago, played to packed houses. I wanted to come to New York with a comprehensible, compelling work, and I believe we've made that work. But . . . no sense beating a dead horse."

The ironies. In the mid-sixties, Blau and Jules Irving, directors of the San Francisco Actor's Workshop, took command of the most publicized theatre in the country, the Repertory Theatre of Lincoln Center. Untold monies had been poured into setting up the operation, some of the biggest names in theatre (Elia Kazan, Robert Whitehead) were being replaced after several seasons of controversy over the quality of work, and the reins were given over to these comparative newcomers. "In a sense," Blau noted, "it was impossible. There was such pressure. Everything we did was subject to incredible scrutiny." And there was dissatisfaction from the beginning. *Danton's Death*, their first production, was mercilessly attacked by the press, some described the acting (several of the principals had come from San Francisco) as inferior to what New Yorkers had a right to expect. Things were destined not to improve. Within a few seasons, Blau packed it in, leaving Jules Irving to fight for whatever victories might still be forthcoming.

Now, after seven long years away, Blau had returned to New York, to discover that, whereas as focal point at Lincoln Center he had everyone watching, now, downtown in Soho, almost no one was watching. Now there was no pressure from the outside, all pressure was internal, now there was no fanfare, no hubbub among theatre people, no gossip, no audience expectations. Except for a handful of us who saw *Donner Party*, it was as if the work had never happened. And here was Blau, preparing to leave New York for a second time, only now very few knew that he had even been here.

But Blau and his performers had been here and had produced a work that I found—need I say it?—of more value, certainly of more significance, than most of the highly acclaimed dramas playing to full houses. "After Lincoln Center I didn't do any theatre work for almost a year. Then I went to the California Institute of the Arts (the Disney-funded project in Valencia) as provost and head of drama and began working with young people, based on the understanding that we had no obligation to produce anything." Blau's tenure proved an unsteady one, there was mutual suspicion instantly between trustees and "the New York liberals and radicals." "Blau resigned," notes James Schevill in his book *Breakout*, "after an ideological hassle with the Disneys and other trustees." His move was to Oberlin College, he took several of his young Cal Arts performers with him, and became director of Oberlin's Inter-Arts Program.

"We concentrate on the technique of reflection. One performer moves into a space, comes up with an idea which is then expressed visually or verbally. By verbally I mean not just sounds but using the English language. At some point a second performer, reflecting on what's seen and heard, begins to make another idea, either in space with the first performer or in the original space. This new idea comments on the first. Then a third will begin to reflect on something provided by the others, either a single idea of theirs or some combination of ideas. And so on, till everyone is visually or verbally reflecting simultaneously.

"It's important to understand that intellectual intelligence is necessary, otherwise the work can't be done properly. Some of the ideas the group has developed through reflections have been incorporated into our pieces, into *Donner Party* and into *The Seeds of Atreus*. In the latter piece, some members of the ensemble would be seated in the audience, reflecting on what was going on in the playing space. When they'd formed a comment based on their reflections, they would move into the playing area. *Atreus*, incidentally, had performers speaking as rapidly as a human voice can speak for an hour and a half. It was part of our effort to reenergize language."

Donner Party is structured as a square dance with numerous variations. In Blau's words, it is meant to be "an analog of the journey of the *Donner Party* (Missouri farmers heading for California in 1846, trapped below the Sierras by an early snowfall, members resorting to cannibalism to stay alive) and an analog of the meaning of the Western experience. We were caught up with the idea of the journey and worked on the meaning of motion. The language is a correlative of that."

I brought up one of my major concerns: politics and theatre. Blau noted that politics had been peripheral to his notion of a working theatre, but then recalled what came to be known as the Christmas bombing of Hanoi. "The Nixon-Kissinger team bombed Hanoi, we had just gotten to Oberlin and a screw got loose in my head. My performers weren't political activists but I proceeded to make my first and only political event. What was it? A series of actions in the street, pageants, puppets, choruses, an audio signal that was transmitted throughout the town. We asked students and townspeople to contribute some possession, something personal that we could hang on a structure we'd created. When we had all those possessions hanging, we burnt the structure to the ground. During the burning, everything became quiet, an austere atmosphere. It occurred to me that someone ought to sit down. (Just as the General Strike people sat down in

Times Square at the conclusion of Strike Week a decade earlier. Curious how these impulses are transferred from place to place, from generation to generation.) I tapped the person next to me and told them quietly to sit down. They did. A little later, two hundred people were sitting on the ground.

"But after the demonstration, my people were concerned because our regular work had been interrupted. We'd been working inwardly and here was a piece that was so blatantly outward. Also, my non-political students couldn't reconcile themselves to what we had just done. They began to feel that I had been manipulating them, and perhaps I had. At any rate, in order to find out who we were, the group developed a piece called *The Enemy*, based on the premise that we define ourselves by the other, by what we're not." What one immediately recalls is Buber's concept, that separate being whom we presumably objectify as the Other. This objectification creates an inviting low road well-traveled through the centuries, we might call it Paranoia Turnpike, where we are seduced into envisioning that which is separate from self as alien force, "the enemy."

There are literally counties, provinces, at times whole land masses that come to be demonized as the enemy. But the demon is also the seducer, offering untold if unspeakable treasures. One of these provinces we speak of alternately with loathing and longing used to be known simply as Broadway, then Off and Off-Off became the respectable offspring, the presumably authentic places, and they gave rise to recent phenomena we call Showcases, "developing theatres," tryouts, readings, and heaven knows what else. "How ya gonna keep 'em down on the farm, after they seen a reading?" That incorrigible, merciless, seemingly idealistic, market-driven outpost we might simply call New York became the focal point of our discourse. I expressed to Blau my ambiguity about this muddy-cultured watering place. On the one hand you face a rigorous audience that at its best won't let itself be taken in by the hottest ticket in town and might actually thirst for something that contains a semblance of an idea, on the other hand you must forget this enticing province with its earthly rewards if you're playing in the boonies and remember that culture is what any community has the possibility and hopefully the responsibility for nurturing, that something always demands that you respond to the moment.

Blau smiled. "On the one hand, New York represents a critical test. On the other hand, audiences everywhere are the same, they see what the critics tell them they're seeing. What's important is the question: what do I know about what I'm doing that is spiritually reliable? It makes no difference to me now where I work as long as I can do my kind of work. I'm after big fish. Bigger fish. Most of the theatre has been after smaller fish and the audiences are content with these smaller fish. When confronted with something new, the audience usually doesn't see it. But I would like to create a work for once that's absolutely inarguable, a work that rises to the audience and the audience rises to the work. An irresistible work."

Why, I asked, was Lincoln Center important back in the middle sixties? Why didn't Blau and Irving just stay in San Francisco where they had a viable theatre? Blau spoke of the appeal of popular theatre. "I'd turned down directing jobs on Broadway, that wasn't what appealed to me about New York. But Lincoln Center represented the possibility of doing important work for mass audiences. Popular theatre isn't in the forefront of my mind now, but none of us know what we may do tomorrow. A part of me hates to yield up these institutions to the barbarians."

Blau thought about what he had just said, he smiled again. "Like Ahab, I've always wanted to penetrate that fugitive figure, in my case the mass audience, and pull out the hot heart of the whale. But the theatre," he went on, perhaps with the image of Ahab's ultimate confrontation with Moby Dick, "the theatre has a hard heart."

∽

30. PETER SCHUMANN

THE BREAD AND PUPPET THEATER

We hear the refrain over and over: it's not the sixties anymore. As if to remonstrate with us, or to speak ruefully. What exactly are we to do now that it's not the sixties? Settle down? Give up our dreams? Make money? Start being old people?

This is no rhapsody for The Bread and Puppets. (Or perhaps it is.) Even the Schumanns, Peter and Elka, are not exactly youngsters, and grandparent-hood, if that condition hasn't already made an appearance, is nevertheless looming, and the work isn't always the most wonderful in the world. But it is quite wonderful more often than that of any other theatre I have come across, it is still enchanting and provocative and the only catering it does is to its own beliefs. Like The Living Theatre, The Bread and Puppet Theater is relentless; Peter is like a magical treadmill artist, there is always a new Crucifixion, a new Resurrection, a new response to the latest idiocy from Washington, and there are wonderful lyrical plays that seem spun off in somebody's spare time, except there never is spare time.

But valued members of this troupe die as the years go on. Recently Margo Sherman learned that Bob Ernsthal, one of the very early and very inspired members of the troupe from its day on Delancey Street on the Lower East Side, died at a comparatively young age in California. And Murray Levy died in New York several years go, died with almost no money to combat the AIDS virus that was afflicting him. And, as I noted in the section on Robert Wilson, there are the ashes of Maurice Blanc, buried in the forest on the Schumann farm in Glover, Vermont. The list is too long. And yet there are always new young people who pick up the banner and proclaim and dance and quarrel with Peter and reenergize the troupe. Are these sixties people? Who cares?

In the best sense of the word, this is an amateur theatre, a theatre of love, not of mammon. It arises from a need to witness, it wants always to express a something about the culture, often as a dissident. Peter usually instigates and shapes this something, and spectators begin to dream, they. begin to watch and hear the sounds of this world as if it were another world, sometimes they even give a little mammon (coin of the realm), they want be touched.

At the end of his recent lecture with fiddle, called "The Old Art of

Puppetry in the New World Order," Peter quotes the rooster talking to the donkey in the *Brementown Musicians*. "Come along, something better than Death we find anywhere." And spectators do come along, they want to find something better than death, even tremulously they want to take the journey to an authenticity they can scarcely imagine but which they can intuit in their bones.

What follows is a reproduction of Peter's booklet, *The Foot*, a "cantastoria" street show with flip-over painted screens, narrator and chorus. It was created by Bread and Puppet Theater in 1982 in New York City for the June 12 Parade for Disarmament. Since then it has taken to the streets and parks of Chicago, Philadelphia, Boston and many other cities in the US, and to England, France, Belgium, Iceland, Germany, Italy, Nicaragua, Puerto Rico, and to Moscow and Siberia during a month-long tour in May of 1990.

✧✧✧

THE FOOT

BREAD & PUPPET 87

FROM THE
GARBAGE

OUT OF NOTHING

②

WITH A LOT OF
HARD WORK

③

WITH THE HELP
OF OUR GRAND-
PARENTS

④

OUR GREAT-GREAT
GREAT-GREAT-

OUR GREAT-
GRANDPARENTS

⑤

GRANDPARENTS

⑥

WE BUILD
A TABLE

A HOUSE

⑦

COOK A SOUP

⑧

INDEX

WOMEN ON THE VERGE:
7 Avant-Garde American Plays
Edited by Rosette C. Lamont

This APPLAUSE anthology gathers together recent work by the finest and most controversial contemporary American women dramatists. Collectively, this Magnificent Seven seeks to break the mold of the well-wrought psychological play and its rigid emphasis on realistic socio-political drama. The reader will imbibe the joyous poetry flowing in these uncharted streams of dramatic expression, a restless search that comes in the wake of European explorations of Dada, Surrealism and the Absurd.

THE PLAYS:

Rosalyn Drexler Occupational Hazard

Tina Howe Birth and After Birth

Karen Malpede Us

Maria Irene Fornes What of the Night?

Suzan-Lori Parks The Death of the Last Black Man in the Whole Entire World

Elizabeth Wong Letters to a Student Revolutionary

Joan M. Schenkar The Universal Wolf

paper • ISBN: 1-55783-148-3

APPLAUSE

THE MADMAN AND THE NUN and THE CRAZY LOCOMOTIVE

THREE PLAYS (including THE WATER HEN)

by Stanislaw Ignacy Witkiewicz

Edited, translated and with an introduction
by Daniel Gerould and C. S. Durer
Foreword by Jan Kott

"It is high time that this major playwright should
become better known in the English-speaking world."
—Martin Esslin

STARTLING discontinuities and surprises erupt
throughout these avant-garde landscapes by
Poland's outstanding modern dramatist. A decadent
poet rebels against society's repressive tyranny
through suicide and last minute resurrection in
Madman and the Nun. A band of degenerate criminals
and artists in *The Crazy Locomotive* commandeer an
engine and seek to bring about God's judgment by
racing at apocalyptic speeds into an oncoming
passenger train. Painter, photographer, novelist,
philosopher, expert on drugs, Witkiewicz exemplifies
in these dramas his mastery of a new art of the theatre.

ISBN: 0-936839-83-X

APPLAUSE

NEW BROADWAYS

THEATRE ACROSS AMERICA AS THE MILLENIUM APPROACHES
by Gerald M. Berkowitz

"AN OUTSTANDINGBOOK OF THE YEAR ...
HIGHLY RECOMMENDED"— CHOICE

"THE MOSTCOMPLETE GUIDE YETCOMPILED"
— AMERICAN THEATRE

In 1950, the terms "American theatre" and "Broadway" were virtually synonymous. As the century ends, Broadway is only a small part of a vital, creative, and varied national theatrical scene. A thorough revision and expansion of the award–winning 1982 book, *NEW BROADWAYS: THEATRE ACROSS AMERICA* treats such subjects as the contributions of the Ford Foundation, the importance of pioneers such as Joseph Papp, the checkered history of Lincoln Center, the evolution of the Broadway musical, and the experimental companies of the 1960s. As the American theatre faces the new millennium, Berkowitz draws on interviews with artistic directors of leading theatres around the country to offer predictions — and some warnings — for the future.

$24.95 • cloth
1-55783-257-9

APPLAUSE